MICHIGAN

Macmillan/McGraw-Hill

Michigan Studies

PROGRAM AUTHORS
James A. Banks
Kevin P. Colleary
Walter C. Parker

STATE CONSULTANT
Mel Miller

 Macmillan/McGraw-Hill

Acknowledgments

PROGRAM AUTHORS

James A. Banks, Ph.D.
Russell F. Stark University
Professor and Director, Center
  for Multicultural Education
University of Washington
Seattle, Washington

Kevin P. Colleary, Ed.D.
Graduate School of Education
Fordham University
New York, New York

Walter C. Parker, Ph.D.
Professor of Education and Chair
  of Social Studies Education
University of Washington
Seattle, Washington

HISTORIANS/SCHOLARS

Patricia A. Bonner, Ph.D
President
Economic Connections
South Lyon, Michigan

Cathy Johnson, Ed.S.
Social Studies Supervisor
Detroit Public Schools
Detroit, Michigan

Marty Mater
Teacher Consultant in Residence
Michigan Geographic Alliance
Central Michigan University
Mt. Pleasant, Michigan

Mel Miller, Ed.S.
Social Studies Consultant
Macomb Intermediate School District
Clinton Township, Michigan

PRIMARY SOURCES RESEARCH

Library of Congress
Publishing Office
Washington, D.C.

GRADE LEVEL CONSULTANTS

Linda Hamilton
Fourth Grade Teacher
Will L. Lee Elementary School
Richmond, Michigan

Greg Pawlusiak
Fourth Grade Teacher
Graveraet Intermediate School
Marquette, Michigan

Mary K. Weaver
K–12 Social Studies Coordinator
Saginaw Public Schools
Saginaw, Michigan

Students with print disabilities may be eligible to obtain an accessible, audio version of the pupil edition of this textbook. Please call Recording for the Blind & Dyslexic at 1-800-221-4792 for complete information.

Macmillan/McGraw Hill would like to acknowledge and thank the Michigan Tribal Education Directors' Consortium for their generous technical contributions to this edition. Over the development of this edition, they have contributed their time and efforts to reviewing material and coverage. Their efforts have contributed to making this edition better and are greatly appreciated.

MICHIGAN TRIBAL EDUCATION DIRECTORS' CONSORTIUM

The Michigan Tribal Education Directors' Consortium consists of Tribal Education Directors from the twelve (12) federally recognized Tribes in Michigan. The purpose of the consortium is to share information and address the educational needs and issues that impact the Native American students of our Tribal communities. The consortium advocates for opportunities, equality and fairness for our Native American students who are attending academic institutions. The consortium also seeks opportunities to inform and educate the public about Native American culture and history.

The McGraw·Hill Companies

Macmillan/McGraw-Hill

Send all inquiries to:
Macmillan/McGraw-Hill
8787 Orion Place
Columbus, OH 43240-4027

ISBN: 978-0-02-153643-6
MHID: 0-02-153643-0

Printed in the United States of America

2 3 4 5 6 7 8 9 10 (079/055) 14 13 12 11 10 09

Contents

Unit 1 — Michigan and Its First People

★Unit 5 How Michigan Works............ 256

Citizenship Handbook C2

Reference Section R1

Skills and Features

Charts, Graphs, and Diagrams

Time Lines

Maps

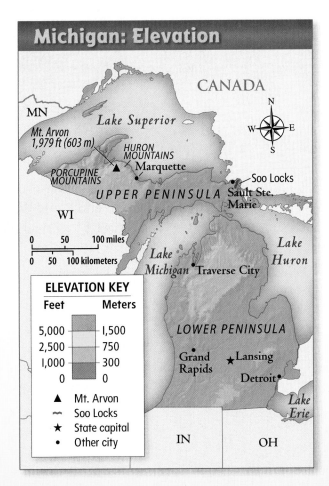

Maps

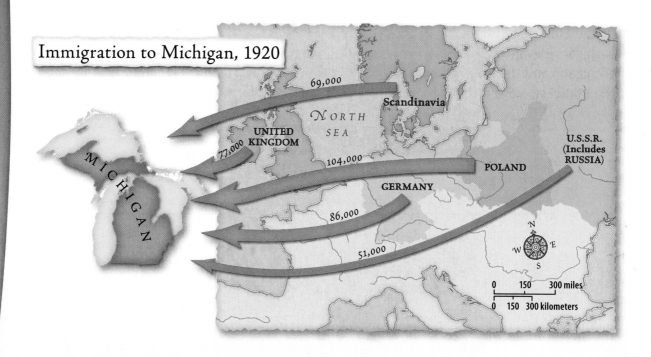

Immigration to Michigan, 1920

ABOUT THE BIG IDEA

The Big Ideas in this textbook are important ideas in social studies. They will help you understand each unit and its Michigan Standards.

The Big Idea question for each unit appears on its opening pages. As you review each lesson, look for the Write About the Big Idea question in the Lesson Review. The question helps you answer the Big Idea question for the unit. When you finish each unit, complete the Big Idea Activities. They will help you review what you have learned. Finally, you will find a list of three books that will help you learn more about the Big Idea.

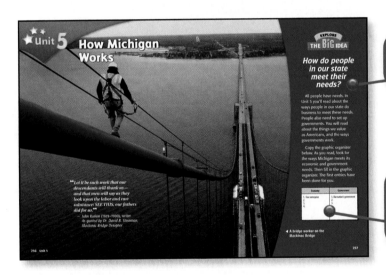

Each unit starts with a Big Idea question.

A graphic organizer helps you answer the Big Idea question.

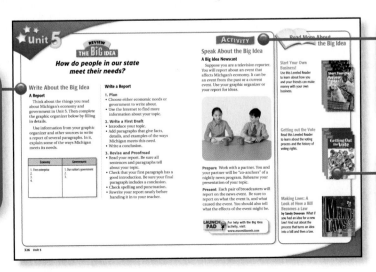

Each unit ends with a Write About the Big Idea to review what you have learned.

The Big Idea Activity lets you work with classmates on a project based on the Big Idea.

Other books can help you learn more about the Big Idea.

Reading Your Textbook

This book is organized to help you understand and apply social studies content and skills as you read.

● **Unit Opener** and **People Who Made a Difference** pages introduce you to people and places in the unit.

The Unit Opener picture and quote capture the excitement of the events of the unit.

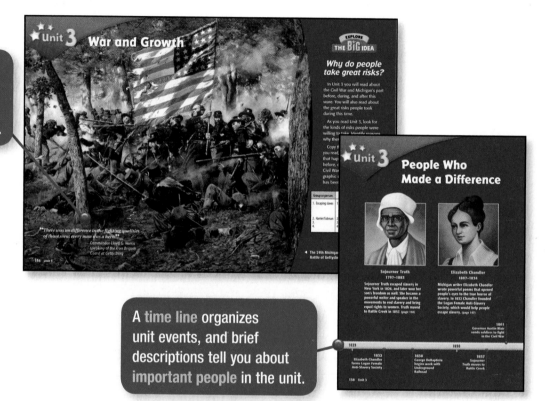

A time line organizes unit events, and brief descriptions tell you about important people in the unit.

● **Chapter Opener** pages introduce you to the time and place of events you will read about.

A map helps you see the locations of places from the chapter.

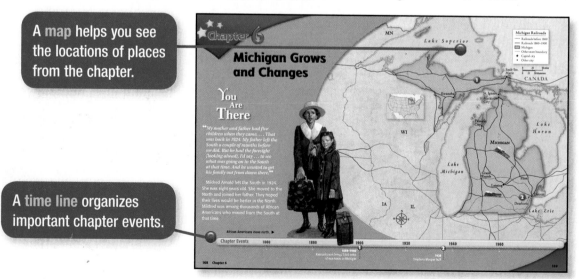

A time line organizes important chapter events.

Lesson Opener pages prepare you before you read.

Focus questions set a purpose for reading.

Graphic organizers help you organize information as you read.

Quick Check questions help you know if you understood the section.

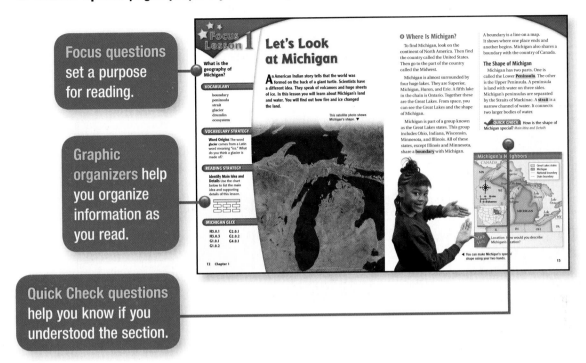

Lesson Review pages test your understanding of the lesson.

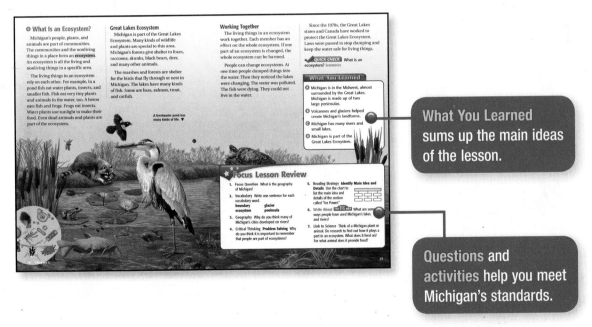

What You Learned sums up the main ideas of the lesson.

Questions and activities help you meet Michigan's standards.

Reading Skills pages help you understand social studies content using important reading skills.

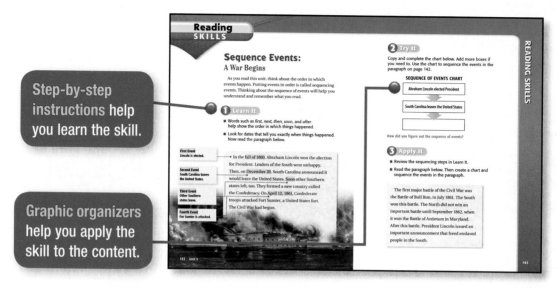

Step-by-step instructions help you learn the skill.

Graphic organizers help you apply the skill to the content.

Biographies and **Primary Sources** bring the past alive.

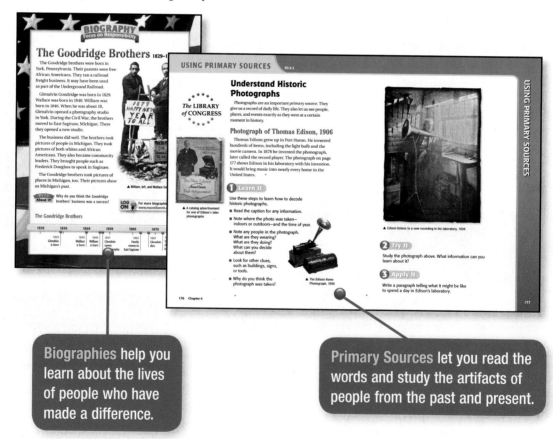

Biographies help you learn about the lives of people who have made a difference.

Primary Sources let you read the words and study the artifacts of people from the past and present.

● **Citizenship** pages show real-life participation in democracy.

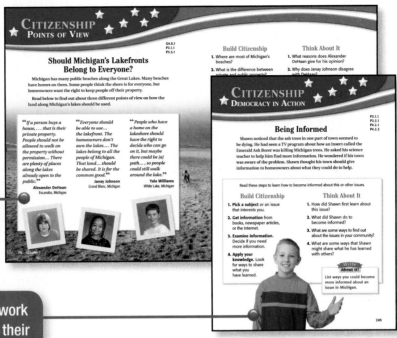

People explain their views on topics important to Michigan.

Third-graders work for changes in their communities.

● **Readers' Theater** and **Literature** bring Michigan history alive.

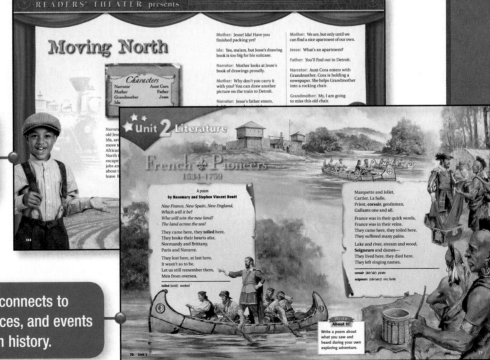

Readers' Theater plays give you a chance to think about events in Michigan in a new way.

Literature connects to people, places, and events in Michigan history.

GEOGRAPHY HANDBOOK

GEOGRAPHY AND YOU

Geography is the study of Earth and the people who live here. Most people think of geography as learning about cities, states, and countries, but geography is more than that. Geography includes learning about bodies of water, such as oceans, lakes, and rivers. Geography helps us learn about land, such as plains and mountains. Geography also helps us learn how to use land and water wisely.

Did you know that people are part of geography, too? Geography includes the study of how people adapt to living in a new place. How people move around, how they move goods, and how ideas travel from place to place are parts of geography.

In fact geography includes so many things that geographers have divided this information into six elements, or ideas, so you can better understand them.

SIX ESSENTIAL ELEMENTS

The World in Spatial Terms: Where is a place located and what land or water features does this place have?

Places and Regions: What is special about a place and what makes it different from another place?

Human Systems: How do people, ideas, and goods move from place to place?

Physical Systems: How and what has shaped the land and climate of a place, and how does this affect the plants, animals, and people there?

Environment and Society: How have people changed the land and water of a place, and how have the land and water affected people of a place?

Uses of Geography: How does geography influence events of the past, present, and future?

You have read about six essential elements. The five themes of geography are another way to divide the ideas of geography. The themes, or topics, are **location**, **place**, **region**, **movement**, and **human interaction**. Using these five themes is another way to understand events you read about in this book.

1. LOCATION

St. James lighthouse
on Beaver Island, Lake Michigan

In geography, location means an exact spot on the planet. A location often means a street name and number. You write a location when you address a letter.

2. PLACE

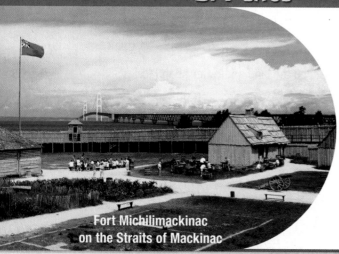

Fort Michilimackinac
on the Straits of Mackinac

A place is described by its physical features, such as rivers, mountains, or valleys. You could also include human features, such as cities, language, and traditions, in the description of a place.

3. REGION

Cornfield in Cadillac, Michigan

A region is larger area than a place or a location. The people in a region are affected by landforms and climate. A region has typical jobs and customs. For example, many people in the southern part of the Lower Peninsula make a living from farming.

4. MOVEMENT

The Sob Locks at Sault Ste. Marie

Throughout history, people have moved to find better land or a better life. Geographers study why these movements occurred. They also study how people's movements have changed a region.

5. HUMAN INTERACTION

The Cityscape of Detroit

Geographers are interested in how people adapt to their environments. Geographers also study how people change their environments. This interaction between people and their environments determines how land is used for cities, farms, or parks.

DICTIONARY OF GEOGRAPHIC TERMS

1 BASIN A bowl-shaped landform surrounded by higher land

2 BAY Part of an ocean or lake that extends deeply into the land

3 CANAL A channel built to carry water for irrigation or transportation

4 CANYON A deep, narrow valley with steep sides

5 COAST The land along an ocean

6 DAM A wall built across a river, creating a lake that stores water

7 DELTA Land made of soil left behind as a river drains into a larger body of water

8 DESERT A dry environment with few plants and animals

9 FAULT The border between two of the plates that make up Earth's crust

10 GLACIER A huge sheet of ice that moves slowly across the land

11 GULF Part of an ocean that extends into the land; larger than a bay

12 HARBOR A sheltered place along a coast where boats dock safely

13 HILL A rounded, raised landform; not as high as a mountain

14 ISLAND A body of land completely surrounded by water

15 LAKE A body of water completely surrounded by land

16 MESA A hill with a flat top; smaller than a plateau

17 MOUNTAIN A high landform with steep sides; higher than a hill

18 MOUNTAIN PASS A narrow gap through a mountain range

19 MOUTH The place where a river empties into a larger body of water

20 OCEAN A large body of salt water; oceans cover much of Earth's surface

21 PENINSULA A body of land nearly surrounded by water

22 PLAIN A large area of nearly flat land

23 PLATEAU A high, flat area that rises steeply above the surrounding land

24 PORT A place where ships load and unload their goods

25 RESERVOIR A natural or artificial lake used to store water

26 RIVER A stream of water that flows across the land and empties into another body of water

27 SOURCE The starting point of a river

28 VALLEY An area of low land between hills or mountains

29 VOLCANO An opening in Earth's surface through which hot rock and ash are forced out

30 WATERFALL A flow of water falling vertically

Looking at Earth

Earth and the Globe

From outer space, Earth looks like a big blue ball with brown and green spots. In order to see a complete view of Earth, we use a globe. A globe is a special map that is shaped like a sphere, or ball. The globe is a model of Earth. It shows what the land and water look like on Earth.

The large areas of land on Earth are called continents. There are seven continents on Earth. Their names are Africa, Antarctica, Asia, Australia, Europe, North America, and South America.

The big bodies of water are called oceans. The names of the four oceans are the Arctic, Atlantic, Indian, and Pacific oceans.

Hemispheres

The equator is an imaginary line on Earth. It divides the sphere of Earth in half. A word for half a sphere is hemisphere. The prefix "hemi" means half. Geographers divide Earth into four hemispheres.

All the land and ocean north of the equator is in the Northern Hemisphere. All the land and ocean south of the equator is in the Southern Hemisphere.

There is another imaginary line on Earth that runs from the North Pole to the South Pole. It is called the prime meridian. It divides Earth into the Eastern Hemisphere and the Western Hemisphere.

🌎 What continents are located on the equator?

🌏 In which two hemispheres is North America?

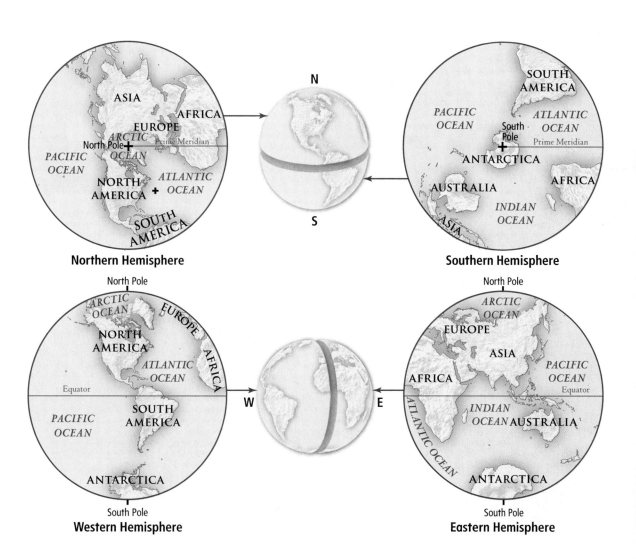

Northern Hemisphere

Southern Hemisphere

Western Hemisphere

Eastern Hemisphere

Reading a Map

Maps are drawings of places on Earth. Most maps have standard features to help you read the map. Some important information you get from a map is direction. The main directions are north, south, east, and west. These are called cardinal directions.

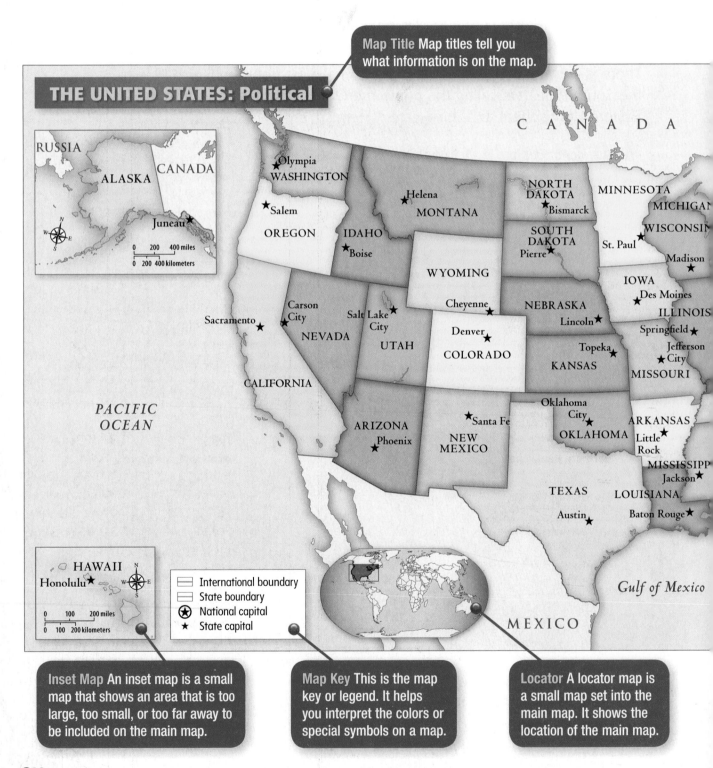

Map Title Map titles tell you what information is on the map.

THE UNITED STATES: Political

CANADA

RUSSIA
ALASKA
CANADA
Juneau
0 200 400 miles
0 200 400 kilometers

Olympia
WASHINGTON
Salem
OREGON
Boise
IDAHO
Helena
MONTANA
NORTH DAKOTA
Bismarck
SOUTH DAKOTA
Pierre
St. Paul
MINNESOTA
MICHIGAN
WISCONSIN
Madison

WYOMING
Cheyenne
NEBRASKA
Lincoln
IOWA
Des Moines
ILLINOIS
Springfield

Carson City
Salt Lake City
Denver
COLORADO
Topeka
Jefferson City
MISSOURI

Sacramento
NEVADA
UTAH
KANSAS

CALIFORNIA

PACIFIC OCEAN

Oklahoma City
Santa Fe
ARKANSAS
OKLAHOMA
Little Rock

ARIZONA
Phoenix
NEW MEXICO

MISSISSIPPI
Jackson

TEXAS
LOUISIANA
Baton Rouge
Austin

Gulf of Mexico

MEXICO

HAWAII
Honolulu
0 100 200 miles
0 100 200 kilometers

International boundary
State boundary
National capital
State capital

Inset Map An inset map is a small map that shows an area that is too large, too small, or too far away to be included on the main map.

Map Key This is the map key or legend. It helps you interpret the colors or special symbols on a map.

Locator A locator map is a small map set into the main map. It shows the location of the main map.

G10

The areas between the cardinal directions are called intermediate directions. They show the directions that are between the cardinal directions. These are northeast, southeast, southwest, and northwest. You use intermediate directions to describe one place in relation to another. For example, Lansing is northeast of Little Rock, Arkansas.

🌐 **In which direction would you travel to go from Lansing, Michigan, to Columbus, Ohio?**

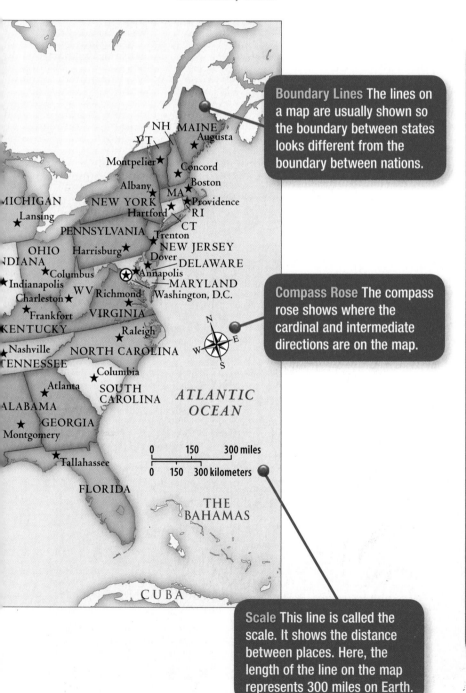

Boundary Lines The lines on a map are usually shown so the boundary between states looks different from the boundary between nations.

Compass Rose The compass rose shows where the cardinal and intermediate directions are on the map.

Scale This line is called the scale. It shows the distance between places. Here, the length of the line on the map represents 300 miles on Earth.

State Abbreviations

The letters on each state are abbreviated, or shortened. The abbreviations were invented by the United States Postal Service to help mail get delivered to the right place. Maps often use them when there is not enough room to write the whole state name.

ALABAMA	AL	MONTANA	MT
ALASKA	AK	NEBRASKA	NE
ARIZONA	AZ	NEVADA	NV
ARKANSAS	AR	NEW HAMPSHIRE	NH
CALIFORNIA	CA	NEW JERSEY	NJ
COLORADO	CO	NEW MEXICO	NM
CONNECTICUT	CT	NEW YORK	NY
DELAWARE	DE	NORTH CAROLINA	NC
FLORIDA	FL	NORTH DAKOTA	ND
GEORGIA	GA	OHIO	OH
HAWAII	HI	OKLAHOMA	OK
IDAHO	ID	OREGON	OR
ILLINOIS	IL	PENNSYLVANIA	PA
INDIANA	IN	RHODE ISLAND	RI
IOWA	IA	SOUTH CAROLINA	SC
KANSAS	KS	SOUTH DAKOTA	SD
KENTUCKY	KY	TENNESSEE	TN
LOUISIANA	LA	TEXAS	TX
MAINE	ME	UTAH	UT
MARYLAND	MD	VERMONT	VT
MASSACHUSETTS	MA	VIRGINIA	VA
MICHIGAN	MI	WASHINGTON	WA
MINNESOTA	MN	WEST VIRGINIA	WV
MISSISSIPPI	MS	WISCONSIN	WI
MISSOURI	MO	WYOMING	WY

Special Purpose Maps

Some maps are drawn to show one feature of an area. For example, some maps show population. Other maps show the amount of rainfall. Each of these maps is called a special purpose map.

Grid Maps

One kind of special purpose map is a grid map, a map which helps you locate things. Each box has a number and a letter. To find St. Ignace in B-3, put one finger on the letter B along the side of the map. Put another finger on the number 3 at the top. Move your fingers down and across until they meet at B-3.

A grid map usually has an index to locate places on the map. Find the place you are looking for in the index, and then use the grid number and letter to locate it on the map.

🌐 Find Escanaba on the map. What grid box is it in?

🌐 What are the grid number and letter for Houghton?

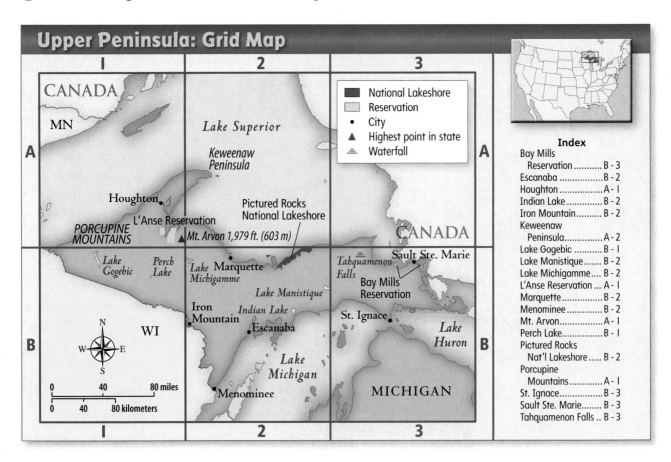

Upper Peninsula: Grid Map

Legend:
- National Lakeshore
- Reservation
- City •
- Highest point in state ▲
- Waterfall ≗

G12

Road Maps

A road map is one kind of special purpose map. Road maps show where the roads in a certain area go. By reading a road map you can figure out how to get from one place to another.

🌐 **Which interstate runs from Sault Ste. Marie to Flint?**

🌐 **Is route 127 a state highway or a U.S. highway?**

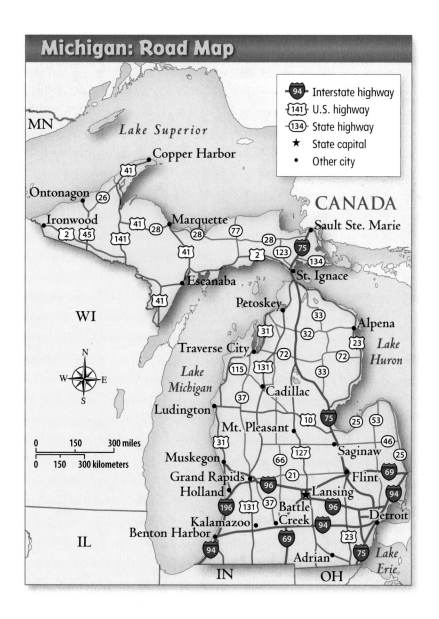

Michigan: Road Map

Legend:
- 94 Interstate highway
- 141 U.S. highway
- 134 State highway
- ★ State capital
- • Other city

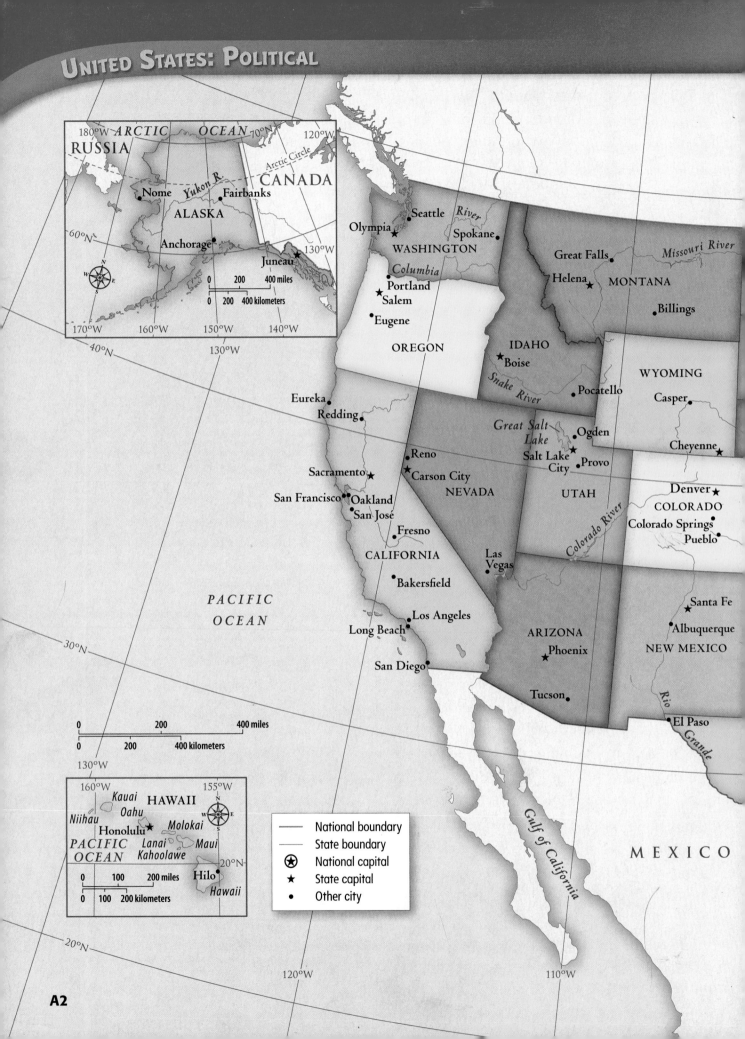

RUSSIA

ARCTIC   OCEAN

180°W   70°N   120°W

CANADA

Arctic Circle

Nome   *Yukon R.*   Fairbanks

ALASKA

60°N

Anchorage

130°W

Juneau

0   200   400 miles
0   200   400 kilometers

170°W   160°W   150°W   140°W

40°N

130°W

Seattle   *River*
Olympia   Spokane
WASHINGTON
Columbia   Great Falls   *Missouri River*
Portland   Helena   MONTANA
Salem
Eugene   Billings
OREGON   IDAHO
Boise   WYOMING
Eureka   *Snake River*   Pocatello
Redding   *Great Salt Lake*   Casper
Ogden   Cheyenne
Reno   Salt Lake City   Provo
Sacramento   Carson City   UTAH   Denver
San Francisco   NEVADA   COLORADO
Oakland   Colorado Springs
San José   Pueblo
Fresno   *Colorado River*
CALIFORNIA   Santa Fe
Las Vegas   Albuquerque
Bakersfield   ARIZONA   NEW MEXICO
Los Angeles   Phoenix
Long Beach
San Diego   Tucson

PACIFIC OCEAN

30°N

El Paso
Rio Grande

0   200   400 miles
0   200   400 kilometers

130°W

160°W   HAWAII   155°W
Kauai   Oahu
Niihau   Molokai
Honolulu
PACIFIC OCEAN   Lanai   Maui
Kahoolawe   20°N
Hilo
Hawaii

0   100   200 miles
0   100   200 kilometers

Gulf of California

MEXICO

	National boundary
	State boundary
★(circle)	National capital
★	State capital
•	Other city

20°N

120°W   110°W

CANADA

NORTH DAKOTA ★ Grand Forks ★ Fargo
Bismarck ★

SOUTH DAKOTA ★ Pierre
Sioux Falls •

NEBRASKA
Omaha •
Lincoln ★
Platte River
Missouri River

Lake Superior
Duluth •
Marquette •
MINNESOTA
St. Paul ★
Minneapolis ★
WISCONSIN
Green Bay •
Milwaukee •
Madison ★
IOWA
Cedar Rapids •
Des Moines ★
Davenport •

MICHIGAN
Lake Huron
Lake Michigan
Grand Rapids •
Lansing ★
Detroit •
Lake Erie
Toledo • Cleveland •

ILLINOIS
Chicago •
Gary •
INDIANA
Indianapolis ★
Springfield ★
OHIO
Columbus ★
Cincinnati •

Lake Ontario
NEW YORK
Buffalo •
Albany ★
Pittsburgh •
PENNSYLVANIA
Harrisburg ★

Hartford ★
Newark •
Trenton ★
Baltimore •
Washington, D.C. ⊛
WEST VIRGINIA
Charleston ★

NEW HAMPSHIRE
VERMONT
Montpelier ★
Concord ★

MAINE
Augusta ★
Portland •

Boston ★
MASSACHUSETTS
Providence ★
RHODE ISLAND
CONNECTICUT
New York City •
NEW JERSEY
Philadelphia •
Dover ★
DELAWARE
Annapolis ★
MARYLAND

KANSAS
Topeka ★
Kansas City •
Kansas City •
Wichita •

MISSOURI
St. Louis •
Jefferson City ★
Evansville •
Ohio River
Louisville •
Frankfort ★
KENTUCKY

Richmond ★
Norfolk •
VIRGINIA

Raleigh ★
NORTH CAROLINA
Charlotte •

OKLAHOMA
Tulsa •
Oklahoma City ★
Arkansas River
Fort Smith •
ARKANSAS
Little Rock ★
Red River

Nashville ★
TENNESSEE
Knoxville •
Tennessee River
Memphis •

Columbia •
SOUTH CAROLINA
Charleston •

TEXAS
Fort Worth •
Dallas •
Austin ★
San Antonio •
Corpus Christi •
Laredo •
Brazos River
Colorado River

Mississippi River
MISSISSIPPI
Jackson ★
LOUISIANA
Shreveport •
Baton Rouge ★
New Orleans •

Birmingham •
ALABAMA
Montgomery ★
Mobile •
Biloxi •

Atlanta ★
GEORGIA
Columbus •
Savannah •
Tallahassee ★
Jacksonville •

Orlando •
FLORIDA
Tampa •
Miami •

ATLANTIC OCEAN

Gulf of Mexico

THE BAHAMAS

CUBA

100°W   90°W   80°W   70°W   50°N   40°N   30°N

N
W E
S

A3

ALASKA inset

ARCTIC OCEAN
70°N
RUSSIA
Bering Strait
Arctic Circle
BROOKS RANGE
ALASKA
CANADA
Mt. McKinley
20,320 ft.
(6,194 m) ▲ RANGE
Yukon River
60°N
Bering Sea
Gulf of Alaska
ALASKA RANGE
Aleutian Islands
0   200   400 miles
0   200   400 kilometers
170°W   160°W   150°W   140°W

Legend

— National boundary
— State boundary
▲ Mountain peak
▲ Highest point
▼ Lowest point

HAWAII inset

160°W   155°W
Kauai
Niihau   Oahu   HAWAII
Molokai
PACIFIC   Lanai   Maui
OCEAN   Kahoolawe
20°N   Hawaii
Mauna Kea
13,796 ft.
(4,205 m)
0   100   200 miles
0   100   200 kilometers

Main map

40°N
130°W
Puget Sound
Mt. Rainier
14,410 ft. (4,392 m)
Mt. St. Helens
8,363 ft. (2,549 m)
Columbia R.
COLUMBIA PLATEAU
ROCKY
Missouri River
Mt. Hood
11,239 ft.
(3,426 m)
CASCADE RANGE
Snake River
Granite Peak
12,799 ft.
(3,901 m)
BLACK HILLS
Mt. Shasta
14,162 ft.
(4,317 m)
Cape Mendocino
COAST RANGES
Sacramento R.
SIERRA NEVADA
CENTRAL VALLEY
San Joaquin R.
Great Salt Lake
GREAT BASIN
GREAT SALT LAKE DESERT
WASATCH RANGE
MOUNTAINS
Lake Tahoe
Kings Peak
13,528 ft.
(4,123 m)
Mt. Elbert
14,433 ft.
(4,399 m)
San Francisco Bay
COLORADO
Pikes Peak
14,110 ft.
(4,301 m)
Mt. Whitney
14,494 ft.
(4,418 m)
Death Valley
-282 ft. ▼
(-86 m)
Lake Mead
River
PLATEAU
Wheeler Peak
13,161 ft.
(4,011 m)
PACIFIC OCEAN
MOJAVE DESERT
Salton Sea
Colorado
Humphreys Peak
12,633 ft.
(3,851 m)
CONTINENTAL DIVIDE
Pecos River
Channel Islands
SONORAN DESERT
Gila River
Guadalupe Peak
8,749 ft.
(2,667 m)
Rio Grande
30°N
Colorado
Gulf of California
0   200   400 miles
0   200   400 kilometers
20°N
120°W
MEXICO
110°W

A4

CANADA

Lake of the Woods

MESABI RANGE

Lake Superior

GREAT LAKES

St. Lawrence River

WHITE MOUNTAINS

GREEN MOUNTAINS

Mt. Washington
6,288 ft.
(1,917 m)

Lake Michigan

Lake Huron

Lake Ontario

ADIRONDACK MOUNTAINS

Hudson River

Cape Cod

Mississippi River

GREAT

Lake Erie

ALLEGHENY PLATEAU

Susquehanna River

Long Island

40°N

CENTRAL PLAINS

River

ALLEGHENY MOUNTAINS

A P P A L A C H I A N   M O U N T A I N S

Delaware Bay

Missouri River

P
L
A
I
N
S

Platte River

Wabash River

Ohio River

Potomac River

PIEDMONT

Chesapeake Bay

Arkansas River

INTERIOR PLAINS

OZARK PLATEAU

River

Tennessee River

Cape Hatteras

▲ Mt. Mitchell
6,684 ft.
(2,037 m)

OUACHITA MOUNTAINS

Mississippi River

Alabama River

Savannah River

ATLANTIC COASTAL PLAIN

ATLANTIC OCEAN

Red River

Brazos River

Chattahoochee River

30°N

Colorado River

EDWARDS PLATEAU

GULF COASTAL PLAIN

Mobile Bay

Galveston Bay

Mississippi River Delta

Lake Okeechobee

THE BAHAMAS

Gulf of Mexico

N
W E
S

Florida Keys

Straits of Florida

CUBA

20°N

100°W

90°W

80°W

A5

80°N
160°W   120°W
60°N
ALASKA (U.S.)
CANADA
NORTH AMERICA
40°N
UNITED STATES
BERMUDA (U.K.)
ATLANTIC OCEAN
MIDWAY ISLANDS (U.S.)
Tropic of Cancer
HAWAII (U.S.)
20°N
See inset below
MEXICO
Caribbean Sea
PACIFIC OCEAN
GUYANA
SURINAME
VENEZUELA
FRENCH GUIANA (France)
GALAPAGOS ISLANDS (Ecuador)
COLOMBIA
0° Equator
ECUADOR
SOUTH AMERICA
PERU
BRAZIL
AMERICAN SAMOA (U.S.)
SAMOA
COOK ISLANDS (N.Z.)
FRENCH POLYNESIA (France)
BOLIVIA
TONGA
PARAGUAY
20°S
PITCAIRN ISLAND (U.K.)
Tropic of Capricorn
URUGUAY
CHILE
ARGENTINA
40°S
FALKLAND ISLANDS (U.K.)
60°S
Antarctic Circle
80°W
120°W
160°W

Central America and West Indies

90°W   80°W   70°W
Gulf of Mexico
FLORIDA (U.S.)
0   200   400 miles
0   200   400 kilometers
Tropic of Cancer
THE BAHAMAS
TURKS & CAICOS ISLANDS (U.K.)
ATLANTIC OCEAN
60°W
20°N
CUBA
20°N
PUERTO RICO (U.S.)   VIRGIN IS. (U.K.)
ST. KITTS & NEVIS
MEXICO
CAYMAN IS. (U.K.)
HAITI
DOMINICAN REPUBLIC
ANTIGUA & BARBUDA
BELIZE
JAMAICA
VIRGIN IS. (U.S.)
GUADELOUPE (France)
GUATEMALA
MONTSERRAT (U.K.)
DOMINICA
MARTINIQUE (France)
HONDURAS
Caribbean Sea
ST. LUCIA
EL SALVADOR
NETHERLANDS ANTILLES (Netherlands)
ST. VINCENT & THE GRENADINES
BARBADOS
NICARAGUA
ARUBA (Netherlands)
GRENADA
TRINIDAD AND TOBAGO
10°N
60°W
COSTA RICA
PACIFIC OCEAN
PANAMA
COLOMBIA
VENEZUELA
GUYANA

ARCTIC OCEAN

GREENLAND (Denmark)
SVALBARD (Norway)
Arctic Circle
ICELAND
See inset below

RUSSIA

EUROPE
AZORES (Portugal)
KAZAKHSTAN
MONGOLIA
ASIA
GEORGIA
UZBEKISTAN
KYRGYZSTAN
NORTH KOREA
JAPAN
PACIFIC OCEAN
CANARY ISLANDS (Spain)
ARMENIA
TURKEY
TURKMENISTAN
TAJIKISTAN
SOUTH KOREA
MOROCCO
TUNISIA LEBANON
SYRIA
IRAQ
AZERBAIJAN
AFGHANISTAN
CHINA
Tropic of Cancer
ALGERIA
LIBYA
ISRAEL
JORDAN
IRAN
KUWAIT
BAHRAIN
QATAR
PAKISTAN
BHUTAN
NEPAL
TAIWAN
WAKE ISLAND (U.S.)
WESTERN SAHARA (Morocco)
EGYPT
SAUDI ARABIA
UNITED ARAB EMIRATES
BANGLADESH
INDIA
NORTHERN MARIANA ISLANDS (U.S.)
MARSHALL ISLANDS
CAPE VERDE
MAURITANIA
MALI
NIGER
CHAD
SUDAN
ERITREA
YEMEN
OMAN
MYANMAR (BURMA)
LAOS
VIETNAM
GUAM (U.S.)
FEDERATED STATES OF MICRONESIA
SENEGAL
GAMBIA
GUINEA-BISSAU
GUINEA
BURKINA FASO
BENIN
NIGERIA
CENTRAL AFRICAN REPUBLIC
DJIBOUTI
ETHIOPIA
THAILAND
PHILIPPINES
PALAU
SIERRA LEONE
LIBERIA
GHANA
AFRICA
SRI LANKA
CAMBODIA
BRUNEI
MALAYSIA
COTE D'IVOIRE TOGO
SAO TOMÉ AND PRINCIPE
CAMEROON
UGANDA
KENYA
SOMALIA
MALDIVES
Equator
KIRIBATI
EQUATORIAL GUINEA
GABON
CONGO
RWANDA
DEM. REPUBLIC OF THE CONGO
BURUNDI
TANZANIA
SEYCHELLES
INDIAN OCEAN
INDONESIA
PAPUA NEW GUINEA
SOLOMON ISLANDS
ATLANTIC OCEAN
ANGOLA
ZAMBIA
MALAWI
COMOROS
EAST TIMOR
TUVALU
ZIMBABWE
MADAGASCAR
NAMIBIA
BOTSWANA
MAURITIUS
REUNION (France)
Tropic of Capricorn
AUSTRALIA
VANUATU
FIJI
MOZAMBIQUE
SWAZILAND
SOUTH AFRICA
LESOTHO
NEW CALEDONIA (France)
N
W   E
S
SOUTH GEORGIA & SOUTH SANDWICH ISLANDS (U.K.)
FRENCH SOUTHERN & ANTARCTIC LANDS (France)
NEW ZEALAND

0   1,000   2,000 miles
0   1,000   2,000 kilometers

ANTARCTICA

Antarctic Circle

Europe

NORWAY
FINLAND
RUSSIA
SWEDEN
North Sea
DENMARK
Baltic Sea
ESTONIA
LATVIA
LITHUANIA
RUSSIA
0   200   400 miles
0   200   400 kilometers
IRELAND
UNITED KINGDOM
BELARUS
N
W   E
S
ATLANTIC OCEAN
NETHERLANDS
POLAND
BELGIUM
GERMANY
LUXEMBOURG
CZECH REPUBLIC
UKRAINE
LIECHTENSTEIN
SLOVAKIA
MOLDOVA
FRANCE
AUSTRIA
HUNGARY
SWITZERLAND
SLOVENIA
ROMANIA
RUSSIA
MONACO
CROATIA
SERBIA AND MONTENEGRO
BULGARIA
Black Sea
GEORGIA
SAN MARINO
BOSNIA AND HERZEGOVINA
ANDORRA
CORSICA (France)
MACEDONIA
PORTUGAL
SPAIN
ITALY
ALBANIA
BALEARIC IS. (Spain)
SARDINIA (Italy)
GREECE
TURKEY
GIBRALTAR (U.K.)
SICILY (Italy)
MOROCCO
ALGERIA
TUNISIA
MALTA
CRETE (Gr.)
CYPRUS
LEBANON
SYRIA
Mediterranean Sea

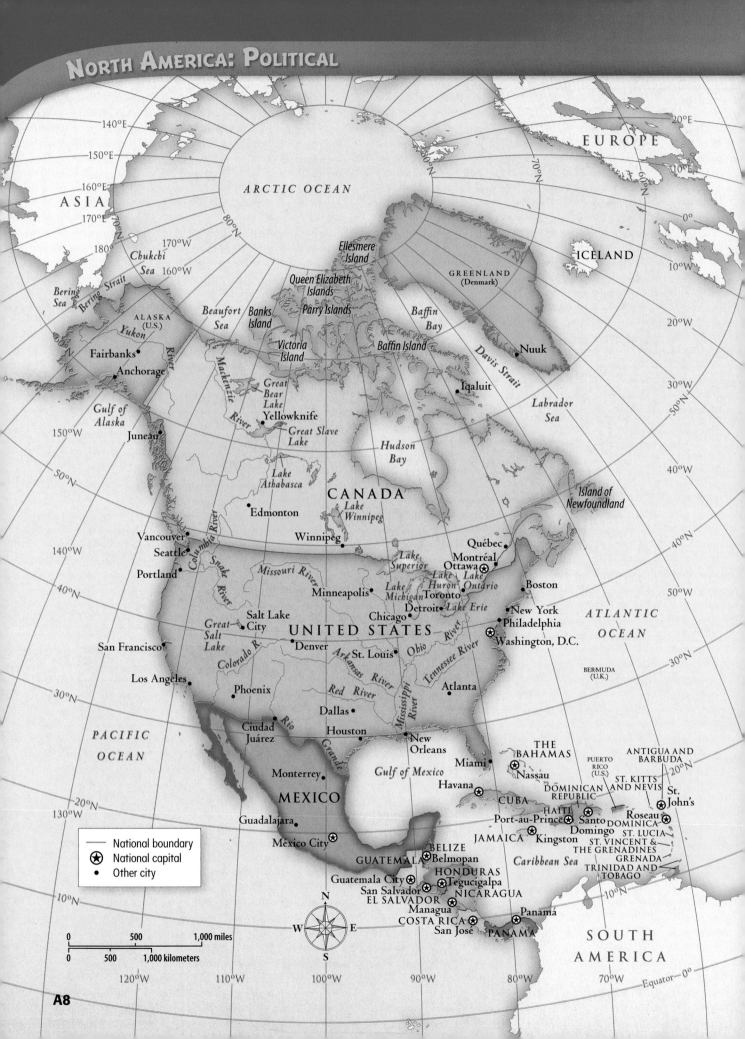

EUROPE

ASIA

ARCTIC OCEAN

Chukchi
Sea

Bering
Strait

Bering
Sea

Ellesmere
Island

ICELAND

Queen Elizabeth
Islands

GREENLAND
(Denmark)

Beaufort
Sea

Banks
Island

Parry Islands

Baffin
Bay

ALASKA
(U.S.)

Yukon
River

Fairbanks

Anchorage

Mackenzie
River

Victoria
Island

Baffin Island

Nuuk

Davis Strait

Gulf of
Alaska

Great
Bear
Lake

Iqaluit

Labrador
Sea

Juneau

Yellowknife

Great Slave
Lake

Hudson
Bay

Lake
Athabasca

CANADA

Island of
Newfoundland

Edmonton

Lake
Winnipeg

Québec

Vancouver

Columbia River

Winnipeg

Montréal

Seattle

Missouri River

Lake
Superior

Ottawa

Boston

Portland

Snake
River

Minneapolis

Lake
Huron

Lake
Michigan

Toronto

Lake
Ontario

New York

Salt Lake
City

Detroit

Lake Erie

Philadelphia

Great
Salt
Lake

UNITED STATES

Chicago

Ohio
River

Tennessee River

Washington, D.C.

ATLANTIC
OCEAN

San Francisco

Denver

St. Louis

Arkansas
River

Colorado R.

Los Angeles

Red
River

Atlanta

BERMUDA
(U.K.)

Phoenix

Dallas

Mississippi
River

PACIFIC
OCEAN

Ciudad
Juárez

Rio
Grande

Houston

New
Orleans

Miami

THE
BAHAMAS

Nassau

PUERTO
RICO
(U.S.)

ANTIGUA AND
BARBUDA

ST. KITTS
AND NEVIS

St.
John's

Monterrey

Gulf of Mexico

Havana

CUBA

DOMINICAN
REPUBLIC

MEXICO

HAITI

Santo
Domingo

DOMINICA

Roseau

Guadalajara

Port-au-Prince

JAMAICA

Kingston

ST. LUCIA

ST. VINCENT &
THE GRENADINES

México City

BELIZE

GRENADA

GUATEMALA

Belmopan

Caribbean Sea

TRINIDAD AND
TOBAGO

Guatemala City

HONDURAS

Tegucigalpa

San Salvador

NICARAGUA

EL SALVADOR

Managua

Panamá

COSTA RICA

PANAMA

San José

SOUTH

AMERICA

National boundary

National capital

Other city

0   500   1,000 miles

0   500   1,000 kilometers

N
W   E
S

140°E
150°E
160°E
170°E
180°
170°W
160°W
150°W

80°N
70°N

20°E
10°E
0°
10°W
20°W
30°W

50°N
40°N
30°N

60°N
50°N
40°N
30°N

150°W
140°W
40°N
30°N
130°W
20°N

120°W   110°W   100°W   90°W   80°W   70°W   Equator—0°

SOUTH AMERICA: POLITICAL

Caribbean Sea

CENTRAL AMERICA

Barranquilla
Maracaibo
Valencia Caracas
Lake Maracaibo
Orinoco River
VENEZUELA
Georgetown
Paramaribo
GUYANA
Cayenne
SURINAME
FRENCH GUIANA (France)

ATLANTIC OCEAN

Medellín
Gulf of Panama
Bogotá
Cali
Magdalena River
COLOMBIA

Negro River
Manaus
River
Belém

Quito
Equator
ECUADOR
Guayaquil
GALAPAGOS ISLANDS (Ecuador)
Iquitos
Amazon River
Madeira River
Tapajos River
Xingu River

Equator

Trujillo
PERU
Callao Lima
Cuzco
BRAZIL
São Francisco River
Recife

Lake Titicaca
Arequipa
La Paz
BOLIVIA
Brasília
Salvador (Bahía)

Sucre
Paraguay River
Paraná River
Belo Horizonte

Antofagasta
Tropic of Capricorn
PARAGUAY
Asunción
São Paulo
Rio de Janeiro
Tropic of Capricorn

Tucumán
CHILE
Paraná River
Paraná
Uruguay River
Porto Alegre

Córdoba
Rosario
URUGUAY
Valparaíso
Santiago
ARGENTINA
Buenos Aires
Montevideo
Rio de la Plata

PACIFIC OCEAN

Concepción
Colorado River

ATLANTIC OCEAN

| National boundary |
| ⊛ National capital |
| • Other city |

FALKLAND ISLANDS (ISLAS MALVINAS) (U.K.)

0   400   800 miles
0   400   800 kilometers

Punta Arenas
Strait of Magellan

SOUTH GEORGIA (U.K.)

15°N   75°W   15°N
0°   Equator   0°
15°S   15°S
Tropic of Capricorn
30°S   30°S
45°S   45°S

105°W   90°W   75°W   60°W   45°W   30°W

N W E S

MICHIGAN: PHYSICAL

48°N

MN

Isle Royale
National Park

Isle Royale

Lake Superior

CANADA

Keweenaw
National
Historical Park

*Keweenaw
Peninsula*

Keweenaw Bay

Hancock

Ontonagon

Gogebic Range

Huron Mts.

Ironwood

Mt. Arvon
1,979 ft.
(603 m)

Marquette

Ottawa
National Forest

UPPER PENINSULA

Menominee Range

Hiawatha
National
Forest

*Tahquamenon
Falls*

Sault Sainte
Marie

*St. Marys
River*

*Drummond
Island*

Pictured
Rocks
National
Lakeshore

Hiawatha
National
Forest

46°N

Manistique

St. Ignace

*Straits
of Mackinac*

Bois Blanc Island

Escanaba

Beaver Island

Cheboygan

*Grand
Traverse
Bay*

Petoskey

Alpena

*Lake
Huron*

Menominee

*N. Manitou
Island*

Bellaire

WI

*S. Manitou
Island*

Kalkaska

Au
Sable River

Manistee River

Traverse
City

Grayling

Huron
National
Forest

Sleeping
Bear Dunes
National
Lakeshore

Manistee

Cadillac

*Houghton
Lake*

44°N

Ludington

Muskegon
River

Manistee
National
Forest

Big
Rapids

Mount
Pleasant

Bay
City

Saginaw Bay

*Lake
Michigan*

Saginaw River

Saginaw

LOWER
PENINSULA

Port
Huron

Muskegon

Flint

Grand Haven

*Grand
River*

Lansing

*Lake
St. Clair*

Grand
Rapids

Pontiac

Holland

Detroit

Battle
Creek

Irish Hills

Kalamazoo

Jackson

Ann
Arbor

Benton
Harbor

Monroe

42°N

IL

St. Joseph River

Adrian

*Lake
Erie*

Niles

IN

OH

N
W · E
S

■	National forest/ park lands
—	International boundary
—	State boundary
★	State capital
●	Other city
▲	Highest point
≡	Waterfall

0 — 50 — 100 miles
0 — 50 — 100 kilometers

90°W   **88°W**   **86°W**   **84°W**

A10

MN

Lake Superior

0   50   100 miles
0   50   100 kilometers

CANADA

Hancock ✈

Ontonagon •

L'Anse

Ironwood •

Marquette •

Sault Sainte
Marie

Lac Vieux
Desert

Bay Mills   Bay Mills

Hannahville
(Potawatomi)

Manistique •

St. Ignace

Escanaba •

Mackinaw City •

Cheboygan •

Menominee •

Petoskey •

Alpena •

Lake
Huron

WI

Grand
Traverse

Bellaire ✈

Kalkaska •

Traverse
City ✈

Grayling •

Manistee •

Cadillac •

Ludington •

Isabella •

Lake
Michigan

Big
Rapids •

Isabella

Midland

Muskegon •

Mount
Pleasant

Bay City •

Saginaw ✈

Grand Haven •

Grand
Rapids ✈

Owosso •

Flint ✈

Port
Huron •

Wyoming •

Lansing ★

Pontiac ✈

Troy ✈

Holland •

Battle
Creek ✈

Jackson •

Dearborn •

Benton
Harbor

Kalamazoo •

✈ Ann
Arbor

Detroit ✈

Niles •

Potawatomi

Potawatomi

Adrian •

Monroe •

Lake
Erie

IL

IN

OH

Legend:

- ▪ American Indian reservation
- ● American Indian reservation
- — International boundary
- — State boundary
- ✈ Airport
- ★ State capital
- • Other city

N
W   E
S

90°W   88°W   86°W   84°W

48°N

46°N

44°N

42°N

A11

MICHIGAN: COUNTIES

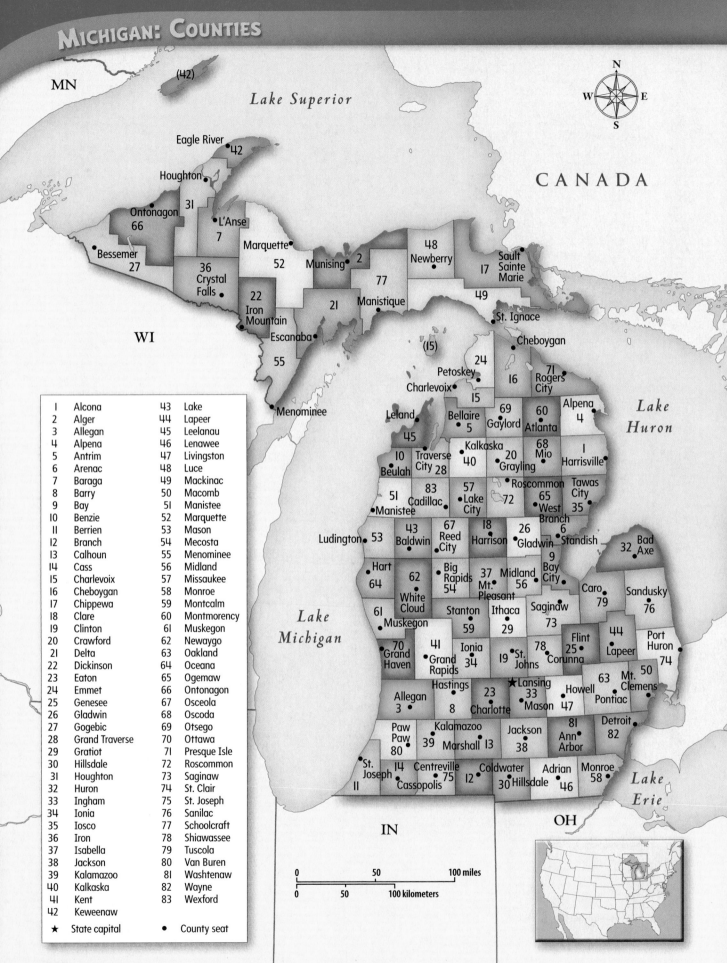

MN

Lake Superior

(42)

CANADA

Eagle River • 42

Houghton •
31

Ontonagon • L'Anse
66 • 7

Marquette •
Bessemer 52 Munising •
27 36 2

Crystal 77
Falls 22 21
Iron 48
Mountain Newberry
Escanaba • 17
55 Manistique

Sault
Sainte
Marie
49

St. Ignace •

WI

Menominee

IN

OH

Lake Huron

Cheboygan •
(15)
24
Petoskey • 16 71
Charlevoix • 15 Rogers
City
Leland • Bellaire 69 60 Alpena
• 5 Gaylord Atlanta 4
45 Kalkaska 68
10 Traverse 40 20 Mio Harrisville
Beulah City 28 Grayling 1
83 57 Roscommon Tawas
51 Cadillac Lake 72 65 City
Manistee • City West 35
43 67 18 26 Branch
53 Baldwin Reed Harrison Gladwin 6
Ludington City 9 Standish 32 Bad
Hart Big 37 Midland Bay Axe
64 62 Rapids Mt. 56 City
White 54 Pleasant Saginaw Caro Sandusky
Cloud Stanton Ithaca 73 79 76
61 59 29
Muskegon 50
41 Ionia 78 Flint Lapeer Port
70 Grand 34 19 St. 25 44 Huron
Grand Rapids Johns Corunna 74
Haven Lansing 63 Mt.
Hastings ★ 33 Howell Clemens
Allegan 23 Mason 47 Pontiac Detroit
3 8 Charlotte 81 82
Paw Kalamazoo Jackson Ann
Paw 39 13 38 Arbor
80 Marshall
St. 14 Centreville Coldwater Adrian Monroe
Joseph 75 12 30 Hillsdale 46 58
11 Cassopolis Lake
Erie

Lake Michigan

Lake Erie

1	Alcona	43	Lake
2	Alger	44	Lapeer
3	Allegan	45	Leelanau
4	Alpena	46	Lenawee
5	Antrim	47	Livingston
6	Arenac	48	Luce
7	Baraga	49	Mackinac
8	Barry	50	Macomb
9	Bay	51	Manistee
10	Benzie	52	Marquette
11	Berrien	53	Mason
12	Branch	54	Mecosta
13	Calhoun	55	Menominee
14	Cass	56	Midland
15	Charlevoix	57	Missaukee
16	Cheboygan	58	Monroe
17	Chippewa	59	Montcalm
18	Clare	60	Montmorency
19	Clinton	61	Muskegon
20	Crawford	62	Newaygo
21	Delta	63	Oakland
22	Dickinson	64	Oceana
23	Eaton	65	Ogemaw
24	Emmet	66	Ontonagon
25	Genesee	67	Osceola
26	Gladwin	68	Oscoda
27	Gogebic	69	Otsego
28	Grand Traverse	70	Ottawa
29	Gratiot	71	Presque Isle
30	Hillsdale	72	Roscommon
31	Houghton	73	Saginaw
32	Huron	74	St. Clair
33	Ingham	75	St. Joseph
34	Ionia	76	Sanilac
35	Iosco	77	Schoolcraft
36	Iron	78	Shiawassee
37	Isabella	79	Tuscola
38	Jackson	80	Van Buren
39	Kalamazoo	81	Washtenaw
40	Kalkaska	82	Wayne
41	Kent	83	Wexford
42	Keweenaw		

★ State capital   • County seat

0 ___ 50 ___ 100 miles

0 __ 50 __ 100 kilometers

Great Lakes states
State capital
Other city

CANADA

Lake Superior

50°N

N
W   E
S

ND

MINNESOTA

MICHIGAN

45°N

Lake Huron

St. Paul
Minneapolis

SD

WISCONSIN

Lake Michigan

Milwaukee
Madison

Lansing
Detroit

Lake Erie

80°W

IA

Chicago

Cleveland

PA

NE

ILLINOIS

OHIO

40°N

INDIANA

Columbus

Springfield

Indianapolis

Cincinnati

WV

KS

St. Louis

MO

KY

VA

OK

TN

NC

AR

MS   AL

0   100   200 miles
0   100   200 kilometers

95°W   90°W   85°W

Michigan and Its First People

"There is not a lake or mountain that had not connected with it some story of delight or wonder, and nearly every beast and bird is the subject of some storyteller...."

— George Copley, Ojibway

How do people adapt to where they live?

◀ Lake Superior shoreline

The first chapter in Unit 1 tells the story of Michigan's land and how this land is used. You'll read about our state's rivers and lakes and hills and valleys. You will also learn about two areas of Michigan. In the second chapter, you will read about how the first people of Michigan lived here.

As you read the unit, think about how Michigan's land has influenced both the people who live here now and the people who lived here long ago.

Copy the graphic organizer below. As you read the chapters in the unit, fill it in with the ways people of long ago and of today have adapted.

Michigan People	Geography	Climate	Natural Resources
People long ago			
People today			

3

People Who Made a Difference

Henry Rowe Schoolcraft
1793–1864

Henry Rowe Schoolcraft studied the land as a geographer and geologist, a person who studies rocks. He also studied American Indian cultures.
(page 42)

Andrew Blackbird
1822–1908

Andrew Blackbird was a member of the Odawa group who worked as a writer, a historian, and a translator of languages. His book about his people provides a wonderful view into the past. (page 10)

1750	1800	1850

1819
Henry Schoolcraft makes geographical survey in Michigan

1861
Andrew Blackbird appointed translator for U.S. government

LOG ON

For more biographies, visit:
www.macmillanmh.com

Marge Anderson
1932–

Marge Anderson served as leader of her band of the Ojibway from 1991 to 2005. She has worked to improve the living conditions of her band and to keep Ojibway traditions alive.
(Page 53)

Frank Ettawageshik
1949–

Frank Ettawageshik is an Odawa storyteller, pottery maker, and teacher. He has recreated a way of making pottery that Odawa artists used hundreds of years ago.
(Page 55)

1900

1950

2000

1957
Mackinac Bridge completed

1974
Frank Ettawageshik begins using traditional pottery methods

1991
Marge Anderson appointed leader of Mille Lacs Ojibway

THE LEGEND OF SLEEPING BEAR

Adapted from the book **by Kathy-jo Wargin**
illustrated by Gijsbert van Frankenhuyzen

American Indians told this story about how the Sleeping Bear Dunes and Manitou Islands were formed:

Long ago, a Mother Bear and her two cubs lived on the edge of a great lake. One day, a forest fire forced the bears to dive into the water. All that day and through the night they swam to reach the other side.

They swam and they swam, growing weary and tired. . . . And as they swam, Mother Bear kept turning her large black face to make sure that her cubs were not far behind. She watched as their paws struggled against the water. And as their small round faces became smaller and smaller between the waves of the mighty lake, Mother Bear grew worried. Soon nighttime fell. . . . Mother Bear . . . swam through the night. Through her tired eyes she noticed the morning sun was beginning to rise. . . . She looked back once more but could not see her cubs.

Mother Bear collapsed on the banks of the shore. Her wet, heavy paws sank into the deep sand. . . . Mother Bear paced up and down the water's edge, but her cubs were nowhere to be found. Mother Bear climbed to the top of the highest hill. She looked out over the

deep dark water, but saw no sign of her cubs.

She waited. And waited. Mother Bear waited, but her cubs never reached the shore. . . .

High upon the hill, Mother Bear fell fast asleep in her sorrow. Years passed, and the winds of Lake Michigan blew blankets of sand upon her, keeping her warm and safe in her slumber.

Over time, the great spirit of the land felt her sadness, recognizing her . . . love for her children. With a tremendous gust of wind, the spirit brought the two cubs near the shore, raising them out of the water as two magnificent islands, placing them forever within the watchful and caring eyes of Mother Bear.

The cubs now stand suspended in time as the North and South Manitou Islands.

Write About It!

Write your own story that explains how something in nature came to be as it is.

Identify Main Idea and Details:
Michigan's Resources

In this unit you will read about Michigan's land and its first people. Looking for main ideas and details when you read will help you understand the important ideas in social studies. The main idea is what a paragraph is about. Often the main idea is stated in the first sentence of the paragraph. The details tell about the main idea. Keeping track of main ideas and details will help you understand what you read.

 **1 Learn It**

- Identify the information in the paragraph.

- Decide whether the first sentence states the main idea.

- Look for details. Think about what these details tell about.

- Now read the paragraph below. Look for the main idea and details.

Main Idea
The first sentence often states the main idea.

Details
Marquette grew because of the discovery of iron. These sentences tell details about the importance of iron to Marquette.

The city of Marquette grew because of the discovery of the mineral iron ore. Until iron ore was discovered nearby in the 1850s, few people lived in Marquette. Then mining companies started to load their ore onto ships at Marquette to send it to factories in other states. Marquette grew rapidly. Today iron mining is still important in Marquette.

2 Try It

Copy and complete the chart below. Then fill in the chart by listing the main idea and supporting details from the paragraph on page 8.

MAIN IDEA AND DETAILS CHART

Marquette grew because of the discovery of iron ore.

How did you find the main idea and details?

3 Apply It

- Review the steps for finding the main idea and details in Learn It.

- Now read the paragraph below. Make a chart to show the main idea and details.

The iron that Michigan produces is used for many things. Most of it is made into steel. The steel is then used to make hundreds of things that are used every day, from automobiles to pots and pans. Michigan supplies one quarter of all the iron in the entire country.

Chapter 1

The Geography of Michigan

You Are There

"*There was . . . an abundance of wild strawberries, raspberries and blackberries that fairly perfumed the air . . . The wild pigeons . . . filled all the groves and in the waters the fishes were . . . plentiful . . .*"

This is how Andrew Blackbird described Michigan in the 1820s. He was the son of an American Indian chief. Michigan has changed a great deal since that time.

In this chapter you will read about Michigan's geography. You will also learn about how Michigan's geography affects the lives of its people.

◀ Andrew Blackbird

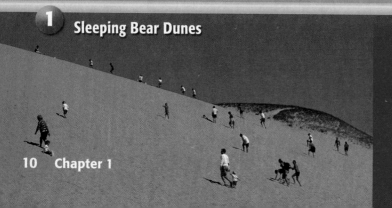

1 Sleeping Bear Dunes

2 Marquette

Isle Royale

Lake Superior

Porcupine Mountains

Houghton

Keweenaw Peninsula

Gogebic Range

Marquette

2

Tahquamenon Falls

3

CANADA

Sault Ste. Marie

UPPER PENINSULA

Escanaba

Straits of Mackinac

WI

1

Traverse City

Au Sable River

Lake Huron

Manistee River

River

LOWER PENINSULA

Saginaw Bay

Muskegon

Lake Michigan

Flint

Grand

River

★ Lansing

Irish Hills

IL

St. Joseph River

Tecumseh

Lake Erie

Michigan's Land

— National boundary
— State boundary
★ State capital
• Other city

N
W E
S

| 0 | 25 | 50 miles |
| 0 | 25 | 50 kilometers |

3 Tahquamenon Falls

What is the geography of Michigan?

boundary
peninsula
strait
glacier
drumlin
ecosystem

Word Origins The word **glacier** comes from a Latin word meaning "ice." What do you think a glacier is made of?

Identify Main Idea and Details Use the chart below to list the main idea and supporting details of this lesson.

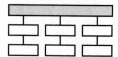

H3.0.1	G2.0.1
H3.0.3	G2.0.2
G1.0.1	G4.0.1
G1.0.2	

Let's Look at Michigan

An American Indian story tells that the world was formed on the back of a giant turtle. Scientists have a different idea. They speak of volcanoes and huge sheets of ice. In this lesson you will learn about Michigan's land and water. You will find out how fire and ice changed the land.

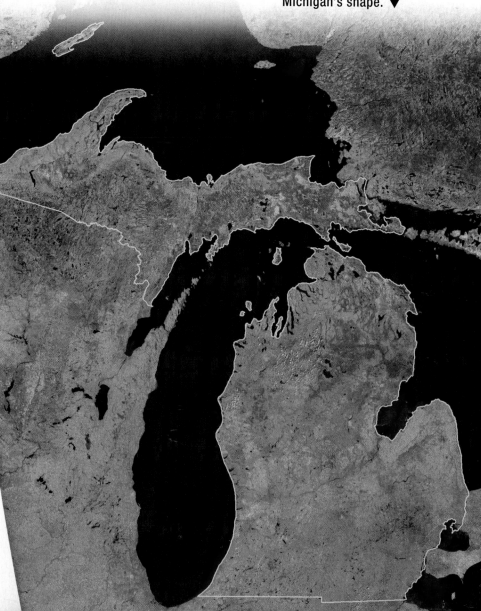

This satellite photo shows Michigan's shape. ▼

Ⓐ Where Is Michigan?

To find Michigan, look on the continent of North America. Then find the country called the United States. Then go to the part of the country called the Midwest.

Michigan is almost surrounded by four huge lakes. They are Superior, Michigan, Huron, and Erie. A fifth lake in the chain is Ontario. Together these are the Great Lakes. From space, you can see the Great Lakes and the shape of Michigan.

Michigan is part of a group known as the Great Lakes states. This group includes Ohio, Indiana, Wisconsin, Minnesota, and Illinois. All of these states, except Illinois and Minnesota, share a **boundary** with Michigan.

A boundary is a line on a map. It shows where one place ends and another begins. Michigan also shares a boundary with the country of Canada.

The Shape of Michigan

Michigan has two parts. One is called the Lower **Peninsula**. The other is the Upper Peninsula. A peninsula is land with water on three sides. Michigan's peninsulas are separated by the Straits of Mackinac. A **strait** is a narrow channel of water. It connects two larger bodies of water.

QUICK CHECK How is the shape of Michigan special? *Main Idea and Details*

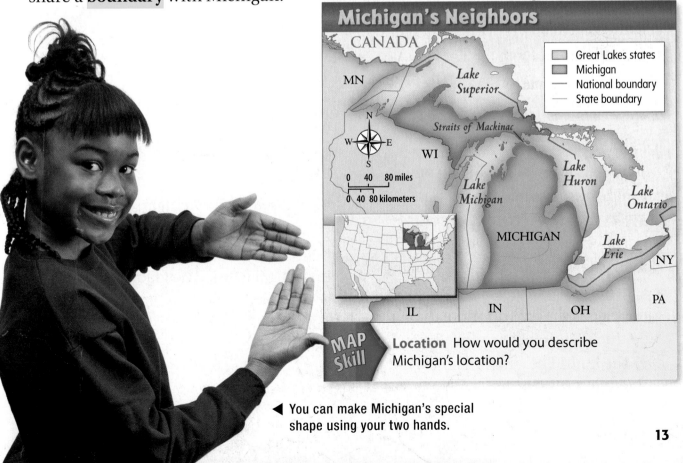

Michigan's Neighbors

CANADA

- Great Lakes states
- Michigan
- National boundary
- State boundary

MN

Lake Superior

Straits of Mackinac

WI

N
W E
S

0   40   80 miles
0   40   80 kilometers

Lake Michigan

Lake Huron

Lake Erie

Lake Ontario

MICHIGAN

NY

IL   IN   OH   PA

MAP Skill **Location** How would you describe Michigan's location?

◀ You can make Michigan's special shape using your two hands.

13

Glaciers like these (above) once moved over the land. They left behind small hills (right) as they melted.

❸ Forming the Land

Powerful forces shaped Michigan over thousands of years. Long ago oceans covered most of the land. Over a long time the waters drained. Dry land appeared. In some places volcanoes erupted. Ash and hot, melted rock came from deep inside Earth. Then the melted rock cooled. It formed the mountains of the Upper Peninsula.

Ice Power

Scientists know that Earth went through a time called the Ice Age. Earth's climate became very cold. Great sheets of ice covered much of North America. We call these moving ice sheets **glaciers** (GLAY shurz). In some places the ice was more than a mile thick! The glaciers moved slowly over the land. They carved holes, valleys, and trenches.

About 10,000 years ago, Earth got warmer. The glaciers began to melt. The melting glaciers left the rocks and sand they had picked up. The dunes along Lake Michigan, including the Sleeping Bear Dunes, were left behind by glaciers.

Southeastern Michigan is dotted with small egg-shaped hills called **drumlins**. The drumlins were left by melting glaciers. The glaciers are long gone, but you can see their marks in many places.

✔ **QUICK CHECK** How did the glaciers shape Michigan's land? *Main Idea and Details*

❻ Lakes and Rivers

Michigan has more than 11,000 small lakes. The lakes were formed when the ice melted. Water filled the holes the glaciers made.

Michigan has many rivers, too. The Grand River is the longest. It winds 260 miles (420 km) through central Michigan. It empties into Lake Michigan at Grand Haven. Other large rivers are the Muskegon in the west and the Au Sable in the east.

The Upper Peninsula has more than 150 waterfalls. The falls on the Tahquamenon River are very beautiful. These falls are 200 feet across. The water falling over them drops 50 feet. That is as tall as a five-story building!

Using the Water

With so many lakes and rivers, Michigan is a good place for fishing, swimming, and boating. Michigan's rivers are important for business, too. In the past rivers were the most important way to travel. Later rivers were used to power sawmills and to make electric power.

Ships still use the lakes and rivers. They carry goods all the way from the Great Lakes to the Atlantic Ocean. Ships carry Michigan's iron, gravel, farm goods, and other products to the rest of the world.

QUICK CHECK How were Michigan's lakes formed? *Summarize*

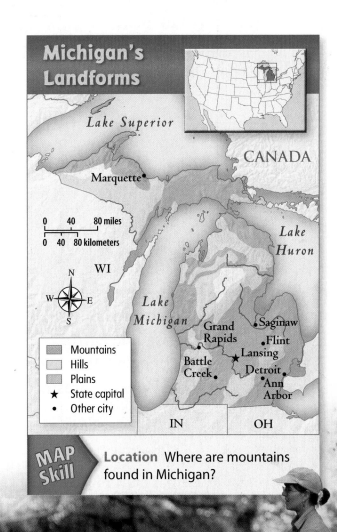

Michigan's Landforms

Lake Superior

CANADA

Marquette

0   40   80 miles
0   40   80 kilometers

WI

N W E S

Lake Michigan

Lake Huron

Grand Rapids
Saginaw
Flint
Lansing
Battle Creek
Detroit
Ann Arbor

Mountains
Hills
Plains
★ State capital
• Other city

IN   OH

MAP Skill

Location Where are mountains found in Michigan?

Many people enjoy fishing on Michigan's rivers. ▶

❶ What Is an Ecosystem?

Michigan's people, plants, and animals are part of communities. The communities and the nonliving things in a place form an **ecosystem**. An ecosystem is all the living and nonliving things in a specific area.

The living things in an ecosystem rely on each other. For example, in a pond fish eat water plants, insects, and smaller fish. Fish eat very tiny plants and animals in the water, too. A heron eats fish and frogs. Frogs eat insects. Water plants use sunlight to make their food. Even dead animals and plants are part of the ecosystem.

Great Lakes Ecosystem

Michigan is part of the Great Lakes Ecosystem. Many kinds of wildlife and plants are special to this area. Michigan's forests give shelter to foxes, raccoons, skunks, black bears, deer, and many other animals.

The marshes and forests are shelter for the birds that fly through or nest in Michigan. The lakes have many kinds of fish. Some are bass, salmon, trout, and catfish.

A freshwater pond has many kinds of life. ▼

Working Together

The living things in an ecosystem work together. Each member has an effect on the whole ecosystem. If one part of an ecosystem is changed, the whole ecosystem can be harmed.

People can change ecosystems. At one time people dumped things into the water. Then they noticed the lakes were changing. The water was polluted. The fish were dying. They could not live in the water.

Since the 1970s, the Great Lakes states and Canada have worked to protect the Great Lakes Ecosystem. Laws were passed to stop dumping and keep the water safe for living things.

 **QUICK CHECK** What is an ecosystem? *Summarize*

What You Learned

A Michigan is in the Midwest, almost surrounded by the Great Lakes. Michigan is made up of two large peninsulas.

B Volcanoes and glaciers helped create Michigan's landforms.

C Michigan has many rivers and small lakes.

D Michigan is part of the Great Lakes Ecosystem.

Focus Lesson Review

1. **Focus Question** What is the geography of Michigan?

2. **Vocabulary** Write one sentence for each vocabulary word.
   boundary   glacier
   ecosystem   peninsula

3. **Geography** Why do you think many of Michigan's cities developed on rivers?

4. **Critical Thinking** **Problem Solving** Why do you think it is important to remember that people are part of ecosystems?

5. **Reading Strategy** **Identify Main Idea and Details** Use the chart to list the main idea and details of the section called "Ice Power."

6. **Write About** 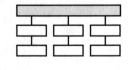 What are some ways people have used Michigan's lakes and rivers?

7. **Link to Science** Think of a Michigan plant or animal. Do research to find out how it plays a part in an ecosystem. What does it feed on? For what animal does it provide food?

Read Elevation Maps

Sometime you might want to go for a hike. How can you find the places where you can hike in Michigan? For this kind of information, you need an **elevation** (el uh VAY shun) map. Elevation is the height of the land above **sea level**, or the level of the surface of the sea. Elevation at sea level is 0 feet.

VOCABULARY

elevation
sea level

1 Learn It

To read elevation maps, follow these steps using the map on page 19.

- Read the map title. The title of the map is "United States: Elevation."

- Elevation maps use colors to show the height, or elevation, of land.

- The map key tells you what each color on the map means. For example, all the light green areas are between 1,000 and 2,500 feet (300 and 750 meters) above sea level.

An elevation map can help you plan a hike. ▼

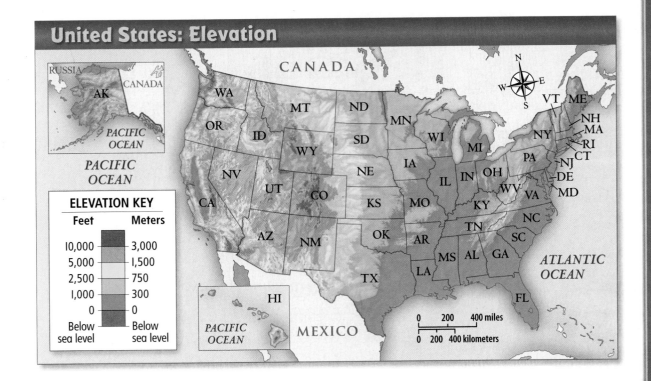

United States: Elevation

ELEVATION KEY

Feet	Meters
10,000	3,000
5,000	1,500
2,500	750
1,000	300
0	0
Below sea level	Below sea level

2 Try It

Use the map to answer these questions.

- Which state has the most area above 10,000 feet?

- Is the elevation of Michigan higher or lower than the elevation of Florida?

- Name 3 states that have an elevation above 5,000 feet.

3 Apply It

- How can an elevation map help you learn about geography?

- What could this elevation map tell you about overland travel from Michigan to California?

What are Michigan's two regions like?

VOCABULARY

region
natural resource
industry
tourism
population

VOCABULARY STRATEGY

Word Origins The Latin word *populus* means "people." Which term above do you think means the number of people in a place?

READING STRATEGY

Compare and Contrast
Use a Venn diagram to compare and contrast Michigan's two regions.

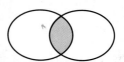

MICHIGAN GLCE

H3.0.1	G4.0.1
H3.0.3	G5.0.1
G1.0.1	G5.0.2
G1.0.2	
G2.0.1	
G2.0.2	

Michigan's Regions

Ernest Hemingway was an American author. When he was a child, he stayed in the Upper Peninsula each summer. Later he filled his books with pictures. The pictures showed the animals, fish, and quiet lakes he first saw in Michigan. He wrote these words in his story "Up in Michigan."

> 66 *The woods ran down to the lake and across the bay. It was beautiful in the spring and summer, the bay blue and bright. . . .* 99

Ⓐ The Upper Peninsula

Michigan's two peninsulas are very different from each other. Each one is a **region**. A region is an area with things in common. It is different from other areas. The Upper Peninsula, or "U.P.," has small mountains and rolling hills.

Using Resources

The Upper Peninsula is rich in **natural resources**. These are things found in nature that people can use. Minerals like iron and copper are mined here. Limestone and gypsum are mined here, too.

The largest city in the area is Marquette. This city grew larger after iron was discovered. Marquette became a shipping center for goods.

Lumber is an important **industry** in the region. An industry is all the businesses that make one kind of product or one kind of service.

Tourism is another industry. Tourism provides services to people on vacation. People come to the Upper Peninsula to hike, ski, and fish. They come to see the great natural beauty. Many people who live here have jobs providing things tourists need.

QUICK CHECK Compare two industries of the Upper Peninsula.
Compare and Contrast

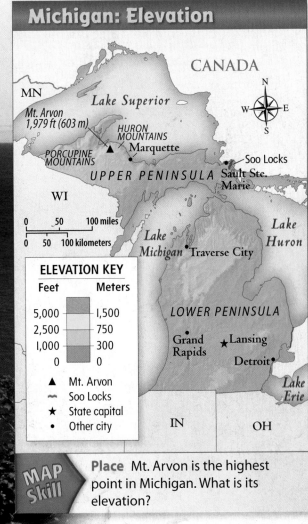

Michigan: Elevation

CANADA

MN

Lake Superior

Mt. Arvon
1,979 ft (603 m)

HURON
MOUNTAINS

PORCUPINE
MOUNTAINS

▲ Marquette

UPPER PENINSULA

Soo Locks

Sault Ste.
Marie

WI

| 0 | 50 | 100 miles |

| 0 | 50 | 100 kilometers |

Lake
Michigan

Traverse City

Lake
Huron

ELEVATION KEY

Feet	Meters
5,000	1,500
2,500	750
1,000	300
0	0

▲ Mt. Arvon
⌁ Soo Locks
★ State capital
• Other city

LOWER PENINSULA

Grand
Rapids

★ Lansing

Detroit •

Lake
Erie

IN

OH

MAP Skill

Place Mt. Arvon is the highest point in Michigan. What is its elevation?

▲ Pictured Rocks
National Lakeshore

ⓑ The Lower Peninsula

Look at the map on page 23. The Lower Peninsula has many cities. It has a much larger **population** than the Upper Peninsula. Population is the number of people that live in one place. Most of Michigan's population lives in the southern part of the Lower Peninsula. Some people think this area is its own region.

Glaciers made the Lower Peninsula low and flat. It has many lakes and rivers. There are millions of acres of forests of pine and hardwood trees in the north. Like the U.P., many people in the Lower Peninsula work in the lumber, furniture, and paper products businesses.

Michigan Agriculture

About one fourth of Michigan's land is used for farming. Most of Michigan's farms are in the southern part of the Lower Peninsula. The area has good soil. It has the longest growing season.

Michigan farmers grow almost one third of the blueberries in the United States. Many fruit orchards are found along the shores of Lake Michigan. This area is called the "Fruit Belt." Peaches, pears, apples, and plums come from the Fruit Belt.

The Lower Peninsula is also "cherry country." More red tart cherries are grown in Michigan than anywhere else. Traverse City is known as the "Cherry Capital of the World." A festival is held there each July.

▼ A pie-eating contest at the National Cherry Festival

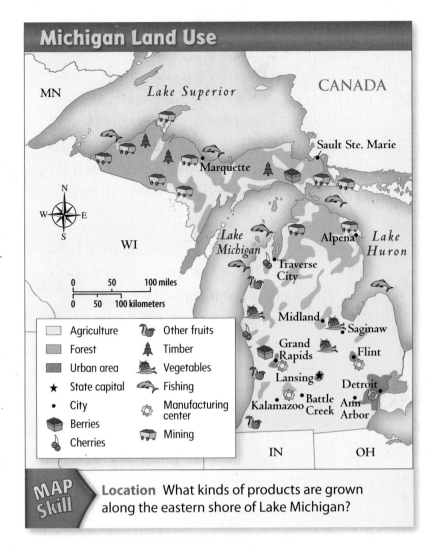

Michigan Land Use

MN

Lake Superior

CANADA

Sault Ste. Marie

Marquette

WI

Lake Michigan

Alpena

Lake Huron

Traverse City

0   50   100 miles

0   50   100 kilometers

Midland

Saginaw

Grand Rapids

Flint

Lansing

Detroit

Kalamazoo   Battle Creek   Ann Arbor

IN   OH

Legend:
- Agriculture
- Forest
- Urban area
- ★ State capital
- • City
- Berries
- Cherries
- Other fruits
- Timber
- Vegetables
- Fishing
- Manufacturing center
- Mining

MAP Skill **Location** What kinds of products are grown along the eastern shore of Lake Michigan?

Detroit is Michigan's largest city. It is called "Motown" or "the Motor City." It is a center of the automobile industry.

The automobile industry is big. It includes the makers of cars and trucks. It includes the factories that make parts for cars and trucks. People who find ways to make cars better are in the auto industry, too.

Besides Detroit, the cities of Flint, Dearborn, Pontiac, and Lansing are also important automobile centers. Cities in the Lower Peninsula make many other things, too. Grand Rapids is known for its furniture. Midland makes chemicals. Kalamazoo makes paper and medicine.

QUICK CHECK Where does most of Michigan's population live?
Main Idea and Details

Farmers in the Lower Peninsula grow other crops, too. Christmas trees are an important crop. Michigan growers cut down about three million Christmas trees a year. Near Saginaw, farmers grow sugar beets. More than one of every ten pounds of sugar made in the United States comes from Michigan sugar beets.

Industry

Most of Michigan's population lives in the southern part of the state. There are many jobs here.

Michigan automakers design cars for the future. ▶

Then and Now

Crossing the Straits

THEN Once the best way to travel between Michigan's two peninsulas was by boat. Here passengers are getting off the Michigan State Ferry. Winter ice often made ferry service impossible.

NOW The Mackinac Bridge was completed in 1957, making travel much easier. Now the bridge carries autos and trucks from one part of Michigan to the other.

 How is transportation in your town different from what it was 50 years ago?

From Here to There

For a long time the only way to get goods to or from the Upper Peninsula was by boat. But boats could not travel from Lake Superior to Lake Huron.

Lake Superior is 21 feet higher than Lake Huron. The St. Marys River connects the two lakes. It drops about 19 feet (6 m) in a series of waterfalls near the town of Sault Ste. Marie (SOO saynt muh REE). Ships could not pass the falls.

Solving the Problem

The problem was solved in the 1850s. The Soo Locks were built. The locks are like a water elevator. They lower or raise a ship to meet the next level.

However, the Upper Peninsula was still cut off from the rest of the state. In 1957 the Mackinac Bridge was completed. The bridge spans the Straits of Mackinac. It connects the Upper and Lower peninsulas. Now it is much easier for people and goods to move from one region of Michigan to the other.

QUICK CHECK Why couldn't ships travel between Lake Superior and Lake Huron before the Soo Locks were built? *Cause and Effect*

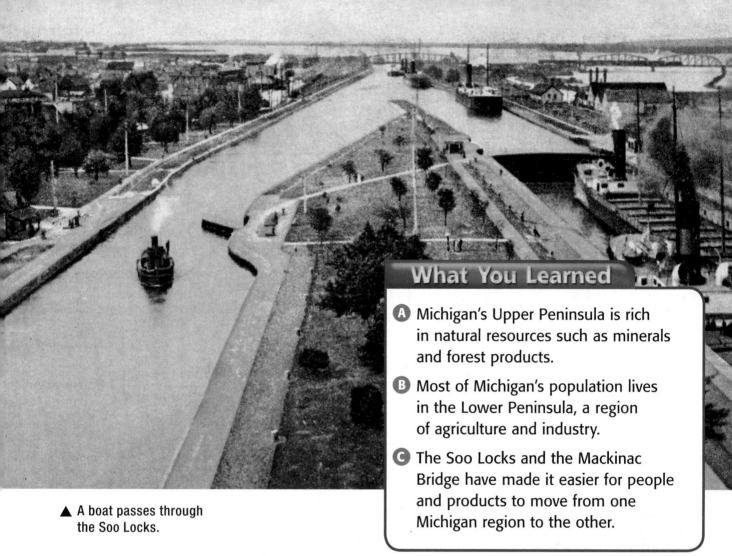

▲ A boat passes through the Soo Locks.

What You Learned

A Michigan's Upper Peninsula is rich in natural resources such as minerals and forest products.

B Most of Michigan's population lives in the Lower Peninsula, a region of agriculture and industry.

C The Soo Locks and the Mackinac Bridge have made it easier for people and products to move from one Michigan region to the other.

Focus Lesson Review

1. **Focus Question** What are Michigan's two regions like?

2. **Vocabulary** Write one sentence for each vocabulary word.
industry	**region**
population	**tourism**

3. **Geography** Which region of Michigan is rich in minerals?

4. **Critical Thinking Problem Solving** How did people solve the difficulty of ships traveling between Lake Superior and Lake Huron?

5. **Reading Strategy Compare and Contrast** Use a Venn diagram to compare the northern Lower Peninsula with the southern Lower Peninsula.

6. **Write About** 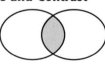 How do people in each region use Michigan's natural resources?

7. **Link to Science** Make a list of minerals mined in the Upper Peninsula. Then do research to find at least two things each is used for.

What Are Primary Sources?

Primary and Secondary Sources

Historians are people who learn about the past. They study two main types of sources. **Primary sources** are spoken or written accounts from a person who has seen or experienced an event. They include objects as well as maps and photographs.

A **secondary source** comes from a person who did not see or experience an event. Secondary sources can tell the basic facts of an event. Examples of secondary sources include encyclopedias and textbooks.

1 Learn It

Throughout this book you will be using many primary sources, including these:

- **Artifacts** are objects such as weapons, clothing, or tools that were made or used by people in the past.

- **Letters** are written messages sent from the writer to another person.

- **Photographs, prints,** and other **pictures** can help you understand more about an event by showing you what the thing looked like at the time the photo was taken.

- **Newspapers** are printed daily or weekly and contain news, opinions, and advertising.

- **Maps** are primary sources if they were made at the time being studied. Maps show the land, who claimed it, how it was used, or events such as battles.

▲ These spear points are artifacts.

The LIBRARY of CONGRESS

VOCABULARY

historian
primary source
secondary source
artifact

2 Try It

Identifying the primary and secondary sources can help you better understand and draw conclusions about events in history.

- Identify the author or maker of the source. What is his or her connection to the source?

- Identify *when* the source was created. Was the author or maker at the event? If you answered "yes," then the source is a primary source.

- Identify *where* the source was created. Was the author or maker in that place during the event? If you answered "yes," then the source is a primary source.

▲ Thomas Edison listening to a record in 1906

3 Apply It

- Write a description of an event you have witnessed recently.

- Describe the event in detail. Share your description with the rest of the class.

A newspaper is a primary source. ▶

G4.0.1
P3.1.1
P3.3.1

Should Michigan's Lakefronts Belong to Everyone?

Michigan has many public beaches along the Great Lakes. Many beaches have homes on them. Some people think the shore is for everyone, but homeowners want the right to keep people off their property.

Read below to find out about three different points of view on how the land along Michigan's lakes should be used.

66*If a person buys a house, . . . that is their private property. People should not be allowed to walk on the property without permission… There are plenty of places along the lakes already open to the public.*99

Alexander DeHaan
Escanaba, Michigan

66*Everyone should be able to use… the lakefront. The homeowners don't own the lakes…. The lakes belong to all the people of Michigan. That land… should be shared. It is for the common good.*99

Janay Johnson
Grand Blanc, Michigan

66*People who have a home on the lakeshore should have the right to decide who can go on it, but maybe there could be [a] path… , so people could still walk around the lake.*99

Yale Williams
White Lake, Michigan

Build Citizenship

1. Where are most of Michigan's beaches?

2. What is the difference between private and public property?

3. Why are the beaches important to Michigan's economy?

Think About It

1. What reasons does Alexander DeHaan give for his opinion?

2. Why does Janay Johnson disagree with DeHaan?

3. Which of the other opinions does Yale Williams most agree with?

Write About It!

Think of some ways this conflict might be solved. Then pick the solution you like best and write a letter to your local newspaper explaining why you think it is the best way to solve the problem.

Focus Lesson 3

How does Michigan's climate affect the way people live in the state?

VOCABULARY

climate
precipitation
lake effect
adapt

VOCABULARY STRATEGY

Prefixes The prefix **ad-** in **adapt** comes from a Latin word meaning "to." *Aptus* means "fit." Can you think of another word that starts with **ad-** and means the same thing?

READING STRATEGY

Summarize Use the chart below to summarize the lesson.

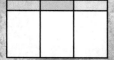

MICHIGAN GLCE

H3.0.1	G1.0.2
H3.0.2	G2.0.1
H3.0.3	G2.0.2
H3.0.7	

Michigan's Climate

Michigan's Keeweenaw Peninsula is in the most northern part of Michigan. In 1978 it began snowing early in the winter, and it kept snowing. By the time winter ended, 392 inches (995 cm) of snow had fallen! It was Michigan's largest-ever snowfall. There was more than 32 feet of snow. That's enough to cover a two-story house!

Ⓐ Weather and Climate

What will the weather be tomorrow? Will it be hot or cold? Will it be dry or wet? Weather is how hot or cold and how wet or dry a place is at any given time. Weather can change from day to day.

Climate is the pattern of weather for an area over time. You have read about the Ice Age in Michigan. The climate gradually grew warmer, and the Ice Age ended.

30 Chapter 1

Four Seasons

Michigan's climate has four seasons: spring, summer, winter, and fall. Spring and fall are warm. Summer is hot. Winter is cold, and there is usually lots of snow.

Michigan's climate has patterns in temperature. The average January temperature on the Upper Peninsula is about 15°F. But it can get as cold as –20° F.

During summer on the Lower Peninsula, the daytime temperature is about 75°F. However, in the town of Mio the temperature reached 112°F in 1936. That's as hot as the California desert! Temperatures in the Upper Peninsula are usually 10 degrees colder than in the Lower Peninsula.

Michigan forests show off their fall colors (below) while winter brings snow (right).

Precipitation is also part of weather. Precipitation is water that falls as rain, snow, sleet, or hail. Michigan gets from 26 to 36 inches of precipitation every year. Most of it falls in winter as snow. In the Lower Peninsula there is more rain. In the Upper Peninsula there is more snow.

QUICK CHECK What kind of climate does Michigan have? *Summarize*

B Water and Weather

Michigan is almost surrounded by water. All this water affects the state's weather and climate.

Water evaporates from lakes and rivers. It forms clouds. Warmer air holds more moisture. As the clouds cool, the moisture changes into droplets. The clouds get very heavy with droplets. Finally the water falls back to Earth as rain or snow.

Lake Effect

Lake Michigan affects Michigan's weather. This is called the **lake effect**. Look at the diagrams on page 33. In summer, the lake water and the air above it are cooler than the land next to it. The lake cools winds blowing across it. Then the winds cool the land.

During winter, the opposite happens. The lake water is usually warmer than the air. The winds blowing across the lake are warmed. They blow across the land. This evens out the land temperature. So Michigan's climate is usually not too hot or too cold.

Sometimes the winds coming across the lake pick up lots of moisture. This causes huge clouds to form. Then the winds blow the clouds across the cool land. The moisture in the clouds falls as snow. This is called lake effect snow. You can read about one lake effect snowstorm in the news report below.

✓ **QUICK CHECK** What happens to winds as they blow across the lake in winter? *Cause and Effect*

PRIMARY SOURCES

From **The Daily News**

of Iron Mountain-Kingsford, Michigan • December 11, 2003

❝ *Marquette broke the record to date with a total of 11.5 inches of snow, according to the National Weather Service in Marquette. The total snow accumulation was 16.1 inches for the storm that began on Tuesday.*

A lake effect snow advisory is in effect for Marquette County until 5 p.m. today. ❞

Write About It! How would you react if this was the weather report for your area?

DATA**GRAPHIC**

Michigan's Climate

A diagram is a type of picture with information. Diagrams can help you understand how something works. Study the diagrams and graph below. Then answer the questions.

The Lake Effect

Summer ▶
Lake water cools the air. Cool breezes blow toward shore.

◀ Winter
Lake water warms the air. Breezes pick up moisture and blow toward land. The moisture is cooled and falls as snow.

Michigan: Annual Snowfall

Inches of Snow

Michigan cities: Monroe, Detroit, Lansing, Marquette, Houghton

Source: *U.S. Weather Bureau*

Think About Michigan's Climate

1. In which season does the lake effect cool the breezes from the lake?

2. How many inches of snow falls in Houghton every year?

3. Houghton is located in the Upper Peninsula of Michigan. Why do you think it gets so much snow?

ⓒ People and Climate

The climate of a place affects the people who live there. In Michigan people **adapt** to four seasons. Adapting means changing to suit your surroundings. People enjoy the warm days of summer. In fall the air is cool. People put on jackets or sweaters. In winter it snows. The air is cold. People adapt by wearing heavier clothes. They also adapt by getting out the snowplows.

Moving with the Seasons

Some people move with the seasons. Many Michiganians have winter homes in the South, where it is warmer. Other people, who love winter sports, visit Michigan in winter to go skiing or snowmobiling.

✔ **QUICK CHECK** Tell one way people in Michigan adapt to the climate in winter.
Cause and Effect

What You Learned

ⓐ Michigan has four seasons. The Upper Peninsula is usually cooler than the southern part of the state.

ⓑ The waters of the Great Lakes have a major effect on Michigan's climate. This lake effect can lead to heavy snowfall.

ⓒ Michigan's climate affects the way people live and work in the state.

★ Focus Lesson Review

1. **Focus Question** How does Michigan's climate affect the way people live in the state?

2. **Vocabulary** Write one sentence for each vocabulary term.
   adapt   lake effect
   climate   precipitation

3. **Economics** Name a Michigan industry that is affected by the climate.

4. **Critical Thinking Problem Solving** How do people adjust to Michigan's weather and climate?

5. **Reading Strategy Summarize** Use the chart to summarize how lake effect works.

6. **Write About** THE **BiG IDEA** Suppose that the Great Lakes dried up. Write a paragraph about how this might affect the lives of people in Michigan.

7. **Link to Science** For one week, keep a record of the daily precipitation in the city or town where you live, and in a Michigan city that is in a different region from yours. Write a report about your findings.

The Wreck of the Edmund Fitzgerald

Music and Lyrics by
Gordon Lightfoot

The leg-end lives on from the Chip-pe-wa on
With a load of iron ore twenty-six thou-sand tons

down of the big lake they called "Git-chee Gu-mee."
more than the Ed-mund Fitz-ger-ald weighed emp-ty,

The lake, it is
that good ship and

said, nev-er_____ gives up her dead when the skies of No-
true was a_____ bone to be chewed when the "Gales of No-

vem-ber turn gloom-y._____
vem-ber" came ear-ly._____

Lake Huron rolls, Superior sings
in the rooms of her ice-water mansion.
Old Michigan steams like a young man's dreams;
the islands and bays are for sportsmen.
And farther below Lake Ontario
takes in what Lake Erie can send her,
and the iron boats go as the mariners all know
with the Gales of November remembered.

**What do you think happened
to the Edmund Fitzgerald?**

READERS' THEATER presents

THE STORY OF PAUL BUNYAN

Characters

*

Narrator
Mother
Father
Paul Bunyan
Babe
Elmer
Sally

*

Narrator: Our tall tale concerns a young boy named Paul Bunyan. Paul is no ordinary boy. You see, he is big—really, really big. How big? Try 10 times the size of a regular two-year-old boy. Our story begins on Paul's second birthday.

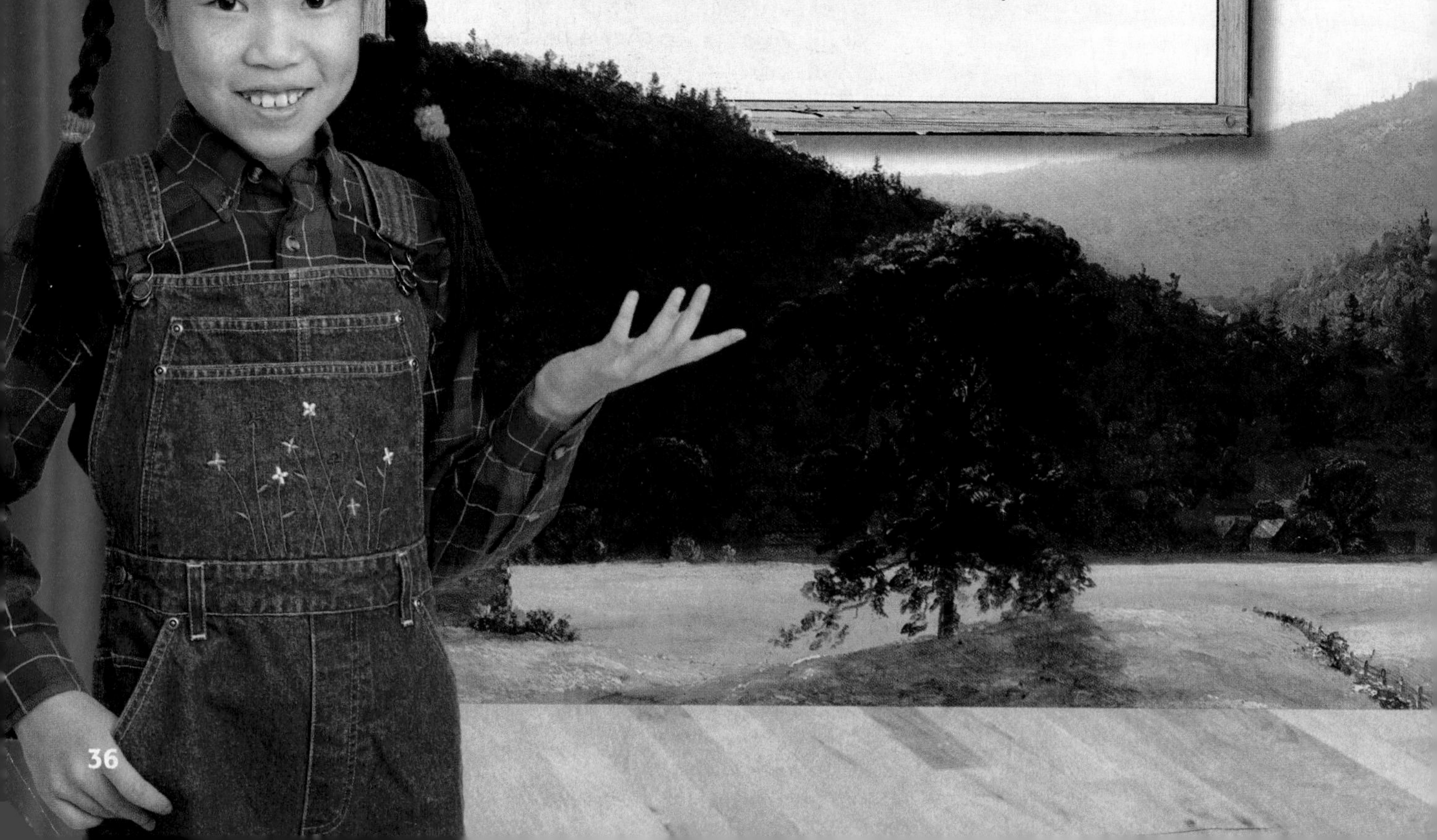

(Mr. and Mrs. Bunyan are at home talking about how to celebrate Paul's birthday.)

Father: Two years old, and he is bigger than we are! I don't know what to do.

Mother: We should love him and care for him like any other child. Let's take him on a ride for his birthday.

Father: I guess you're right. *(leaving)* I'll bring around the lumber wagon.

Mother: What for?

Father: If we are going to take him for a ride, nothing else can hold him.

Narrator: Paul continued to grow bigger and bigger. He did get into mischief, as children often do.

Mother: *(walks in, holding Paul by the hand)* The baby crawled into town. Now the town is destroyed. He just can't help it!

Father: Let's face facts. Paul isn't like other babies. Most babies play with toys. Paul plays with an ax. The other day he dragged his ax behind him and carved out the Grand Canyon.

Mother: When he started to walk, his footprints made the Great Lakes.

Father: *(disappointed)* I think we need to find someplace big enough for Paul, someplace where he can't get into so much mischief.

Narrator: So young Paul went to live in the woods, where he continued to grow bigger and bigger. He became a lumberjack. He brushed his teeth with the tops of pine trees and wrestled polar bears for fun. He whacked down 20 trees with one swing of his mighty ax. His best friend was a giant blue ox named Babe. Soon Paul was famous. One day he got a letter.

Paul: *(holding a letter)* It says here the President wants me to chop down all the trees in North and South Dakota. He wants to make room for new settlers coming in. I think that even I will need some help to do that.

Narrator: So Paul made some new friends.

(Elmer and Sally enter.)

Paul: *(shaking hands with Elmer)* Elmer, I hear you're a really good lumberjack. Is that true? You, Sally, are the best cook west of the Mississippi River. Can you help me?

Elmer and Sally: *(together)* Sure.

Paul: Great. Let's get started. Sally, can you cook enough food for 10,000 lumberjacks?

Sally: No problem. Just find a lake and dump in all the pork and beans you can lay your hands on. Then, build a few fires to boil the lake, and I'll make you the best soup you've ever tasted.

(Sally stirs the lake of soup. Elmer and Paul chop trees furiously.)

Narrator: The lumberjacks worked all winter long, day and night. Sally's soup kept them strong. By spring they had finished the job.

Sally: Well, you did it. Look! That's the first wagon bringing settlers here.

Paul: I should be happy, but I'm not.

Elmer: Why?

Paul: All I can think of is how the settlers will never hear the wind through the trees.

Elmer: So?

Paul: Well, that's wrong. I just chopped one thousand trees. Now I'm going to plant one thousand more.

Narrator: That's exactly what Paul did. Many more stories have been told about Paul Bunyan. These tall tales entertained women, men, and children all over the United States. Paul's spirit gave them courage. Paul's energy, size, and strength became a symbol for the United States.

Write About It!

Write a tall tale of your own. Use the tall tale to explain how your community came to be.

Chapter 1 Review

FOCUS Vocabulary Review

Copy the sentences below on a separate sheet of paper. Use the list of vocabulary words to fill in the blanks.

drumlin   strait
peninsula   climate
population   tourism

1. Michigan's two regions are separated by a _____.

2. A _____ is a body of land that is almost surrounded by water.

3. The _____ of Detroit is about 900,000.

4. What you wear might depend on the _____ where you live.

5. _____ is the business of providing services to people on vacation.

6. A _____ is a small egg-shaped hill.

7. **Test Preparation** The average weather conditions of a region make up its _____ .

A **climate**   C **boundary**
B **ecosystem**   D **plateau**

FOCUS Comprehension Check

8. How were the Great Lakes formed?

9. Name three important products grown in Michigan.

10. What are some natural resources found in the Upper Peninsula?

11. How would you describe the shape of Michigan's land?

12. Name one kind of ecosystem and list three members of that ecosystem.

13. Describe how Lake Michigan affects Michigan's weather in summer.

14. What states other than Michigan make up the Great Lakes states?

15. **Critical Thinking** How did building the Mackinac Bridge make it easier to reach the Upper Peninsula?

16. **Critical Thinking** Why does most of Michigan's population live in the Lower Peninsula?

Read Elevation Maps

Write a complete sentence to answer each question.

17. Which part of the U.P. has a higher elevation, the western part or the eastern part?

18. Is western Kansas (KS) higher or lower than eastern Kansas?

The Midwest: Elevation

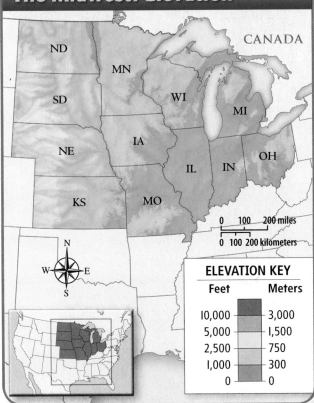

ELEVATION KEY

Feet		Meters
10,000		3,000
5,000		1,500
2,500		750
1,000		300
0		0

Primary and Secondary Sources

Look again at the photograph below.

19. Would this photograph be considered a primary or secondary source?

20. When is a map a primary source?

21. **Draw a Sketch Map** Draw a sketch map of Michigan. Use different colors to show the regions. Show rivers and cities. Make a key for your map.

22. **Narrative** Write a letter to a friend in which you describe some part of Michigan's geography that you like.

 For help with the process of writing, visit: www.macmillanmh.com

Chapter 2

Michigan's First People

You Are There

"It was a period when . . . the Indians used skins for clothing, and flints for arrowheads. It was long before the time that the flag of the white man was seen in these lakes, or the sound of an iron axe had been heard."

These words tell of a time in Michigan long ago. They are from an American Indian story. Henry Rowe Schoolcraft wrote down this story. He lived in Michigan in the early 1800s.

In this chapter you will learn about Michigan's first people. Their story is an important part of Michigan's history.

◀ Ojibway woman

1 Michigan's First People

2 Odawa Artifact

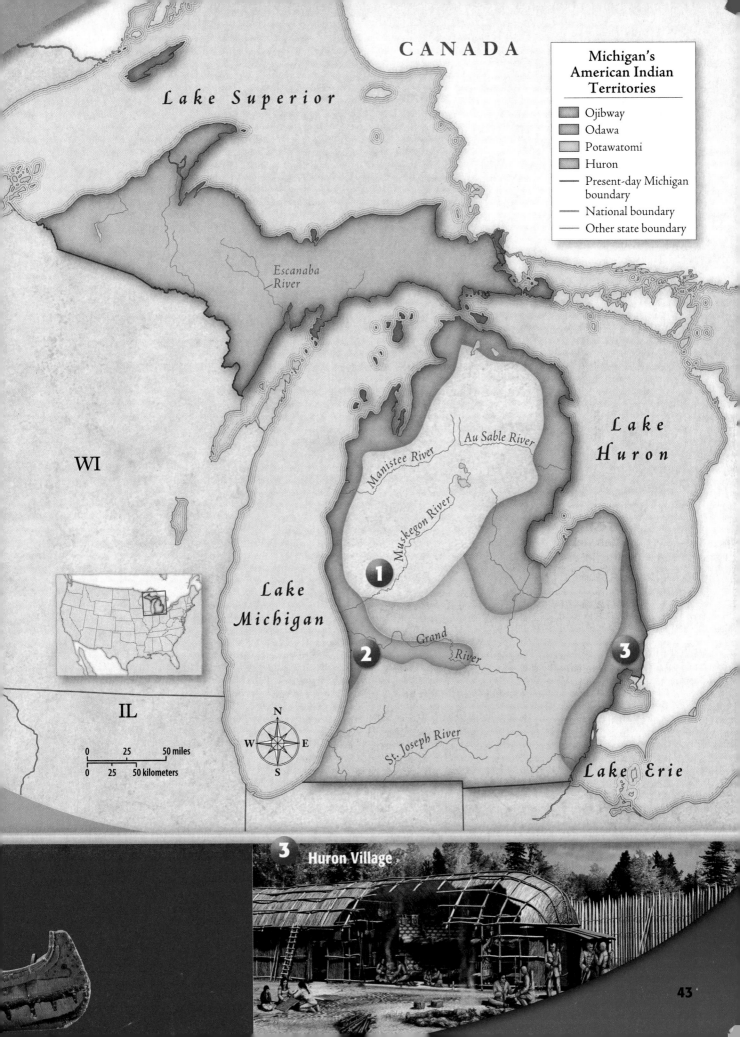

CANADA

Lake Superior

WI

IL

Escanaba River

Lake Michigan

Manistee River

Au Sable River

Muskegon River

1

2

Grand River

St. Joseph River

3

Lake Huron

Lake Erie

N
W E
S

| 0 | 25 | 50 miles |
| 0 | 25 | 50 kilometers |

Michigan's American Indian Territories

- Ojibway
- Odawa
- Potawatomi
- Huron
- Present-day Michigan boundary
- National boundary
- Other state boundary

3 Huron Village

The Early American Indians

How did the first people of Michigan use its natural resources?

VOCABULARY

Paleo-Indian
archaeologist
culture
artifact

VOCABULARY STRATEGY

Suffixes The suffix **-ologist** means "a person who studies a particular subject." *Archaic* means "ancient." Can you guess what subject an **archaeologist** studies?

READING STRATEGY

Identify Main Idea and Details Use the chart below to list the main idea and supporting details of this lesson.

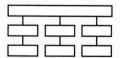

MICHIGAN GLCE

H3.0.1	G1.0.1
H3.0.3	G1.0.2
H3.0.4	G2.0.1
H3.0.5	G4.0.2
H3.0.8	

For a long time, Michigan was once under ice. But it became warm, and the ice melted. In its place, grass began to grow. Caribou soon came to feed on the grass. Then came hunters. They used weapons made of stone and bone.

Who were these first people of Michigan?

Ⓐ The First Michiganians

In the last chapter, you read about glaciers. They once covered much of what is now North America. This happened thousands of years ago. Much of the world's water was ice, so the oceans were not so deep. A strip of dry land appeared between Asia and North America. This land made a bridge between the two continents.

Changes in Land and Climate

Animals came across the land bridge from Asia. Later people also moved across the land bridge into North America. Over time these people spread across North America. Some scientists think that people also came from Europe and Asia by boats to North America. Many American Indians say through their stories that they were always here.

▲ Stone spear points

About 11,000 years ago, the climate warmed. Michigan's glaciers melted, and many animals came to the area. Soon after that people followed.

These ancient people are called **Paleo-Indians**. Their name means "old" or "early" Indians. We know of them through **archaeologists**. An archaeologist studies things left from the past. For example, archaeologists have found ancient stone tools near Flint and in other places in Michigan.

Archaeologists think Paleo-Indians lived in small groups. They probably hunted small animals and caribou. Caribou move from place to place. People may have followed the caribou as they moved.

QUICK CHECK Who were the Paleo-Indians, and why are they important?
Main Idea and Details

◄ Michigan's first people followed caribou herds north as the glaciers melted.

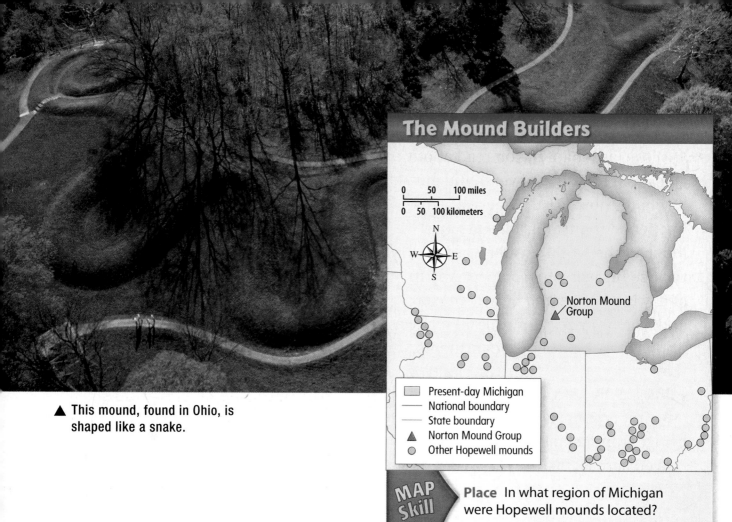

▲ This mound, found in Ohio, is shaped like a snake.

The Mound Builders

0 50 100 miles
0 50 100 kilometers

Norton Mound Group

Present-day Michigan
National boundary
State boundary
Norton Mound Group
Other Hopewell mounds

MAP Skill

Place In what region of Michigan were Hopewell mounds located?

ⓑ The Hopewell

About 2,000 years ago, a new group of people called the Hopewell moved into Michigan. They came from south of the state. The most well-known Hopewell site in Michigan is the Norton Mounds. It is near where Grand Rapids is today.

Mound Builders

The Hopewell lived in groups. They were spread out over a large area. They probably did not all speak the same language. But all the Hopewell people were mound builders. They used these mounds to bury their dead.

Hopewell groups shared the same **culture**. This means they had similar art, beliefs, and customs.

Building mounds is a Hopewell custom. To build a mound, gravel is covered with fine dirt. Then logs are added on top. The body is placed on the logs. Next, drains are made in the mound so rainwater drains off.

Special things, such as beads and knives, were placed in the mound. The body and special things were covered with dirt. Then, a large mound formed.

Learning from Artifacts

Archaeologists have learned a lot from the **artifacts** they found buried in the mounds. Artifacts are things made or used by people who lived in the past.

The Hopewell made things they could use, such as tools and pots. They also made works of art such as jewelry. The Hopewell could make many things from metal. They even made instruments for music.

The artifacts show us other things, too. They show that the Hopewell traded with others. Archaeologists have found pearls in the mounds. They came from the Gulf of Mexico. Archaeologists have also found shark teeth. They came from the Atlantic Ocean.

The End of Hopewell Culture

About the year 400, signs of Hopewell groups began to decline. Archaeologists are not sure why this happened. Some think it was because of changing weather and disease.

Archaeologists think that some of the American Indians who live in Michigan are descended from the Hopewell.

QUICK CHECK How do we know about the Hopewell culture? *Summarize*

◀ A toad decorates this Hopewell pipe.

What You Learned

Ⓐ Ancient people known as Paleo-Indians lived in Michigan about 11,000 years ago.

Ⓑ The Hopewell built huge burial mounds. They traded for goods with other groups across North America.

Focus Lesson Review

1. **Focus Question** How did the first people of Michigan use its natural resources?

2. **Vocabulary** Write one sentence for each vocabulary term.
   archaeologist   culture
   artifact   Paleo-Indian

3. **Geography** Look at the map on page 46. Why do you think Hopewell culture did not move farther north than southern Michigan?

4. **Critical Thinking Make Decisions** The Hopewell mounds are burial places. Do you think archaeologists should be allowed to dig the mounds? Why or why not?

5. **Reading Strategy Identify Main Idea and Details** Find the main idea and supporting details about Hopewell culture.

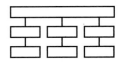

6. **Write About THE BiG IDEA** How did the climate influence the lives of the Paleo-Indians?

7. **Link to Language Arts** Suppose you are an archaeologist who has just discovered artifacts in a Hopewell mound. Write about what artifacts you have found and what they seem to tell us about the Hopewell.

Understand Latitude and Longitude

Every place on Earth has an address based on its location. To describe the "address" of a place, geographers use special maps with grids. Grids are lines that cross each other on a map. Earth's grid system is based on a set of lines called **latitude** and **longitude**. Lines of latitude measure how far north or south a place is from the equator. Lines of longitude measure distance east or west. Lines of latitude and longitude measure distance in **degrees**. The equator is 0 degrees. The symbol for degrees is °.

1 Learn It

- Lines of latitude are also called **parallels**. Look at Map A. Lines of latitude north of the equator are labeled N. Lines of latitude south of the equator are labeled S.

- Lines of longitude are also called **meridians**. The **prime meridian** is the starting place for measuring distance from east to west. Look at Map B. Lines of longitude east of the prime meridian are labeled E. Lines of longitude west of the prime meridian are labeled W.

- Look at Map A. Lines of longitude and latitude cross to form a **global grid**. It can be used to locate any place on Earth.

- When you locate a place on a map, give the latitude first and the longitude second.

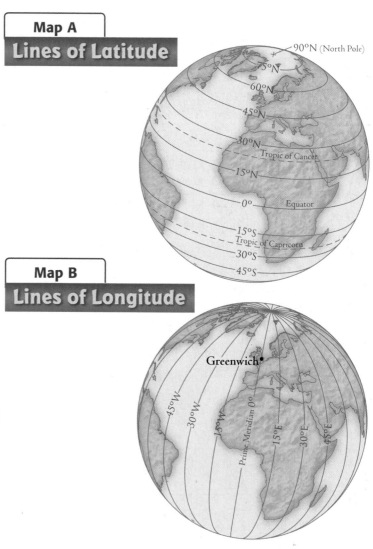

Map A
Lines of Latitude

Map B
Lines of Longitude

Map C
Global Grid

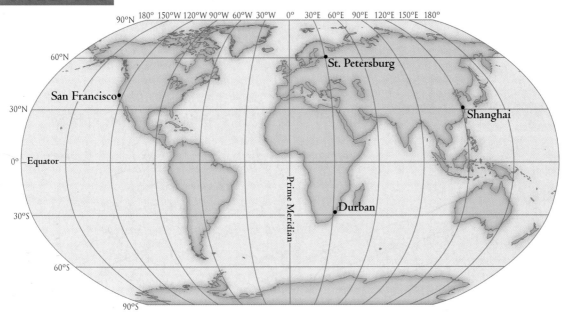

2 Try It

■ Locate Durban on Map C. Is Durban east or west of the prime meridian? It is east. Durban is located at about 30°S, 30°E.

■ Use Map C to locate the cities closest to the latitude and longitude "addresses" below. Name each city.
    30°N, 120°E
    60°N, 30°E

■ Use Map D to find the nearest latitude and longitude to Flint.

3 Apply It

■ Look at Map D. Find the longitude and latitude that is closest to where you live.

Map D
Michigan: Latitude and Longitude

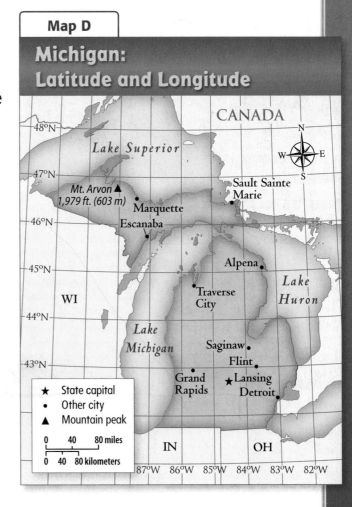

Who are the Anishinaabeg?

VOCABULARY

migrate
confederacy
wigwam
band
clan

VOCABULARY STRATEGY

Word Origins Wigwam is a form of an American Indian [Ojibway] word, *wigwaum* or *wigiwam*. It means "their house." The word came into English as soon as Europeans met American Indian people in the early 1600s.

READING STRATEGY

Summarize Use the chart below to summarize information about the Three Fires.

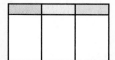

MICHIGAN GLCE

H3.0.1	H3.0.7
H3.0.2	H3.0.8
H3.0.3	G1.0.1
H3.0.4	G1.0.2
H3.0.5	G4.0.4

The Anishinaabeg

Beatrice Taylor is an American Indian elder. Here is what she says about passing down her culture:

> **❝***We teach our children and grandchildren about the different ways our People have lived and the things we do. For example, in the fall, the Ojibway traditionally go out to harvest wild rice. I taught my daughters and my sons what they're supposed to do when they go ricing, and hopefully they will pass that knowledge on to their children.*❞

Ⓐ The Three Fires

The Anishinaabeg (uh NISH nuh beg) once lived near the Atlantic Ocean. About 1,000 years ago, they **migrated** from the Atlantic coast to the land near the Great Lakes. To migrate is to move from one place to settle in another.

A New Homeland

The Anishinaabeg came to what is now Sault Ste. Marie. They formed three groups. One group was the Ojibway (also called the Chippewa). Another was the Odawa (also called the Ottawa). The third group was the Potawatomi. You can see on the map where each group lived.

The groups called themselves the Three Fires. They were like a family. The Ojibway were called the older brother. The Odawa were the middle brother. The Potawatomi were the younger brother. They formed the Three Fires **Confederacy**. A confederacy is a group with a common purpose. Together the Three Fires were very powerful.

QUICK CHECK Who were the Three Fires? *Summarize*

The Anishinaabeg Migration

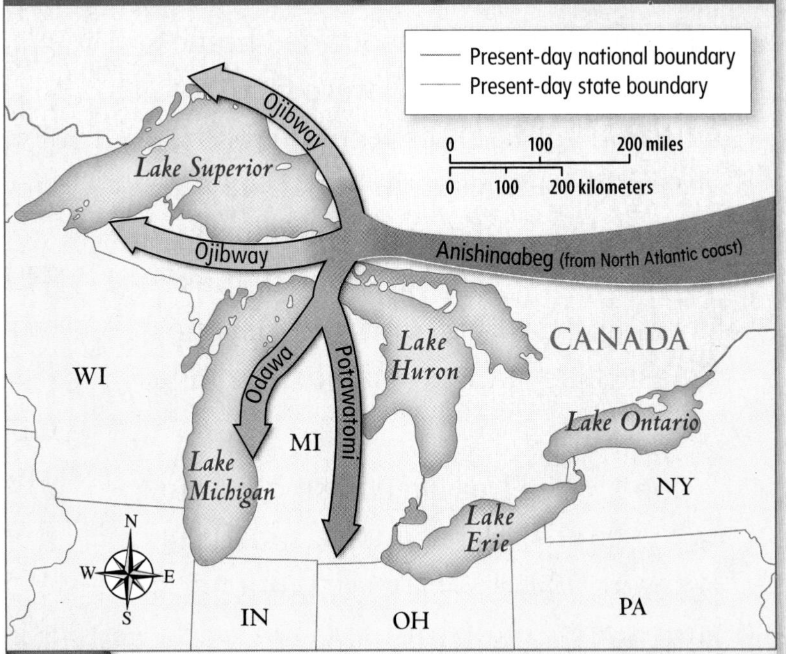

— Present-day national boundary
— Present-day state boundary

0   100   200 miles
0   100   200 kilometers

Ojibway
Lake Superior
Ojibway
Anishinaabeg (from North Atlantic coast)
WI
Odawa
Potawatomi
Lake Huron
CANADA
Lake Ontario
Lake Michigan
MI
NY
Lake Erie
N W E S
IN
OH
PA

MAP Skill

Movement Once they reached the Great Lakes, in what directions did the Anishinaabeg move?

◀ Harvesting wild rice

51

ⓑ The Anishinaabeg Way of Life

The Three Fires had the same culture. Most lived in rounded homes called **wigwams**. They were made of bark and young trees. The Three Fires also made canoes from bark. They hunted deer and moose in the forests. They used the skins and furs to make clothing. They grew corn, beans, and squash. They tapped maple trees in spring for their sap.

The Three Fires lived in small groups called **bands**. Each band was made up of several **clans**. A clan is a group of families with the same ancestor.

A totem is something from nature that is special to a person or group. Each clan had a totem. Totems could represent an animal such as a bear, eagle, or turtle. Or totems could represent other parts of nature. Children had the same totem as their father.

The Ojibway

The Ojibway had more people than the other two groups. About 30,000 Ojibway lived in the Upper Peninsula. They grew corn and squash. They mostly fished for their food, too. They also picked wild rice from the marshes near the Great Lakes.

This model birch-bark canoe was made by an Odawa chief.

The Odawa

The Odawa often traded with other groups. The name *Odawa* comes from a word that means "to trade." The Odawa traveled in canoes. They traveled all around the Great Lakes.

The Odawa once lived on the Upper Peninsula. Another group, the Iroquois (IR uh kwoy), came from New York. They pushed the Odawa out of the Upper Peninsula. The Odawa then migrated to the Lower Peninsula.

The Potawatomi

The Potawatomi lived in southern Michigan. In winter they hunted for food. In summer they returned to their farming villages.

The Potawatomi were very good farmers. They grew vegetables, fruit and tobacco. When the soil was no longer good, they burned brush to make new fields for planting. They would even move a whole village to a new place so the soil would not be overused.

QUICK CHECK How did the Anishinaabeg get the things they needed from their environment? *Summarize*

Marge Anderson
Ojibway tribal leader

66 *Our People are rediscovering the traditions of our ancestors that give us pride in our past, and <u>vision</u> for our future. . . . I used to fear that, when my generation passed on, the Ojibway language would die with us. . . . I now have great confidence that the Ojibway language— and the Ojibway People—will live 'as long as the grass grows, and the rivers flow'.* 99

<u>vision</u> something imagined or dreamed

Write About It! Why does Marge Anderson feel traditions are important?

⒞ The Anishinaabeg Today

More than 60,000 American Indians live in Michigan today. Many are Ojibway. Most live on the Upper Peninsula.

Keeping Culture Alive

Art is part of American Indian culture. Some artists try to keep their culture alive. Frank Ettawageshik is an Ojibway artist who does this. You will read about him on the next page.

The Ojibway people know it is important to keep their language alive. Their language helps them to hold on to their culture. Some Ojibway children learn the language in school.

✓ **QUICK CHECK** What is the one way the Anishinaabeg work to keep their culture alive? *Summarize*

▼ These Ojibway moccasins are made of deerskin and decorated with beadwork.

★★★ Focus Lesson Review

1. **Focus Question** Who are the Anishinaabeg?

2. **Vocabulary** Write one sentence for each vocabulary word.
   band   confederacy   wigwam
   clan   migrate

3. **Government** Why do you think the Anishinaabeg formed a confederacy?

4. **Critical Thinking Main Idea and Details** What are some things the Three Fires had in common?

5. **Reading Strategy Summarize** Summarize what you learned about the Potawatomi.

6. **Write About** THE **BIG IDEA** How did the geography of Michigan affect how the Anishinaabeg lived?

7. **Link to Art** The Ojibway are known for their beautiful beadwork. Use the Internet to research Ojibway bead designs. Choose one to draw, using colored pencils.

Frank Ettawageshik 1949–

Frank Ettawageshik (etta wah GHEE shick) lives in Michigan. He grew up listening to his father tell the stories of the Odawa (Ottawa) of Michigan.

Ettawageshik became an artist who works with pottery. He decided to bring back an Odawa tradition. He learned how Odawa artists made pottery hundreds of years ago. In time he learned how to make his own pottery the same way. He only uses clay and granite. He makes them hard over a wood fire.

Ettawageshik is tribal leader of the Odawa people. He often speaks out about saving the Great Lakes.

"What we learn in our traditions is to honor the other beings in creation. To respect the waters and lands within and upon which they and we live. Our very existence is in peril when we forget these simple truths."

Write About It! How does Frank Ettawageshik keep the traditions of his people alive?

LOG ON For more biographies, visit: www.macmillanmh.com

The Life of Frank Ettawageshik

1945	1965	1985	2005
1949 Frank Ettawageshik born	1974 Begins studying traditional Odawa pottery methods	1991 Begins first term as Tribal Chairman	2005 Elected Tribal Chairman of Executive Branch

Understand Artifacts

The LIBRARY *of* CONGRESS

Artifacts are one kind of primary source. Archaeologists examine artifacts such as tools, pottery, and cave paintings to find out how people lived long ago.

Ojibway Song Board and Drum

Music has always been an important part of Ojibway culture. Songs were used in healing ceremonies. Singers often played a drum as they sang. The Ojibway often decorated the objects they made with designs and symbols of birds and other animals. They used paints made from berries, minerals, and other natural materials.

1 Learn It

You may have a chance to study actual artifacts at a museum. You may be able to touch them. Many times, though, you will be looking at photographs of artifacts. Here are things to think about when studying an artifact.

▲ Song boards like this one helped singers learn and remember songs.

- Look closely at the artifact to see what it is made of. Think about what this might tell you about the people who made it.

- Read any information given with the artifact.

- Try to understand what the artifact was used for.

2 Try It

Look at the photograph of the song board on page 56.

- What does the label tell you about it?

- What does it seem to be made of?

- What do the materials used tell you about this artifact and the people who made it?

3 Apply It

- In what way is the drum similar to the one shown in the photograph?

- What is something you cannot tell about the drum from looking at this picture of it?

- What more do you want to know after studying the artifact?

▲ Ojibway holy man holding ceremonial drums

An Ojibway drum ▶

Use Reference Materials

If you want to learn more about the American Indians of Michigan, you can do research using **reference materials**. These are books and other sources that contain facts about many different subjects. Some of them can be found in a part of the library called the reference section. Others are on the Internet.

1 Learn It

1. Use a Dictionary

■ You might want to learn the exact meaning of the word *archaeologist.* To find out, you can use a **dictionary**. A dictionary gives meanings of words. It also shows you how to pronounce and spell them.

■ The words in a dictionary are arranged in alphabetical order. The **guide words** at the top of each page tell you the first and last words defined on the page.

2. Use an Encyclopedia

■ Suppose you want to know more about the Menominee. You can look up this topic in an **encyclopedia**. This book or set of books gives information about people, places, things, and events. Like dictionaries, encyclopedia entries are arranged in alphabetical order.

3. Use Reference Sources on the Internet

■ The **Internet** is another reference source. It is a computer network. You can read more on how to search the Web for information on pages 236–237.

2 Try It

Look at the sample dictionary page below.

- What are the guide words for this page?

- What is the last word defined on the page?

- Would the word *extra* be defined on the page?

3 Apply It

- Choose a topic from the last lesson to research. Use reference sources to find out about it.

- Write a short research report about what you learn.

---

experimental ➤ explosive

experimental From or relating to experiments: *The scientists were working on an experimental project in the chemistry laboratory.* **ex·per·i·ment·al** (ek sper′ə ment′əl) *adjective.*

expert A person who knows a great deal about some special thing: *One of our teachers is an expert on American history. Noun.*
○ Having or showing a great deal of knowledge: *The swimming coach gave the team expert advice on how to dive. Adjective.*
ex·pert (eks′pûrt *for noun*; eks′pûrt *or* ek spûrt′ *for adjective*) *noun, plural* **experts;** *adjective.*

expiration 1. The act of coming to an end or close: *I must get a new library card before the expiration of my old one.* 2. The act of breathing out air: *The sick child's expirations were weak.* **ex·pi·ra·tion** (eks′pə rā′shən) *noun, plural* expirations.

expire 1. To come to an end: *Your membership at the pool expires at the end of the month.* 2. To breathe out; exhale: *When we expire, our bodies let air out of our lungs.* 3. To die. **ex·pire** (ek spīr′) *verb,* **expired, expiring.**

The art teacher is explaining **paintings to the class.**

explain 1. To make something plain or clear; tell the meaning of: *Explain how to get the answer to this mathematics problem.* 2. To give or have a reason for: *Can you explain why you were late for school?* **ex·plain** (ek splān′) *verb,* **explained, explaining.**

explanation for why the vase was broken. **ex·pla·na·tion** (eks′plə nā′shən) *noun, plural* **explanations.**

explicit Stated clearly or shown clearly: *Our teacher gave explicit instructions on how we should do the work.* **ex·pli·cit** (ek splis′it) *adjective.*

explode 1. To burst or cause to burst suddenly and with a loud noise; blow up: *I pumped too much air into the tire, and it exploded.* 2. To show an emotion noisily or forcefully: *The audience exploded with laughter at the funny joke.* **ex·plode** (ek splōd′) *verb,* **exploded, exploding.**

exploit A brave deed or act: *The story is about the daring exploits of a knight. Noun.*
○ 1. To use in an unfair or unjust way for selfish reasons: *The American colonists felt that the British government exploited them by taxing the tea they drank.* 2. To make the fullest possible use of: *This new drill will enable us to exploit oil buried far under the ground. Verb.*
ex·ploit (ek′ sploit *for noun;* ek sploit′ *for verb*) *noun, plural* **exploits;** *verb,* **exploited, exploiting.**

exploration The act of exploring: *Sometimes people really mean conquest when they talk about exploration.* **ex·plo·ra·tion** (ek′splə rā′shən) *noun, plural* **explorations.**

explore 1. To go to a place that one knows nothing about: *Astronauts explored the moon and brought back rocks.* 2. To try to figure out: *Doctors explore the causes of diseases.* **ex·plore** (ek splôr′) *verb,* **explored, exploring.**

explorer A person who explores. **ex·plor·er** (ek splôr′ər) *noun, plural* **explorers.**

explosion 1. The act of bursting or expanding suddenly and noisily: *The explosion of the bomb broke windows in the buildings nearby.* 2. A sudden outburst: *The funny joke caused an explosion of laughter.* **ex·plo·sion** (ek splō′zhən) *noun, plural* **explosions.**

explosive 1. Likely to explode or cause an explosion: *A bomb is an explosive device.* 2. Likely to cause a lot of trouble: *an explosive political situation. Adjective.*

The Huron

How did the Huron live long ago?

VOCABULARY

stockade
longhouse
kinship

VOCABULARY STRATEGY

Root Words The word *kin* means "a person's relatives." Can you think of some terms that describe **kinship**?

READING STRATEGY

Identify Main Idea and Details Use the chart below to list the main idea and supporting details of the lesson.

MICHIGAN GLCE

H3.0.1
H3.0.3
H3.0.4
H3.0.5
G4.0.4

The Huron is another group of American Indians. In 1999 members of the Huron from Mighigan, two other states, and Ontario, Canada, met. They got to know one another. They were proud of their Huron ancestors. These words from *The Wendat Confederacy* tell us about how they felt:

" *Over 10 generations ago, the Wendat [Huron] people were driven to many directions from our beloved homeland. Today, 350 years later, we . . . light the council fire and invite all who come in a spirit of peace and brotherhood to enjoy its warmth.* "

Slabs of tree bark covered the sides and roofs of Huron houses. ▼

Ⓐ People of the Peninsula

Other groups lived in Michigan besides the Anishinaabeg. The Huron and the Iroquois (IR uh kwoy) moved into Michigan. They came from New York. The Menominee also lived in Michigan.

The Huron and the Iroquois

The Huron and the Iroquois spoke the same language. They had the same ancestors, but they were enemies. The Huron lived in what is now Mackinac County. The Iroquois moved there too. They wanted that land.

Fierce fighting took place between the two groups. The Iroquois pushed the Huron out. Then, the Huron moved south. They made their home in southeastern Michigan. They lived near Lake Erie.

The Huron probably had more people than any other upper Great Lakes group. Huron villages stretched south from Canada along Lake Huron and Lake Erie. They stretched as far east as New York.

QUICK CHECK How did the Huron get along with the Iroquois? *Main Idea and Details*

Ⓑ Village Life

The Huron lived in large villages. They grew most of the food they ate. The men cleared the forest to make fields. Huron women and children planted and took care of the crops. The most important crops were corn, beans, and squash. The men also fished and hunted.

The Huron were farmers. They lived near their fields and did not move from place to place very often. Instead, if soil was no longer good for farming, Huron men would clear new fields.

A Huron village could have almost 2,000 people. Villages were from one to ten acres—about five football fields in size. High fences called **stockades** circled the villages. Stockades protected villages from attack. People lived in **longhouses**. These large houses were about 25 feet wide and 200 feet long.

Family Relationships

The Huron way of life was based on **kinship**, or family relationships. Children were part of their mother's clan, not their father's. When a man married, he became part of his wife's clan. He would go live in her longhouse.

The Huron were loving parents. They believed that children learned from example, not from punishment. Huron children knew their families would be disappointed if they did not behave. Because of this, they learned to do the right thing.

◀ A Huron wife helps her husband prepare for a journey. Baskets like this one were used for storage.

Government

The Huron were ruled by a council of men. Clan mothers chose the men to be on the council. The council made important decisions for the group. Huron women also met in councils. They would then give advice to the men's council.

Huron councils did not make decisions by taking a vote. Instead they talked about things until there was agreement.

The Huron believed that people were free. They believed that no one had the right to make others do something. It was important for just about everyone to agree on any plans. A kind of agreement that includes everyone is called a consensus.

QUICK CHECK How did Huron children learn the right way to behave? *Summarize*

▲ This Huron pouch was made of deerskin and decorated with moose-hair embroidery.

What You Learned

A The Huron lived first in the Upper Peninsula, and after being forced to move by the Iroquois, in southeastern Michigan.

B The Huron were excellent farmers who lived in villages near their fields. Huron life was based on kinship through the mother's clan. The governing council made decisions by consensus.

Focus Lesson Review

1. **Focus Question** How did the Huron live long ago?

2. **Vocabulary** Write one sentence for each vocabulary word.
   kinship   longhouse   stockade

3. **Government** How did the Huron leaders make decisions?

4. **Critical Thinking Draw Conclusions** How do you think living in a longhouse would be different from living in a modern house?

5. **Reading Strategy Identify Main Idea and Details** Use the chart to show the main idea and details about Huron villages.

6. **Write About THE BIG IDEA** How did geography influence the way the Huron lived?

7. **Link to Mathematics** About 20 people lived in each Huron longhouse. If a village had 100 houses, about how many people did it have?

A Young Anishinaabeg Child Long Ago

Anishinaabeg children helped their parents from an early age. Girls learned to make clothing from animal skins and furs. They learned which plants were good to eat, and how to grow squash and corn. Boys learned to make canoes and to fish. Both found time to play.

◄ The jingle dress this girl is wearing is a special Ojibway tradition.

Children learned skills, such as canoe-making, by working with adults. ▼

The Anishinaabeg used this stick to play a game like lacrosse. ▼

Ojibway boy wearing traditional clothing ▼

▲ The Ojibway decorated clothing with beadwork.

◄ Anishinaabeg girls played with dolls like this one. Its hair is made from horse hair.

Write About It!

Write about ways an Anishinaabeg child's life was like your life today.

LOG ON — For more about young people in history, visit: www.macmillanmh.com

Chapter 2 Review

Copy the sentences below on a separate sheet of paper. Use the list of vocabulary words to fill in the blanks.

archaeologist	migrate
clan	stockades
longhouse	

1. Several related Huron families lived together in a(n) _____ .

2. A(n) _____ can learn about the Hopewell by studying the things found in their mounds.

3. The Huron belong to their mother's _____ .

4. The Iroquois forced the Huron to _____ to southeastern Michigan.

5. High fences called _____ protected villages from attack.

6. **Test Preparation** People of the Three Fires lived in dome-shaped _____ .

   A bands   C kinship
   B wigwams   D longhouses

7. **Test Preparation** A group's _____ is passed down from parent to child.

   A culture   C band
   B confederacy   D artifact

8. Who were the first people to live in what is now Michigan?

9. Which custom did all Hopewell have in common?

10. What three groups make up the Three Fires?

11. How do we know the Hopewell were skilled metalworkers?

12. How did the Anishinaabeg travel Michigan's lakes and rivers?

13. How did Huron governing councils make decisions?

14. What are some crops the Anishinaabeg grew?

15. **Critical Thinking** Why didn't the Huron move from place to place?

16. **Critical Thinking** How do we know the Hopewell traded with people far away?

17. **Critical Thinking** Why was it good that the members of the Three Fires remained close?

Understand Latitude and Longitude

Write a complete sentence or choose from the answer choices to answer each question.

18. What are the east/west grid lines on the map called?

19. Look at the map. On which line of latitude is the city of Flint located?

20. Which city is closest to 43° N, 86° W?

Michigan: Latitude and Longitude

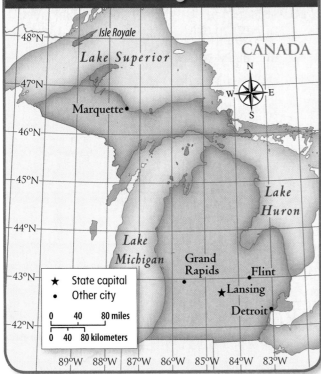

Artifacts

Ojibway moccasins

Study the photograph. Then answer the questions.

21. Why are these moccasins a primary source?

22. Tell two things you could learn about the Ojibway by studying this artifact.

23. **Be an Archaeologist** Form groups and place any three items in a paper bag. Exchange bags with another group. Take the items out one at a time. What could you learn about a culture based on those objects? Write a list.

24. **Narrative** Write a paragraph describing what a member of the Huron group did long ago on a typical spring day. Give as many details as you can.

LOG ON For help with the process of writing, visit: www.macmillanmh.com

★ Unit 1 Review and Test Prep

Comprehension and Critical Thinking Check

Write one or more sentences to answer each question.

1. What states share a **boundary** with the state of Michigan?

2. Describe what a **peninsula** is, using facts about Michigan's geography.

3. Explain how human beings are part of an **ecosystem**.

4. What **natural resources** can be found in Michigan's Upper Peninsula?

5. What is the difference between **climate** and weather?

6. Who were the **Paleo-Indians**?

7. What can **artifacts** tell you about the past? Provide an example from what you've learned about Michigan's history.

8. What was the Three Fires **Confederacy**?

9. **Critical Thinking** How do **archaeologists** help us know about the past?

10. **Critical Thinking** How do you think living in a **longhouse** would affect how people interacted with one another?

Reading Skills Check

Main Idea and Details

Copy this graphic organizer. Recall what you read in this unit about Michigan's climate. Use the graphic organizer to help you identify the main idea and details about the climate of this Great Lakes state and how it affects the way people live.

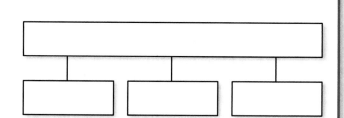

11. How do the climates of Michigan's two regions differ?

12. How does Lake Michigan moderate, or even out, the land temperatures of the state?

13. How are people affected by Michigan's climate?

Study the map and use it with what you already know to answer the questions.

American Indian Territories

14. How does geography help explain why the Potawatomi did more farming than the Ojibway or the Odawa?

   A The Upper Peninsula was good for growing vegetables.

   B The Upper Peninsula was covered with forests.

   C The coastal area of the northern Lower Peninsula is good for farming.

   D The southern Lower Peninsula has a good climate for farming.

15. Which answer BEST explains why the Odawa were great traders?

   A Their land was good for farming.

   B They lived along lakes and rivers.

   C They built mounds.

   D They had wagons.

Write About History

16. **Narrative** Imagine that you are on a trip to Michigan's Upper Peninsula. Write a postcard to a friend describing what you are doing and seeing.

17. **Expository** Create an outline of the life of one of Michigan's American Indian groups. Include main ideas and details.

18. **Expository** Suppose you are a Michigan farmer. You have been asked to organize a farm festival. Write a speech to give on the opening day of the festival explaining what crop you are celebrating and why it is important to Michigan.

LOG ON

For help with the process of writing, visit: www.macmillanmh.com

Unit 1

REVIEW
THE BIG IDEA

How do people adapt to where they live?

Write About the Big Idea

Expository Essay

An expository essay is a written composition that explains something. You will use your graphic organizer to help you write an essay about one geographic region in Michigan. Your essay should answer the Big Idea question "How do people adapt to where they live?"

Think about what you learned about Michigan's geography, climate, people, and natural resources as you read Unit 1. Go back and reread lessons if you need to. Use the details to complete the graphic organizer.

Michigan People	Geography	Climate	Natural Resources
People long ago			
People today			

Write an Expository Essay

1. Plan
- Often you will need to choose a topic. Here it has been given to you.
- Do more research if you need to.
- Decide how to organize your essay. You could write a paragraph for each section of the graphic organizer.

2. Write a First Draft
- Write an introduction that tells what the essay is about.
- Write a main idea sentence for each paragraph. You will have one paragraph for each section of the graphic organizer.
- Now add details to each paragraph that tell more about the main idea.
- Write a conclusion.

3. Revise and Proofread
- Read your essay. Be sure you stated your main idea in the introduction.
- Be sure each paragraph has a main idea sentence that is explained with examples and details.
- Proofread your essay. Check the spelling, capitalization, and punctuation.
- Rewrite your essay neatly.

ACTIVITY

Speak About the Big Idea

Travel Commercial

Create a television advertisement for a region of Michigan. You will want to explain and describe the positive things that would make people want to visit the region. You might make a colorful brochure or poster that you can show during your commercial.

Prepare Work in small groups. Each group should choose a region to promote. Include information about your region's climate, natural resources, tourist attractions, cities, or national parks. Use information from Unit 1 and your notes. Find additional information by using the Internet, or at your library.

Present Have each group present their advertisement to the class. Each member should present some of the information.

LAUNCH PAD   For help with the Big Idea activity, visit: www.macmillanmh.com

Read More About the Big Idea

Ojibwe Legends

Read this Leveled Reader to learn about how the Ojibwe, also spelled Ojibway, used their stories to teach lessons about how to live.

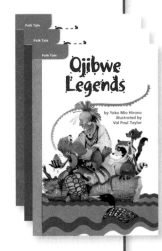

The National Museum of the American Indian: A Living Museum

Explore this Leveled Reader to take a tour of the National Museum of the American Indian in Washington, D.C.

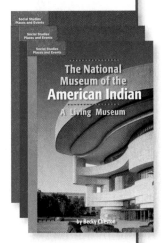

A Curious Glimpse of Michigan

by Kevin and Stephanie Kammeraad Explore this delightful collection of fun and fascinating Michigan facts.

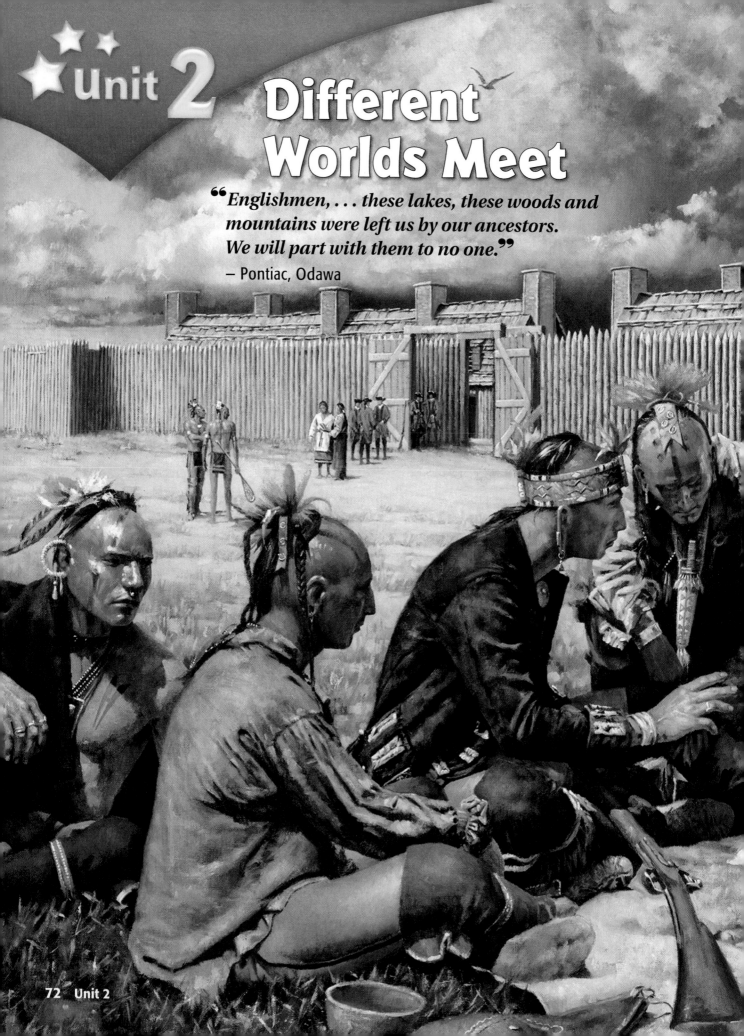

Different Worlds Meet

"*Englishmen, . . . these lakes, these woods and mountains were left us by our ancestors. We will part with them to no one.*"

— Pontiac, Odawa

What happens when different peoples first meet?

In Unit 2 you'll learn how the lives of Michigan's American Indians changed when European explorers, soldiers, and others arrived. You will also read about how Michigan grew and became part of the United States.

As you read the unit, look for changes caused by the meeting of Europeans and American Indians in Michigan. Then copy the graphic organizer. After you read, fill in details telling how different groups affected American Indians.

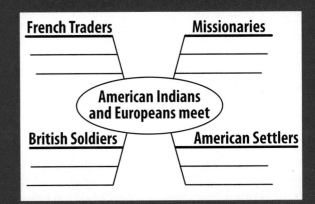

French Traders   Missionaries

American Indians and Europeans meet

British Soldiers   American Settlers

◀ American Indians discuss what to do about Europeans in their land.

73

People Who Made a Difference

Jacques Marquette
1637–1675

Jacques Marquette was a French explorer and priest. He founded Michigan's first European settlement in 1668. (page 84)

Pontiac
about 1720–1769

Pontiac was an Odawa chief. In 1763 he convinced several American Indian groups to fight the British settlement. (page 93)

Jean du Sable
about 1750–1818

Jean du Sable is considered the founder of the city of Chicago. He was captured by the British during the American Revolution. (page 100)

1670	1700	1730	1760

1668
Marquette founds mission at Sault Ste. Marie

1763
Pontiac leads American Indians to fight British settlers

LOG ON

For more biographies, visit:
www.macmillanmh.com

Tecumseh
about 1768–1813

Tecumseh was a leader of the Shawnee. He visited many American Indian groups in order to unite them to fight for their homelands. (page 108)

Oliver Hazard Perry
1785–1819

Oliver Hazard Perry was an officer in the United States navy. During the War of 1812, he led the U.S. fleet to victory. (page 114)

Stevens T. Mason
1811–1843

Stevens T. Mason helped lead Michigan to statehood, and was Michigan's first state governor. He was elected to office at the age of 23. (page 129)

about 1809
Tecumseh tries to unify American Indians to protect their homelands

1790	1820	1850	1880

1779
Jean du Sable captured by British during the American Revolution

1813
Perry defeats British in Battle of Lake Erie

1835
Stevens T. Mason elected governor of Michigan

Unit 2 Literature

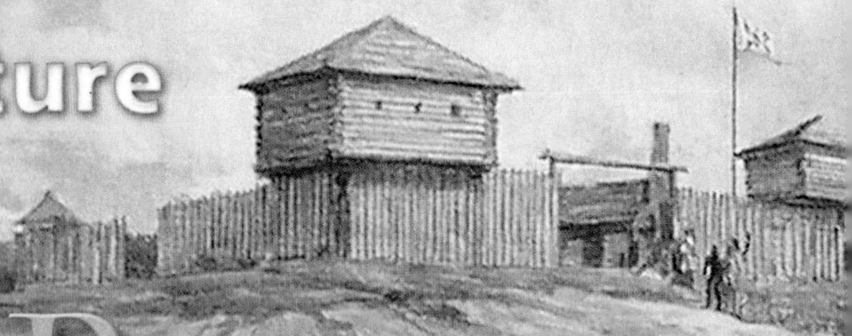

French Pioneers
1534-1759

A poem

by Rosemary and Stephen Vincent Benét

New France, New Spain, New England,
Which will it be?
Who will win the new land?
The land across the sea?

They came here, they **toiled** here,
They broke their hearts afar,
Normandy and Brittany,
Paris and Navarre.

They lost here, at last here,
It wasn't so to be.
Let us still remember them,
Men from oversea.

---

toiled (toild) worked

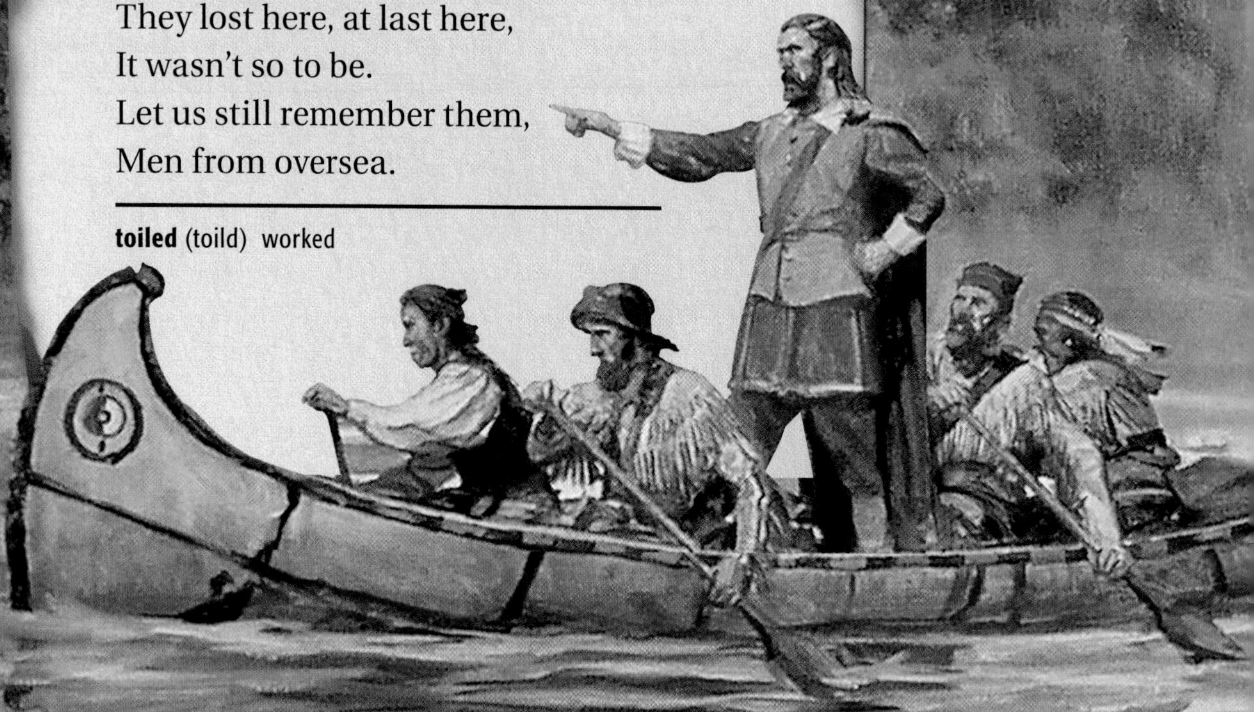

Marquette and Joliet,
Cartier, La Salle,
Priest, **corsair**, gentleman,
Gallants one and all.

France was in their quick words,
France was in their veins.
They came here, they toiled here.
They suffered many pains.

Lake and river, stream and wood,
Seigneurs and dames—
They lived here, they died here,
They left singing names.

corsair (kôr′sår) pirate

seigneurs (sān′yerz) sirs; lords

Write About It!

Write a poem about what you saw and heard during your own exploring adventure.

Reading
SKILLS

Summarize:
Exploring North America

In this unit you will learn about the first Europeans to explore North America. Summarizing, or stating the important ideas in a reading selection, will help you understand social studies better. A summary states the main ideas but leaves out minor details. Summarizing will also help you understand and remember what you read.

 **Learn It**

- First find the main ideas of a selection. Then restate these ideas briefly in your summary.

- Find important details and combine them in your summary.

- Leave out details that are not important.

Now read the selection below and think about how you would summarize it.

Main Idea
The first sentence is a main idea.

Detail
These details can be combined.

Main Idea
This main idea is about Henry Hudson.

Detail
This detail is about Hudson's trips.

Early explorers thought that there was a Northwest Passage that would take them from the Atlantic Ocean to the Pacific. John Cabot was the first to try. He did not find it. Many other explorers followed him in the search.

Henry Hudson came the closest to finding a successful route. He tried to find the Northwest Passage twice. His trips spanned the years 1609–1611. The closest he came was a bay north of the Great Lakes that is now named after him.

 **Try It**

Copy the summary chart below. Finish filling in the chart by summarizing the second paragraph on page 78.

SUMMARIZE

Paragraph 1	Paragraph 2
Cabot and other explorers looked for a Northwest Passage.	

What did you look for to summarize the paragraph?

3 Apply It

■ Review the steps for summarizing in Learn It.

■ Read the passage below. Then, create a summary chart to summarize both paragraphs.

Jacques Cartier hoped to find the Northwest Passage. He did not find it, but he claimed all the land he explored including parts of today's Michigan. He named the land New France.

Jacques Cartier was hoping to find riches in New France. Instead of gold and diamonds he found "fool's gold" and crystal quartz, which were worthless. The source of wealth he did find in New France was furs.

Chapter 3

Europeans Come to Michigan

You Are There

"He wore a grand robe of China damask [fabric], all strewn with flowers and birds of many colors. . . . The news of his coming quickly spread. . . ."

This passage is from a French history book. It tells of explorer Jean Nicolet's first meeting with an American Indian group. They were probably the Winnebago. In this chapter you will learn what happened when Nicolet and other Europeans came to Michigan.

Missouri River

◀ Jean Nicolet

Chapter Events

| | 1660 | 1680 | 1700 |

1
1668
Michigan's first European settlement founded at Sault Ste. Marie

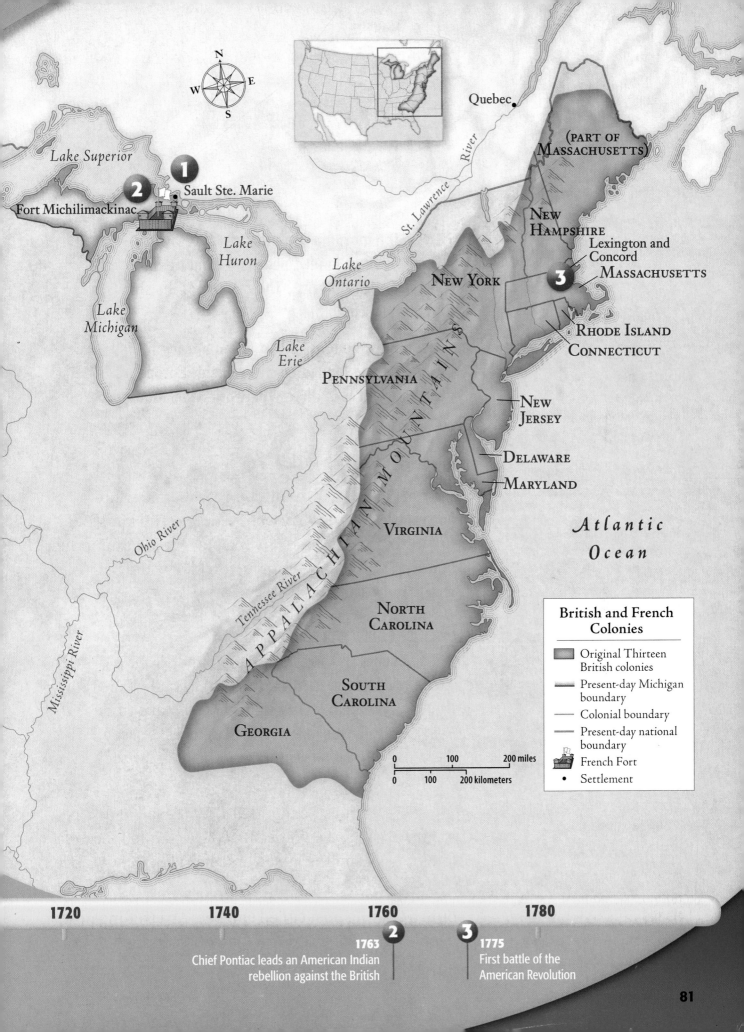

N
W · E
S

Quebec

Lake Superior

1 Sault Ste. Marie

2 Fort Michilimackinac

Lake Huron

Lake Michigan

Lake Ontario

Lake Erie

(PART OF MASSACHUSETTS)

St. Lawrence River

NEW HAMPSHIRE

Lexington and Concord
MASSACHUSETTS

3

NEW YORK

RHODE ISLAND
CONNECTICUT

PENNSYLVANIA

APPALACHIAN MOUNTAINS

NEW JERSEY

DELAWARE

MARYLAND

Ohio River

VIRGINIA

Atlantic Ocean

Tennessee River

NORTH CAROLINA

Mississippi River

SOUTH CAROLINA

GEORGIA

British and French Colonies

- Original Thirteen British colonies
- Present-day Michigan boundary
- Colonial boundary
- Present-day national boundary
- French Fort
- • Settlement

0   100   200 miles
0   100   200 kilometers

1720   1740   1760   1780

2 1763
Chief Pontiac leads an American Indian rebellion against the British

3 1775
First battle of the American Revolution

Why did the French come to Michigan?

VOCABULARY

colony
Northwest Passage
expedition
trading post
alliance
missionary
barter
voyageur

VOCABULARY STRATEGY

Root Words The root of **alliance** is ally. An ally is a friend or partner. What do you think it means for two nations to make an alliance?

READING STRATEGY

Summarize Use the chart below to summarize this lesson.

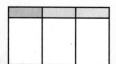

MICHIGAN GLCE

H3.0.1   H3.0.9
H3.0.3   H3.0.10
H3.0.5
H3.0.6

Europeans Arrive

It was the morning of October 12, 1492. Three small Spanish ships landed near an island. It was off the coast of North America. The captain of the ship was Christopher Columbus.

Columbus thought he had found a trade route to Asia. Instead he had landed on a continent. Europeans had not even known it was there. The world was about to change.

A Claiming Land

After Columbus, many countries sent explorers across the ocean. They were sent to claim land and to build **colonies**. A colony is a place ruled by another country. The French and the English would both play a part in Michigan's history.

French Explorers

The French hoped to find gold and silver in North America. They also hoped to find a water route to the Pacific Ocean. This route would make trade with Asia easier. It was called the **Northwest Passage**. The French made **expeditions**, or journeys of discovery, to find the route.

In 1534 Jacques Cartier (kahr TYAY) sailed to the mouth of the St. Lawrence River. He claimed the area for France. Later the land would be called New France.

In 1608 Samuel de Champlain (sham PLAYN) built a **trading post** called Quebec. At a trading post, people can trade goods for food and supplies. It was on the St. Lawrence River.

1534
Jacques Cartier claims
New France

1608
Samuel de Champlain
develops New France

1701
The founding
of Detroit

◀ Samuel de Champlain

Champlain made an agreement with the Huron. This agreement of friendship is called an **alliance**. The Huron agreed to supply the French with furs. The furs could be sold in Europe for a lot of money. In return the French would help the Huron fight the Iroquois.

The Iroquois were enemies with the Huron. Because the French helped the Huron, the Iroquois would be enemies of France for years to come.

Champlain also sent explorers to look for a Northwest Passage. Étienne Brulé (broo LAY) was the first European to reach Michigan. He canoed to Sault Ste. Marie in 1620. Jean Nicolet (nik oh LAY) came to the Upper Peninsula in 1634. Neither found a Northwest Passage.

QUICK CHECK What did the French hope to find in North America? *Summarize*

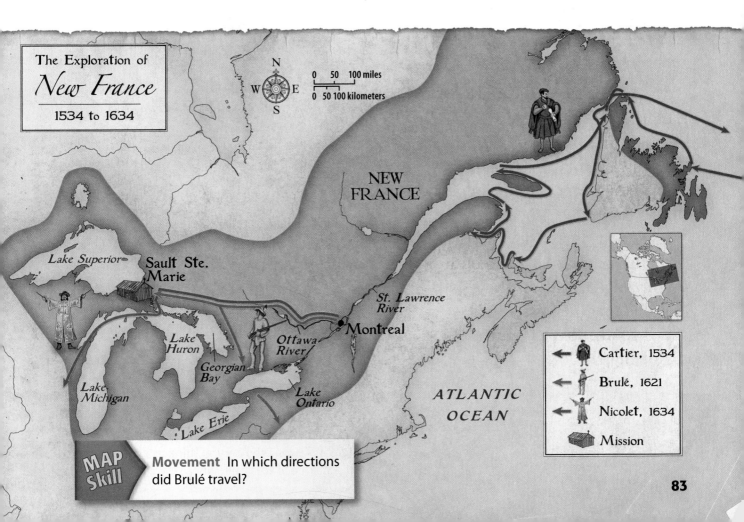

The Exploration of
New France

1534 to 1634

0 50 100 miles
0 50 100 kilometers

NEW
FRANCE

Lake Superior

Sault Ste.
Marie

Lake
Superior

Lake
Huron

Georgian
Bay

Ottawa
River

St. Lawrence
River

Montreal

Lake
Michigan

Lake
Ontario

Lake Erie

ATLANTIC
OCEAN

← Cartier, 1534

← Brulé, 1621

← Nicolet, 1634

Mission

MAP Skill **Movement** In which directions did Brulé travel?

ⓑ The First Settlements

Some people who came to New France were explorers or traders. Others were Catholic **missionaries**. A missionary teaches religious beliefs to people who have other beliefs. The missionaries in New France wanted to teach Christianity to American Indians.

Jacques Marquette

One missionary, Père (Father) Jacques Marquette, founded the first European settlement in Michigan in 1668. It was called Sault Ste. Marie. A few years later, he founded St. Ignace, above the Straits of Mackinac. Marquette became friends with the Huron and Odawa. But he did not convince many of them to become Christians.

In 1673 Marquette joined Louis Jolliet (joh lee AY). They went on an expedition down the Mississippi River. The men hoped the river would lead them to the Pacific Ocean. See their route on the map. They met American Indians at the mouth of the Arkansas River. They learned that the Mississippi flows south. So they returned to Michigan.

French Forts

Explorers built forts to protect their land. Robert La Salle built the first fort on the Lower Peninsula in 1679. He called it Fort Miami. Today it is the city of St. Joseph. The forts became centers of trade with American Indians.

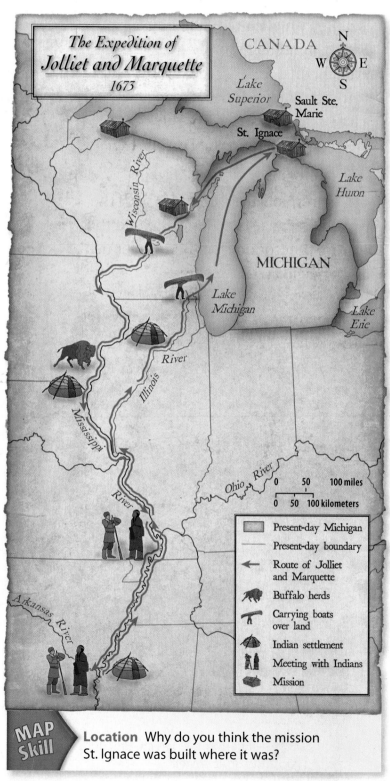

The Expedition of *Jolliet and Marquette* 1673

Present-day Michigan
Present-day boundary
Route of Jolliet and Marquette
Buffalo herds
Carrying boats over land
Indian settlement
Meeting with Indians
Mission

MAP Skill

Location Why do you think the mission St. Ignace was built where it was?

▲ French traders often paddled as much as 100 miles a day.

The Fur Trade

The French did not find silver or gold. They found furs instead. Furs were popular in Europe. Europeans would pay high prices for mink, beaver, and fox pelts, or skins. French explorers saw that American Indians used fur for clothing. They knew the furs would be a good way to make money.

The French **bartered** with American Indians. To barter is to trade goods without using money. For the furs the French gave the American Indians beads, pots, knives, guns, and clothing. American Indians taught European traders their language and how to track animals.

Traders sent furs to Quebec on canoes. Then the furs were shipped from Quebec to France. In France, they were made into expensive hats and clothing.

Young men transported the furs by canoe. They were called **voyageurs**. A voyageur's life had a lot of adventure. But it was a hard life, too. They got up before sunrise and paddled all day.

Changes to American Indian Life

Contact with the French changed American Indian life forever. American Indians began to depend on Europeans for many of their needs. The Huron gave up their old way of life to trap animals for the fur trade.

The French brought diseases to American Indian lands. They brought smallpox, measles, and mumps. American Indians had never had these diseases. As a result, thousands died from these diseases.

✓ **QUICK CHECK** How did the arrival of Europeans change American Indian life?
Cause and Effect

▲ This painting shows Antoine de la Cadillac landing at Detroit.

New France Settlements in Michigan

Lake Superior

Sault Ste. Marie

St. Ignace

Fort Michilimackinac

Lake Michigan

Lake Huron

Lake St. Clair

Fort Pontchartrain (Detroit)

Fort Miami

Lake Erie

0 40 80 miles
0 40 80 kilometers

— Present-day national boundary
— Present-day state boundary
🏰 Fort
• Settlement

MAP Skill   **Location** Which French fort was located farthest west?

ⓒ The Founding of Detroit

In the late 1600s, France and England were enemies. Now English traders began moving into French territory in North America. Antoine de la Cadillac was the commander of the fort at St. Ignace. He thought France needed a fort in the south. A fort in the south would stop the English from reaching the upper Great Lakes.

In 1701 Cadillac took 50 soldiers, 50 workers, 100 American Indians, and 2 priests south. They built Fort Pontchartrain. The town that grew around the fort was called "LaVille d'Etroit" (City of the Strait) or "Detroit."

Soon farms appeared along the Detroit River. The town grew into a busy colony. Men, women, and children worked together to provide food and clothing. They also prepared furs for trading.

France offered a pig, a wagon, and farmland to anyone who moved to Detroit. ▶

American Indians at the Fort

American Indians now trapped many more animals than before the French arrived. When there were no more animals left in an area, trappers moved to another area. This led to wars over land. The Iroquois got guns from Europeans. In 1648 they used the guns to attack the Huron and other groups.

Thousands of Anishinaabeg and Huron moved near Fort Pontchartrain. They wanted to be safe. The fort was surrounded by a stockade fence. Problems also grew between the French and the British. By 1718 there were French forts in each corner of Michigan. The forts did not stop the British from coming.

QUICK CHECK Why did the French build Fort Pontchartrain? *Summarize*

What You Learned

Ⓐ The French came to the Great Lakes area in the 1500s and 1600s looking for riches and a Northwest Passage to Asia.

Ⓑ Catholic missionaries played a key role in exploring and settling New France.

Ⓒ In 1701 the French founded the settlement that became Detroit.

Focus Lesson Review

1. **Focus Question** Why did the French come to Michigan?

2. **Vocabulary** Write one sentence for each vocabulary word.
alliance	colony	missionary
barter	expedition	voyageur

3. **Geography** What role did geography play in the way the voyageurs transported goods?

4. **Critical Thinking Make Inferences** What kind of person do you think would make a good voyageur?

5. **Reading Strategy Summarize** Use the chart to summarize why French explorers, traders, and missionaries came to Michigan.

6. **Write About THE BIG IDEA** How did the fur trade change life in Michigan?

7. **Link to History** Suppose that you are an archaeologist. List three artifacts you think you might find at Fort Michilimackinac. Why do you think you would find them there?

Read Time Lines

To understand history, you need to know *when* things happened. You also need to know the *order* in which things happened. A **time line** can help you do this. A time line is a diagram that shows when events took place. You can use this useful tool to learn about the past. A time line also shows whether one event happened before or after another event. You can use the notches on the time line to find out how much time passed between each event.

1 Learn It

- Read the title of the time line below. The title summarizes what the time line is about.

- Time lines are usually divided into parts. Each part covers a certain number of years. On the time line below, each part is 15 years.

- Read the time line from left to right. The earliest event is shown on the left side. Each event to the right happened after that. On the time line below, you can see the date of Marquette's birth on the left and his death on the far right.

- Some time lines show events both above and below the line.

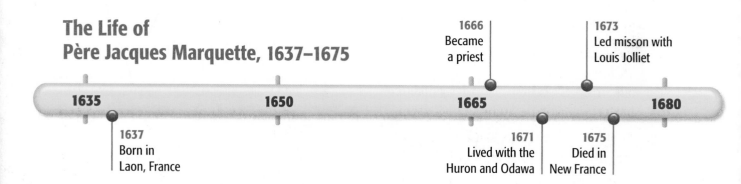

The Life of Père Jacques Marquette, 1637–1675

1666 Became a priest

1673 Led misson with Louis Jolliet

1635   1650   1665   1680

1637 Born in Laon, France

1671 Lived with the Huron and Odawa

1675 Died in New France

② Try It

Use the time line on page 88 to answer these questions.

- Did Marquette live with the Huron and Odawa before or after he led a mission?

- When did Marquette become a priest?

- How many years did Marquette live?

③ Apply It

Use the time line below to answer the questions.

- When was Cadillac born?

- In what year did Cadillac found the city of Detroit?

- How many years were there between the year Cadillac came to New France and the year he founded Detroit?

The Life of Antoine de la Cadillac, 1658–1730

1655	1670	1685	1700	1715	1730

1658
Born in France

1683
Sailed to New France

1694
Became commandant of Mackinac

1701
Founded city of Detroit

1710
Appointed governor of Louisiana territory

1730
Died in France

Marquette and Jolliet traveled down the Mississippi River. ▼

How did the French and Indian War affect Michigan?

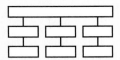
The French and Indian War

From 1607 to 1750, about two million people came to the Atlantic coast. They settled in the 13 English colonies. New France had about 80,000 people. They did not have enough people to fight in the battle ahead.

Ⓐ The English in North America

In the late 1500s and 1600s, many countries had colonies in North America. English colonies started along the Atlantic coast in 1607.

American Indians watch as a European fort is built. ▼

1607
English settle colony of Jamestown in Virginia

1707
England and Scotland unite to form Great Britain

1750
Two million people live in British colonies of North America

1754
French and Indian War begins

1763
Treaty of Paris ends war

The English traded with American Indians for furs. They also wanted new settlements. Thousands of English families moved to North America to farm. Their farms produced tobacco, rice, and other crops. These crops were sent back to England for money.

Conflict Over Land

In 1707 England and Scotland joined together. This made the country of Great Britain. British settlers kept moving to North America. Land along the coast became scarce. Settlers began to move across the mountains to the northwest **frontier**. A frontier is the far edge of a country. It is where people are just beginning to settle.

France said they owned this land. The area was known as the Ohio **Territory**. A territory is land owned by a country. The land can be within or outside the country's borders. France and Great Britain were already enemies in Europe. Now both countries wanted the same land in North America.

QUICK CHECK How did Great Britain's colonies in America differ from New France? *Main Idea and Details*

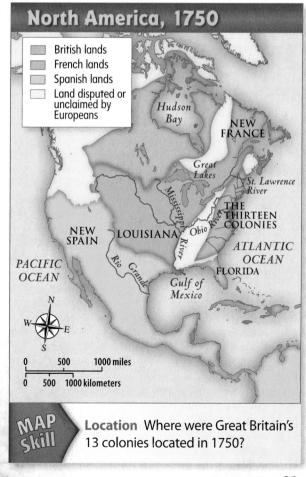

North America, 1750

- British lands
- French lands
- Spanish lands
- Land disputed or unclaimed by Europeans

Hudson Bay

NEW FRANCE

Great Lakes

St. Lawrence River

THE THIRTEEN COLONIES

NEW SPAIN

LOUISIANA

Ohio River

Mississippi River

ATLANTIC OCEAN

PACIFIC OCEAN

FLORIDA

Rio Grande

Gulf of Mexico

0   500   1000 miles
0   500   1000 kilometers

MAP Skill   **Location** Where were Great Britain's 13 colonies located in 1750?

▲ In the 1750s the British army was the best in the world.

ⓑ War Breaks Out

As the British moved into land the French claimed, the French wanted more protection. In 1754 they built Fort Duquesne (doo KANE) near present-day Pittsburgh. The British also claimed this land. They attacked the fort. One of the leaders of the attack was 22-year-old George Washington. He was from the colony of Virginia.

This attack started a war known as the French and Indian War. Actually American Indians fought on both sides. Most fought for the French. But the Iroquois sided with the British. No battles were fought in Michigan. However, the side that won would control all of the western frontier.

The Fall of New France

At first, France won battles in New York. Their American Indian allies helped them. But the British army was larger and had better weapons. As time went on, the British began winning against the French. In 1760 the British captured Montreal. They gained control of the St. Lawrence River. Soon, more and more French forts, including Detroit, fell to the British.

The war ended in 1763 with the **Treaty** of Paris. A treaty is a formal agreement between nations. France lost all of its territory in North America, including what is now Michigan. Great Britain also took over the fur trade. It was now the strongest nation in the world.

Chief Pontiac ▶

American Indians Resist

In the French and Indian War, many American Indians were killed. Many villages were burned to the ground. After the war American Indian leaders were angry. Great Britain would not stop colonists from pushing into their land.

Pontiac's Rebellion

Pontiac was an Odawa chief. He talked the Huron and Potawatomi into a **rebellion** against Great Britain. A rebellion is a struggle against a government or other authority.

In May 1763, Pontiac's men attacked Fort Pontchartrain with burning arrows. They also attacked other forts in the region.

At Fort Michilimackinac, Odawa warriors played a lacrosse game outside the fort. Women near the gates hid weapons under blankets. When the ball rolled into the gate, the warriors grabbed the weapons. They killed 20 soldiers and took over the fort.

Pontiac's men surrounded Fort Pontchartrain. The British were cut off from supplies for 153 days. But they did not give up. By fall, the American Indians had to return home. They needed to gather crops for the winter. Pontiac realized his rebellion could not succeed.

 **QUICK CHECK** What did Pontiac try to do? *Summarize*

ⓒ The Proclamation of 1763

Pontiac had alliances with other groups. He visited these allies. He wanted them to "bury their hatchets" and make peace with the British. The British wanted peace. They had just finished an expensive war. They did not want to spend any more on war.

In 1763 the British king made a **proclamation**, or announcement. The Proclamation of 1763 said that American Indians could keep the land west of the Appalachian Mountains. But this promise did not stop the American colonists. They still crossed the mountains and took American Indian land.

QUICK CHECK What did the Proclamation of 1763 say?
Summarize

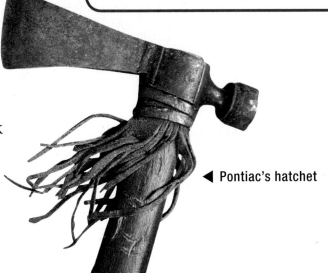
◄ Pontiac's hatchet

What You Learned

ⓐ The British conflicted with the French and the American Indians when they moved onto land claimed by France.

ⓑ The British won the French and Indian War and took France's North American territory.

ⓒ After Pontiac led a rebellion against the British in 1763, the British promised the frontier would remain under American Indian control.

★ Focus Lesson Review

1. **Focus Question** How did the French and Indian War affect Michigan?

2. **Vocabulary** Write one sentence for each vocabulary word.
   frontier   rebellion
   proclamation   treaty

3. **Economics** What was the main goal of the British in North America?

4. **Critical Thinking Problem Solving** Did Pontiac make the right decision in making peace with the British? Explain your answer.

5. **Reading Strategy Identify Main Idea and Details** Re-read pages 92–93. Use the chart to show the main idea and details of the section.

6. **Write About THE BiG IDEA** Explain which three groups wanted the Ohio Territory, and why each wanted it.

7. **Link to Language Arts** Write a newspaper article (including a headline) describing an event from this lesson.

Pontiac about 1720–1769

Pontiac was probably born near Detroit around 1720. As a young man, he may have traded with the French. He may have fought with them against British soldiers. Pontiac was brave and smart. By 1755, he had become an Odawa chief.

Great Britain had won against France in the French and Indian War. After the war was over, British colonists began moving onto American Indian lands. This made Pontiac angry. He once said about British colonists:

" You can see well that they are seeking our ruin. Therefore, my brothers, we must all swear their destruction and wait no longer."

In 1763 Pontiac led warriors from several groups. They attacked British forts. But his rebellion failed. He was finally able to make peace with the British in 1766. It is believed that Pontiac was killed by another American Indian in 1769.

Pontiac knew that the British settlers would change his people's way of life. He fought with courage to stop his land from being taken.

 Write About It! Why do you think Pontiac was courageous?

 For more biographies, visit: www.macmillanmh.com

The Life of Pontiac

1710	1730	1750	1770
	about 1720 Pontiac is born	1763 Pontiac's forces attack Detroit	1766 Pontiac makes peace with British	1769 Pontiac dies

Compare Maps at Different Scales

All maps are drawn to scale. A **map scale** uses a unit of measure, such as an inch, to represent a real distance on Earth. A map scale like the one below will tell you the size of an area on a map.

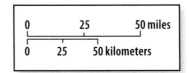

A **small-scale map** such as Map A covers a large area but cannot include many details. A **large-scale map** such as Map B shows many details of a smaller area.

1 Learn It

■ If you want to see the entire area of Pontiac's Rebellion, use a small-scale map, or Map A. This map gives you information without many details.

■ If you want to know only about the area around southern Michigan of Pontiac's Rebellion, you would need the large-scale map, or Map B. It shows a smaller area with more details and more information. It is as if you "zoomed in" on Map A.

■ Compare the scales on the two maps.

■ Map A has a scale of 150 miles. It shows a large area.

■ Map B has a scale of 50 miles. It shows a small area.

2 Try It

■ Which map shows the largest area?

■ Use the scale on Map A and measure the distance from Miami to St. Joseph. Now do the same with Map B, using the scale on Map B. What did you find out?

3 Apply It

■ Using the map scale on Map A, find out about how many miles Pontiac's Rebellion covered from east to west.

■ What detail is on Map B that is not on Map A?

Map A, Small-Scale Map

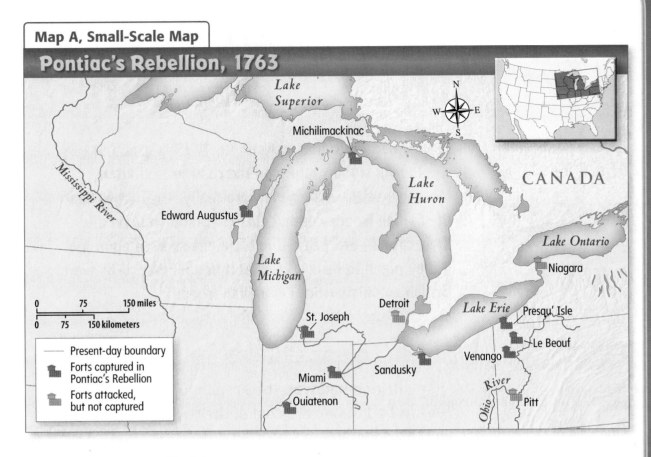

Pontiac's Rebellion, 1763

Lake Superior

Michilimackinac

CANADA

Lake Huron

Edward Augustus

Lake Ontario

Lake Michigan

Niagara

Detroit

Lake Erie

Presqu' Isle

St. Joseph

Le Beouf

Venango

Sandusky

River

Mississippi River

Miami

Ohio

Pitt

Ouiatenon

0   75   150 miles
0   75   150 kilometers

— Present-day boundary

Forts captured in Pontiac's Rebellion

Forts attacked, but not captured

Map B, Large-Scale Map

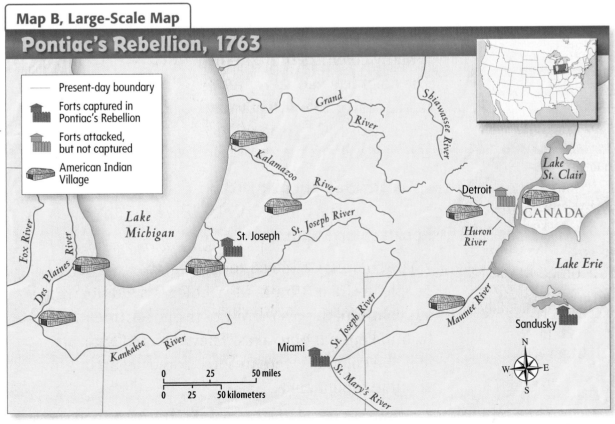

Pontiac's Rebellion, 1763

— Present-day boundary

Forts captured in Pontiac's Rebellion

Forts attacked, but not captured

American Indian Village

Grand River

Shiawassee River

Kalamazoo River

Lake St. Clair

Detroit

CANADA

Fox River

Des Plaines River

Lake Michigan

St. Joseph

St. Joseph River

Huron River

Lake Erie

Kankakee River

St. Joseph River

Maumee River

Sandusky

Miami

St. Mary's River

0   25   50 miles
0   25   50 kilometers

How did the American Revolution affect Michigan?

VOCABULARY

tax
representation
revolution
fortification

VOCABULARY STRATEGY

Root Words The root of **fortification** is the Latin word *fortis* or the Old French word *fort*, both of which mean "strong." What do you think a fortification does?

READING STRATEGY

Summarize Use the chart below to summarize the information about the American Revolution.

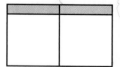

MICHIGAN GLCE

H3.0.1	H3.0.10
H3.0.3	G1.0.1
H3.0.6	
H3.0.9	

Michigan and the Revolution

In the early morning of April 19, 1775, a group of colonists stood waiting on the road to Lexington, Massachusetts. Their guns were ready. They could hear the British troops coming closer. "Stand your ground," their captain ordered. "Don't fire unless fired upon, but if they mean to have a war, let it begin here." Why were British colonists firing on British troops?

Ⓐ The Colonists Rebel

The British had won the French and Indian War. Britain had to pay the cost of the war. The British government passed **taxes** on American colonists. A tax is money paid to support the government. The taxes would help repay the money.

Many colonists thought the new taxes were unfair. The colonists had no **representation**, or voice in the British government. They had no say in decisions about taxes. "No taxation without representation!" some cried.

The Proclamation of 1763 upset colonists, too. Many colonists wanted the land beyond the Appalachian Mountains.

The colonists also wanted the same rights as people in Great Britain. Most colonists did not want a **revolution**, the overthrow of the government. But Britain kept passing taxes. They even put a tax on tea! The colonists were furious. Some began talking about independence.

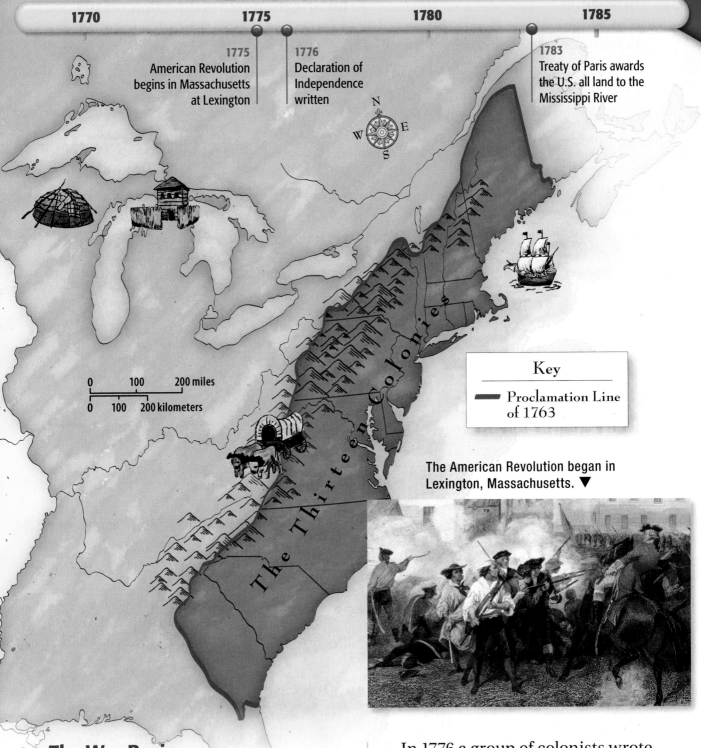

1775
American Revolution begins in Massachusetts at Lexington

1776
Declaration of Independence written

1783
Treaty of Paris awards the U.S. all land to the Mississippi River

N W E S

0   100   200 miles
0   100   200 kilometers

The Thirteen Colonies

Key

▬ Proclamation Line of 1763

The American Revolution began in Lexington, Massachusetts. ▼

The War Begins

The colonists dumped a ship full of tea into the sea. British troops were sent to punish them. This made the colonists angrier. In 1775 soldiers and colonists started fighting at Lexington. The revolution had begun.

In 1776 a group of colonists wrote the Declaration of Independence. It told the world why the colonies wanted independence. It was a declaration of war.

QUICK CHECK Why did the colonists think the new taxes were unfair? *Summarize*

ⓑ War on the Frontier

No Revolutionary War battles were fought in Michigan. But Michigan's location was important to the British. They moved the French Fort Michilimackinac to Mackinac Island. In 1780 they took down the wooden stockade fence. They put up stone

PRIMARY SOURCES

The Declaration of Independence • 1776

❝ *We, therefore, the Representatives of the United States of America . . . solemnly publish and declare, That these United Colonies are, and of Right ought to be Free and Independent States; . . . and that all political connection between them and the State of Great Britain, is and ought to be totally dissolved . . .* ❞

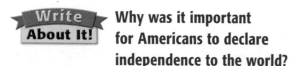

Why was it important for Americans to declare independence to the world?

fortifications. A fortification makes something strong, like a wall. Many Michiganians, especially in Detroit, supported Great Britain. They gave soldiers food and guns.

American Indians in the Revolution

Most American Indians supported the British in the war. They did not like the colonists. The colonists were moving west and taking their lands. British commander Henry Hamilton came to Detroit in 1775. He planned to raid the colonial areas. American Indians joined in his attacks.

During one raid, the British captured Jean du Sable. He was one of the first people of African ancestry in the area. The British thought he was a spy. They held him in prison at Fort Mackinac.

In 1779 American troops got ready to attack Detroit. They were led by George Rogers Clark. They captured Hamilton before they reached the city. They put Hamilton in prison. After Clark's victory, many American Indian groups stopped fighting on the British side.

Independence

George Washington fought for Great Britain in the French and Indian War. He now led American colonists to fight against Great Britain. However, American colonists would not have won the war without France. France was Britain's old enemy. It sent soldiers, money, and ships to help the colonists.

The French also played a role when the British surrendered at Yorktown, Virginia, in 1781.

The British and Americans signed a second Treaty of Paris in 1783. The treaty ended the American Revolution. The British agreed to American independence. They gave the new United States all the land east of the Mississippi River.

The treaty, however, did not protect the rights of American Indians. The British also refused to leave their fort on Mackinac Island. They stayed there until 1796. The rest of the Michigan territory belonged to the United States. Americans now were eager to move west.

✓ **QUICK CHECK** How did France help the Americans win the American Revolution? *Main Idea and Details*

What You Learned

Ⓐ American colonists declared independence from Great Britain because they wanted greater freedom.

Ⓑ Most American Indians fought on the British side during the American Revolution. The Treaty of Paris granted the United States its independence.

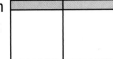

George Washington led American troops against Great Britain. ▶

☆ Focus Lesson Review

1. **Focus Question** How did the American Revolution affect Michigan?

2. **Vocabulary** Write one sentence for each vocabulary word.
   fortification   revolution
   representation   tax

3. **Geography** How was Detroit important to British military strategy?

4. **Critical Thinking Make Judgments** Do you agree that the British government had no right to tax the colonists?

5. **Reading Strategy Summarize** Reread the section "War on the Frontier." Use the chart to summarize the section.

6. **Write About** THE BIG IDEA How did the American Revolution change relations between American Indians and European settlers?

7. **Link to Language Arts** Why did the country's founders call it the United States of America instead of the United Colonies of America?

Field Trip to ___
Mackinac Island

Mackinac Island is located between the Upper Peninsula and the Lower Peninsula. Long ago it was a yearly gathering place for the Anishinaabeg. They thought the island resembled the back of a giant turtle. Today many tourists enjoy visiting the island to see the sights there. They can tour by horse and carriage — no cars are allowed!

Mackinac Island

◄ **1** Blacksmith Shop
Watch a blacksmith at work, and buy a horseshoe or a candleholder to take home.

2 The Grand Hotel ►
The hotel, opened in 1887, has been the setting for several movies.

3 Wings of Mackinac ▼

Visit the butterfly conservatory, where you can see as many as 200 kinds of live butterflies.

4 Fort Mackinac ▶

Built by British soldiers during the Revolutionary War, the fort watches over the Straits of Mackinac.

ACTIVITY

Research more attractions on Mackinac Island and then design and write a travel brochure describing several sights.

LOG ON ↑ For virtual field trips, visit:
www.macmillanmh.com

Chapter 3 Review

FOCUS Vocabulary Review

Copy the vocabulary words on a separate sheet of paper, and then match them with their proper definitions.

colony   revolution
frontier   treaty

1. a formal agreement between nations

2. the overthrow of a government

3. the far edge of a country, where people are just beginning to settle

4. a place ruled by another country

5. **Test Preparation** The two groups made a(n) _____ of friendship.

A alliance   C rebellion
B expedition   D fortification

FOCUS Comprehension Check

6. Why did Europeans want to find the Northwest Passage?

7. What was the cause of the French and Indian War?

8. What did Pontiac try to do?

9. Why did American settlers dislike the Proclamation of 1763?

10. Why did the taxes passed by the British government make the colonists angry?

11. **Critical Thinking** Why do you think most American Indians supported the British in the American Revolution?

12. **Critical Thinking** Why was the Declaration of Independence a declaration of war?

FOCUS Use the Time Line

Use the time line below to answer each question.

13. How many years passed between Pontiac's rebellion and the beginning of the American Revolution?

14. Which came first: the American Revolution or the French and Indian War?

| 1750 | 1755 | 1760 | 1765 | 1770 | 1775 | 1780 |

1754
French and Indian War begins

1763
Pontiac's rebellion

1775
American Revolution begins

Compare Maps at Different Scales

Use the maps below to answer each question.

15. How does a map scale show distance?

16. Which map would you use to find the distance between Marquette and Munising?

17. **Test Preparation** About how many miles is it from Marquette to Mackinac Island?

A 100 miles   C 160 miles

B 140 miles   D 200 miles

Islands of the Great Lakes

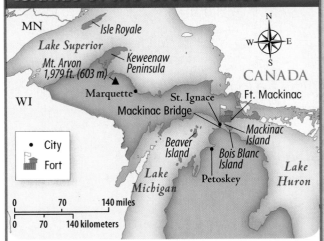

Central Upper Peninsula

Official Documents

Use the passage from the Declaration of Independence to answer the questions below.

> ❝ *We, therefore, Representatives of the United States of America . . . solemnly publish and declare, That these United Colonies are, and by Right ought to be Free and Independent States; . . . . and that all political connection between them and the State of Great Britain, is and ought to be totally dissolved . . . .* ❞

18. Why is this document a primary source?

19. How did our country get its name from the Declaration?

20. Why was this declaration written?

Hands-on Activity

21. **Make a Poster** Work in small groups to make posters that the leaders of the American Revolution might have used to convince people to join them.

Write About History

22. **Descriptive** Suppose you are a French explorer. Write a letter to the king of France describing what you have found in the area that would become Michigan.

 For help with the process of writing, visit: **www.macmillanmh.com**

Chapter 4

Territory and Statehood

You Are There

"The interior of Michigan is delightful—a mixture of prairies, oak openings, and woodlands, abounding in clear streams, fine lakes, and cold springs."

–from a letter by a Michigan settler

New settlers came to the land that is now Michigan. They wrote to their friends and families back home. They told them about all that the land had to offer.

In this chapter you will read about how Michigan grew. You will learn how it became a state.

Michigan settler ▶

Chapter Events	1800	1810	1820

1805 ①
Detroit burns in a major fire

1812–1815 ②
War of 1812

Settlers' Routes to Michigan

Present-day Michigan
Toledo Strip
Canal
Pioneers' route to Michigan
National boundary
Other state boundary
Battle

Map shows boundaries of 1837.

CANADA

Lake Superior

MICHIGAN

WISCONSIN TERRITORY

Lake Huron

NEW YORK

Lake Ontario

Erie Canal

St. Lawrence River

Buffalo

Lake Michigan

Hudson River

1

Detroit

4

TOLEDO STRIP

2 Put-in-Bay

Lake Erie

ILLINOIS

OHIO

PENNSYLVANIA

NEW JERSEY

MARYLAND

DELAWARE

INDIANA

Ohio River

APPALACHIAN MOUNTAINS

KENTUCKY

VIRGINIA

0   100   200 miles
0   100   200 kilometers

1830   1840   1850

3
1825
Pioneers follow Erie Canal to Michigan

4
1837
Michigan fights Ohio over the Toledo Strip

How did Michigan settlers come into conflict with American Indians?

VOCABULARY

ordinance
township
slavery
pioneer

VOCABULARY STRATEGY

Suffixes In the word **township,** the suffix **-ship** refers to members of a group. You can see the same ending in the word *membership*.

READING STRATEGY

Summarize Use the chart below to summarize this lesson.

MICHIGAN GLCE

H3.0.3
H3.0.6
H3.0.9
H3.0.10

The Michigan Territory

Tecumseh was a Shawnee chief. He believed that no one owned the land. He spoke to William Henry Harrison. One day Harrison would be President. Tecumseh said:

> "No groups among us have a right to sell, even to one another, and surely not to outsiders who want all, and will not do with less. . . . Sell a country! Why not sell the air, the clouds, and the Great Sea, as well as the earth? Did not the Great Spirit make them all for the use of his children?"

◀ On the frontier, about 1800

1785	1795	1805	1815
1787 Northwest Ordinance law	**1794** Battle of Fallen Timbers	**1805** Michigan Territory formed	**About 1809** Tecumseh and Tenskwatawa try to unify American Indians to resist settlers

Ⓐ A New Frontier

In 1781 the United States stretched to the Mississippi River. Michigan was part of the Northwest Territory. Settlers rushed to the territory to claim land.

The new Congress passed two **ordinances**, or laws. They would be used to govern the territory. The first law was the Land Ordinance of 1785. It called for the mapping of land sold or lost by American Indians. The land would be made into **townships**. A township is a block of land six miles long and six miles wide.

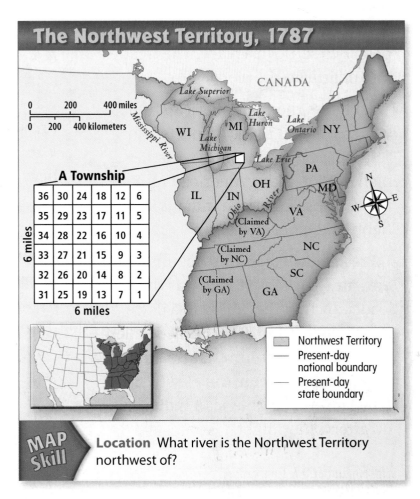

The Northwest Territory, 1787

A Township

36	30	24	18	12	6
35	29	23	17	11	5
34	28	22	16	10	4
33	27	21	15	9	3
32	26	20	14	8	2
31	25	19	13	7	1

6 miles

6 miles

Northwest Territory
— Present-day national boundary
— Present-day state boundary

MAP Skill **Location** What river is the Northwest Territory northwest of?

Becoming a State

The second law was the Northwest Ordinance of 1787. It was a plan to make states in the Northwest Territory. The plan said that a state could be made as soon as 60,000 people lived in a place. Five states would be made from the Northwest Territory. The map shows these states.

The Northwest Ordinance made **slavery** against the law in the territory. Slavery is keeping people against their will and making them work for no pay.

The law said that people in the territory could not take new enslaved people. But many people in the United States already had enslaved people. The new rules let people who had enslaved people continue to keep them.

QUICK CHECK Which two laws helped govern the Northwest Territory? *Summarize*

109

B Growth and Conflict

American Indians had made treaties with the British. The treaties protected their land. With the British gone, more **pioneers** moved to the Northwest Territory. A pioneer is one of the first people to settle in a place. The treaties meant little to the pioneers.

Congress thought American Indians would sell land to the pioneers. Most refused. They were angry with the pioneers for taking American Indian lands. Some American Indians started fighting the pioneers.

President George Washington sent an army. Anthony Wayne was their leader. In 1794 they came to a place near Toledo, Ohio. It was called Fallen Timbers. Wayne's army started fighting an American Indian army led by Chief Blue Jacket. The American Indians gave up after a short fight.

The signing of the Treaty of Greenville. ▼

After the battle a group of American Indian chiefs signed a treaty. The chiefs were led by Bad Bird. They signed the Treaty of Greenville. This treaty gave away large amounts of land in parts of Ohio and Michigan.

A Capital City

In 1805 the Territory of Michigan was made. Its capital was Detroit. President Thomas Jefferson sent William Hull to the territory. Hull became its first governor.

In 1805 a fire started in a bakery. The fire burned Detroit to the ground. Augustus Woodward was a judge in the territory. He made new plans for the city. Detroit's people began to build the city again.

Michigan made treaties with any American Indians who would sign away their land. In 1807 American Indians signed the Treaty of Detroit. In doing so they lost southeast Michigan.

New Conflicts

Two Shawnee chiefs wanted to stop the settlers. One was Tenskwatawa, who was also called "The Prophet." The other was his brother, Tecumseh. Tecumseh wanted American Indians to fight back. He went to visit other American Indian groups. He told them they had to join together to stop the settlers.

At the same time, American Indians got help from the British in Canada. The British gave them weapons. This made the Americans angry. Soon war would break out again.

◀ Tecumseh led resistance against American settlers.

QUICK CHECK How did Tecumseh believe American Indians could defeat the settlers? *Main Idea and Details*

What You Learned

A The Land Ordinance of 1785 and the Northwest Ordinance of 1787 laid out plans to govern the Northwest Territory.

B Settlers in the Northwest Territory came into conflict with American Indians, who resisted American settlement.

Focus Lesson Review

1. **Focus Question** How did Michigan settlers come into conflict with American Indians?

2. **Vocabulary** Write one sentence for each vocabulary word.
   ordinance   slavery
   pioneer   township

3. **Geography** What states were formed from the Northwest Territory?

4. **Critical Thinking Draw Conclusions** Why do you think it was difficult for American Indians to unite to fight together?

5. **Reading Strategy Summarize** Use the chart to summarize the section of this lesson called "A New Frontier."

6. **Write About THE BIG IDEA** What happened when settlers from the United States moved into the frontier?

7. **Link to Language Arts** Tecumseh tried to unite American Indian groups to oppose American expansion. Write a speech you would use to unite your classmates for a cause you care about.

The War of 1812

How did the War of 1812 affect the settlement of Michigan?

VOCABULARY

impressment
reservation

VOCABULARY STRATEGY

Root Words The word *reserve* means "to save or set aside." What do you think a **reservation** is?

READING STRATEGY

Identify Main Idea and Details Use the chart below to list the main idea and details of this lesson.

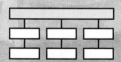

MICHIGAN GLCE

H3.0.1	H3.0.6
H3.0.2	G1.0.2

Francis Scott Key saw the British attack an American fort. When the smoke was gone he saw a flag. He wrote about what he saw. He used these words:

> "*Oh say, can you see, by the dawn's
>   early light,
> What so proudly we hail'd at the twilight's
>   last gleaming?
> Whose broad stripes and bright stars,
>   through the perilous fight,
> O'er the ramparts we watch'd, were so
>   gallantly streaming?*"

United States naval officer Oliver Hazard Perry led forces into battle on Lake Erie. ▼

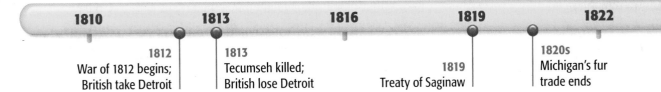

1810	1813	1816	1819	1822

1812
War of 1812 begins; British take Detroit

1813
Tecumseh killed; British lose Detroit

1819
Treaty of Saginaw

1820s
Michigan's fur trade ends

Ⓐ War with Great Britain

American Indians still had an alliance with Great Britain. They got weapons from British traders and used them to fight the settlers. Some American settlers wanted even more land. They wanted to move north, into Canada. The British ruled Canada. They did not want American settlers to move to Canada.

At the same time, the British Navy was stopping American ships in the Atlantic Ocean. They took American sailors from those ships. They made the sailors work on British ships. This practice is called **impressment**. Americans did not like it. Many people wanted the United States to go to war.

Detroit Surrenders

In 1812 Congress decided to go to war against Great Britain. The British and American Indians were on the same side. The two groups rushed into Michigan. First they took Fort Mackinac. The British then fired on Fort Pontchartrain at Detroit. Governor Hull did not have enough people to fight. He had to surrender the city.

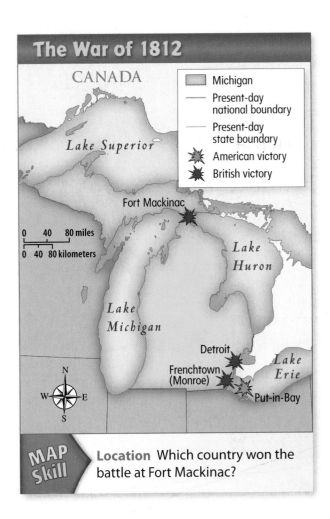

The War of 1812

CANADA

- ⬜ Michigan
- — Present-day national boundary
- — Present-day state boundary
- ✸ American victory
- ✴ British victory

Lake Superior

Fort Mackinac

0   40   80 miles
0   40   80 kilometers

Lake Huron

Lake Michigan

Detroit

Frenchtown (Monroe)

Lake Erie

Put-in-Bay

N W E S

MAP Skill **Location** Which country won the battle at Fort Mackinac?

Early in 1813, William Henry Harrison led a group of soldiers to take back Detroit. They lost a fight near Frenchtown. The British were taking over even more land. More American soldiers hurried in. They went to stop the British.

✓ QUICK CHECK Why did some Americans want to go to war with Great Britain in 1812? *Main Idea and Details*

113

▲ Perry's victory on Lake Erie helped to end the War of 1812.

ⓑ The War and Afterward

The British needed control of the Great Lakes in order to move supplies. The Americans and British fought each other on the Great Lakes.

One important battle was at Put-in-Bay on Lake Erie in late 1813. After hours of fighting, the British gave up. Oliver Hazard Perry was a young officer. He had led the American ships. He sent out a message, "We have met the enemy and they are ours." The Americans took back the Great Lakes.

Winning the War

Without the Great Lakes, the British could not keep Michigan. News of Perry's win reached Detroit. The British burned many buildings. Then they left.

The British and American Indians went toward Canada. Harrison's army chased after them. They met at the Thames River. The two sides began fighting. Harrison won the battle.

Tecumseh was killed in the Battle of the Thames. We do not know much about how he died. Many believe American Indians took his body. The Shawnee said, "No white man knows, or ever will know, where we took the body of our beloved Tecumseh."

In 1814 the British and Americans signed the Treaty of Ghent. It ended the war. It said the British had to give all the lands they took back to the United States. The treaty also called for a meeting to take place. That meeting would decide where the border between the United States and Canada would be.

Taking More Land

In 1813 Michigan Territory got a new governor. His name was Lewis Cass. He pushed American Indians in the territory to sign the Treaty of Saginaw. They signed it in 1819. This treaty added much land to the Michigan Territory. In return American Indians got $3,000. They were told they would also get $1,000 each year.

American Indians lost their land in the territory bit by bit. By 1836 they had lost the Lower Peninsula and moved away. Some went to the Upper Peninsula. Others lived on **reservations**. These are lands given to American Indians by the government.

QUICK CHECK Why was Oliver Perry's victory important? *Summarize*

American Indian Land Losses in Michigan 1795 – 1836

Lake Superior
CANADA
Lake Huron
WI
Lake Michigan
Detroit
Lake Erie
IN   OH

0   40   80 miles
0   40   80 kilometers

- Current reservations
- Greenville Treaty, 1795
- Detroit Treaty, 1807
- Saginaw Treaty, 1819
- Washington Treaty, 1836
- Other treaties

MAP Skill **Human Interaction** In which year was the Detroit Treaty signed?

PRIMARY SOURCES

▲ The Treaty of Saginaw, 1819

Ojibway Chief O-ge-maw-ke-ke-to

Speaking to Territorial Governor Lewis Cass during talks over the Treaty of Saginaw, September 1819:

66 *Your people trespass upon our hunting grounds. . . . Our possessions grow smaller and smaller. The warm wave of the white man rolls in upon us and melts us away. . . . Our children want homes. Shall we sell from under them the spot where they spread their blankets?* 99

Write About It! Why does O-ge-maw-ke-ke-to compare the American settlers to a warm wave?

115

C Americans Indians Forced Out

By the 1820s, life had changed in Michigan. Many forests had been cut down. The fur trade had disappeared. With no fur trade, the settlers did not need the American Indians. The settlers pushed for the American Indians to leave Michigan.

Soldiers rounded up Potawatomi and marched them away. They went to Kansas. Many Huron also went to Kansas. Others left for Canada. They were welcome there. Many other American Indians had died from diseases brought by the settlers. Their old way of life was gone forever.

QUICK CHECK How did the end of the fur trade affect American Indians?
Draw Conclusions

These Potawatomi were among those who stayed in Michigan. ▶

What You Learned

Ⓐ The United States defeated Great Britain in the War of 1812, some of which was fought in Michigan.

Ⓑ After the war the U.S. took American Indian lands.

Ⓒ Many groups were forced out of Michigan.

Focus Lesson Review

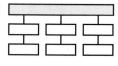

1. **Focus Question** How did the War of 1812 affect the settlement of Michigan?

2. **Vocabulary** Write one sentence for each vocabulary word.
   impressment   reservation

3. **Geography** Why did both armies need to control the Great Lakes in the War of 1812?

4. **Critical Thinking Make Predictions** What might have happened if Hull had not surrendered Detroit?

5. **Reading Strategy Identify Main Idea and Details** Use the chart to list the main idea and details of the section "American Indians Forced Out."

6. **Write About THE BiG IDEA** Why do you think many American Indians fought alongside the British in the War of 1812?

7. **Link to Math** In the Treaty of Saginaw, American Indians sold 6 million acres of land for $3,000. How much was that for 1 million acres?

Problem Solving

Problems are part of daily life, and a big part of history. Problem solving is finding answers, or **solutions**. You can use the following method to solve big problems or small ones.

VOCABULARY

solution

option

consequence

1 Learn It

- **Identify the problem.** You need to know what the problem is before you can solve it.

- **Gather information.** Find out as much as you can.

- **Identify the options.** Options are the different choices you can make to solve a problem.

- **Think about the consequences.** Every option has a result, or **consequence**. Some are good and others are bad.

- **Choose a solution.** The best solutions have the best results.

Identify the problem

↓

Identify options and consequences

↓

Choose a solution

2 Try It

In Lesson 2 you read about problems American Indians faced as United States settlers moved onto their land. Use the problem-solving method and what you have read to answer the questions. Organize your information in a graphic organizer.

- What problems did American Indians face?

- What information can you find on pages 114–116?

- What options did the groups have? What might have been some consequences of those options?

- What do you think would have been the best solution? Explain.

3 Apply It

Identify a problem in your school or community. Use the problem-solving method to suggest a solution.

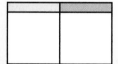
What was life like on the Michigan frontier in the 1830s?

VOCABULARY

canal
steamboat
self-reliant

VOCABULARY STRATEGY

Compound Words The word **steamboat** is a compound word. What do you think makes a steamboat go? Can you think of another compound word using the word *boat*?

READING STRATEGY

Summarize Use the chart below to summarize the lesson.

MICHIGAN GLCE

H3.0.1
H3.0.3
G1.0.1
G1.0.2
G4.0.2

Life on the Frontier

Will Carleton lived in Michigan in the 1800s. He was a poet. Students in Michigan used to learn his poems. Today each October 21 is Will Carleton Day in Michigan. Carleton's poems often tell what it was like living on the frontier. These lines are from one of his poems. It is called "The First Settler's Story."

"It ain't the funniest thing a man can do—
Existing in a country when it's new"

The *Walk-in-the-Water* was one of the first steamboats to carry settlers to Michigan. ▼

Pioneer Routes to Michigan, 1840

MN
Lake Superior
CANADA
N
W E
S
WI
Lake Huron
MICHIGAN
Lake Michigan
Saginaw
Grand Rapids
St. Joseph
Detroit
Lake Erie
IN
Cleveland
OH

NY
VT
NH
ME
Lake Ontario
Erie Canal
Buffalo
Albany
Boston
MA
RI
Hudson River
CT
PA
New York City

Water routes
Land routes
Land routes in Michigan
• City

MAP Skill ▶ **Movement** Describe the water route a pioneer might have taken from New York City to Detroit.

▼ Erie Canal

Ⓐ Moving to Michigan

In 1820 land in Michigan did not cost much. But it was too hard for people to get there. That was about to change.

The Erie Canal

In 1825 the state of New York finished the Erie **Canal**. A canal is a waterway made by people. The Erie Canal linked the Hudson River to the Great Lakes.

Settlers could now get to Michigan from New York City. Many people came. By the middle of the 1830s, there were 175,000 people there. People in Michigan used the canal, too. They used it to send wheat, flour, and lumber to cities in the East.

Canal boats were pulled by horses and other animals. They walked on paths next to the canal's banks. In Buffalo, people boarded **steamboats**. A steamboat is a boat run by steam. The journey to Detroit took three days.

In 1810 it took 30 days to get from New York to Michigan by land. In 1830 the same trip along the canal and lake took only 14 days.

QUICK CHECK How did travel from New York to Michigan change between 1810 and 1830? *Summarize*

B Frontier Life

Mary Lewis was four years old in 1836. That year her family came to Michigan. They came by covered wagon from New York. When she grew up she talked about what she saw. She said, "After leaving Detroit the road was mostly through dense woods." In Michigan she saw small groups of cabins. They later became cities like Marshall, Battle Creek, and Kalamazoo.

Mary's father was Bill Lewis. He was called "Yankee." He bought land in Barry County. This land was in southern Michigan. It was good for farming. First, Mary's father cut down trees. In their place he planted crops. Then he built a log cabin from the trees he had cut down.

Family Chores

Log homes in Michigan often had a loft and one large room. A loft is an open top floor. Families would often sleep, eat, and play in the same room.

Most people on Michigan's frontier lived in log homes like the one below. ▼

Light came from oil-burning lamps. Fireplaces or wood-burning stoves warmed rooms. There was no running water. Families had to get water from a well or carry it from a stream.

Women sewed the family's clothes. They washed clothes by hand. They churned butter, baked bread, and cooked meals.

Families often had many children. The children fed animals and took care of crops. They gathered eggs and milked cows. The school year was short. Children were needed on the farm.

Work and Play

Pioneers had to be **self-reliant**. This means that they had to take care of themselves. Relatives and neighbors also helped each other out.

Pioneer children still had time to play together. They ran races and played horseshoes and tug-of-war.

In 1838 Mary's Lewis's father invited his neighbors for Thanksgiving dinner. After they ate, a guest played the violin, and people danced.

By 1844 Mary's father started running a stagecoach stop. It was at Yankee Springs. He ran an inn, too. It was a busy stop on the trip between Grand Rapids and Kalamazoo.

QUICK CHECK What were some ways pioneers entertained themselves?
Summarize

What You Learned

A The Erie Canal helped Michigan's population grow by making the state easier to reach.

B Life on the frontier was hard but could also be fun. Settlers helped each other.

Focus Lesson Review

1. **Focus Question** What was life like on the Michigan frontier in the 1830s?

2. **Vocabulary** Write one sentence for each vocabulary term.
   canal   self-reliant   steamboat

3. **Technology** How did the completion of the Erie Canal affect the settlement of Michigan?

4. **Critical Thinking Draw Conclusions** Would you have liked living on a farm in Michigan in 1830? Explain your answer.

5. **Reading Strategy Summarize**
   Use the chart to summarize the section "Frontier Life."

6. **Write About THE BIG IDEA** List some of the first things a pioneer family had to do when they reached the frontier.

7. **Link to Math** A barge on the Erie Canal traveled about 2 miles per hour. The trip from Albany to Buffalo was 360 miles. How long did it take?

Understand Letters

Letters are an important kind of primary source. Letters tell historians how people felt and what they thought at the time events occurred.

The Letters of Elijah Allen Spooner

Elijah Allen Spooner left Adrian, Michigan, in 1849. His wife remained behind in Adrian. Spooner wrote to her often. His letters tell of encounters with American Indians, buffalo hunting, and traveling conditions.

 Learn It

Read the steps below to help you find information in letters.

- Look for the date and place the letter was written.

- Scan the letter to see if any events are mentioned or to find background information.

- Review what you know about the letter writer.

- Read to find out why the letter was written.

- Look up any unfamiliar words as you read.

The **LIBRARY** *of* **CONGRESS**

Elijah Spooner's original letter ▼

2 Try It

Read the letter below. Then answer the questions.

Place and Date →

Tiffin, Ohio, March 22d, 1849

Dearest Friend

Having a little leisure I again call my pen into requisition for the purpose of informing you of my progress, . . . From Sylvania, we made 12 ms. [miles] and crossed the Maumee river. . . .

The bridge across the Maumee was swept away about a week before we left Adrian. Consequently

Background information →

we had to cross the river, which now is quite rapid, in an old scow boat. This is done by fastening the boat to a long rope which is made fast in the middle of the river, in this case on an island. It is then hauled up to the side and loaded and then by giving it a right direction over and working the rudder, the current carries it across the river. . . .

Give my love to all the Family and believe me
Yours as ever,

Letter writer →

E.A. Spooner

- What is the place and date of this letter?

- How did the travelers cross the river? Why was this necessary?

3 Apply It

- Write a letter to a friend in which you describe what you saw on a trip you took. Include how you felt while on the trip.

VOCABULARY STRATEGY

Compound Words You probably know what lumber is, but what is a jack? A jack is someone who works at a trade. A steeplejack builds or fixes steeples (or high structures). What do you think a **lumberjack** does?

READING STRATEGY

Sequence Events Use the chart below to list the events in the lesson in order.

Changes on the Frontier

In the 1800s the people of Michigan would sing this folk song. It showed that they liked living in Michigan.

> "Come all ye Yankee farmer boys,
> Who would like to change your lot;
> With spunk enough to travel
> Beyond your native spot.
> And leave behind the village
> Where Pa and Ma do stay.
> Come go with me and settle
> In Michigania."

Loggers used trains to ship lumber out of Michigan. ▼

1835	1840	1845	1850	1855

1837
Michigan becomes 26th state

1841
Copper deposits discovered in Keweenaw Peninsula

1847
Michigan's capital moved from Detroit to Lansing

1855
Soo Locks completed

Ⓐ Growing into Statehood

Between 1830 and 1840, Michigan grew fast. It grew faster than any other place in the country. It wanted to become a state. To do that, Michigan needed a **constitution**, or plan of government. On May 11, 1835, 91 men met in Detroit. They wrote a constitution.

The people of Michigan approved the constitution in October. They picked a governor. His name was Stevens Mason. He was 23 years old. But Congress refused to let Michigan become a state. The problem was a small piece of land. It was known as the Toledo Strip.

The Toledo Strip

In 1832 Ohio began to build a canal. It would link the Ohio and Maumee rivers. Michigan claimed some of this land for the canal. This area was known as Toledo. It was near the mouth of the Maumee.

Ohio and Michigan both sent soldiers to fight for the "Toledo Strip" in the Toledo War. The "war" was no more than a lot of shouting. Michigan and Ohio could not agree.

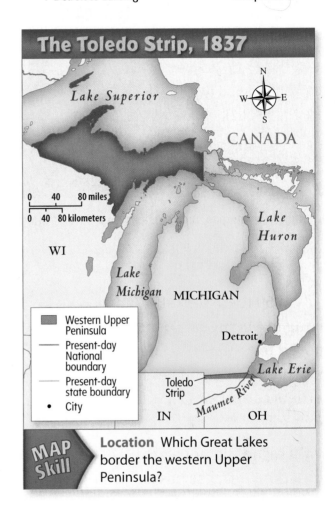

The Toledo Strip, 1837

Legend:
- Western Upper Peninsula
- Present-day National boundary
- Present-day state boundary
- City

MAP Skill **Location** Which Great Lakes border the western Upper Peninsula?

In time Congress came up with a **compromise**. In a compromise, each side gives up something. Congress asked Michigan to give up the Toledo Strip. In return Congress gave the state part of the Upper Peninsula.

Michigan liked the compromise. On January 26, 1837, Michigan became a state. It was the 26th state.

✔ **QUICK CHECK** List the events that led to Michigan statehood. *Sequence Events*

125

▲ Loggers would pile huge stacks of logs after cutting.

ⓑ A Population Boom

By 1850 there were 400,000 people living in Michigan. So many people moved to Michigan that it was said they had "Michigan Fever." Most settlers came from New England and New York.

Michigan did not want all of the settlers. A law was passed to stop African Americans from moving in. After 1830, though, free African Americans began to buy land in Calvin Township. They later joined the fight to end slavery.

Many **immigrants** moved to Michigan, too. Immigrants are people who leave one country to live in another. They came to Michigan from many different countries. Before 1860, though, most immigrants to Michigan came from countries in Europe.

Making Lumber

In the 1840s Michigan used the logs from its many trees for lumber. Michigan made more lumber than any place in the country.

A person who cuts down trees and sends them to sawmills is called a **lumberjack**. Michigan's lumberjacks were well paid, but the work was dangerous. "River hogs" stood on moving logs and guided them down rivers to sawmills. Lumber was shipped across the Great Lakes to other parts of the country. Cities like Saginaw grew because of the lumber industry.

In 1847 Michigan's capital moved from Detroit to Lansing. It was now closer to the middle of the state and the lumber industry.

QUICK CHECK Why was it dangerous to work in the lumber industry?
Main Idea and Details

Moving Michigan's Resources

In the 1800s thousands of people moved to Michigan to take jobs in the lumber industry, or in copper and iron mines. The Soo Locks, opened in 1855, helped businesses ship Michigan's resources out of the state. Study the diagram and map below. Then answer the questions.

How a Canal Works

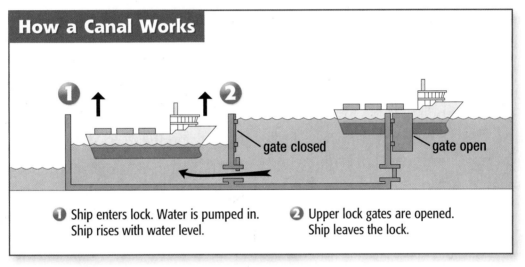

gate closed   gate open

1 Ship enters lock. Water is pumped in. Ship rises with water level.

2 Upper lock gates are opened. Ship leaves the lock.

Michigan's Natural Resources, 1860

Copper Harbor
Houghton
Lake Superior
Marquette
Soo Locks
Ishpeming
Manistique
Escanaba
Menominee
Alpena
Lake Huron
Manistee
Ludington
Saginaw
Muskegon
Grand Rapids
Lansing
Lake Michigan
Detroit
Lake Erie

Timber area
Copper mine
Iron mine
Sawmill
★ State capital
• Other city

N W E S

Think About Michigan's Resources

1. What happens before a ship sails out of the Soo Locks?

2. Which resource could you find near Saginaw?

3. In which direction did copper and iron have to be shipped to reach the Soo Locks?

127

The Copper Rush

In 1841 copper was discovered on the Keweenaw Peninsula. Douglass Houghton was the first person to find copper there. After that there was a mining boom. People rushed to the Upper Peninsula to get rich from mining. Until the 1920s Michigan had some of the world's best copper deposits.

Iron was discovered in Michigan in the late 1840s. Another boom took place. Michigan had more iron than any other state until the early 1900s. Today only Minnesota has more iron. Houghton and Hancock were mining camps in Michigan. They became cities.

◀ Copper was used for many common items.

The Soo Canal

You have already read about the Soo Canal. It was built because of mining. The canal opened on May 31, 1855. It linked Lake Huron and Lake Superior. Now ships could carry iron and copper from the mines. They carried them to other cities. People used the iron and copper to make things.

QUICK CHECK Why did the population of the Upper Peninsula grow in the 1840s? *Cause and Effect*

What You Learned

A On January 26, 1837, Michigan became the 26th state.

B Thousands of people moved to Michigan between 1830 and 1850, from eastern states and northern Europe.

C The Soo Locks were completed in 1855.

Focus Lesson Review

1. **Focus Question** Why did people get "Michigan Fever"?

2. **Vocabulary** Write one sentence for each vocabulary word.
   compromise   immigrant
   constitution   lumberjack

3. **Citizenship** Why do you think a territory needed to write a constitution before it could become a state?

4. **Critical Thinking** Draw Conclusions Was it a good idea to move Michigan's capital from Detroit to Lansing?

5. **Reading Strategy** Sequence Events Use the chart to sequence events in the section "The Copper Rush."

6. **Write About** THE BIG IDEA In what ways did immigrants change Michigan's way of life?

7. **Link to Music** Write your own song lyrics encouraging people to come to Michigan today.

Stevens T. Mason 1811–1843

Stevens Thomson Mason was born in Virginia. He was from a well-known family. When he was a baby, his father moved the family to Kentucky. He hoped to make a lot of money there. In 1830 President Andrew Jackson made Mason's father Secretary of the Michigan Territory. The Masons moved to Detroit.

A year later, Jackson sent Mason's father to Mexico. Stevens, then 19 years old, took his father's place as Secretary. Three years later he became Territorial Governor. People called him the "boy governor." He did not like that name though.

Mason was eager for Michigan to become a state. He ordered a census, or a count of all the people in a place. The census showed that the territory had 86,000 people. This was far more than the 60,000 needed for a territory to become a state. When Michigan became a state, the people picked Mason to be its first governor. He said,

❝*No country has ever been settled by more enterprising, intelligent and industrious citizens.*❞

 What part of the text shows that Stevens Mason was a good leader?

LOG ON For more biographies, visit:
www.macmillanmh.com

The Life of Stevens T. Mason

1810	1830		1850
1811 Mason born	1831 Appointed Secretary of Michigan Territory	1835 Elected first governor of the state of Michigan at age 23	1843 Mason dies

Chapter 4 Review

Vocabulary Review

Copy the sentences below on a separate sheet of paper. Use the list of vocabulary words to fill in the blanks.

immigrant   reservation
compromise   steamboat

1. After leaving the Erie Canal at Buffalo, a traveler took a(n) _____ to Michigan.

2. The Toledo War was settled by a(n) _____.

3. A(n) _____ is a person who moves from one country to another.

4. Some American Indians live on a(n) _____.

5. **Test Preparation** The first people to enter or settle a region are known as _____.

   A townships   C lumberjacks
   B voyageurs   D pioneers

Comprehension Check

6. Why was Tecumseh important?

7. How did the War of 1812 affect Michigan?

8. Why did the Erie Canal lead to an increase in the population of Michigan?

9. What was the reason for the Toledo War?

10. What were Michigan's major industries in the 1800s?

11. **Critical Thinking** Why were Tecumseh and Mason both good leaders?

12. **Critical Thinking** Who got the better deal in the compromise that ended the Toledo War? Explain your answer.

Use the Time Line

Use the time line below to answer each question.

13. How many years passed between the Northwest Ordinance and Michigan becoming a state?

14. Was Michigan a state at the time of the War of 1812? How do you know?

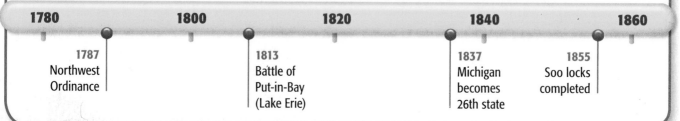

1780	1800	1820	1840	1860

1787
Northwest
Ordinance

1813
Battle of
Put-in-Bay
(Lake Erie)

1837
Michigan
becomes
26th state

1855
Soo locks
completed

Problem Solving

Write a complete sentence to answer each question below.

15. What are the steps you can follow to solve a problem?

16. **Test Preparation** What problems did the first Michigan pioneers face, and how did they solve them?

Letters

Read this passage from a letter written by a Michigan pioneer. Then write complete sentences to anwer the questions.

> ❝ *There is to be a new road laid out shortly between Adrian and Tecumseh, which will run through our place, and probably but a short distance from the house; and if so, make it rather more lively for us, or less retired than at present.* ❞

17. What does this letter tell you about life at the time the letter was written?

18. How do you think the letter writer feels about the new road?

19. **Write a Play** Work in small groups to write a short play about an incident that led to the War of 1812. Include at least two speaking characters with differing points of view. Make sure your play has a conclusion.

20. **Narrative** Write a diary entry as if you were a 10-year-old living with your family in the 1820s on the Michigan frontier. Include details about work, play, and the way you live.

LOG ON For help with the process of writing, visit: **www.macmillanmh.com**

Unit 2 Review and Test Prep

Comprehension and Critical Thinking Check

Write one or more sentences to answer each question.

1. Why were European explorers trying to find the **Northwest Passage**?

2. What is a **missionary**?

3. Describe how French trappers **bartered** with American Indians.

4. What was the goal of the **Proclamation of 1763**?

5. Why did American colonists begin a **revolution** against Great Britain?

6. How did the Northwest **Ordinance** affect the development of Michigan?

7. What did it mean for pioneers on the frontier to be **self-reliant**?

8. How did a **compromise** with Ohio help Michigan become a state?

9. **Critical Thinking** Why do you think it is important for people to live under a **constitution**?

10. **Critical Thinking** Why do you think **immigrants** are important to a growing territory?

Reading Skills Check

Summarize

Recall what you read in this unit about how American Indians were affected by European explorers and settlers. Copy the graphic organizer. Use it to help you summarize important facts about how life changed for American Indians. Then answer the questions.

11. What was the difference between American Indian relationships with the French and with the British?

12. How did American Indians resist the settlement of their lands by European colonists?

13. What is a summary? Why is summarizing an important skill?

Read the paragraphs. Then use them with what you already know to answer the questions.

Life for early pioneers in Michigan was difficult. Settlers had to be self-reliant. They made use of the resources of the land. Pioneers cut trees to build log cabins. They cleared land to make farmlands and grow corn. They built mills along rivers to grind the corn into flour and cornmeal.

Everyone in a pioneer family had to work hard, including children. Boys and girls helped build houses and clear land. Young people also had daily farm chores, such as feeding animals and planting crops.

14. Which conclusion makes the MOST sense?

  A Pioneers would rather work hard than take it easy.

  B Life for children on the frontier was boring.

  C Settlers considered pioneer life to be worth the hardships they had.

  D Michigan's resources were difficult to use.

15. What is probably the BEST reason settlers usually had large families?

  A Having many children made the families happier.

  B Life for children on the frontier would be very interesting.

  C Michigan needed more people.

  D Large families were needed to help with the work.

Write About History

16. Dialog Write a dialog between Tecumseh and an American Indian he tries to convince to join the fight against American settlers.

17. Letter Suppose that you have been named the first governor of the Michigan territory. Write a speech in which you declare your goals for the territory.

18. Summary Write a summary that lists the American Indian leaders you read about in the unit. Describe what they did and why they were important.

 For help with the process of writing, visit: www.macmillanmh.com

REVIEW
THE BIG IDEA

What happens when different peoples first meet?

Write About the Big Idea

Narrative Essay

A narrative essay is a composition that tells how something happened. You will use your graphic organizer to help you write an essay about what happened as the native peoples of Michigan and Europeans met. Your essay should answer the Big Idea question "What happens when different peoples first meet?"

Think about what you learned in Unit 2. What happened when Europeans met the American Indians who lived in Michigan? Go back and reread lessons if you need to. Then, use the information to complete the graphic organizer.

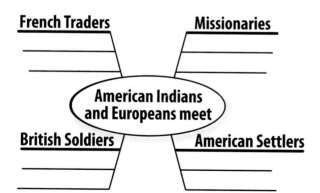

Write a Narrative Essay

1. Plan
- Get organized. Do more research or reread parts of the unit if you need to.
- Use the graphic organizer to organize your information.

2. Write a First Draft
- Write an introduction that tells what the essay is about.
- Write a main idea sentence for each paragraph. You will have one paragraph for each section of the graphic organizer.
- Now add sentences that give details about the main idea.
- Write a conclusion.

3. Revise and Proofread
- Read your essay. Be sure you stated your main idea in the introduction.
- Be sure each paragraph has a main idea sentence, and that you explained with examples and details.
- Be sure your essay tells what happened when the different groups met.
- Proofread your essay. Check the spelling and punctuation.
- Rewrite your essay neatly.

ACTIVITY

Speak About the Big Idea

An Interview

Recall the people you read about in Unit 2. Create an interview about how life changed. For example, you might interview an American Indian about life before the French explorers and the changes after they arrived.

Prepare Work in pairs. One person in the pair will be the interviewee. That person will tell about personal observations and experiences. The other will conduct the interview. Together, prepare a list of questions and answers. Gather information from your textbook, your graphic organizer, and other research. Practice your interview.

Present The interviewer should introduce his or her guest. Then partners should take two or three minutes to act out their interview for the rest of the class.

LAUNCH PAD For help with the Big Idea activity, visit: www.macmillanmh.com

Read More About the Big Idea

Laura Ingalls Wilder
Explore the lives of early pioneers in this Leveled Reader about the travels of one young American woman.

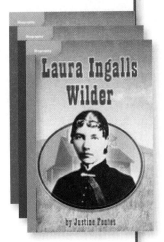

The Amish: Living a Simple Life
Read this Leveled Reader to learn about daily lives of the Amish people.

A Place Called Home
by Janie Lynn Panagopoulos
This blend of fact and fiction tells the story of the sawmill on Mill Creek that supplied the wood for the new fort on Mackinac Island.

War and Growth

> "There was no difference in the fighting qualities of those men; every man was a hero."
>
> — Commander Lloyd G. Harris
> *speaking of the Iron Brigade Guard at Gettysburg*

Why do people take great risks?

In Unit 3 you will read about the Civil War and Michigan's part before, during, and after this war. You will also read about the great risks people took during this time.

As you read Unit 3, look for the kinds of risks people were willing to take. Identify reasons why these people took risks.

Copy the graphic organizer. As you read, think about the events that happened in Michigan before, during, and after the Civil War. Then complete the graphic organizer. The first one has been done for you.

Group or person	Risk taken	Reason or goal
1. Escaping slaves	1. Returning to slavery; punishment	1. Freedom
2. Harriet Tubman	2.	2.
3.	3.	3.
4.	4.	4.

◀ The 24th Michigan at the Battle of Gettysburg

People Who Made a Difference

Sojourner Truth
1797–1883

Sojourner Truth escaped slavery in New York in 1826, and later won her son's freedom as well. She became a powerful writer and speaker in the movements to end slavery and bring equal rights to women. Truth moved to Battle Creek in 1857. (page 150)

Elizabeth Chandler
1807–1834

Michigan writer Elizabeth Chandler wrote powerful poems that opened people's eyes to the true horror of slavery. In 1832 Chandler founded the Logan Female Anti-Slavery Society, which would help people escape slavery. (page 147)

1861
Governor Austin Blair sends soldiers to fight in the Civil War

1825

1850

1832
Elizabeth Chandler forms Logan Female Anti-Slavery Society

1838
George DeBaptiste begins work with Underground Railroad

1857
Sojourner Truth moves to Battle Creek

LOG ON

For more biographies, visit:
www.macmillanmh.com

George DeBaptiste
1815–1875

George DeBaptiste moved to Detroit in 1846, where he became a successful businessman and helped many enslaved people escape from the South. He also organized a troop of free black men to fight for the North in the Civil War. (page 156)

Austin Blair
1818–1894

Politician Austin Blair was one of the Republican party leaders who nominated Abraham Lincoln for President. As governor of Michigan in 1861, he sent the first troops from a western state to fight for the North in the Civil War. (page 160)

1875

1900

1863
Battle of Gettysburg

1865
Civil War ends

1900–1920
Southern and eastern European immigrants flock to Michigan

Harriet Tubman

A poem
by Eloise Greenfield

Harriet Tubman didn't take no stuff
Wasn't scared of nothing neither
Didn't come into this world to be
   no slave
And wasn't going to stay one either

"Farewell!" she sang to her friends one night
She was mighty sad to leave 'em
But she ran away that dark,
   hot night
Ran looking for her freedom

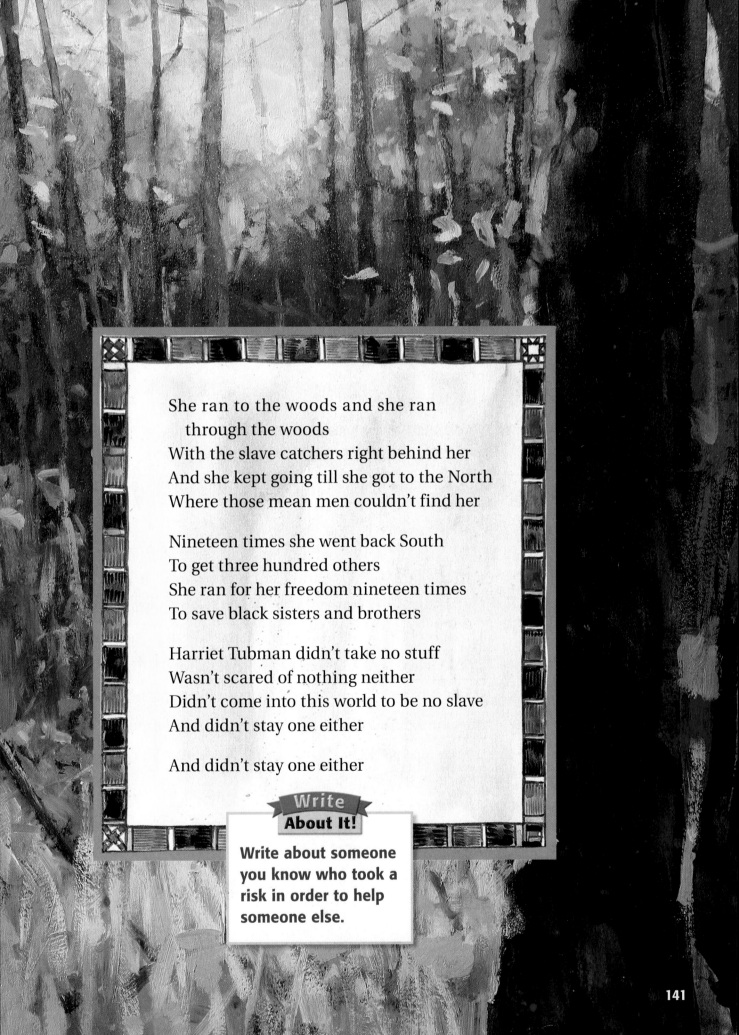

She ran to the woods and she ran
   through the woods
With the slave catchers right behind her
And she kept going till she got to the North
Where those mean men couldn't find her

Nineteen times she went back South
To get three hundred others
She ran for her freedom nineteen times
To save black sisters and brothers

Harriet Tubman didn't take no stuff
Wasn't scared of nothing neither
Didn't come into this world to be no slave
And didn't stay one either

And didn't stay one either

Write About It!

Write about someone you know who took a risk in order to help someone else.

Sequence Events:
A War Begins

As you read this unit, think about the order in which events happen. Putting events in order is called sequencing events. Thinking about the sequence of events will help you understand and remember what you read.

1 Learn It

- Words such as *first*, *next*, *then*, *soon*, and *after* help show the order in which things happened.

- Look for dates that tell you exactly when things happened. Now read the paragraph below.

First Event
Lincoln is elected.

Second Event
South Carolina leaves the United States.

Third Event
Other Southern states leave.

Fourth Event
For Sumter is attacked.

In the fall of 1860, Abraham Lincoln won the election for President. Leaders of the South were unhappy. Then, on December 20, South Carolina announced it would leave the United States. Soon other Southern states left, too. They formed a new country called the Confederacy. On April 12, 1861, Confederate troops attacked Fort Sumter, a United States fort. The Civil War had begun.

Try It

Copy and complete the chart below. Add more boxes if you need to. Use the chart to sequence the events in the paragraph on page 142.

SEQUENCE EVENTS CHART

> Abraham Lincoln elected President

> South Carolina leaves the United States

> [ ]

How did you figure out the sequence of events?

Apply It

- Review the sequencing steps in Learn It.

- Read the paragraph below. Then create a chart and sequence the events in the paragraph.

The first major battle of the Civil War was the Battle of Bull Run, in July 1861. The South won this battle. The North did not win an important battle until September 1862, when it won the Battle of Antietam in Maryland. After this battle, President Lincoln issued an important announcement that freed enslaved people in the South.

Chapter 5

Michigan and the Civil War

You Are There

DAKOTA TERRITORY

NEBRASKA TERRITORY

COLORADO TERRITORY

NEW MEXICO TERRITORY

"*Marching orders received today—two days more and the Army of the Potomac will be on its way to Bull Run. . . . Oh, what excitement and enthusiasm that order produced—nothing could be heard but the wild cheering of the men, as regiment after regiment received their orders. The possibility of a defeat never seemed to enter the mind of any.*"

Sarah Emma Edmonds was a Civil War nurse. She dressed as a man and became a soldier and a spy.

She wrote the words above to describe the days before the first major battle of the war. That battle started on July 21, 1861.

◀ Sarah Emma Edmonds

Chapter Events   1840   1845   1850

1850
Fugitive
Slave Act

CANADA

ME

VT

NH

MA

MN

Lake Superior

MICHIGAN

WI

Lake Huron

Lake Ontario

NY

CT

RI

Lake Michigan

2
Jackson

Lake Erie

PA

3
Gettysburg

NJ

Hudson River

IA

OH

MD

DE

IL

IN

WV

1

⭐ Washington, D.C.

KS

MO

KY

Ohio River

Richmond

4

VA

Tennessee River

Atlantic Ocean

NC

AR

TN

Mississippi River

SC

MS

AL

GA

LA

TX

FL

Gulf of Mexico

0	100	200 miles
0	100	200 kilometers

States and Territories, 1861

⬛ Union States, 1861
⬛ Confederate States, 1861
— Michigan boundary
— State boundary, 1861
— National boundary

West Virginia became a Union state in 1863.

1855 **1860** **1865**

2
1854
Republican
Party formed

3
1863
Battle of
Gettysburg

4
1865
Civil War
ends

145

How was slavery dividing the nation?

VOCABULARY

plantation
illegal
abolitionist
fugitive
liberty

VOCABULARY STRATEGY

Root Words The word *abolish* means "to end" or "to stop." What do you think an **abolitionist** wanted to end?

READING STRATEGY

Sequence Events Use the chart below to sequence the events in this lesson.

MICHIGAN GLCE

H3.0.1
H3.0.3

A Divided Nation

In 1844 Adam Crosswhite and his family escaped from slavery in Kentucky. They went to Marshall, Michigan. They could live as free people there.

In 1847 slave catchers found the Crosswhites. The people of Marshall stopped the slave catchers from taking the Crosswhites. Charles Gorham was a banker in Marshall. He spoke for the crowd.

"*You have come here after some of our citizens. You can't have them, or take them; this is a free country, and these are free persons. . . .***"**

▲ In the South, enslaved people lived in small cabins like this one.

Ⓐ Slavery in the United States

From the early 1600s until the end of the 1700s, men and women in Africa were kidnapped. They were taken against their will and brought to North America. They were forced to work without pay.

Most enslaved people worked on large farms called **plantations**. These farms were in the South. Plantation owners needed workers to grow tobacco, cotton, rice, and sugar. By 1860 there were 4 million enslaved people in the South.

Many people in the North used slave labor, too. But farms in the North were not as large. More and more immigrants came to the United States. Farmers and business owners in the North found they had enough workers.

Ideas Change

Many people began to feel that slavery was wrong. By the early 1800s, most states in the North made slavery **illegal**. It was against the law to own enslaved people.

Then slaveholders began moving to the West. They wanted to take enslaved people with them. Northerners wanted the West to stay "free soil."

▲ Enslaved people picking cotton

The Northwest Ordinance of 1787 said each new state could choose whether to allow slavery. When Michigan became a state, it made slavery illegal. States where slavery was illegal were called free states.

Abolitionists

People who wanted to abolish, or end, slavery were called **abolitionists**. The Logan Female Anti-Slavery Society was the first Michigan abolitionist group. (*Anti-* means "against.") Elizabeth Chandler founded the group. She was a Quaker.

QUICK CHECK When did slavery become illegal in Michigan? *Sequence Events*

147

ⓑ Michigan Fights Slavery

For many years, Congress tried to balance the number of slave states and free states. Each time a territory wanted to become a state, there was a debate.

The Fugitive Slave Act

In 1850 California asked to join the United States. It wanted to be a free state. People from the South did not want California to be a state. It would give the country more free states than slave states.

Finally, Congress reached a compromise. It was known as the Compromise of 1850. California would be a free state. In return, Congress also passed the **Fugitive** Slave Act. A fugitive is someone who tries to escape.

The law said that fugitives had to be returned to their "owners." This included enslaved people in the free states, too. Anyone who helped them escape could go to jail.

Abolitionists hated the new law. Michigan was already known for refusing to help "slave catchers." In 1847 a Missouri man came to Detroit. He wanted to find a fugitive named Robert Cromwell. Abolitionists helped Cromwell escape to Canada. Then they put the Missouri man in jail for kidnapping.

In 1855 Michigan passed the Personal **Liberty** Law. It protected formerly enslaved people. Liberty means "freedom from another person's control." This law gave fugitives the right to a trial to win their freedom.

Slaveholders put announcements in newspapers offering rewards for the capture of runaways (left). Some people helped runaways reach freedom (below).

$150 REWARD

RANAWAY from the subscriber, on the night of the 2d instant, a negro man, who calls himself *Henry May*, about 22 years old, 5 feet 6 or 8 inches high, ordinary color, rather chunky built, bushy head, and has it divided mostly on one side, and keeps it very nicely combed; has been raised in the house, and is a first rate dining-room servant, and was in a tavern in Louisville for 18 months. I expect he is now in Louisville trying to make his escape to a free state, (in all probability to Cincinnati, perhaps he may try to get employment on a steamboat. He is handy in any capacity as a house servant. Had on when he left, a cassinett coatee, and dark striped cassinett pantaloons, new—they are good clothing. I will give $50 reward if taken in Louisville; 100 dollars if taken one hundred miles from Louisville in this State, and 150 dollars if taken out of this State, and delivered to me, or secured in any jail so that I can get him again. WILLIAM BURKE.

Bardstown, Ky., September 3d, 1838.

▲ Frederick Douglass

135,000 SETS, 270,000 VOLUMES SOLD.

UNCLE TOM'S CABIN

FOR SALE HERE.

AN EDITION FOR THE MILLION, COMPLETE IN 1 Vol., PRICE 37 1-2 CENTS.
"   "   IN GERMAN, IN 1 Vol., PRICE 50 CENTS.
"   "   IN 2 Vols., CLOTH, 6 PLATES, PRICE $1.50.
SUPERB ILLUSTRATED EDITION, IN 1 Vol., WITH 153 ENGRAVINGS,
PRICES FROM $2.50 TO $5.00.

The Greatest Book of the Age.

◄ *Uncle Tom's Cabin* became the best-selling book of the 1800s.

Talking about Slavery

Abolitionists told people about slave life. People who were enslaved would tell how they were treated. Some had been whipped by plantation owners. Others were kept in chains. They told about how husbands and wives or parents and children could be sent away to live far from each other.

Abolitionist Leaders

Frederick Douglass had escaped slavery in Maryland. He gave speeches across the country. Douglass also spoke at the Second Baptist Church in Detroit.

In speeches he said, "I expose slavery in this country, because to expose it is to kill it. Slavery is one of those monsters of darkness to whom the light of truth is death."

In 1851 Harriet Beecher Stowe wrote *Uncle Tom's Cabin*. This book was an important story about slavery. It told how enslaved people tried to keep their families together. It was translated into other languages. People in Europe read it. It made many people think that slavery should end.

QUICK CHECK How did formerly enslaved people work to end slavery? *Summarize*

C Sojourner Truth

Sojourner Truth was enslaved in New York. She escaped in 1826. Then, in 1827, New York ended slavery. Sojourner's son was sold illegally and sent to a plantation in Alabama. She went to court and won her son's freedom.

Sojourner Truth began writing and speaking out against slavery. In 1857 she and her family moved to Battle Creek, Michigan. There, she kept working to end slavery.

Many abolitionists were part of history's great rescue stories. In the next lesson, you will read about a special "railroad." It carried people from slavery to freedom.

QUICK CHECK Why did Sojourner Truth go to court? *Summarize*

◀ Sojourner Truth

What You Learned

A By the early 1800s, slavery was illegal in most of the North, but Southern plantation owners depended on slave labor. Michigan was a free state.

B In 1850 Congress passed the Fugitive Slave Act, which said that persons escaping slavery must be returned to their "owners."

C Abolitionists such as Sojourner Truth worked to convince people that slavery was wrong.

Focus Lesson Review

1. **Focus Question** How was slavery dividing the nation?

2. **Vocabulary** Write one sentence for each vocabulary word.
   abolitionist   liberty
   fugitive   plantation

3. **Geography** Michigan shares a border with Canada, where slavery was illegal. How did Michigan's location affect what some escaping slaves decided to do?

4. **Critical Thinking Make Decisions** Do you think the people of Michigan were right to help escaping enslaved people? Why or why not?

5. **Reading Strategy Sequence Events**
   Reread the section "Sojourner Truth" on this page. Use the chart to help sequence the events in her life.

6. **Write About THE BiG IDEA** How did the abolitionists work to change the way people thought about slavery?

7. **Link to Music** Enslaved people created work songs to sing while they worked in the fields. Ask your music teacher or librarian to help you find some of these songs. Play or sing them for your class.

Identify Fact and Opinion

VOCABULARY

fact

opinion

In Lesson 1 you read about slavery. Some of the sentences in the lesson were facts. A **fact** is a statement that can be proven true. You can prove a fact by checking it in an encyclopedia, for example.

Other statements in the lesson were opinions. An **opinion** tells what someone believes or feels. Opinions cannot be proven true or false.

1 Learn It

- Facts can be proven true. Statements with dates and amounts are often facts.

- Opinions state feelings and beliefs. Words like *better, probably, should,* and *believe* signal opinions.

Now look for facts and opinions in this paragraph.

No one cared more about the cause of abolition than Frederick Douglass. He had been enslaved in Maryland. Then, in 1838, he escaped to New York. He later started an antislavery newspaper called the *North Star.* He was probably the best known of the abolitionists.

2 Try It

Read the paragraph about Frederick Douglass again. Then answer the questions.

- Is the first sentence a fact or an opinion? How do you know?

- Is the second sentence a fact or an opinion? How do you know?

- Would you be able to prove the third sentence? Explain.

3 Apply It

Write two statements of fact about your school or classroom. Then write two statements of opinion.

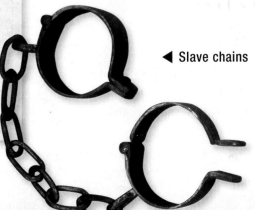

◀ Slave chains

H3.0.8

What Did Michiganians Think About the Fugitive Slave Law?

Many Michiganians were strongly opposed to slavery. Some were active as abolitionists. Others opposed slavery, but believed that the nation's laws must be obeyed. Read below to find out about three different points of view on the Fugitive Slave Law.

❝*[We] hold our liberty dearer than we do our lives, and we will organize and prepare ourselves with the determination, live or die, sink or swim, we will never be taken back into slavery . . . for we are not slaves but human beings.*❞

Henry Bibb
Abolitionist
Detroit, Michigan

❝*[The Fugitive Slave Law] will be enforced in this judicial district. . . . If experience proves . . . the [incorrectness] of the [law, it can be repealed], but until that repeal occurs, the law must be regarded as supreme. . . .*❞

Ross Wilkins
District Court Judge
Detroit, Michigan

❝*It shall be the duty of [government officials] within [Michigan], whenever [anyone living in] this state is arrested or claimed as a fugitive slave . . . to use all lawful means to protect and defend [that] slave. . . .*❞

Erastus Hussey
Newspaper Editor
Lansing, Michigan

Build Citizenship

1. Which of three speakers spoke from personal experience of slavery?

2. What was the purpose of the Fugitive Slave Law?

3. What did Erastus Hussey think was the duty of Michigan officials?

Think About It

1. What reasons does Ross Wilkins give for supporting the enforcement of the Fugitive Slave Law?

2. Why does Henry Bibb say he will never again be taken into slavery?

3. Does Erastus Hussey support Henry Bibb's viewpoint or Ross Wilkins's viewpoint? Explain your answer.

Write About It!

If you had been a lawyer in a Michigan court in 1852, how would you defend a man who had escaped from slavery? Write a few paragraphs telling what you would say to the jury about this man.

Slavery and Freedom

How did the people of Michigan help fugitives from slavery?

VOCABULARY

Underground Railroad
secede

VOCABULARY STRATEGY

Synonyms The **Underground Railroad** was neither underground nor a railroad. It was a secret way to help escaped slaves find freedom. In this case underground means "hidden."

READING STRATEGY

Summarize Use the chart below to summarize this lesson.

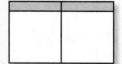

MICHIGAN GLCE

H3.0.1
H3.0.3
G1.0.1
G1.0.2
G4.0.2

In the 1850s Seymour Finney owned a hotel in Michigan. He hid fugitives on their way to freedom in Canada.

Many people trying to escape slavery hid in the large barn next to Finney's hotel. Slave catchers from the South would stay in Finney's hotel. They did not know the people they were looking for were right next door.

Fugitives traveled by night, using the North Star as a guide ▼

1835	1840	1845	1850	1855	1860

1836
Detroit's Second Baptist
Church founded

1854
Republican Party
formed in Jackson

1860
Abraham Lincoln
elected President

Ⓐ The Underground Railroad

Enslaved people risked their lives for freedom. Abolitionists had an **Underground Railroad** to help them. The Underground Railroad was not a real railroad. It was a system of secret routes. People used these routes to escape slavery. The fugitives headed for states in the North. Slavery was illegal there. Others went to Canada. There they could be free.

Secret Codes

The Underground Railroad used railroad terms. A *station* was a safe place to stay. A *conductor* helped fugitives find their way. *Station agents* were people who lived at stations. Fugitives traveled by night. During the day they hid in barns, secret rooms, or churches.

Stations in Michigan

Michigan was an important part of the Underground Railroad. Escape routes went through towns shown on the map. Many "passengers" passed through Cass County. Some stayed and built a new community there.

✓ **QUICK CHECK** How did the Underground Railroad work? *Summarize*

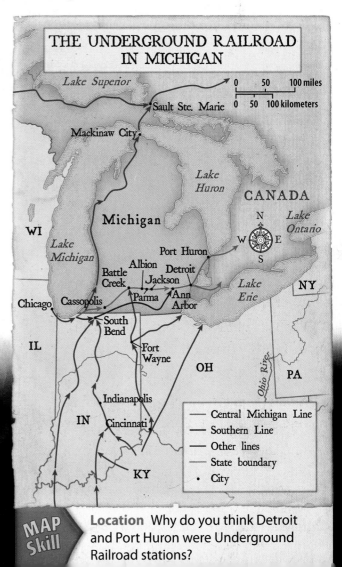

THE UNDERGROUND RAILROAD IN MICHIGAN

Legend:
— Central Michigan Line
— Southern Line
— Other lines
— State boundary
• City

MAP Skill **Location** Why do you think Detroit and Port Huron were Underground Railroad stations?

ⓑ Michigan's Heroes

The leaders of Michigan's Underground Railroad were heroes. They risked their lives to help other people. Laura Haviland was a Quaker. She helped thousands escape to Canada through Michigan. She hid so many runaways that she was called the Superintendent of the Underground Railroad.

George DeBaptiste was a free African American. He was another leader of the Underground Railroad. Like other free African Americans who helped runaways, DeBaptiste risked his own freedom. If he was caught helping people escape, he could have been forced into slavery.

Helping Fugitives

The Second Baptist Church in Detroit was an important Underground Railroad station. The church was founded in 1836 by 13 people who were once enslaved. Almost 5,000 fugitives got food and shelter there.

The Underground Railroad was very strong in Michigan. Detroit newspapers even printed the number of daily "arrivals" in the city's stations. Very few people in Michigan would help slave catchers.

The Underground Railroad ran for about 30 years. It is hard to be sure, but about 40,000 people may have used it to get to freedom. But in 1860, there were still 4 million enslaved people in the United States. The Railroad could not help them all.

QUICK CHECK Why was working on the Underground Railroad dangerous? *Draw Conclusions*

Fugitives that reached Detroit might be helped by George DeBaptiste (left) or find shelter in the Second Baptist Church (below).

Underground Railroad

Before 1865, the year slavery was abolished, thousands of enslaved persons followed the Underground Railroad to freedom. Study the map and the chart below. Then answer the questions.

▲ Slave identification tag

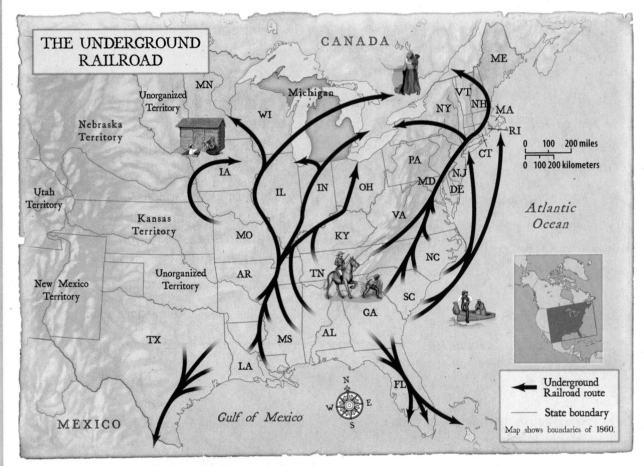

THE UNDERGROUND RAILROAD

Map shows boundaries of 1860.

← Underground Railroad route

— State boundary

Five Top Slave States in 1860

State	Enslaved People
Virginia	490,865
Georgia	462,198
Mississippi	436,631
Alabama	435,080
South Carolina	402,406

Source: *U.S Census, 1860*

Think About the Underground Railroad

1. Which state had the most enslaved people in 1860?

2. Why do you think the routes from Texas headed south instead of north?

C A New Political Party

The nation was arguing over slavery. During this time, 3,000 people met in Jackson, Michigan, on July 6, 1854. They thought the country's leaders were not doing enough to keep slavery from spreading to the West. That day they started a new political party. It was called the Republican party.

Abraham Lincoln

In 1860 the Republicans chose Abraham Lincoln to run for President. He was an Illinois lawyer. Most people in the South did not want him to be President. They thought he would try to end slavery.

The November election was close. Lincoln won. Angry Southern leaders quickly made plans. They voted to **secede** from the United States.

To secede means "to withdraw from a group or country." The country was about to split in two.

QUICK CHECK How did Southern leaders react when Lincoln was elected President? *Cause and Effect*

What You Learned

A Michiganians played an important role in the Underground Railroad, which helped fugitives.

B Famous conductors of the Underground Railroad included Laura Haviland and George DeBaptise.

C After Abraham Lincoln was elected President in 1860, Southern states made plans to secede from the United States.

Abraham Lincoln ▶

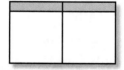

★ Focus Lesson Review

1. **Focus Question** How did the people of Michigan help fugitives from slavery?

2. **Vocabulary** Write one sentence for each vocabulary term.
   secede
   Underground Railroad

3. **Citizenship** Do research to find out who Abraham Lincoln's vice president was.

4. **Critical Thinking** **Identify Fact and Opinion** Read the first sentence on page 156. Is this statement an example of fact or opinion?

5. **Reading Strategy** **Summarize** Use a chart to summarize the section of this lesson called "A New Political Party."

6. **Write About** THE **BiG** IDEA Why do you think the North and the South could not agree about slavery?

7. **Link to Math** Look again at the chart on page 157. What is the total number of enslaved people in the states shown on the chart?

Laura Haviland 1808–1898

Laura Smith Haviland was born in Canada and raised in New York. As a child Laura loved to read. One night she read a book about the slave trade. It made her think slavery was wrong.

When she was 17, Laura married Charles Haviland. Together they moved to Raisin in southeastern Michigan. Laura helped start the first Michigan Underground Railroad station. She helped so many enslaved people that slaveholders offered a reward of $3,000 for her, dead or alive.

Laura was also concerned about children in the nearby poorhouse. She began teaching them in her home. Then, in 1837, she and Charles started a school. It was called the Raisin Institute. The school was not like most schools. It was open to students of all races.

During the Civil War, Haviland worked as a nurse. After the war she taught newly freed African Americans. In her autobiography she wrote,

❝*In whatever condition or station in life we find ourselves, are we not our brother's keeper?*❞

Write About It! How did Laura Haviland try to help others?

For more biographies, visit:
www.macmillanmh.com

The Life of Laura Haviland

1800	1820	1840	1860	1880	1900

1808 Born in Canada

1825 Marries Charles Haviland

c. 1832 Organizes first Michigan Underground Railroad station

1898 Haviland dies

Michigan at War

How did Michigan help the Union win the Civil War?

VOCABULARY

Confederacy
cavalry
brigade
Emancipation
   Proclamation
regiment

VOCABULARY STRATEGY

Word Origins Sometimes a word's origin gives a clue to its meaning. **Brigade** comes from an Italian word that means "to fight." Can you guess what a brigade is?

READING STRATEGY

Identify Main Idea and Details Use the chart below to list the main idea and details of this lesson.

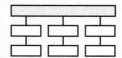

MICHIGAN GLCE

H3.0.2
G1.0.1
G1.0.2

Governor Austin Blair spoke to Michigan lawmakers on January 2, 1862. That day they agreed that "Michigan does not hesitate to say that . . . slavery should be swept from the land, and our country maintained."

Ⓐ The Country Divides

On December 20, 1860, South Carolina seceded from the United States. Ten more Southern states soon followed. They formed the Confederate States of America. It was also called "the **Confederacy**."

1860	1861	1862	1863	1864	1865

1861
Civil War
begins

1862
Lincoln issues
Emancipation
Proclamation

1863
Battle of
Gettysburg

April 1865
Civil War
ends

The Confederacy had its own President. His name was Jefferson Davis. It had its own Constitution, too. It was not like the United States Constitution. The Confederate Constitution allowed slavery everywhere.

The First Shots

Most Americans didn't want a war. However, on April 12, 1861, Confederate soldiers attacked Fort Sumter off the coast of South Carolina. The Civil War began.

News of the attack reached Michigan. Almost 1,000 Michiganians rushed to join the fight. They were among the first soldiers from the west to join the army of the Northern states. Many people now called the Northern states "the Union." The men reached Washington, D.C., on May 16. When Lincoln saw them, he said, "Thank God for Michigan!"

QUICK CHECK How did the Civil War begin? *Main Idea and Details*

◄ These men are dressed as soldiers of the 24th Michigan Infantry, part of the Iron Brigade.

161

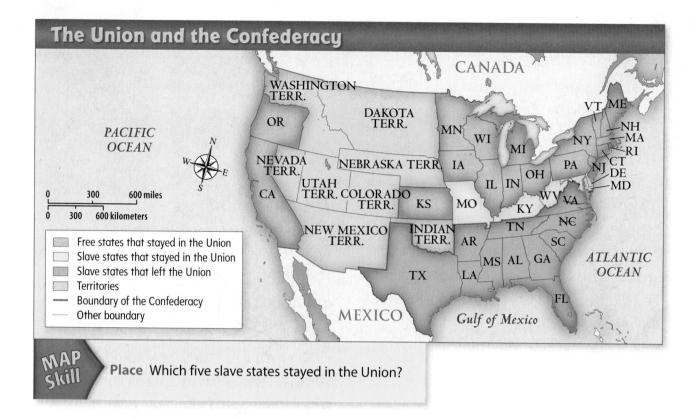

The Union and the Confederacy

Map legend:
- Free states that stayed in the Union
- Slave states that stayed in the Union
- Slave states that left the Union
- Territories
- Boundary of the Confederacy
- Other boundary

0   300   600 miles
0   300   600 kilometers

PACIFIC OCEAN

CANADA

MEXICO

Gulf of Mexico

ATLANTIC OCEAN

MAP Skill **Place** Which five slave states stayed in the Union?

B Joining the Fight

More than 90,000 Michigan men fought in the Civil War. That was one of every four men in the state. Some were born in Michigan. Others came from New York, New England, and other countries.

The Cavalry and Sharpshooters

George Custer from Monroe led the Michigan **Cavalry Brigade**. Cavalry troops fight on horseback. A brigade is a large group of soldiers. Custer led troops into battle yelling, "Come on, you Wolverines!" At age 23 he became the youngest American major general.

The Michigan Sharpshooters were a group of about 150 Ojibway and Odawa men. They were expert shooters. They fought in some of the worst battles.

Women in the War

Women were not allowed to fight in the war. But some did anyway. Sarah Edmonds of Flint dressed up like a man and called herself Frank Thompson. She was a spy for the Union. She was also in several battles. As herself, Edmonds was a nurse for injured Union soldiers.

Helping at Home

Men who stayed behind also helped the Union. They mined iron and copper. These were needed to make bullets, trains, and boat engines. Lumberjacks chopped wood. The wood was used for wagons and gun handles.

While men were at war, their families did extra work. Women took care of farms. Children did extra chores.

Michiganians in Battle

A soldier's life was hard. Diseases spread through the camps. Men were tired, lonely, and bored. Sometimes they had to wait a long time before a battle. Many men were hurt in battles. You can read part of a Michigan soldier's diary below.

Michigan's most famous unit was the 24th Michigan Infantry. It was part of the famous Iron Brigade. Most men in the 24th came from Wayne County. In July 1863, the brigade fought in the Battle of Gettysburg in Pennsylvania. They held off a group of Confederate troops. They kept these troops away from the main part of the battle.

QUICK CHECK How did Michigan soldiers help win the Battle of Gettysburg?
Summarize

▲ "Johnny Shiloh," Michigan drummer boy

PRIMARY SOURCES

Charles Wunderlick, Jr. Private, Company G
1st Michigan Infantry • May 1864

❝*If you find this book with me when I am dead you may keep all but the book . . . do please my parents and send the book and state my death as near as you can. . . . Although hoping that it may not make you much trouble, but I beg of you in the field of battle, be you a Rebel or not I ask your honor to fulfil my request as an honest man of Nature. I remain yours, a friend forever, C. J. Wunderlick*❞

Write About It! If you had found this diary in 1865, what might you have done with it?

⊙ Freedom and Victory

Early in the war, the South seemed to be winning. Then, on September 17, 1862, there was a terrible battle. It was at Antietam Creek, Maryland. Almost 23,000 men were killed or hurt. The Union won. People on both sides were shocked at how many died. They were getting tired of the fighting.

Lincoln had been waiting for the Union to win. A few days later, on September 22, 1862, he made a decision. He issued the **Emancipation Proclamation**. To emancipate means to free someone. The proclamation said that all enslaved people living in the Confederate states were free.

The Civil War was now about ending slavery. Some Northerners did not agree with the President. They did not want the war to be about freedom.

Lincoln said, "In giving freedom to the slave, we assure freedom to the free." In other words, the United States could not be a free country unless everyone in it was free. The proclamation was read to everyone in Detroit's Second Baptist Church. Free African Americans celebrated.

The Union army took over many towns. It would often free enslaved people in those towns. Many of these people joined the Union army.

▲ The Emancipation Proclamation freed enslaved people in the Confederacy.

By the end of the war, 200,000 former enslaved people and free African Americans fought in the army. This included more than 1,500 from Michigan. Most of them were part of the 1st Michigan Colored **Regiment**. A regiment is a military group made of several small units.

Celebration and Sadness

From the beginning the Union was better prepared for the war. It had more soldiers and supplies. It also had more money than the Confederacy.

In the two years after Gettysburg, the Union won many battles. In April 1865 the Union army captured Richmond, Virginia. It was the Confederate capital. Soon the Confederacy surrendered. In the four years of fighting, about 620,000 Union and Confederate soldiers were killed. The war was over. The United States was whole again. Now 4 million enslaved people were free.

Just five days later, a Southerner named John Wilkes Booth shot and killed President Lincoln. Back in Michigan, people mourned the President. They also mourned almost 15,000 Michigan men who died fighting for the Union.

QUICK CHECK What were the results of the Civil War? *Summarize*

◄ Kinchen Artis was a member of the 1st Michigan Colored Regiment.

Focus Lesson Review

1. **Focus Question** How did Michigan help the Union win the Civil War?

2. **Vocabulary** Write one sentence for each vocabulary term.
   Emancipation Proclamation
   regiment

3. **Geography** Why do you think no battles of the Civil War were fought in Michigan?

4. **Critical Thinking Make Inferences** How do you think Confederate soldiers felt about the Emancipation Proclamation?

5. **Reading Strategy Identify Main Idea and Details** Reread pages 164–165. Use the chart to list the main idea and details of this section.

6. **Write About THE BIG IDEA** Why do you think so many Michigan men risked their lives as soldiers?

7. **Link to Language Arts** Do some research about Michigan soldiers in the Battle of Gettysburg. Then write a diary entry that a soldier might have written after the battle.

Chapter 5 Review

FOCUS Vocabulary Review

Copy the sentences on a separate sheet of paper. Use the list of vocabulary terms to fill in the blanks.

Confederacy	plantation
Emancipation Proclamation	Underground Railroad

1. Many enslaved people worked on a cotton _____.

2. President Lincoln issued the _____.

3. Southern states formed the _____.

4. The _____ helped enslaved people escape to the North and to Canada.

5. **Test Preparation** A _____ is someone who tries to escape.

   A **regiment**   C **fugitive**
   B **plantation**   D **Union**

FOCUS Comprehension Check

6. What did the Fugitive Slave Act do?

7. Why did Michigan pass a Personal Liberty Law?

8. Who was Sojourner Truth?

9. What happened because of the election of 1860?

10. Look at the map on page 162. List the 11 states that formed the Confederacy.

11. **Critical Thinking** Why did abolitionists tell others about the cruel treatment of enslaved people?

12. **Critical Thinking** Why do you think so many Michiganians joined the Union army?

FOCUS Use the Time Line

Use the time line below to answer each question.

13. Which event came first: the attack on Fort Sumter or the Battle of Gettysburg?

14. How many years had Lincoln been President when the Civil War ended?

1860	1861	1862	1863	1864	1865
1860 Lincoln elected President	1861 Confederates attack Fort Sumter		1863 24th Michigan at Battle of Gettysburg		1865 Civil War ends

Identify Fact and Opinion

Write a complete sentence or choose the correct option to answer each question.

15. What is the difference between a fact and an opinion?

16. **Test Preparation** Which of the following statements is an opinion?

    A Harriet Beecher Stowe wrote *Uncle Tom's Cabin.*

    B Lincoln was elected President.

    C Eleven Southern states seceded from the United States.

    D The Union army had the bravest soldiers.

Diaries

Reread the diary entry and then answer the questions.

From the diary of Charles Wunderlick, Jr.

> **"** *If you find this book with me when I am dead you may keep all but the book . . . do please my parents and send the book and state my death as near as you can. . . .***"**

17. What does the entry tell you about what Charles Wunderlick was thinking about as he went to war?

18. What makes this diary entry a primary source?

19. **Draw a Map** Work in small groups to draw a map that would help a fugitive get from one station to another on the Underground Railroad. Include physical features such as rivers, mountains, swamps, and cities. Draw a clear route for people to take.

20. **Persuasive** Write a letter to the editor of a local newspaper for the date April 20, 1861. Give your opinion on the attack on Fort Sumter and the start of the Civil War. Try to convince other readers that your position is correct.

For help with the process of writing, visit: **www.macmillanmh.com**

Chapter 6

Michigan Grows and Changes

You Are There

"*My mother and father had five children when they came. . . . That was back in 1924. My father left the South a couple of months before we did. But he had the foresight [looking ahead], I'd say . . . to see what was going on in the South at that time. And he wanted to get his family out from down there.*"

Mildred Arnold left the South in 1924. She was eight years old. She moved to the North and joined her father. They hoped their lives would be better in the North. Mildred was among thousands of African Americans who moved from the South at that time.

African Americans move north. ▶

Chapter Events   1860   1880   1900

1860–1900
Railroad boom brings 7,000 miles
of new tracks to Michigan

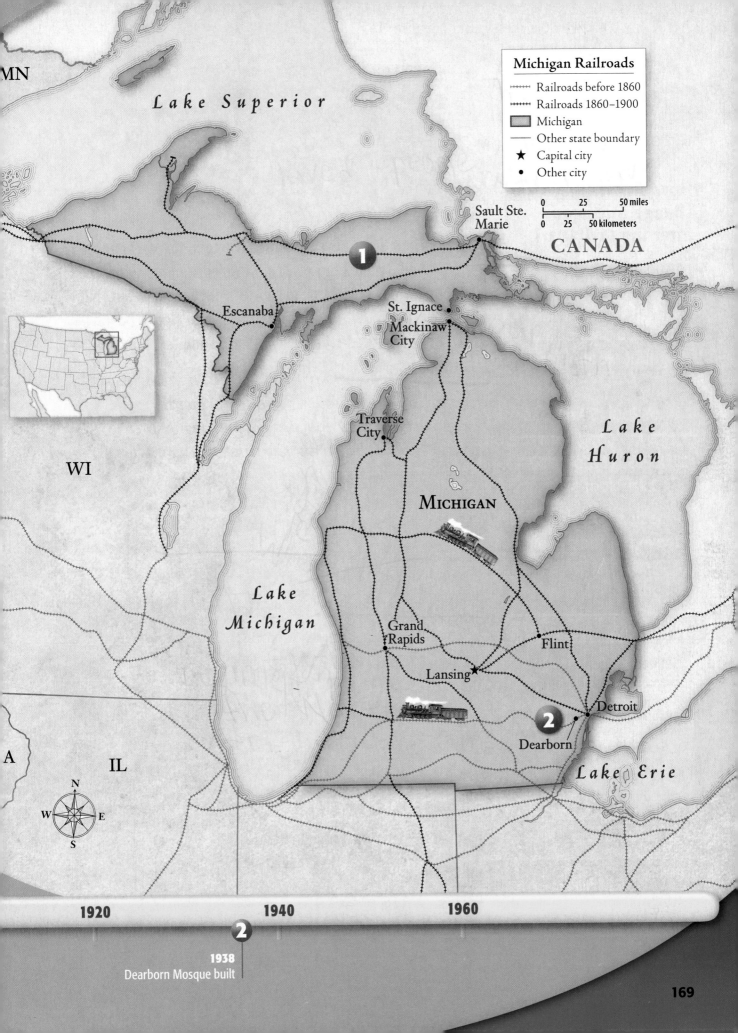

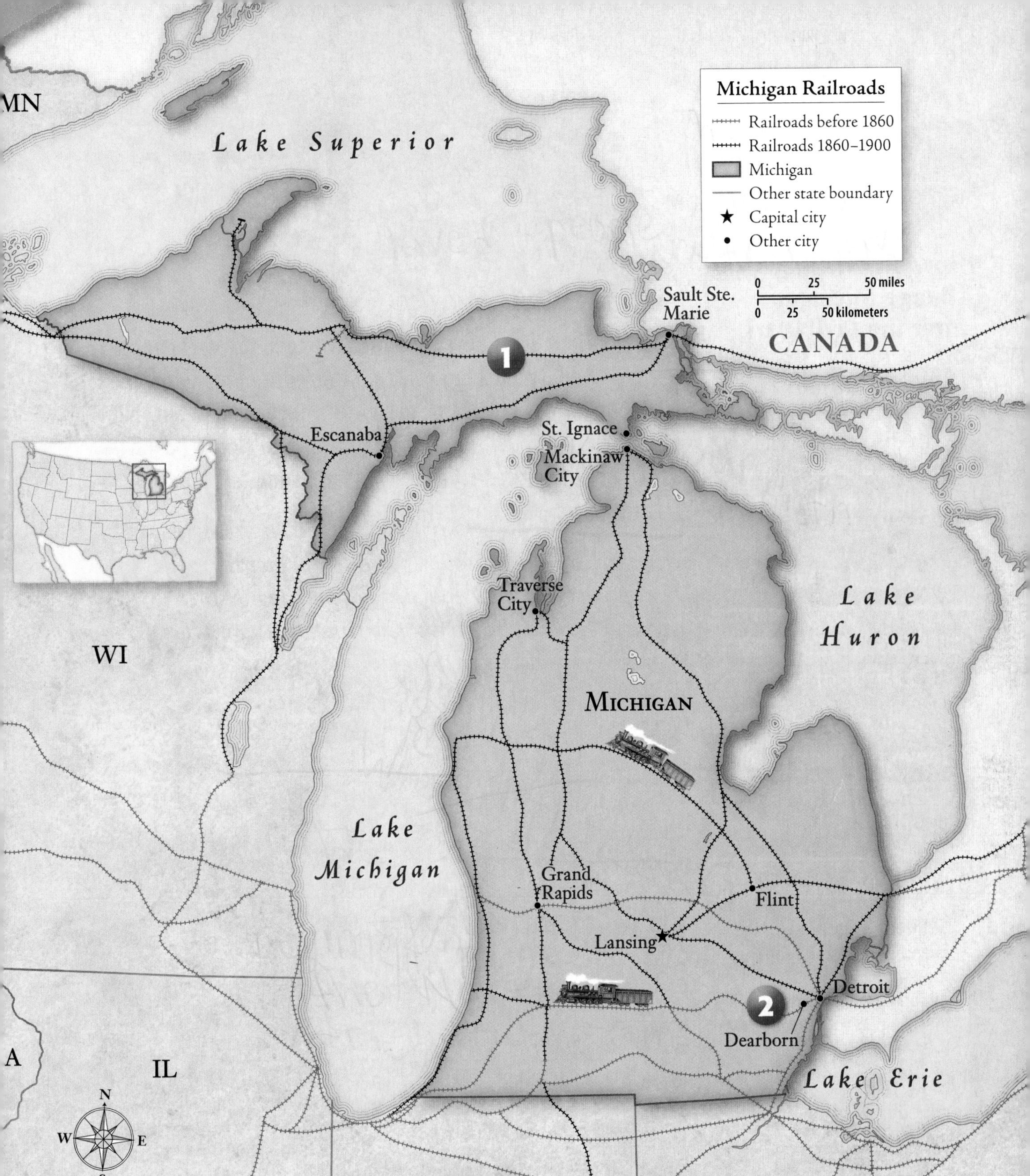
Michigan Railroads
Railroads before 1860
Railroads 1860–1900
Michigan
Other state boundary
Capital city
Other city
0 25 50 miles
0 25 50 kilometers
MN
Lake Superior
Sault Ste. Marie
CANADA
1
Escanaba
St. Ignace
Mackinaw City
Traverse City
Lake Huron
WI
MICHIGAN
Lake Michigan
Grand Rapids
Flint
Lansing
Detroit
2
Dearborn
Lake Erie
A
IL
N
W
E
S

1920 1940 1960

2
1938
Dearborn Mosque built

New Ways and New People

How did technology change Michigan after the Civil War?

VOCABULARY

technology
cash crop
raw materials
manufacturer
diverse
discrimination

VOCABULARY STRATEGY

Word Origins The word *manufacture* comes from the Latin phrase *manu factus,* or "made by hand." Today, however, most manufacturing is done by machine.

READING STRATEGY

Sequence Events Use the chart below to sequence the events from this lesson that led to greater immigration to Michigan.

MICHIGAN GLCE

H3.0.1
H3.0.3
G4.0.2

In the 1800s new machines changed the way people lived. A machine could do the work of many people. Machines made work easier. But they also meant that many workers were no longer needed. Here's how a newspaper described a new harvesting machine:

> "*The saucy machine has driven the scythe from the field . . . and the principal work of harvest, now, is to drive the horse about the field a few times, and lo! The harvest is gathered.*"

1860	1870	1880	1890	1900

1860
Congress gives Michigan 4 million acres of land to build new railroad tracks

1870
African American men gain the right to vote

1890
One in four Michigan residents born outside the United States

Ⓐ New Technologies

Michigan farmers began using new **technology** during the Civil War. Technology is the use of machines to meet people's needs. Hand tools were replaced by horse-drawn plows, reapers, and mowers. Later these machines would be run by steam.

With machines, farmers could grow more **cash crops**. These are crops that farmers grow to sell to others.

Moving Goods

Raw materials are things found in nature that can be made into products. It was hard to get raw materials to factories. During warm months, rivers were used. But the rivers froze in the winter and turned to mud in the spring. This made shipping difficult.

Manufacturers use machines to make goods. They also needed ways to move goods.

◀ Machines like this began to change farm production.

◀ In 1872 Elijah McCoy of Detroit invented the first automatic oil cup. It helped trains run more smoothly. McCoy later created a company that sold oil cups worldwide.

A Railroad Boom

The answer was railroads. Congress gave Michigan 4 million acres of land for railroads. By 1900 Michigan had about 8,000 miles of track, mostly in the south. People and goods could easily be moved to the Upper Peninsula from Chicago and Milwaukee. They could also get to the Lower Peninsula. Now it was easy to move raw materials and goods.

QUICK CHECK What happened after Congress gave Michigan land to build railroads? *Sequence Events*

ⓑ Newcomers to Michigan

Michigan became a center of business. There were now many jobs. People came from everywhere for work. These people helped Michigan to grow. In 1860 about 750,000 people lived in Michigan. Many had come from New England and New York.

Between 1860 and 1890, about 700,000 more people moved to Michigan. Most came from northern European countries. They came from Germany, Finland, Great Britain, and Ireland. Others came from Italy.

By 1890 one in four people in Michigan had been born outside the United States. The people of Michigan were **diverse**. They came from many different places.

Many people found jobs in logging. Others got work in factories. Michigan's growing cities had many new factories.

Rights for African Americans

Many African Americans moved to Michigan after the Civil War. Some had gone through Michigan to Canada on the Underground Railroad. They returned to Michigan when the war ended. Others moved from the South.

In 1867 Michigan passed a new law. It said anyone in Michigan had the right to go to any school. But no one followed the law. African Americans and whites were forced to go to different schools. In 1870 the parents of two African American children went to court. They wanted their children to go to Duffield Union, a white school in Detroit.

Many European immigrants landed in New York Harbor. ▼

They won their case. The African American children were allowed to go to school at Duffield Union. For the first time white and African American children went to the same public school in Michigan.

African Americans had other new rights, too. Starting in 1870, African American men could vote. But women of all races were still not allowed to vote. **Discrimination** also kept African Americans from living and working in some places. Discrimination is an unfair difference in the way people are treated. In the coming years, many people in Michigan would work to stop discrimination.

QUICK CHECK Where did newcomers to Michigan come from after the Civil War? *Main Idea and Details*

A German immigrant's doll from 1870 ▶

Focus Lesson Review

1. **Focus Question** How did technology change Michigan after the Civil War?

2. **Vocabulary** Write one sentence for each vocabulary term.
   cash crop   diverse
   discrimination   manufacturer

3. **Government** How did the government help the railroad industry in Michigan?

4. **Critical Thinking Draw Conclusions** Why do you think many communities ignored laws meant to help end discrimination against African Americans?

5. **Reading Strategy Sequence Events** Use the chart to sequence the section "A Railroad Boom," on page 171.

6. **Write About THE BIG IDEA** How did new technology change life for Michigan farm families?

7. **Link to Geography** How did the growth of railroads change where people could live and work in Michigan?

Use Line and Circle Graphs

You just read about how Michigan changed after the Civil War. Suppose you wanted to know how many miles of railroad track Michigan built during those years, or whether Michigan companies still use railroads to ship goods today. You can find out by looking at a **graph**. A graph is a diagram that shows information in a clear way. A **line graph** shows how something has changed over time. A **circle graph** shows how the parts of something make up the whole. Circle graphs are also called pie graphs because each part looks like a slice of a pie.

1 Learn It

- To find out what a graph is about, look at the title. For example, the title of the line graph on the next page is "Growth of Michigan Railroads, 1860–1900."

- Next, study the labels on the graphs. On the line graph, the numbers on the left side show, in thousands, the number of miles of railroad track in Michigan. The labels at the bottom of the graph show the years that the graph covers.

- By looking at the red line on the graph, you can see the increase in total miles of railroad track over these years.

- The labels within the circle graph tell you how many tons of exports were shipped using a certain type of transportation.

2 Try It

- During which 10-year period did Michigan build the most new miles of railroad track?

- About how many miles of new railroad track were built in Michigan from 1860 to 1900?

- Which form of transportation was used to ship the most Michigan exports in 2002?

- Were more exports shipped by train or by air?

Apply It

- Based on the two graphs, what can you conclude about Michigan companies' use of railroads since 1900?

- Make a circle graph of your own showing how many trips you take in a week or a month using different forms of transportation.

Growth of Michigan Railroads 1860 – 1900

Miles of Railroad Track (in thousands)

Year

Source: *Michigan Department of Treasury*

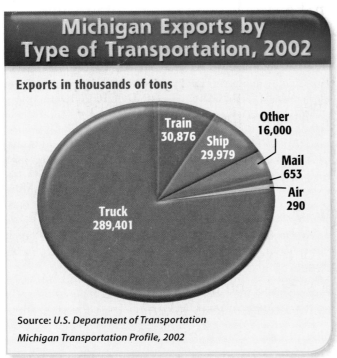

Michigan Exports by Type of Transportation, 2002

Exports in thousands of tons

Train 30,876
Ship 29,979
Other 16,000
Mail 653
Air 290
Truck 289,401

Source: *U.S. Department of Transportation*
Michigan Transportation Profile, 2002

Understand Historic Photographs

Photographs are an important primary source. They give us a record of daily life. They also let us see people, places, and events exactly as they were at a certain moment in history.

Photograph of Thomas Edison, 1906

Thomas Edison grew up in Port Huron. He invented hundreds of items, including the lightbulb and the movie camera. In 1878 he invented the phonograph, later called the record player. The photograph on page 177 shows Edison in his laboratory with his invention. It would bring music into nearly every home in the United States.

▲ A catalog advertisement for one of Edison's later phonographs

1 Learn It

Use these steps to learn how to decode historic photographs.

■ Read the caption for any information.

■ Note where the photo was taken—indoors or outdoors—and the time of year.

■ Note any people in the photograph. What are they wearing? What are they doing? What can you decide about them?

■ Look for other clues, such as buildings, signs, or tools.

■ Why do you think the photograph was taken?

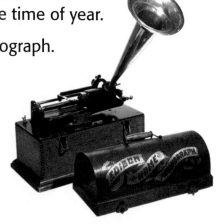

▲ The Edison Home Phonograph, 1896

▲ Edison listens to a new recording in his laboratory, 1906

2 Try It

Study the photograph above. What information can you learn about it?

3 Apply It

Write a paragraph telling what it might be like to spend a day in Edison's laboratory.

Why did people come to Michigan in the early 1900s?

VOCABULARY

economy
mosque

VOCABULARY STRATEGY

Foreign Words A **mosque** is a house of worship for followers of Islam. It comes from the French *mosquée*, which came from the Arabic *masjid*, meaning "temple."

READING STRATEGY

Summarize Use the chart below to summarize who came to Michigan and why in the early 1900s.

MICHIGAN GLCE

H3.0.1
H3.0.2
H3.0.3
G1.0.2
G4.0.2

A Wave of Newcomers

Many European immigrants came to Michigan in the early 1900s. Irene Jordan's great-grandfather was one of them. Like many people, he came to Michigan looking for a better life. Irene Jordan said:

❝*Our great-grandfather, Stanislaw Namiotka, fled Poland at the age of 16, alone. He came to avoid conscription [being forced] into [Russia's] army. . . . He boarded the ship SS Greisnaur in the harbor of Bremen [Germany] in March 1905 and sailed away . . . to America. He landed . . . with 75 cents in his pocket.*❞

1900	1910	1920	1930	1940

1900s–1920s
Southern and eastern European immigrants flock to Michigan

1930
170,000 African Americans live in Michigan

1938
Dearborn mosque built

Ⓐ The New Immigrants

As the 1900s began, Michigan's **economy** was strong. An economy has to do with how a place makes and uses resources, goods, and services. The economy was so strong that almost anyone could find a job. When others learned of this, even more people came to Michigan.

Many new immigrants came to Michigan from southern and eastern Europe. In the early 1900s, more than 100,000 people came to Michigan from Poland alone. These people did not work in mining or logging jobs. Most of them worked in city factories.

▲ These tools were brought by an immigrant tailor from Russia.

The new immigrants wanted to feel at home in Michigan. Polish, Irish, Greek, Italian, and African American neighborhoods grew.

Why They Came

Most people came to Michigan to make money. Some left their homes because of war. Others wanted religious freedom. For them Michigan had great promise.

✓ **QUICK CHECK** How did immigration to Michigan change in the early 1900s? *Summarize*

◀ Immigrant children from the Netherlands at a Grand Rapids school

Immigration to Michigan, 1920

Many of Michigan's new manufacturing jobs were filled by European immigrants. They left their homelands seeking opportunities in the United States, and found them in Michigan's factories.

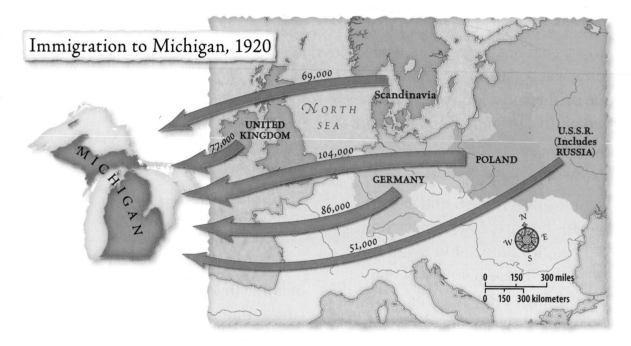

Immigration to Michigan, 1920

European Immigrants to Michigan, 1920

Poland 104,000

Other European countries 119,000

Germany 86,000

U.S.S.R. (Includes Russia) 51,000

United Kingdom** 77,000

Scandinavia* 69,000

*Denmark, Norway, and Sweden
**Includes Ireland

Source: U.S Census

Think About Immigration

1. Looking at the map, which countries bordering the North Sea had immigrants go to Michigan?

2. Looking at the chart and map, were you more likely to hear Russian or German spoken in Michigan? Why?

3. Which country or region had about half as many immigrants as Poland?

ⓑ The Great Migration

Between 1890 and about 1920, many African Americans migrated, or moved, north. One such person was Lily McKnight. Read more about her below.

Groups like the Detroit Urban League helped newcomers to Michigan. They helped people find jobs and homes.

So many African Americans migrated north that this was called the Great Migration. By 1930, 170,000 African Americans lived in Michigan.

Unfair Treatment

Most African Americans came north looking for better-paying jobs. Many wanted to leave the problems they faced in the South. African Americans still faced discrimination in the South. They lived in hard times.

In the South, African Americans could not get high-paying jobs. They could not eat in the same places or shop in the same stores as white people. They were kept from voting.

African Americans lived only a little better in Michigan. They still got the hardest jobs. Many whites would not work with them. African Americans were not welcome in many areas. They made their own neighborhoods, like Black Bottom in Detroit. It was named for the rich, black soil found there.

In the neighborhoods, African Americans built their own churches, stores, and jazz clubs. Many of these clubs were on Hastings Street in Detroit. Jazz music was very popular there.

QUICK CHECK How did the Urban League help new arrivals to Detroit?
Main Idea and Details

PRIMARY SOURCES

Lily McKnight
from 1983 interview

❝*Just some clothes, that's all. Suitcases, that's all. I sold and gave away all of my furniture, but I didn't bring nothin' but my clothes, that's all. Just packed a suitcase and got a train and came on up here. That's nerve, isn't it?*❞

 What does McKnight mean when she says, "That's nerve, isn't it?"

C Arab Americans

Many Arab immigrants moved to Michigan. Most came from countries in the Middle East, such as Syria, Lebanon, and Egypt. The city of Dearborn is near Detroit. Many Arab immigrants moved to Dearborn. Today more Arab Americans live in Dearborn than any other place in the country.

The Dearborn Mosque ▼

Most Arabs are Muslim. They follow the religion of Islam. Dearborn's Muslims decided to build a **mosque**. It was one of the first in the country. A mosque is a Muslim place of worship. Dearborn is also home to the Arab American National Museum.

QUICK CHECK From which Middle Eastern countries did Michigan's Arab immigrants come?
Main Idea and Details

What You Learned

A In the early 1900s, immigrants came from southern and eastern Europe.

B From 1890 to about 1920, many African Americans moved north in a movement called the Great Migration.

C Many Arab immigrants settled in Dearborn.

Focus Lesson Review

1. **Focus Question** Why did people come to Michigan in the early 1900s?

2. **Vocabulary** Write one sentence for each vocabulary word.
   economy   mosque

3. **Economics** How did Michigan's booming industries affect immigration?

4. **Critical Thinking Make Decisions** Do you think most immigrants to Michigan found what they were looking for? Explain your answer.

5. **Reading Strategy Summarize** Use the chart to summarize the section "The Great Migration" on page 181.

6. **Write About THE BIG IDEA** How did immigrants living in Michigan help newcomers from their own countries?

7. **Link to Music** Read more about Detroit's jazz clubs. Who played there? What were their songs about?

The Goodridge Brothers 1829–1922

The Goodridge brothers were born in York, Pennsylvania. Their parents were free African Americans. They ran a railroad freight business. It may have been used as part of the Underground Railroad.

Glenalvin Goodridge was born in 1829. Wallace was born in 1840. William was born in 1846. When he was about 18, Glenalvin opened a photography studio in York. During the Civil War, the brothers moved to East Saginaw, Michigan. There they opened a new studio.

The business did well. The brothers took pictures of people in Michigan. They took pictures of both whites and African Americans. They also became community leaders. They brought people such as Frederick Douglass to speak in Saginaw.

The Goodridge brothers took pictures of places in Michigan, too. Their pictures show us Michigan's past.

▲ William, left, and Wallace Goodridge

 Write About It! Why do you think the Goodridge brothers' business was a success?

LOG ON For more biographies, visit: www.macmillanmh.com

The Goodridge Brothers

1820	1830	1840	1850	1860	1870	1880

- 1829 Glenalvin is born
- 1840 Wallace is born
- 1846 William is born
- 1847 Glenalvin opens photography studio
- 1863 Family moves to East Saginaw
- 1867 Glenalvin dies
- 1872 Studio destroyed by fire

Moving North

Characters

Narrator	Aunt Cora
Mother	Father
Grandmother	Jesse
Ida	

Narrator: It is September 1917. Nine-year-old Jesse and his twelve-year-old sister, Ida, are leaving their home in Georgia to move to Detroit. Like thousands of other African Americans, their family is going North to begin a new life. They want to escape discrimination and find better jobs and schools. Although Jesse is excited about this big change, he doesn't want to leave his best friend.

Mother: Jesse! Ida! Have you finished packing yet?

Ida: Yes, ma'am, but Jesse's drawing book is too big for his suitcase.

Narrator: Mother looks at Jesse's book of drawings proudly.

Mother: Why don't you carry it with you? You can draw another picture on the train to Detroit.

Narrator: Jesse's father enters, holding several train tickets.

Father: I have tickets for everyone. We'll meet the other club members at the station at noon.

Jesse: What club is that?

Father: It's called a migration club, son. About 40 of us are traveling to Detroit together. Up North, we can help each other find jobs and homes.

Jesse: I thought we were staying with Uncle Jacob and Aunt Sara.

Mother: We are, but only until we can find a nice apartment of our own.

Jesse: What's an apartment?

Father: You'll find out in Detroit.

Narrator: Aunt Cora enters with Grandmother. Cora is holding a newspaper. She helps Grandmother into a rocking chair.

Grandmother: My, I am going to miss this old chair.

Father: I'll buy you a new one in Detroit, as soon as I get a job. That's a promise.

Ida: Where will you work?

Father: Maybe Mr. Henry Ford will hire me to make cars in his factory. I hear he's paying five dollars a day.

Grandmother: Five dollars a day!

Father: It's a lot more than I earn working at the mill here.

Aunt Cora: The newspaper says there are plenty of jobs up North. All the factories are hiring workers because of the war. Your cousin Lewis makes trucks for the army.

Mother: Maybe I can get a job in one of those big Detroit hotels.

Grandmother: As long as none of you ever has to work in the fields the way I did. I never rested from morning till night. If I wasn't planting, I was cooking, or washing clothes.

Narrator: Mother hugs her.

Mother: We're taking care of you now, Mama. In Detroit, I want you to rest and take in all the sights.

Ida: I can't wait to go to a school in a real school building.

Narrator: Jesse looks upset.

Jesse: What's wrong with our school here? I like it fine.

Ida: Well, I don't! It's not a real school at all. It's just an old store with a leaky roof. It doesn't have enough books.

Jesse: I don't need a big, fancy school with lots of books. You can all go to Detroit without me!

Narrator: Jesse runs out to the porch. His father follows him.

Jesse: Why can't I stay here like Joe? He's my best friend.

Father: We're starting a new life in Detroit, son . . . as a family.

Jesse: It's not fair.

Father: No. People mistreating you because of who you are isn't fair. In Michigan you'll be able to stand up and speak your mind. In his last letter, Cousin Lewis told me he can vote.

Jesse: Have you ever voted before?

Father: Son, I've never voted in my entire life. But I will in the North. And one day, so will your mother.

Narrator: Jesse looks up and his father smiles.

Father: Now, come help me with the suitcases. We don't want to be late.

Jesse: Yes, sir.

Narrator: Jesse stops and looks back.

Jesse: I'm going to write a letter to Joe from Detroit. Maybe his family will move up North, too.

Father: If they do, they'll have plenty of friends to stay with.

Write About It!

Write your own Readers' Theater scene about the family's life in Detroit a year after they move there.

Chapter 6 Review

Vocabulary Review

Copy the sentences below on a separate sheet of paper. Use the list of vocabulary terms to fill in the blanks.

economy   manufacturer
discrimination   raw materials

1. African Americans faced _____ in Michigan even after the Civil War.

2. Factories need _____ to create their products.

3. A(n) _____ uses machinery to make or process things.

4. The _____ of Michigan depended on farms, lumber, and mining.

5. **Test Preparation** The use of skills, ideas, and tools to meet people's needs is _____.

   A diverse   C mosque
   B cash crop   D technology

Comprehension Check

6. How did new technology help Michigan farmers?

7. Why was it difficult to move raw materials in Michigan before railroads?

8. How did Michigan's population become more diverse after the Civil War?

9. What were two reasons that African Americans migrated from the South to Michigan?

10. What kind of work did immigrants find in Michigan after 1900?

11. **Critical Thinking** What would have been the best part of coming to Michigan as an immigrant after 1900? What would have been some of the biggest challenges?

12. **Critical Thinking** What were the advantages for immigrants moving to neighborhoods with other people from their homelands?

Use the Time Line

Use the time line below to answer each question.

13. How many years after African American men gained the right to vote did Michigan's African American population reach 170,000?

14. How many years does this time line show?

1840	1860	1880	1900	1920	1940

1860 Railroad boom begins

1870 African American men gain the right to vote

1900s–1920s Southern and eastern European immigrants flock to Michigan

1930 170,000 African Americans live in Michigan

1938 Dearborn Mosque built

Read Line and Circle Graphs

Use the graph to answer these questions.

15. About how many more African Americans lived in Detroit in 1940 than in 1900?

16. During which decade did the most African Americans move to Detroit?

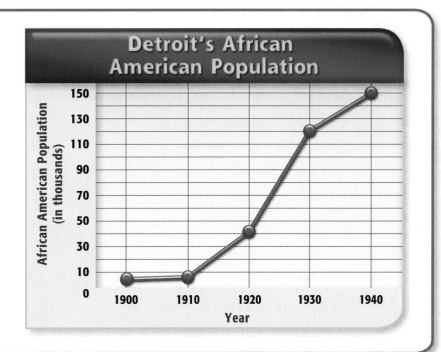

Detroit's African American Population

African American Population (in thousands) vs *Year*

Using Primary Sources

Historic Photographs

Use the photo to answer the questions.

1879 HAPPY NEW YEAR TO ALL

17. What can we learn from historic photographs?

18. When was this photograph taken?

Hands-on Activity

19. Make a Poster Work in groups to create posters that would convince people to move to Michigan in 1910.

Write About History

20. Expository Suppose you are an immigrant to Michigan from Europe in the early 1900s. Write a letter home to a relative telling what your life is like in the United States.

 LOG ON For help with the process of writing, visit: www.macmillanmh.com

Comprehension and Critical Thinking Check

Write one or more sentences to answer each question.

1. Why did **plantation** owners feel they needed enslaved workers?

2. What did **abolitionists** want to abolish?

3. How did the **Underground Railroad** help enslaved people?

4. When did some states in the South begin to **secede** from the United States?

5. What did the **Emancipation Proclamation** do?

6. Which Michigan **regiment** fought in the Battle of Gettysburg?

7. How did the use of new technology after the Civil War make **cash crops** possible?

8. How did Michigan's **raw materials** get to the factories that needed them?

9. **Critical Thinking** Did African Americans escape **discrimination** when they moved north?

10. **Critical Thinking** Why was building a **mosque** important to Dearborn's Arab American community?

Reading Skills Check

Sequence Events

Copy this graphic organizer. Reread Chapter 5, Lesson 3, "Michigan at War." Use the graphic organizer to list the events from Lesson 3 in order. Then answer the questions.

11. How did you decide which event to put first?

12. How did you decide which event to put last?

13. How does listing events from the text in the order they happened help you to remember what you read?

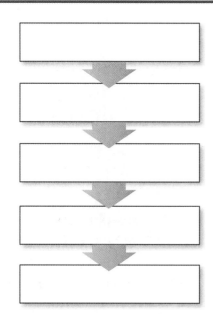

Study the map and use it with what you already know to answer the questions.

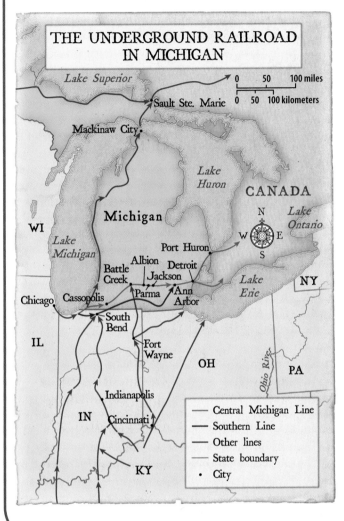

THE UNDERGROUND RAILROAD IN MICHIGAN

14. Based on the map, which conclusion can you draw?

   A There was no slavery in Canada.

   B All of Michigan's Underground Railroad stations were in the Lower Peninsula.

   C The safest way to travel to Canada was by water.

   D The only way to get to Canada on the Underground Railroad was through Michigan.

15. Why did many people escaping slavery want to get to Canada instead of the free states of the northern United States?

   A If they reached Canada, they would not have to fight in the Civil War.

   B From Canada they could sail to Europe.

   C Canada's government promised homes to people escaping slavery.

   D The Fugitive Slave Law did not apply in Canada.

Write About History

16. **Narrative** Suppose that you are a conductor on the Underground Railroad. Write about the work you do.

17. **Letter** Do research to find more about the role of the 24th Michigan at the Battle of Gettysburg. Then write a letter a Michigan soldier might have written after the battle.

18. **Expository** Make a list of ways life in Michigan changed in the 40 years after the Civil War.

LOG ON For help with the process of writing, visit: www.macmillanmh.com

Why do people take great risks?

Write About the Big Idea

Journal Entry

Think about the events that happened to Michigan people before, during, and after the Civil War. Then, complete the graphic organizer you started on page 137.

Group or person	Risk taken	Reason or goal
1. Escaping slaves	1. Returning to slavery; punishment	1. Freedom
2. Harriet Tubman	2.	2.
3.	3.	3.
4.	4.	4.

Use your graphic organizer to help you write a journal entry about the experiences of one of the groups or people from the organizer. Be sure to include details in your journal entry and to give it a date and setting.

Write a Journal Entry

1. Plan
- A journal entry is similar to writing a page in a diary. It is a personal account of something that has happened in your life.
- Journal entries often include a date and a setting. They include as many details as possible.

2. Write a First Draft
- Tell the story of a day in your life in Michigan. Include details that will be interesting and important to others.
- Use the word *I* as you tell about your life.

3. Revise and Proofread
- Read your journal entry. Does it include interesting details? Does it include a date and setting?
- Proofread your entry. Be sure you spelled words correctly. Check capitalization and punctuation.
- Rewrite your journal entry neatly before handing it in.

ACTIVITY

Speak About the Big Idea

Stories of Experience

Tell stories about the experiences of Michiganians in the Civil War.

Prepare Work in groups organized by the graphic organizer you completed. All the people who wrote about the same person or group should work together. Use your journal entries, information from Unit 3, and other sources. Practice telling stories from the perspective of these people. Make your stories brief, but interesting.

Present Give each member of the group time to tell his or her story. Then have one person from the group summarize the experiences of the group.

For help with the Big Idea activity, visit: www.macmillanmh.com

Read More About the Big Idea

Levi Coffin: My Home Is Your Home
Read this Leveled Reader to learn about how one man used his own home in the fight against slavery.

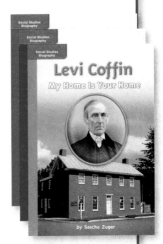

Harriet Tubman
Read this Leveled Reader to discover the story of Harriet Tubman's life and her work with the Underground Railroad.

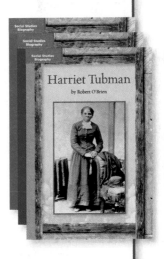

Civil War
by John Stanchak
Discover the war that turned brother against brother in this book packed with fascinating information, maps, and photographs.

Michigan and the Twentieth Century

"*Our greatest primary task is to put people to work. This is no unsolvable problem if we face it wisely and courageously.*"

— President Franklin Delano Roosevelt
First Inaugural Address

How do people solve conflicts?

In Unit 4 you'll learn about how events both at home and far away affected life in Michigan. You'll also read about the people who helped bring changes to Michigan.

As you read, look for information about how people worked to solve conflicts and bring about change.

Copy the graphic organizer. After you read the chapters in this unit, fill in details about each conflict. An example has been done for you.

Group	Conflict	Solution
1. Supporters of women's rights	1. Wanted women to have the right to vote.	1. Passage of the 19th Amendment
2.	2.	2.
3.	3.	3.

◀ This mural by Diego Rivera shows workers at the Ford River Rouge automobile factory.

People Who Made a Difference

Hazen Pingree
1840–1901

Hazen Pingree served as mayor of Detroit from 1890 to 1897. As mayor, and later as governor of Michigan, he worked to improve the lives of workers and immigrants. (page 207)

Anna Howard Shaw
1847–1919

Anna Howard Shaw was a Michigan minister and doctor. She worked in the state and around the country to help give women the right to vote. (page 208)

Henry Ford
1863–1947

Henry Ford changed the auto industry and the nation when he introduced production methods that helped him make autos more quickly and cheaply. (page 212)

1903
Henry Ford opens the Ford Motor Company

1935
Walter Reuther brings a union to General Motors

1890 — 1900 — 1910 — 1920 — 1930 — 1940

1890
Hazen Pingree is mayor of Detroit

1904
Anna Howard Shaw becomes president of the National American Woman Suffrage Society

1920
Women gain the right to vote

1941
United States enters World War II

LOG ON For more biographies, visit:
www.macmillanmh.com

Walter Reuther
1907–1970

In 1935 Walter Reuther brought the United Auto Workers (UAW) union to General Motors. The union was able to work together for better pay and conditions for its members. (page 220)

Rosa Parks
1913–2005

Known as the "mother of the civil rights movement," Rosa Parks helped spark change for African Americans. She later moved to Detroit, where she worked to help young people. (page 244)

Coleman Young
1918–1997

Coleman Young, Detroit's first African American mayor, served five terms, during which he worked to open up city government to all people. (page 242)

1963
Martin Luther King, Jr., leads Freedom March in Detroit

| 1950 | 1960 | 1970 | 1980 | 1990 | 2000 |

1955
Rosa Parks arrested in Montgomery, Alabama

1973
Coleman Young elected mayor of Detroit

1992
The Scenic Rivers Act protects 500 miles of Michigan's rivers

Willow Run

A Selection from **Willow Run**
by Patricia Reilly Giff

It is 1944, the United States is fighting World War II, and Meggie Dillon's world has been turned upside down. Her brother Eddie is a soldier somewhere in Europe. Her father has been offered a job in an airplane factory in Willow Run, Michigan. Meggie and her parents pack the car and make the long drive from their Long Island, New York, home. Meggie is sad to leave her grandpa and her friends, but tells herself that this will be an adventure.

The car was filthy, caked with mud from a thunderstorm in Rochester, grist from a blast of wind in Chicago, and a smear of greasy yellow dirt on the fender from somewhere in Michigan.

"We're here," Dad said.

Here was nowhere. A long building that went on forever, cars pulling up in front, people streaming in and out the doors like Macy's. What had I expected Willow Run to be like? I tried to think. Maybe the Emerald City in *The Wizard of Oz*. At least someplace shiny and beautiful.

"It's the factory." Dad waved his hand. "Henry Ford's assembly line for the war effort."

I didn't know who Henry Ford was, didn't know what an assembly was, and I didn't care. I was sticking to the backseat of the car, boiling hot, while the two cats were fur coats covering my feet. "We're going to live in a factory?"

"Come on, get out. I'll show you," he said.

We walked through the gates. Dad showed a tag to a woman at a table; then we poked our heads into the wide doorway. It was hot, it was noisy, people were all over the place, and pieces of metal were on tables and . . .

"Enough for now," Dad said. "Mom is hot in the car."

We slid back in and Dad waved his arm toward the factory. "Instead of cars, Ford is making bombers, B-24s. The same way though—everyone working on one piece at a time." His round glasses glinted in the sunlight. "It's a mile long, this factory, the largest in the world. If only I could fly one of those B-24s . . ." He broke off. "But the next best thing is to build them."

Mom turned toward him, her plump hand on his arm, her face red from the heat. "I know how much you miss flying."

For a moment no one said anything. We watched people going in and out, hundreds of them, it seemed. If Dad had been able to fly, he'd have been in the war like Eddie. I was glad he wasn't, glad he wore these owl glasses. "I might die of thirst in this car," I said to make him laugh.

He did laugh. "Just the last few streets to go." He started the car and drove along blocks of apartment houses with a few trailers here and there and a couple of shacks leaning against each other. Not a garden in sight.

Grandpa would hate it.

"All this was thrown up in about two minutes to house the workers," Dad said. "It must have been beautiful before the war, green fields and trees, and once maybe a stream."

"It'll be lovely again," Mom said. "Someday soon."

I knew she was thinking about Eddie coming home, wishing it were soon.

Dad turned the key and the hum of the motor stopped. It was strange to hear the silence. "Anyway," he said. "We're here for the **duration**." He opened the door and wandered up the walk.

A kindergarten kid could have drawn it: a long low box that stretched from one end of the paper to the other, no paint, no color. And if you divided the box into tiny sections, each family would have one to live in. Worst of all, there was no grass, nothing growing, only tree stumps near the curb, their tops pale and raw. I remembered what Grandpa had said once, shaking his head in anger. "To kill a tree!"

I could see that Mom was as disappointed as I was. I handed the cats to her, one by one, then backed out of the car.

Dad was already turning the key in the lock. Mom looked over her shoulder at me, her roly-poly face flushed. "It's just for the duration."

The duration again. Hadn't I heard that a hundred times! As if the war were going to end tomorrow.

---

duration (duhr RAY-shun) the length of time during which something continues

Write About It!

Write a letter that Meggie might have sent to her grandpa telling about their arrival in Willow Run.

Compare and Contrast:
Transportation in Michigan

In this unit you will learn about changes in Michigan during the twentieth century. One of the big changes was in how people got around. Learning how to compare and contrast will help you understand the changes you read about in social studies.

1 Learn It

- To compare two or more things, note how they are similar, or alike.

- To contrast two or more things, note how they are different.

- Now read the passage below. Think about how you would compare and contrast ways of traveling.

Find Similarities
Both the train and the automobile made travel faster in the United States.

Find Differences
Automobiles could go anywhere, but trains could go only where there were tracks.

Find Differences
People trusted trains, but automakers had to convince people their automobiles would not break down.

The train and the automobile changed the way people could travel in the United States. Trips that took weeks by horse and carriage took just days with trains and automobiles. The train was fast, but it could take people only where there were railroad tracks. Automobiles could take people almost anywhere.

People trusted the railroads to get them where they needed to go. Early automobiles, however, often broke down. Most people thought they were better off on horses. Automakers like Ransom Olds had to convince people that their automobiles would not break down.

2 Try It

Copy the Venn diagram below. Then fill it in with details from the paragraphs on page 202.

VENN DIAGRAM

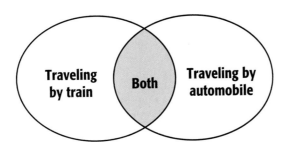

Traveling by train | Both | Traveling by automobile

What did you look for in the reading to compare and contrast?

3 Apply It

- Review the steps for comparing and contrasting.

- Read the passage below. Then create a diagram to compare and contrast the information you read.

Ransom Olds and Henry Ford started two of Michigan's first automobile companies. Olds was the first to build factories that could make autos in large numbers. In 1904 he sold more autos than anyone else.

However, when Henry Ford designed a new assembly method, it helped him make autos faster and more cheaply than anyone else could. By 1908 his Model T was the most popular auto in the country.

▲ The Ford Model T

The Twentieth Century

You Are There

"We women do not want the ballot [vote] in order that we may fight, but we do want the ballot in order that we may help men to keep from fighting....

You can no more build up homes without men than you can build up the state without women."

Anna Howard Shaw of Big Rapids gave this speech in 1915. She wanted to convince people that women should have the right to vote.

In the early part of the twentieth century, Americans lived through war. Times were tough. People like Shaw tried to make some important changes in this country.

MN

IA

◀ Woman demonstrating for the right to vote

Chapter Events	1900	1910	1920

1 Early 1900s
Caroline Bartlett Crane works to improve the quality of life in Michigan

2 1908
Henry Ford sells his first Model T automobile

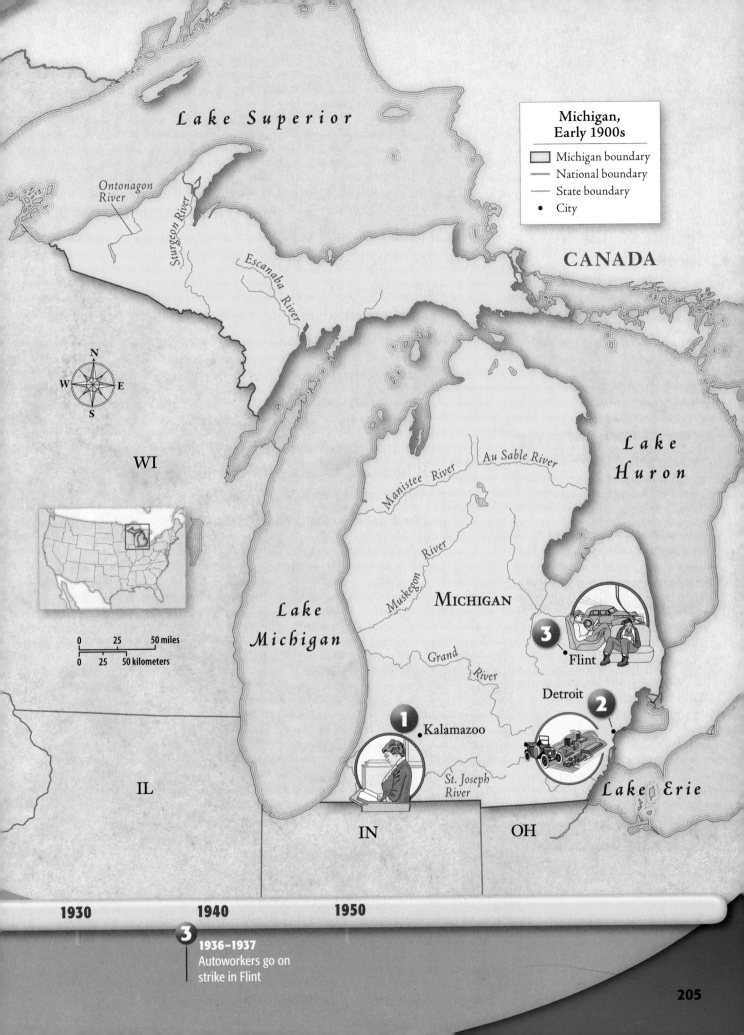

Lake Superior

Ontonagon River

Sturgeon River

Escanaba River

CANADA

Michigan, Early 1900s

▢ Michigan boundary
— National boundary
— State boundary
• City

WI

N
W · E
S

Manistee River

Au Sable River

Lake Huron

Muskegon River

MICHIGAN

Grand River

0   25   50 miles
0   25   50 kilometers

Lake Michigan

1 • Kalamazoo

St. Joseph River

3 • Flint

Detroit

2

Lake Erie

IL

IN

OH

1930   1940   1950

3
1936–1937
Autoworkers go on
strike in Flint

The Progressives

VOCABULARY

Progressive
reform
suffrage
amendment

VOCABULARY STRATEGY

Root Words Amend means "to fix or change." What do you think an **amendment** to the United States Constitution does?

READING STRATEGY

Compare and Contrast Use the Venn diagram to show how the Progressives changed life in Michigan. Label each side of the chart.

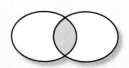

MICHIGAN GLCE

H3.0.1
H3.0.2
H3.0.3
P3.1.3
P3.3.1

Hazen Pingree was mayor of Detroit from 1890 to 1892. Voters thought he was a great man. He tried to help people who did not have much. One thing he did was to make sure people had enough to eat.

Paul Laurence Dunbar was an African American poet. He wrote a poem about Pingree. It was called "Vote for Pingree and Vote for Bread":

> "Come comrades [friends], hear the record fair
> That clings about the present mayor—
> The man who gives us gas galore,
> For two-thirds what we paid before;
> Who takes out pavements rough and old
> And makes them worthy to behold . . .
> For Pingree's at the city's head,
> We'll vote for him and vote for bread."

Streetcars helped people get around in busy cities like Holland. ▼

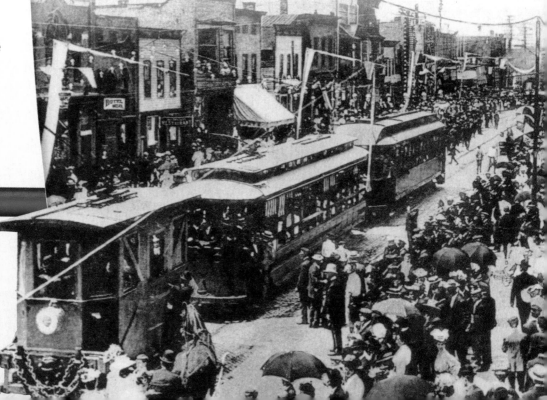

1890	1900	1910	1920

1890
Hazen Pingree elected
mayor of Detroit

1904
Anna Howard Shaw becomes
president of the National American
Woman Suffrage Society

1920
Women gain
right to vote

Ⓐ Making Life Easier

At the end of the 1800s, life in Michigan had changed. It was easier in many ways. More buildings had electric lights. There was gas heat and running water. People could take the streetcar, or trolley, to get around. They did not have to walk.

Life was not easier for everyone. Immigrants and low-paid workers could not afford these changes. A Detroit streetcar ride was five cents. Most working women made less than 10 cents a day.

A new group of politicians worked to make life better for the poor. This group was known as the **Progressives**. They tried to make life in the state and the country better.

Hazen Pingree

Hazen Pingree was a Progressive Republican. In 1890 he became mayor of Detroit. He pushed for **reforms**, or changes for the better. Soon the cost of a streetcar ride fell to three cents. The price of gas heat was cut in half.

In 1893 the United States economy was not doing well. Many Detroit workers had lost their jobs.

▲ Detroit mayor Hazen Pingree helped plant potato fields for the needy.

Pingree talked to landowners. He asked them to let people plant gardens on land that wasn't being used. Many families grew potatoes on this land. People started calling the mayor "Potato Patch" Pingree.

Pingree was elected governor of the state in 1896. He had a hard time getting Michigan lawmakers to pass his reforms. In time, many became laws across the country.

QUICK CHECK How did Detroit change while Hazen Pingree was mayor?
Compare and Contrast

ⓑ Women Take the Lead

Several Michigan women were leaders in the fight to help the poor. Caroline Bartlett Crane was from Kalamazoo. She was a teacher, reporter, and minister.

In 1889 she became pastor of First Unitarian Church in Kalamazoo. There she started a free public kindergarten. She opened a cafeteria and a school.

Crane also spoke out about Kalamazoo's meat-packing factories. She told people they were not clean. She fought for a new state law. The law let towns make tougher rules for meat-packing companies.

News of her reforms spread. More than 60 city leaders from across the country came to see Crane. They asked for her ideas to improve public health in their communities.

The Right to Vote

Progressives also wanted to reform politics. Since the 1840s many Americans wanted women to vote. The right to vote is called **suffrage**. Senator Thomas Palmer of Michigan gave a speech in the United States Senate in 1885. This was the first speech in the Senate in favor of women's suffrage.

Anna Howard Shaw came to Big Rapids with her parents in 1859. She became a doctor, a minister, and a leader in the fight for suffrage. From 1904 to 1914, she was president of the National American Woman Suffrage Society. She gave speeches across the country.

Finally, in 1920, the Nineteenth **Amendment** gave women the right to vote. An amendment is a formal change to the Constitution.

The Nineteenth Amendment was a great victory for women. It was also one of the greatest victories for Progressives in the United States.

✓ **QUICK CHECK** Why do you think leaders of other cities came to Caroline Bartlett Crane for advice? *Draw Conclusions*

A parade for women's suffrage, 1912 ▶

★ Focus Lesson Review

1. **Focus Question** How did Michiganians try to improve life for the poor?

2. **Vocabulary** Use each of the following words in a sentence.
   amendment   reform   suffrage

3. **History** How did Caroline Bartlett Crane make Michigan's food supply safer?

4. **Critical Thinking Draw Conclusions** How did lowering the price of a streetcar ride help the poor?

5. **Reading Strategy Compare and Contrast** Reread the first paragraph on page 207. Using the diagram, compare life in Michigan at the beginning of the 1800s with life at the end of the 1800s.

6. **Write About** THE **BIG** IDEA Describe one way the Progressives improved the lives of others.

7. **Link to Language Arts** The Progressives made speeches to convince people that their ideas were right. Write a speech you would give to improve life in your own town.

The Birth of the Automobile

How did Detroit become the center of the world's automobile industry?

VOCABULARY

mass production
assembly line

VOCABULARY STRATEGY

Root Words Product is the root word of **production**. One meaning of *mass* is "a large quantity." What do you think **mass production** means?

READING STRATEGY

Identify Main Idea and Details Use the chart to show the main idea and details of this lesson.

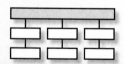

MICHIGAN GLCE

H3.0.1
H3.0.3

The first hit song about an automobile was "In My Merry Oldsmobile." It was one of America's most popular songs in 1905.

> *Come away with me Lucille in my merry Oldsmobile. Down the road of life we'll fly, automo-bubbling you and I.*

❶ Horseless Carriages

Until the early 1800s, there were only two ways to travel on land. People could walk. They could ride or be pulled by an animal. The animal was usually a horse.

The railroad was the biggest change to land travel in the 1800s. People could get from one place to another in days instead of weeks. But trains could only travel where there were tracks. The horse and carriage were still needed to get around.

Inventors around the world were working on a "horseless carriage." This carriage would run on steam or gasoline.

1897
Ransom Olds
opens the state's
first auto company

1908
Henry Ford
sells the first
Model T

1929
Michigan has more
than 1 million cars
on the road

Michigan's First Car Company

Car making in Michigan began in 1897. Ransom Eli Olds opened the state's first automobile company in Lansing. Two years later, he opened a factory in Detroit. In 1903 Olds sold 4,000 "Oldsmobiles." They cost $650 each.

Early carmakers needed to show that their cars would work. They also needed to teach people how to use them. In 1901 Olds hired a driver. The man drove an Oldsmobile from Detroit to New York. The trip was 820 miles. It only took seven-and-a-half days. The trip caused Oldsmobile sales to increase.

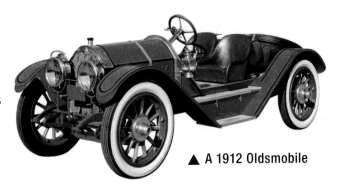

▲ A 1912 Oldsmobile

Olds also made the first driver's manual. It told new car owners, "Don't do anything to your motor without a good reason or without knowing just what you are doing."

QUICK CHECK How did travel by land change from the early 1800s to the early 1900s? *Main Idea and Details*

New Oldsmobiles lined up at Ransom Olds's factory in Lansing in 1901. ▼

211

Assembly Line

ⓑ Ford's Model T

By 1907 there were about 250 carmakers in the Detroit area. Most made very expensive cars. Henry Ford wanted to make cars everyone could buy. His ideas made him the world's most successful carmaker.

Henry Ford stands with a Model T in 1920.

Ford opened the Ford Motor Company in 1903. In 1908 he began making the famous Model T. It was also called the "Tin Lizzie." The Model Ts were used as fire trucks, ambulances, and police cars. They were also used by families. Farmers could even use the Model T to haul crops and animals.

Ford sold 25,000 Model Ts the first year. In 1923 his company sold 1,800,000. Ford Motor Company would produce 15 million Model Ts in all.

The Assembly Line

Ford used **mass production** to make cars. Mass production means making large numbers of one product quickly.

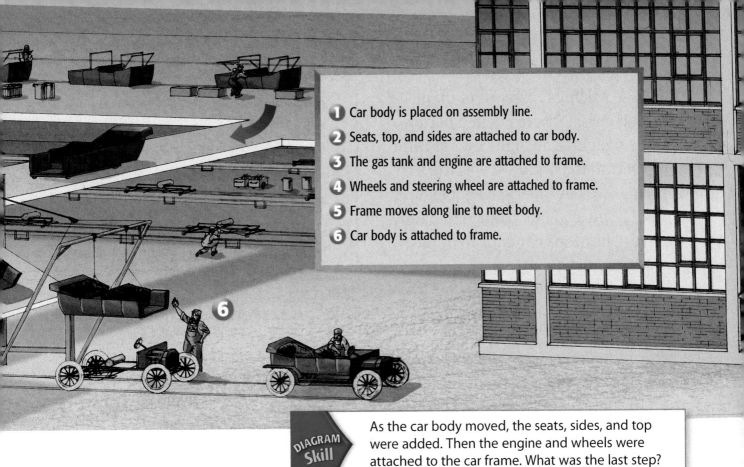

1. Car body is placed on assembly line.
2. Seats, top, and sides are attached to car body.
3. The gas tank and engine are attached to frame.
4. Wheels and steering wheel are attached to frame.
5. Frame moves along line to meet body.
6. Car body is attached to frame.

DIAGRAM Skill As the car body moved, the seats, sides, and top were added. Then the engine and wheels were attached to the car frame. What was the last step?

Ford had huge factories. Workers stood next to moving belts that moved cars in a line. This was the **assembly line**. Workers and machines were put in the right order to make a car. When the belt stopped, each worker did just one job. One worker might put on windshields. The next worker might put on doors. A car could be assembled in 93 minutes.

Many Ford employees were new immigrants. They had never done factory work before. That did not matter because each worker only had to learn one job.

The assembly line was a success. It was cheaper for Ford to build his cars this way. In 1908 a Model T cost $850. By 1916 the price was $360.

The Motor City

Ford and Olds were not the only carmakers in Detroit. Companies like Dodge, Buick, and Chrysler opened factories in the city. They opened factories around the city, too. Detroit had been a French fort. Now it was America's "Motor City."

Ford's own "motor city" was his River Rouge factory. In time, the factory had more than 100,000 workers. They worked in 93 buildings. This factory produced a new car every 49 seconds.

QUICK CHECK Why were workers with no experience able to work in Ford's factories? *Cause and Effect*

◉ Cars Bring Change

By 1929 Michigan had more than 1 million cars. Drivers wanted better roads. An eight-lane highway was built from Detroit to Pontiac. It was the first superhighway in America. People now bought homes farther from where they worked. They took car trips to other parts of the country.

New Workers

The car business grew quickly. Factories needed more workers. Carmakers wanted African Americans from the South to move to Michigan. The Great Migration continued. By 1930, Detroit was the country's fourth-largest city.

QUICK CHECK What events led Detroit companies to ask African Americans to come to work in their factories?
Sequence Events

▼ Before modern roads were built, drivers could get stuck in the mud.

⭐ Focus Lesson Review

1. **Focus Question** How did Detroit become the center of the world's automobile industry?

2. **Vocabulary** Use the following terms to write a paragraph about how Henry Ford changed the automobile industry.
   assembly line   **mass production**

3. **Technology** How did technology help Henry Ford sell more cars than other automakers?

4. **Critical Thinking** **Draw Conclusions** Why do you think more people moved farther from where they worked after cars became available?

5. **Reading Strategy** **Identify Main Idea and Details** Use the chart to show the main idea and details of the first paragraph on page 214.

6. **Write About** THE BIG IDEA How did workers cooperate with each other on the assembly line?

7. **Link to Music** Using the song on page 210 as a model, write a song lyric about driving today.

Ransom Eli Olds 1864–1950

Growing up in Lansing, Ransom Olds tinkered with engines in his father's machine shop. By age 22, he had already built his first "horseless carriage."

In 1897 Olds opened Michigan's first auto company in Lansing. He said he would build cars

"*in as nearly perfect a manner as possible.*"

Olds made only six cars that year. The business grew after he moved to a larger factory in Detroit. In 1901 he sold 425 "Oldsmobiles." Two years later, he sold 4,000. Olds said his car was "built to run, and it does!"

Olds left his company in 1904. Then he started the REO (Ransom E. Olds) Motor Car company in Lansing. Olds left REO in 1936. He was spending much of his time and fortune helping charities.

In 1908 Oldsmobile became part of the General Motors company. In 2004 the last new Oldsmobile was made. It was 106 years after Olds had built the first.

 How did Ransom Olds show leadership?

 For more biographies, visit:
www.macmillanmh.com

Life of Ransom Eli Olds

1860	1880	1900	1920	1940	1960
1864 Born in Geneva, Ohio	1880 Moves with family to Lansing	1897 Starts Olds Motor Vehicle Company	1904 Starts REO Motor Car Company	1936 Leaves automobile business	1950 Dies in Lansing

Why was Michigan hurt so much by the hard times of the 1930s?

VOCABULARY

stock market
Great Depression
unemployed
union
strike
closed shop

VOCABULARY STRATEGY

Word Origins A union is a group of workers with a common goal. The word **union** comes from a Latin word meaning "one."

READING STRATEGY

Cause and Effect Use the chart below to show the causes and effects of the 1937 events in auto factories.

MICHIGAN GLCE

H3.0.1
H3.0.3

World War I and Hard Times

In 1932 Michigan workers were hit by hard economic times. Yip Harburg wrote a song. It was called "Brother, Can You Spare a Dime?" It described how many people felt:

> "*They used to tell me I was building a dream, with peace and glory ahead,*
> *Why should I be standing in line, just waiting for bread?*
> *Once I built a railroad, I made it run, made it race against time.*
> *Once I built a railroad; now it's done. Brother, can you spare a dime?*"

A A World at War

In 1914 a huge war began in Europe. Great Britain, France, and Russia were at war with Germany, Turkey, and Austria-Hungary. So many countries fought that the war was later called World War I.

At first many Americans didn't want to get into the war. Then, in 1915, a German submarine sank the British ship *Lusitania*. It killed 123 Americans. On April 6, 1917, Congress declared war on Germany.

During the war some Americans feared that German immigrants were spies for Germany. Speaking German was against the law in some places. Berlin, Michigan, had the same name as Germany's capital. They changed the name to Marne. People even started calling frankfurters, named for a German city, "hot dogs" instead.

1910	1920	1930	1940

1914
World War I
begins

1918
World War I
ends

1929
Stock market
crashes

1935
Walter Reuther
brings the United
Auto Workers to GM

1936–1937
GM workers
strike in Flint

Michigan Gets Involved

Almost 175,000 Michiganians were sent to fight in World War I. About 5,000 of them died. Soldiers had not seen this kind of war before. For the first time, tanks and machine guns were used. Fighter planes and poison gas were used, too.

At home, Michigan factories made thousands of trucks and tanks. They also made ambulances and airplane engines. Children got days off from school to work on state farms. They helped to harvest extra fruits and vegetables.

World War I ended on November 11, 1918. The United States and its allies won. Americans hoped it was the last war ever. They called it "the war to end all wars."

QUICK CHECK Why did the United States fight in World War I? *Cause and Effect*

Government posters encouraged Michiganians to ship out for the war. ▶

JOIN THE
AIR SERVICE
and
SERVE
in
FRANCE

DO IT
NOW

▲ During the Depression, unemployed men lined up for free meals at soup kitchens.

⑬ From Good Times to Bad

The end of World War I brought good times for many people. The economy was strong in the 1920s. Michigan families could afford new things like radios and electric refrigerators.

People also began spending more. They put money into the **stock market**. The stock market is where shares of companies, or stocks, are bought and sold. People thought buying stocks was a quick way to get rich. They borrowed money to buy as much as they could. Then the prices of stocks began to drop in 1929. People began to sell them.

As stocks lost their value, people began to panic. Finally, on October 29, 1929, stock prices "crashed." Everybody wanted to sell. Almost nobody wanted to buy. Americans lost billions of dollars. The good times were over.

Michigan Is Hit Hard

The **Great Depression** was the worst economic time in American history. It was a hard time for other countries as well. Factories closed. Banks that had loaned money to businesses failed. Families lost their savings. Many farmers lost their land.

The Depression hit Michigan harder than most states. Most Americans did not have much money. They could no longer afford expensive goods like new cars.

Many factory workers lost their jobs. By 1930 one in five Michigan workers was **unemployed**. This meant that they did not have jobs. In Detroit almost half of all adults did not have jobs. Because of discrimination, more African Americans lost their jobs than white workers.

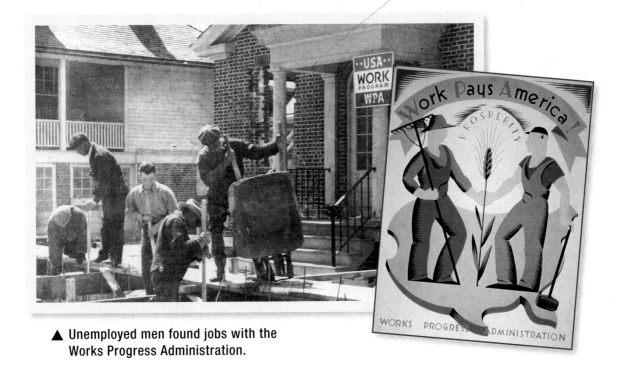

▲ Unemployed men found jobs with the Works Progress Administration.

A "New Deal"

In 1930 Frank Murphy became the mayor of Detroit. Murphy was like Hazen Pingree from years before. Murphy helped people find jobs and grow food. Still, life was hard for many families. They sewed clothes from burlap sacks. They made furniture from old crates.

In 1933 Franklin Delano Roosevelt became President. He was from New York. He told Americans, "The only thing we have to fear is fear itself." He promised a "new deal." It would get people working.

Roosevelt's New Deal programs made many jobs. The Works Progress Administration (WPA) hired workers to build roads, bridges, and playgrounds. The WPA also hired artists, writers, and musicians. They made murals and other works. You can still see them around Michigan.

The Civilian Conservation Corps (CCC) paid workers to build roads. Workers also planted more than 200 million trees. Even with these jobs, the Great Depression lasted for 10 years.

QUICK CHECK How did Roosevelt help unemployed people? *Summarize*

President Franklin Delano Roosevelt ▼

219

ⓒ Workers Unite

A **union** is a group of workers who join together to get better pay and working conditions. There had been some unions in Michigan. Most factory workers did not belong to them. Factory workers were often better paid than other workers. Also, there were often more factory jobs than workers to fill them.

The Great Depression changed that. Many factory workers lost their jobs. Those who kept their jobs were paid less. They also worked longer days. If they complained, bosses told them that many men would be happy to take their place.

The United Auto Workers

Walter Reuther was a young Detroit autoworker. Reuther was the son of a union leader from West Virginia. He said, "There is no greater contribution than to help the weak."

In 1935 he wanted to start a union at General Motors (GM). GM was the world's largest automaker. Reuther and others talked to thousands of workers. They got the men to join the United Auto Workers (UAW).

By 1936 the UAW was ready to make demands. It wanted GM to change the way it treated its workers.

QUICK CHECK Why did autoworkers want to join unions in the 1930s? *Summarize*

This union rally brought 150,000 people to downtown Detroit. ▼

Walter Reuther ▶

Prices Then and Now

The chart below lists prices of some things in 1930 and today. It seems as though things were pretty cheap back then, but weekly salaries were much lower, too.

Prices Then and Now		
Item	1930	Today
hamburger	.15	$3.50
hot dog	.10	$2.50
boy's shirt	$1.00	$10.00
loaf of bread	.10	$2.50
quart of milk	.10	$1.25
refrigerator	$99.50	$800.00
electric stove	$124.50	$1,000.00
new car	$700.00	$20,000.00

Source: www.michigan.gov/hal

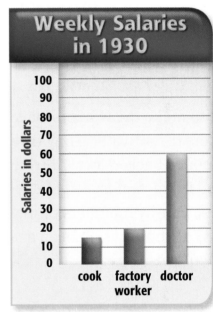

Source: www.michigan.gov/hal

Think About Salaries and Prices

1. How much did a boy's shirt cost in 1930 compared to today?

2. Which job shown on the graph paid the most in 1930?

3. How many weeks did a factory worker have to work to pay for a new car in 1930? How many weeks would it take the factory worker at today's prices and salary?

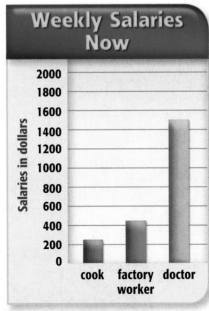

Source: www.michigan.gov/hal

221

ⓓ The Sit-Down Strike

On December 30, 1936, UAW workers at a GM factory in Flint, Michigan, went on **strike**. They stopped working. They wanted better working conditions. The Flint strike was a "sit-down" strike. This meant the workers came to work but would not do their jobs until GM agreed to their demands. The workers stayed inside the factory. The company could not bring in other workers to do their jobs.

Reaching an Agreement

On January 11, 1937, Flint police tried to make the workers leave. The workers threw water. They threw bolts. The police backed away. Strikers stayed in the factory for 44 days and nights. Family members brought them food. The food was made at a "strike kitchen" close by.

Finally GM agreed to meet with the union's leaders. Frank Murphy was now Michigan's governor. He helped the two sides reach an agreement on February 11. Each side gave up some of its demands. The UAW got better pay and working conditions. GM also agreed that the union could speak for the company's workers.

Chrysler, another automaker, also agreed to let the UAW represent its workers. Henry Ford would not let the UAW come to his factories. In a book Ford wrote, "The strike . . . only makes the situation worse whether you win or lose."

Ford fought the UAW in court for years. He fired workers who tried to sign up union members. Finally, in May 1941, Ford agreed to let the UAW represent his workers. Now all automakers were a **closed shop**. This means all workers had to join a union.

◀ Workers in a GM plant during the Flint sit-down strike; (below) a union pin

The Spread of Unions

Other workers soon followed the ideas of the UAW. Young women working in a Woolworth's department store in Detroit went on strike. After an eight-day sit-down strike they got a raise of five cents per hour. After the Depression, more workers joined unions. By 1950 the UAW had more than 1 million members.

The unions asked Congress to protect workers. New laws said workers could not be asked to work more than 40 hours a week. They could not be paid less than a "minimum wage." The wage would be set by the government.

QUICK CHECK Why do you think Chrysler allowed the UAW to represent its workers? *Draw Conclusions*

▲ Workers' children supported the strikers.

What You Learned

A Michigan factories made vehicles for the army in World War I.

B The Great Depression brought hard times to many Michigan families. President Franklin Roosevelt's New Deal gave jobs to many unemployed workers.

C During the Depression, unions fought for better conditions for autoworkers.

D A strike in Flint encouraged other workers to join unions.

☆ Focus Lesson Review

1. **Focus Question** Why was Michigan hurt so much by the hard times of the 1930s?

2. **Vocabulary** Write one sentence for each vocabulary term.
   closed shop   unemployed
   strike   union

3. **Economics** Why did the stock market "crash" of 1929 hurt so many Americans?

4. **Critical Thinking Cause and Effect** Why were African Americans particularly hard hit during the Great Depression?

5. **Reading Strategy Cause and Effect** Use the chart to show how President Roosevelt's New Deal affected Michigan.

6. **Write About**  **THE BIG IDEA** How did new technology change the way nations fought in World War I?

7. **Link to Art** In the 1930s, unions used posters to recruit workers. Sketch a poster you would use to convince workers to join a union.

The LIBRARY *of* CONGRESS

Understand Newspapers

A newspaper is a paper that is usually printed daily or weekly. Newspapers contain news, opinions, and advertising. They report on current events, or things that happen every day. Newspapers can be important primary sources because they usually contain first-hand reports of events, or opinions about events, at the time they are happening.

The Flint Sit-Down Strike

In the last lesson you learned about the Flint autoworkers' strike. The primary source on page 225 is a newspaper account of the event.

 **Learn It**

Read the steps below to help you find information in newspapers.

- **Identify the name of the newspaper.**

- **Identify the kind of article you are reading.** A news article, or story, describes a recent event. A feature article gives a detailed report on one topic. An editorial offers an opinion about a topic.

- **Identify the parts of the article you are reading.** The article's headline is usually printed in larger letters and tells the main idea of the story. The byline tells you who wrote the story. Not all articles have a byline. The dateline tells you when and where the story was written.

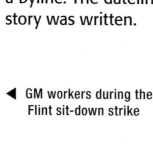

◀ GM workers during the Flint sit-down strike

 **Try It**

Read the newspaper account below to understand what people can find out from newspapers.

■ **A news article should answer five questions:** *Who* was involved? *What* took place? *When* did it happen? *Where* did it happen? *Why* did it happen?

Name of Newspaper →

The New York Times

Dateline → Flint, Michigan, Tuesday, Feb. 2

Headline → **Troops Surround Plants Following Riots in Flint**

"Marching orders issued at midnight to troops mobilizing [gathering] over the state will concentrate the full National Guard strength of 4,000 soldiers today in Flint where a regiment took over last night an area in which new rioting in the General Motors strike occurred in the afternoon. . . . The Military Intelligence Service reported that 1,150 men were in the occupied Chevrolet No. 4, of whom 250 were sit-down strikers, 700 outsiders and 200 "loyal" workers who would like to get out but could not.

3 Apply It

■ Read an article from a recent newspaper for your town. Does it answer the five questions?

■ Does the article have a headline or a byline?

Chapter 7 Review

FOCUS Vocabulary Review

Copy the sentences below on a separate sheet of paper. Use the list of vocabulary terms to fill in the blanks.

suffrage   unemployed
mass production   union

1. A(n) _____ is an organization formed to improve working conditions and pay.

2. A person without a job is _____.

3. _____ is the system of making things in large quantities quickly and easily.

4. _____ is the right to vote.

5. **Test Preparation** A(n) _____ is a business where all workers must join a union.

   A assembly line   c stock market
   B Progressive   D closed shop

FOCUS Comprehension Check

6. Who was Anna Howard Shaw?

7. Why was World War I a difficult time for German Americans?

8. How did Michigan factories help the war effort during World War I?

9. Why did people call early automobiles "horseless carriages"?

10. Why did workers hold a sit-down strike in Flint in 1936–1937?

11. **Critical Thinking** Why do you think the people of Detroit built a large statue of Hazen Pingree?

12. **Critical Thinking** What did Franklin Roosevelt mean when he said, "The only thing we have to fear is fear itself"?

FOCUS Use the Time Line

Use the time line below to answer each question.

13. Did the stock market crash before or after women got the right to vote?

14. In what years did World War I begin and end?

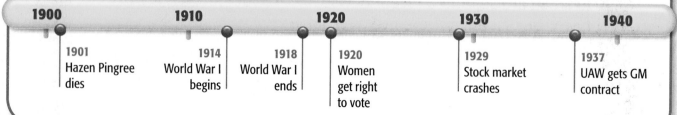

1900	1910	1920	1930	1940
1901 Hazen Pingree dies	1914 World War I begins	1918 World War I ends	1920 Women get right to vote	1929 Stock market crashes	1937 UAW gets GM contract

Use Line and Circle Graphs

Use the line graph to answer the questions.

15. About how many thousands of miles of track were there in Michigan in 1860?

16. In what year were the total miles of track twice as many as in 1880?

Growth of Michigan Railroads, 1860–1900

Miles of Railroad Track (in thousands) vs. *Year*

Source: *Michigan Department of Treasury*

Using Primary Sources

Newspapers

Use the newspaper article below to answer the questions.

The New York Times, January 5, 1937

Sit-Downers Get a Chef

FLINT, Mich., Jan. 4 — An expert chef today took over the task of feeding sit-down strikers in the Fisher Body Plants here as volunteer workers found themselves overtaxed [unable to keep up]. Strike headquarters said 2,100 men were in the plants; General Motors offices said the number was not more than 700.

17. Why do you think the union and GM gave the reporter different estimates of how many strikers were in the factories?

18. How does this newspaper article answer the question *why*?

Hands-on Activity

19. **Make a Poster** The Works Progress Administration hired artists to create murals for city halls, schools, and other buildings across Michigan. These murals often showed the history of a place, or pictured the different people who lived or worked there. Make a sketch of a mural you would put in your school today. You may want to work in a group with other classmates.

Write About History

20. **Narrative** In the years before women got the right to vote, leaders like Anna Howard Shaw made speeches to convince other people to support the idea. Write a newspaper article about an event where Shaw spoke, describing how the audience reacted to her message.

LOG ON For help with the process of writing, visit: www.macmillanmh.com

Chapter 8

Struggles at Home and Abroad

You Are There

MN

"*For anything and everything,
there's stamps you got to use,
The D's and G's are groceries and
I think the T's are shoes.
You have to be an FBI man, to figure
all the clues
And that's the situation,
When you've got the Duration Blues.*"

During World War II people had to change the way they lived. They needed special stamps to buy things. Words from songs like this helped people find humor in their new world In this chapter, read about how people of Michigan changed during and after the second big war.

IA

World War II soldier ▶

Chapter Events	1930	1940	1950

1 1943
Willow Run
factory opens

2 1957
Mackinac
Bridge opens

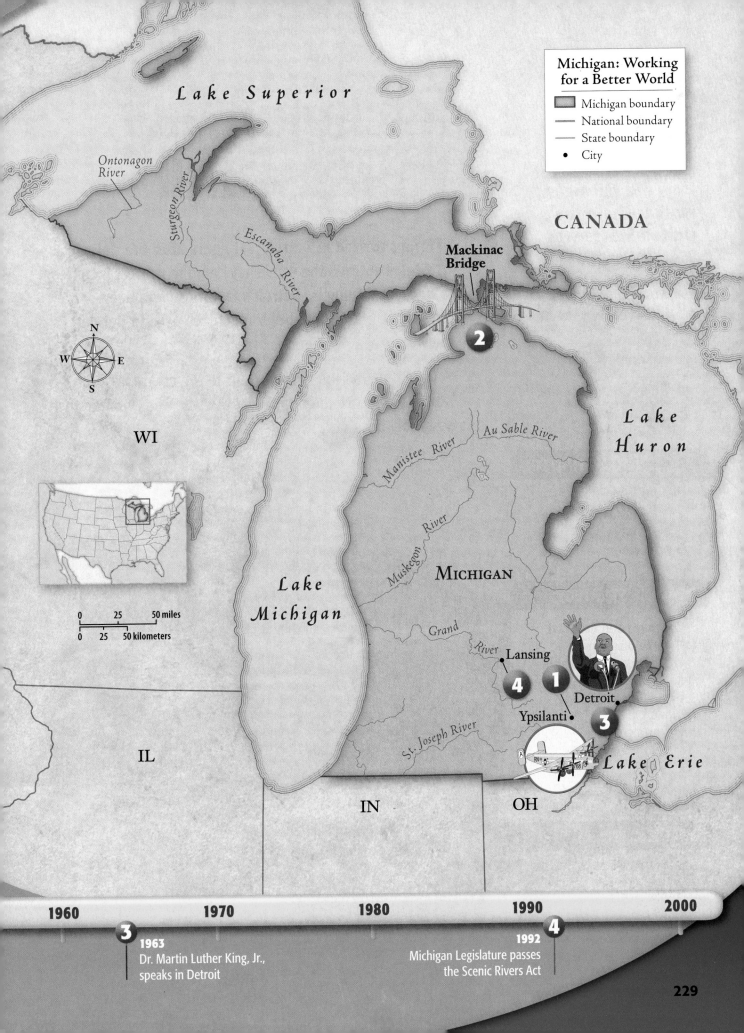

Michigan: Working for a Better World

- Michigan boundary
- National boundary
- State boundary
- • City

CANADA

Lake Superior

Ontonagon River

Sturgeon River

Escanaba River

Mackinac Bridge

2

WI

Lake Huron

Au Sable River

Manistee River

Muskegon River

MICHIGAN

Lake Michigan

Grand River

Lansing

4 **1**

Detroit

Ypsilanti

3

Lake Erie

IL

St. Joseph River

IN

OH

0 25 50 miles
0 25 50 kilometers

N
W   E
S

1960   1970   1980   1990   2000

3
1963
Dr. Martin Luther King, Jr., speaks in Detroit

4
1992
Michigan Legislature passes the Scenic Rivers Act

How did Michigan workers help the United States win World War II?

dictator
arsenal
riveter
scarcity
ration

Root Words The word *dictate* means "to order by power." What do you think a **dictator** is?

Compare and Contrast Use the diagram to compare and contrast the kinds of jobs Michiganians did before and during World War II.

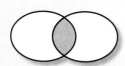

H3.0.1
G4.0.3

Michigan and World War II

Troops arrived in Detroit just hours after the United States entered the war. They came to protect factories, bridges, and tunnels. Detroit's factories were busy building airplanes and other machines used in fighting the war.

This effort was very important to the country. Union leader Walter Reuther said that the war was "won on the assembly lines of Detroit."

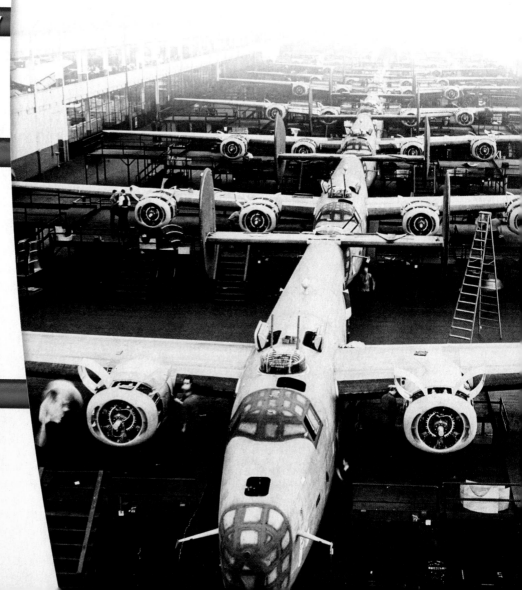

1935   1940   1945

1939
World War II
begins in Europe

1941
United States
enters the war

1945
World War II
ends

Ⓐ World War II Begins

In the 1930s Adolf Hitler ruled Germany. Hitler was a **dictator**— a person who takes over a country and rules alone. In 1939 Germany invaded Poland. This attack started another war.

Different countries took sides. Great Britain, China, the Soviet Union, and France made up the Allies. They fought against the Axis powers of Germany, Italy, and Japan.

The United States stayed out of the war at first. However, in late 1941 Japan attacked the United States. It shot down planes and bombed ships in Pearl Harbor, Hawaii. The United States now decided to enter the war. It joined the Allies.

Michigan's Role

Thousands from Michigan joined the fight. Some joined the army. Others helped from "the home front."

The United States was not ready for war. It did not have many ships, airplanes, or weapons. Michigan's car factories were ordered to build trucks, tanks, and airplanes for the army.

Henry Ford built a plant at Willow Run near Ypsilanti. It was the largest factory in the world. B-24 bomber airplanes were made there.

Michigan was called the "**arsenal** of democracy." An arsenal is a place where weapons are made or stored.

QUICK CHECK How was the work in Michigan auto factories different before the war and during the war?
Compare and Contrast

◀ The U.S.S. *Arizona* (left) and many other ships were sunk in the attack on Pearl Harbor. Plants like Willow Run (far left) made planes and tanks.

This wartime poster expressed the feelings of women workers. ▼

We Can Do It!

▲ Workers could assemble a B-24 in just over one hour. They used rivets like these (right).

ⓑ New Workers for the War

The war helped end the Great Depression. There were now more jobs than workers. More than 600,000 people from Michigan were fighting in the war. There were not enough workers to keep the factories running.

People rushed to cities like Detroit to take the jobs. Many came from the South. There was not enough housing for all of them. Many would sleep in tents or in their cars.

Working Women

More workers were needed, so the government asked women to work in the factories. One poster said, "Do the Job He Left Behind!" Many women had never worked outside the home. Now they felt it was their patriotic duty.

The women workers were nicknamed "Rosie the **Riveter**." A riveter uses rivets, or bolts, to put together pieces of metal. More than 15,000 women worked at the Willow Run factory.

Rationing

Those fighting in the war needed food and supplies. There was a **scarcity**, or shortage, of foods such as butter, sugar, coffee, and beef. There was also a scarcity of supplies such as rubber and gasoline. Scarce things were **rationed**, or limited. Gasoline and shoes were rationed. People used ration stamps to buy things.

Help from Kids

Children did their part by planting "victory gardens." Young people also found old bits of rubber and metal that factories could use.

V Is for Victory!

In 1945 the Allies won the war. Many soldiers returned home. But almost 13,000 soldiers from Michigan had died. Those who made it back took part in celebrations.

Many people in Michigan were now ready for their lives to be normal. Michigan had another problem, though. The war had not stopped discrimination. African Americans continued to face discrimination at home. They were ready for change. Soon changes would come.

✔ **QUICK CHECK** Why did thousands of people move to Detroit during the war?
Draw Conclusions

What You Learned

A When the United States entered World War II in 1941, Michigan's factories switched from making cars to making planes and tanks.

B Many workers found jobs in Michigan's factories during the war. Everyone pitched in for the war effort.

★ Focus Lesson Review

1. **Focus Question** How did Michigan workers help the United States win World War II?

2. **Vocabulary** Write one sentence for each vocabulary word.
arsenal	ration
dictator	scarcity

3. **Economics** How did the beginning of World War II help end the Great Depression?

4. **Critical Thinking Draw Conclusions** Why do you think Michigan factories stopped making cars during the war?

5. **Reading Strategy Compare and Contrast** Use the diagram to compare and contrast life in Michigan before the war and during the war.

6. **Write About THE BIG IDEA** Write about the different ways men, women, and children helped the war effort.

7. **Link to Art** Think of one way Michigan people were asked to help win the war. Design a poster to convince people to help in this way.

On the Home Front During World War II

During World War II those at home pitched in to help win the war. Even children did their part. They grew vegetables in Victory Gardens and collected metal scrap. Of course they still found time for playing games and having fun.

Ration coupons were used to buy many items. ▼

▲ Children collected scrap metal to help the war effort.

Children enjoyed baseball and played with toy soldiers.

▲ Students learn to shop with ration coupons.

Write About It!

Suppose you are living during World War II. Write a diary entry telling something you did to help.

LOG ON ➤ For more about young people in history, visit: www.macmillanmh.com

Use the Internet

The **World Wide Web** is a collection of information on the Internet. The Web has billions of **Web sites**. The Michigan government has its own Web site. So do most Michigan companies, cities, and schools.

You can use a search engine to help you sort through the sites. A search engine is a computer program that finds information on the Web.

VOCABULARY

World Wide Web
Web site
keyword
URL

1 Learn It

- Type a keyword in a search engine to start a search. A **keyword** is a topic word that helps you find information.

- Your search engine will then give you a list of Web sites that match your search. Read the Web sites' titles and descriptions to see if they have information you might want.

- Look at the **URL**, or address, for each site. The last three letters in each URL tell you the kind of site it is.
  Government sites have .gov.
  Private companies have .com.
  Schools use .edu.
  Research groups use .org.

- Don't trust everything you find. Always find at least two sources for your information so you can compare what one site says with what the other says.

2 Try It

Compare the sample search engine pages on page 237 to answer the following questions.

- What are the keywords used in each? Which keywords would you choose to find out more about the war on the home front?

- What is the URL for Michigan National Guard in Search 1?

- Which site would you trust to offer the most reliable information about the Michigan National Guard? Explain your answer.

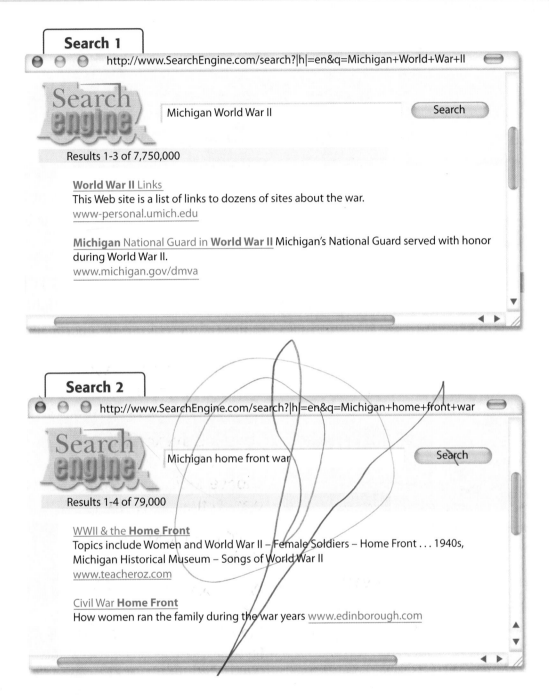

Search 1

http://www.SearchEngine.com/search?|h|=en&q=Michigan+World+War+II

Search engine

Michigan World War II   Search

Results 1-3 of 7,750,000

World War II Links
This Web site is a list of links to dozens of sites about the war.
www-personal.umich.edu

Michigan National Guard in **World War II** Michigan's National Guard served with honor during World War II.
www.michigan.gov/dmva

Search 2

http://www.SearchEngine.com/search?|h|=en&q=Michigan+home+front+war

Search engine

Michigan home front war   Search

Results 1-4 of 79,000

WWII & the **Home Front**
Topics include Women and World War II – Female Soldiers – Home Front . . . 1940s, Michigan Historical Museum – Songs of World War II
www.teacheroz.com

Civil War **Home Front**
How women ran the family during the war years www.edinborough.com

3 Apply It

Think about how you would do your own Internet search to find out about Michigan's products.

- Start with more general keywords such as *Michigan Products*. You may also choose to search for specific products.

- What other keywords will help you find information?

- How would you decide which Web sites have the most reliable information?

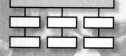

The Struggle for Equal Rights

How did Michiganians work to improve civil rights?

VOCABULARY

racist
segregate
civil rights
boycott
integrate

VOCABULARY STRATEGY

Root Words The word **segregate** comes from a Latin word that means "to set apart." Which word do you think is its opposite?

READING STRATEGY

Identify Main Idea and Details Use the chart below to list the main idea and details for the lesson.

MICHIGAN GLCE

H3.0.1
H3.0.2

Malcolm X lived in Lansing as a child. People burned his house to the ground. They did not want his family to live there. Malcolm grew up to become a leader of African Americans.

Malcolm said, "Human rights are something you were born with. Human rights are your God-given rights. Human rights are the rights that are recognized by all nations of this earth."

1955	1960	1965	1970

1955
Rosa Parks refuses to give up her seat on a Birmingham bus

1963
Martin Luther King, Jr., speaks in Detroit

1967
Civil unrest breaks out in Detroit

Ⓐ Problems in Michigan

During World War II, more than 50,000 African Americans moved to Michigan. They came to find jobs and a better life. But they found hatred, too.

In the 1920s the Ku Klux Klan came to Michigan. The Klan is a **racist** group. A racist believes that a person of one race or group is better than another. Many white people joined the Klan. The Klan hated Catholics and Jews. It hated anyone who was not white. The Klan terrorized African Americans.

Fighting for Our Country

African Americans were **segregated**, or kept separate, from whites just about every place they went. They could not eat in the same restaurants as whites. They could not join the same clubs or go to the same schools as whites.

African Americans had hoped that World War II would change this. After all, many had fought for our country just as white people had. But even the army separated people of different races.

◀ Tensions in Detroit erupted in a riot in 1943.

Detroit

In Detroit black workers were paid less than whites. If a black worker got a better job, white workers sometimes went on strike. This made many people angry. Some wanted to fight back.

▲ Malcolm X

In June 1943 there was a heat wave. A fight broke out between a white man and a black man. It started at Belle Isle Park near Detroit. The fight turned into a riot, a clash that gets out of control. The army was called in to stop the riot. When it was over, 34 people were dead.

QUICK CHECK What were conditions like for African Americans in Michigan during World War II? *Main Idea and Details*

Sign in front of the Sojourner Truth Homes in Detroit ▼

WE WANT WHITE TENANTS IN OUR WHITE COMMUNITY

239

Ⓑ Marching Toward Civil Rights

Many Americans were tired of segregation. Once the war was over, they formed groups. They took a stand against discrimination. These people were part of the **civil rights** movement. Civil rights are the rights of all people to be treated equally under the law. African Americans wanted full civil rights. They wanted to be treated equally.

Bus Boycott

In many cities there was segregation on buses. In 1955 a woman in Montgomery, Alabama, refused to give up her seat. Her name was Rosa Parks. She had been riding on a city bus when a white man asked her to move. She refused and was arrested.

African Americans decided to **boycott** Montgomery city buses. A boycott is refusing to buy or use something. The bus boycott lasted almost a year. It brought much attention to the fight for civil rights. It ended in 1956 when the Supreme Court ruled that segregating buses was against the law.

The Freedom March

Dr. Martin Luther King, Jr., was a leader of the boycott. When it was over, Dr. King spoke out for civil rights throughout the country. In June 1963 he came to Detroit. He led 125,000 people in a "Freedom March." See what King said below. He asked people to take a peaceful stand.

Soon after the march, people of Michigan took a stand. They wanted equal rights for all people. A new constitution was passed.

PRIMARY SOURCES

Dr. Martin Luther King, Jr.

Speech at the Great March on Detroit • June 23, 1963

❝*I have a dream . . . that one day we will recognize the words of Jefferson that 'all men are created equal, that they are endowed by their Creator with certain <u>unalienable</u> Rights, that among these are Life, Liberty, and the pursuit of Happiness.'*❞

---

unalienable cannot be taken away

 Where did the words Dr. King quoted come from? What do you think they mean?

▲ Many businesses were destroyed during the 1967 Detroit civil unrest.

The new constitution created the Michigan Civil Rights Commission. It was the first commission like it in the country. Its job would be to stop discrimination. The Michigan Department of Civil Rights would help the Civil Rights Commission. Its job was to help resolve civil rights problems.

Problems in Detroit

The Civil Rights Commission made some changes. Real change was slow. In 1967 African American families were still kept out of many neighborhoods. African Americans could not eat in many restaurants. Banks would not give them loans. Few could get jobs as teachers or police officers.

On July 23, 1967, new fighting broke out in Detroit. It was another hot night. A fight started between police officers and a group of young African American men. The fighting sparked civil unrest that lasted five days. Again the army came to the city to stop the fighting. Hundreds of homes and businesses were destroyed. When the fighting ended, 43 people had died.

The city tried to find new ways to solve its problems. But many people living in Detroit would not wait. Instead they moved to the suburbs.

✓ **QUICK CHECK** What changes did Michigan make to be sure that all people had equal rights? *Main Idea and Details*

▲ Congressman John Conyers

John Conyers, Jr., was elected to Congress in 1964. Conyers was from Detroit. He represented the people in Detroit and Dearborn. He helped start the Congressional Black Caucus. This group works to pass laws that help African Americans.

Coleman Young

In 1973 Detroit elected its first African American mayor, Coleman Young. He was elected five times as mayor. He changed the city. As mayor, Young worked to **integrate** city jobs. This means he wanted city jobs to be open to people of all races. Now more African Americans worked for the police and in other city jobs.

Young had once worked for labor unions. He knew many businesspeople. He convinced them to stay in Detroit. He also convinced them to put more money into the city.

ⓒ New Leaders

It was hard to see how Detroit's many problems could be solved. The city had almost no money. It seemed that anyone who could was moving out of the city. But some people began working together to solve Detroit's problems.

The Detroit skyline ▼

Coleman Young was the first African American mayor of Detroit. ▶

The city began to get better. New office towers were built. Hotels and sports arenas were also built. African Americans said they now felt they had a voice in how the city was run.

In the 1970s more laws were passed to protect people's rights. More African Americans were able to go to college. They could get good jobs and buy homes. Today the people of Michigan still work to make sure that all Michiganians have the same rights.

✓ **QUICK CHECK** What are some of the changes Coleman Young made as mayor of Detroit? *Compare and Contrast*

What You Learned

A African Americans came to Michigan for better jobs and a better life, but they faced discrimination and violence.

B In the 1950s and 1960s, the civil rights movement worked for change through boycotts and marches. Progress was slow. Detroit had more civil unrest in 1967.

C In 1973, Coleman Young became mayor of Detroit and brought many changes.

★ Focus Lesson Review

1. **Focus Question** How did Michiganians work to improve civil rights?

2. **Vocabulary** Write one sentence for each vocabulary term.
   civil rights   **racist**
   integrate   **segregate**

3. **Government** Give an example of how Michigan's government leaders worked to end discrimination.

4. **Critical Thinking** **Draw Conclusions** Why might many African Americans in Detroit have thought it was a good sign when Coleman Young was elected mayor?

5. **Reading Strategy** **Identify Main Idea and Details** Reread page 239. Use the chart to write the main idea and details for the section.

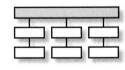

6. **Write About** THE **BiG IDEA** What are some peaceful ways people worked to solve conflicts during the 1950s and 1960s?

7. **Link to Art** Research leaders of the civil rights movement. Then make a poster that tells about one or more of them.

Rosa Parks 1913–2005

Rosa Parks was born in Tuskegee, Alabama. "I remember," she said, "going to sleep as a girl hearing the Klan ride at night and . . . being afraid the house would burn down."

When Rosa grew up, she wanted to make the lives of African Americans better. She joined the NAACP (the National Association for the Advancement of Colored People). She began in small ways to fight segregation. She would take the stairs. That way she would not have to take the "blacks only" elevator. She would often walk instead of sitting on a segregated bus.

On December 1, 1955, Rosa decided enough was enough. She took the bus and was asked to give up her seat. She refused.

> **❝*He said 'I'll have you arrested.' And I told him he could do that.*❞**

Rosa Parks inspired others to take a stand. Changes started to happen. Segregation on buses was stopped. Rosa Parks moved to Detroit in 1957.

 Write About It! **How did Rosa Parks show courage?**

LOG ON For more about biographies, visit: www.macmillanmh.com

The Life of Rosa Parks

1900	1920	1940	1960	1980	2000	2020

1913
Born in Tuskegee, Alabama

1955
Refuses to give up bus seat in Montgomery, Alabama

1999
Receives Congressional Gold Medal

2005
Dies in Detroit

P3.1.1
P3.3.1
P4.2.1
P4.2.2

Being Informed

Shawn noticed that the ash trees in one part of town seemed to be dying. He had seen a TV program about how an insect called the Emerald Ash Borer was killing Michigan trees. He asked his science teacher to help him find more information. He wondered if his town was aware of the problem. Shawn thought his town should give information to homeowners about what they could do to help.

Read these steps to learn how to become informed about this or other issues.

Build Citizenship

1. **Pick a subject** or an issue that interests you.

2. **Get information** from books, newspaper articles, or the Internet.

3. **Examine information.** Decide if you need more information.

4. **Apply your knowledge.** Look for ways to share what you have learned.

Think About It

1. How did Shawn first learn about this issue?

2. What did Shawn do to become informed?

3. What are some ways to find out about the issues in your community?

4. What are some ways that Shawn might share what he has learned with others?

Write About It!

List ways you could become more informed about an issue in Michigan.

Michigan Today

The Mackinac Bridge is more than four miles long. Some drivers are afraid to drive across it. They are called "timmies" (timid people). The Bridge Authority helps timmies by having someone drive their car across the bridge for them!

VOCABULARY

suspension bridge
embargo
renewable resource
nonrenewable resource
development
recycle

VOCABULARY STRATEGY

Word Origins The word *suspend* means "to attach by hanging." What do you think a **suspension bridge** is?

READING STRATEGY

Summarize Use the chart below to summarize what the lesson says about issues facing Michigan today.

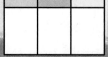

A Getting Around Michigan

Cars have always been important to Michigan. The state has been a leader in building modern roads. In the 1950s new highways made driving across Michigan fast and easy.

MICHIGAN GLCE

H3.0.1	G5.0.1
G4.0.1	G5.0.2
G4.0.3	

1957
Mackinac Bridge
opens

1973
OPEC oil
embargo

1976
Michigan voters
pass the Beverage
Container Act

2002
Jennifer Granholm
elected Michigan's first
woman governor

There was no highway to connect the Upper and Lower Peninsulas. People had to take a ferry across the Straits of Mackinac. It took an hour.

In 1954 about 3,500 workers began building the Mackinac Bridge. It is a **suspension bridge**, held up by cables hung from towers. The bridge opened in 1957. Now it took less time to go from one peninsula to the other.

Changing Times for Carmakers

In 1973 there was a war between Israel and Egypt. This war would have a big impact on Michigan. The Organization of the Petroleum Exporting Countries (OPEC) sided with Egypt. The United States backed Israel. OPEC started an oil **embargo**. It refused to sell oil to the United States.

Without oil from OPEC, the United States faced a gas shortage. The price of gas rose. People began buying small cars that used less gas. Michigan made mostly big cars. Japan made mostly small cars. More people bought Japanese cars. Sales of cars made in Michigan fell. By 1974 many people in Michigan were out of work.

Michigan's car companies now work with companies in other countries. Today some Japanese car companies even make cars in Michigan.

QUICK CHECK What problems did the 1973 oil embargo cause in Michigan? *Summarize*

◄ The cables that hold up the Mackinac Bridge contain 42,000 miles of wire and weigh almost 12,000 tons.

247

The Ontonagon River (left) is one of many rivers protected by the Scenic Rivers Act. Recycling (above) also helps protect the environment.

ⓑ Protecting Natural Resources

Michigan is rich in natural resources. Some, like trees, are **renewable resources**. New trees can grow and take the place of old trees. Oil is a **nonrenewable resource**. Once oil is used, it is gone. Most cars run on gasoline, which is made from oil. Today carmakers try to make cars that use less gas or no gas at all.

Protecting Resources

Factories in Michigan sometimes cause pollution. Putting waste into lakes and rivers harms the things that live there. In addition, new **developments** use up open land. A development is a group of houses and buildings in the same place.

The people of Michigan have decided to protect the water, air, and open land. The Scenic Rivers Act of 1992 protects rivers. It stopped development on more than 500 miles of rivers. In 2002 Michigan also said that no one could drill for oil under the Great Lakes.

One way to protect resources is to **recycle**. To recycle means to reuse items instead of throwing them away. There is less waste if people recycle. In 1976 Michigan passed the Beverage Container Act. People have to pay an extra 10 cents for goods in cans or bottles. The 10 cents is returned when people return the containers. The containers are then recycled.

Working Together

Michigan has the eighth-largest population of all of the states. There are over 10 million people in Michigan. It takes a lot of resources to meet the needs of so many people. The people of Michigan do not want to run out of their resources.

In 2004 Governor Jennifer Granholm talked about what's next for Michigan. She said, "The road to a healthy people in a healthy land merges with the road to good jobs. Let it be said that we did it together."

QUICK CHECK How does the Michigan Beverage Container Act protect the environment?
Cause and Effect

What You Learned

A In 1957 workers completed the Mackinac Bridge connecting the Upper and Lower Peninsulas. A 1973 oil embargo drove up the price of gas, causing the Michigan auto industry to suffer.

B Michigan has passed many laws to protect its environment and preserve natural resources.

▲ The Mackinac Bridge is a popular symbol of Michigan.

Focus Lesson Review

1. **Focus Question** How does Michigan protect its natural resources?

2. **Vocabulary** Write one sentence for each vocabulary term.
   development   nonrenewable resource
   embargo   recycle

3. **Geography** Why did Michigan's geography make building the Mackinac Bridge important?

4. **Critical Thinking** **Analyze** What advice would you give the auto industry as it looks toward the future?

5. **Reading Strategy** **Summarize** Reread the section on page 246 called "Getting Around Michigan." Then use the chart to summarize the section.

6. **Write About** THE **BiG IDEA** Write about how people in your town protect the environment.

7. **Link to Art** Create a poster showing ways Michigan can protect its resources.

Write a sentence using each term.

1. scarcity

2. home front

3. nonviolence

4. recycle

5. **Test Preparation** A law that says a certain racial group must attend separate schools is an example of _____.

   A **civil rights**
   B **integration**
   C **segregation**
   D **nonviolence**

6. After which event did the United States enter World War II?

7. How did Michigan earn the nickname "arsenal of democracy"?

8. How did rationing help the war effort?

9. What did the Scenic Rivers Act do?

10. **Critical Thinking** Why were many Detroit autoworkers out of work in 1974?

11. **Critical Thinking** Explain how people at home helped the United States win the war.

12. **Critical Thinking** Explain why it is important to use natural resources wisely.

Use the time line below to answer each question.

13. Did the United States enter World War II before or after the Willow Run plant opened?

14. How many years after the U.S. Supreme Court ruling on bus segregation did Coleman Young become mayor of Detroit?

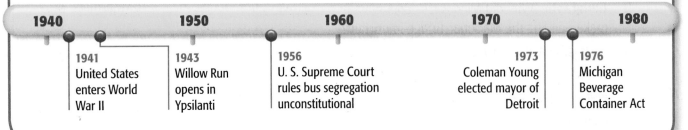

| 1940 | 1950 | 1960 | 1970 | 1980 |

1941
United States
enters World
War II

1943
Willow Run
opens in
Ypsilanti

1956
U. S. Supreme Court
rules bus segregation
unconstitutional

1973
Coleman Young
elected mayor of
Detroit

1976
Michigan
Beverage
Container Act

Skills Check

Use the Internet

Write a complete sentence to answer each question below.

15. What is a search engine?

16. Suppose you wanted to find the entire speech that Dr. King gave in Detroit in June 1963. What keywords could you use to help you find it on the Internet?

17. Which Web site would you trust most to give you information about Michigan's laws, one that ends in .com, or one that ends in .gov? Why?

18. Why should you always try to find two sources for the information you need?

Using Primary Sources

Speeches

Use the excerpt below to answer the questions.

> **❝***I have a dream . . . that one day we will recognize the words of Jefferson that 'all men are created equal, that they are endowed by their Creator with certain unalienable Rights, that among these are Life, Liberty, and the pursuit of Happiness.'***❞**

Dr. Martin Luther King, Jr.

19. Why is this speech excerpt a primary source?

20. What rights does Dr. King mention in his speech?

Hands-on Activity

21. **Create a Display** Do research to find out which planes were built at Willow Run. Find or draw pictures of them. Label the pictures and make a display.

Write About History

22. **Narrative** Write a short story that tells what it is like to be a child during World War II. Include details that tell how the war has affected your everyday life.

LOG ON For help with the process of writing, visit: www.macmillanmh.com

Comprehension and Critical Thinking Check

Write one or more sentences to answer each question.

1. What were some of the things the **Progressives** worked for?

2. What kinds of **reforms** did Hazen Pingree work for when he was mayor of Detroit?

3. What important change did the Nineteenth **Amendment** make?

4. Describe how an **assembly line** works.

5. How did **mass production** help Henry Ford?

6. What is a **union**?

7. How did Michigan contribute to building the **arsenal** the United States used to fight in World War II?

8. What effect did the 1973 oil **embargo** have on life in the United States?

9. **Critical Thinking** How did President Roosevelt create more jobs during the **Great Depression**?

10. **Critical Thinking** Why is it important to **recycle**?

Reading Skills Check

Compare and Contrast

Copy this graphic organizer. Recall what you have read in this unit about the civil rights movement. Use the graphic organizer to help you compare and contrast life for African Americans before and after (through the 1970s) the civil rights movement.

11. What were some examples of segregation before the civil rights movement?

12. What changes did the civil rights movement bring to Michigan?

13. How do you decide what information to include in each section?

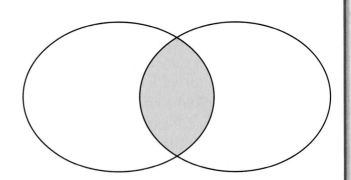

Read the passage and use it with what you know to answer the questions.

At the end of World War I, people in the United States began spending more and more money buying shares in companies, called stocks, because they thought stocks were a quick way to get rich. Then the value of the shares began to fall and people panicked. Soon everyone wanted to sell their shares, and no one wanted to buy. Thousands of Americans lost their entire savings. This "crash" of the stock market caused a worldwide depression known as the Great Depression.

During the Great Depression, many banks went out of business. Factories closed and many people lost their jobs. In Detroit almost half of all workers were without jobs. It wasn't until the United States entered World War II that there were plenty of jobs once again.

14. Factories probably closed during the Great Depression because

  A people were making things at home.

  B people couldn't afford to buy the things the factories made.

  C people were buying goods from Europe.

  D the workers were all on strike.

15. Which is the BEST reason jobs became plentiful during World War II?

  A People began buying stocks again.

  B Europe was buying our goods.

  C The President announced the New Deal.

  D Factories began making things needed for the war.

Write About History

16. **Descriptive** Think about what life was like in cities like Detroit in the 1890s. Suppose that you had been a Progressive reformer. Write a paragraph describing a situation that you would like to change to help the daily lives of citizens.

17. **Expository** Write a paragraph about the life of Henry Ford. Remember to include a main idea and details. You may need to use the school library or the Internet to do more research.

18. **Letter** Suppose you are working in the Willow Run factory in 1943. Write a letter to a cousin in another state that will convince her to move to Michigan to find work.

LOG ON For help with the process of writing, visit: www.macmillanmh.com

Unit 4

REVIEW
THE BIG IDEA

How do people solve conflicts?

Write About the Big Idea

A Report

Think about the conflicts you read about in Unit 4. Then, complete the graphic organizer. List some of the conflicts and then show how each was solved.

Use information from your graphic organizer and other sources to write a report of several paragraphs. In your report you will explain how Michigan people solved a conflict.

Group	Conflict	Solution
1. Supporters of women's rights	1. Wanted women to have the right to vote.	1. Passage of the 19th Amendment
2.	2.	2.
3.	3.	3.

Write a Report

1. Plan
- Choose one conflict and solution to write about.
- Use the Internet to find more information about your topic. Do a Web search. Remember that your purpose is to give information.

2. Write a First Draft
- In your first paragraph, introduce your topic.
- Add paragraphs that explain what the conflict was about and what people did to solve it.
- In your final paragraph, write a conclusion.

3. Revise and Proofread
- Read your report. Be sure your sentences and paragraphs all tell about your topic.
- Check to see that your first paragraph makes a good introduction. Edit your final paragraph to make a good summary of your reasons.
- Proofread your report. Did you indent all your paragraphs?
- Rewrite your report neatly before handing it in to your teacher.

ACTIVITY

Speak About the Big Idea

Make a Presentation

Choose a person you read about in Unit 4. Think about that person's contribution to Michigan. The person may have contributed to reforms for people who live and work in Michigan.

Prepare Explain what your chosen person contributed to Michigan. Give details and examples. In your presentation, you might want to dress in clothing similar to what the person would have worn. Use information from Unit 4, your graphic organizer, and any information you learned from your research.

Present Make a presentation about this person, or you might role-play this person dressed in period clothing. Explain his or her contribution to solving conflicts in Michigan.

For help with the Big Idea activity, visit:
www.macmillanmh.com

Read More About the Big Idea

Martin Luther King, Jr.: A Man with a Dream

Explore this Leveled Reader to learn about the life and struggles of one of the most important figures of the civil rights movement.

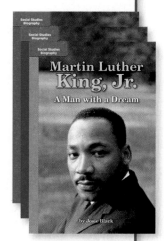

Bright Ideas: Inventions that Changed History

Read this Leveled Reader to discover important inventions throughout history.

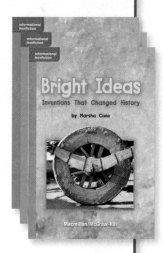

Rosa Parks: From the Back of the Bus to the Front of a Movement

by Camilla Wilson Read the story of the woman whose courageous action changed the country.

How Michigan Works

"Let it be such work that our descendants will thank us . . . and that men will say as they look upon the labor and wrought substance: SEE THIS, our fathers did for us."

— John Ruskin (1819–1900), writer
As quoted by Dr. David B. Steinman, Mackinac Bridge Designer

How do people in our state meet their needs?

All people have needs. In Unit 5 you'll read about the ways people in our state do business to meet these needs. People also need to set up governments. You will read about the things we value as Americans, and the ways governments work.

Copy the graphic organizer below. As you read, look for the ways Michigan meets its economic and government needs. Then fill in the graphic organizer. The first entries have been done for you.

Economy	Government
1. Free enterprise 2. 3. 4.	1. Our nation's government 2. 3.

◄ A bridge worker on the Mackinac Bridge

People Who Made a Difference

Will Keith Kellogg
1860–1951

Will Keith Kellogg and his brother John began the cereal industry in Michigan. Will went on to do important charity work. (page 277)

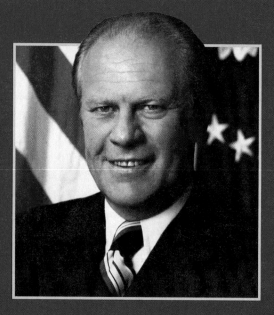

Gerald Ford
1913–2006

Gerald R. Ford grew up in Grand Rapids and served 13 straight terms in the U.S. House of Representatives. He became the President of the United States in 1974. (page 290)

| 1780 | 1800 | 1820 | 1840 | 1860 | 1880 |

1787
U.S. Constitution written

1835
Michigan's first state constitution written

LOG ON For more biographies, visit:
www.macmillanmh.com

Shelley Goodman Taub
1939–

Once an elementary school teacher, Shelley Goodman Taub was elected to the Michigan legislature in 2002. She helped pass a bill to allow children with asthma to bring their medicine to school. (page 306)

Jennifer Granholm
1959–

Jennifer Granholm was elected Michigan's governor in 2002. Previously she served as the state attorney general, and she was the first woman to hold both of these offices. (page 309)

1963
Michigan's current state constitution written

1900   1920   1940   1960   1980   2000

1894
Will and John Kellogg invent a new breakfast cereal

1974
Gerald Ford of Michigan becomes 38th U.S. President

2002
Jennifer Granholm elected; Shelley Goodman Taub elected

PURPLE MOUNTAIN MAJESTIES

Selection from **Purple Mountain Majesties**
by Barbara Younger

When Katharine Lee Bates took a train across America, she was so inspired by the beautiful country that she wrote a poem. Purple Mountain Majesties *is about how she came to write that poem. Today many people sing the words to her poem to show how proud they are to be American.*

"Pikes Peak or bust," Katharine noted in her diary that evening. "Most glorious scenery I ever beheld." Into her notebook she penciled the lines of poetry that had come to her that day. *O beautiful for **halcyon** skies/For amber waves of grain./ For purple mountain majesties/Above the **enameled** plain! America! America! God shed his grace on thee. . . .*

halcyon (HAL see uhn) calm, peaceful

enameled (ee NAM eld) covered with beautiful colors

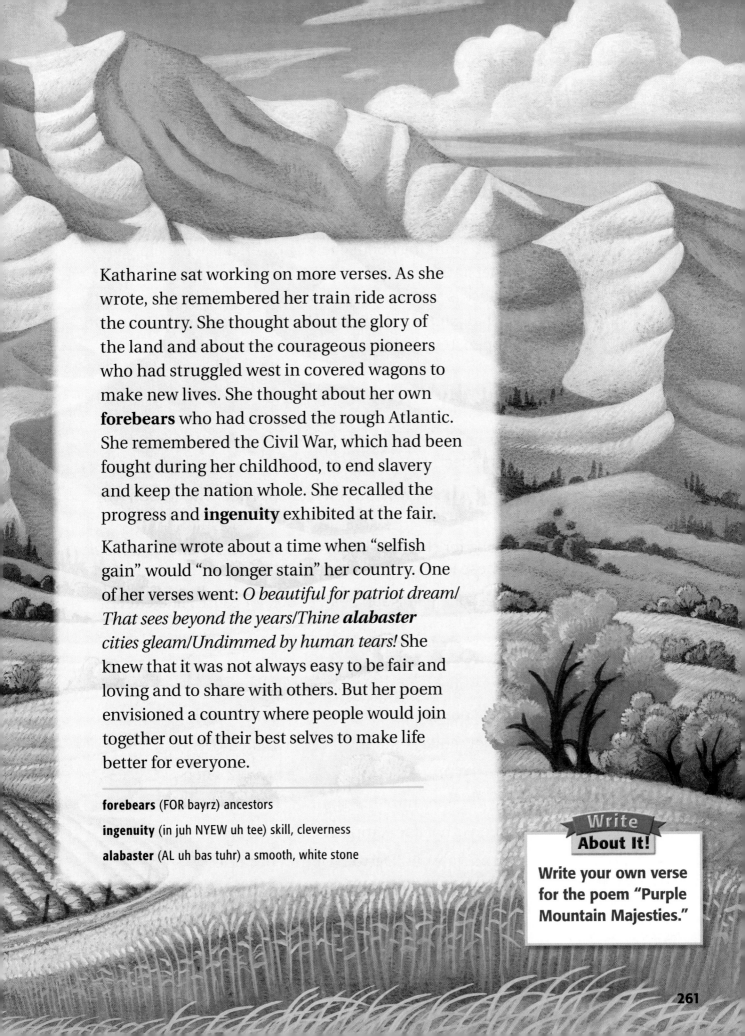

Katharine sat working on more verses. As she wrote, she remembered her train ride across the country. She thought about the glory of the land and about the courageous pioneers who had struggled west in covered wagons to make new lives. She thought about her own **forebears** who had crossed the rough Atlantic. She remembered the Civil War, which had been fought during her childhood, to end slavery and keep the nation whole. She recalled the progress and **ingenuity** exhibited at the fair.

Katharine wrote about a time when "selfish gain" would "no longer stain" her country. One of her verses went: *O beautiful for patriot dream/ That sees beyond the years/Thine **alabaster** cities gleam/Undimmed by human tears!* She knew that it was not always easy to be fair and loving and to share with others. But her poem envisioned a country where people would join together out of their best selves to make life better for everyone.

---

forebears (FOR bayrz) ancestors

ingenuity (in juh NYEW uh tee) skill, cleverness

alabaster (AL uh bas tuhr) a smooth, white stone

Write About It!

Write your own verse for the poem "Purple Mountain Majesties."

Identify Cause and Effect:
Michigan and the Auto Industry

In this unit you will read about Michigan's economy today. Thinking about causes and effects will help you understand how and why Michigan's economy has changed. A cause is an event that makes something happen. An effect is what happens. When one thing causes another thing to happen, they have a cause-and-effect relationship.

1 Learn It

- As you read, ask what happened. *What happened* is an effect.

- Ask yourself *why* this effect happened. The reason *why* is a cause.

- Look for clue words such as *because, so,* and *as a result.* These words signal causes and effects.

- Read the paragraph below. Look for causes and effects.

Cause
This sentence tells why Olds moved his plant to Michigan. It is a cause.

Effect
The word *so* helps you know this is an effect.

Effect
This tells what happened as a result of becoming the automotive center of the world. This is an effect.

Samuel L. Smith promised to loan Ransom Olds money to expand his automobile company if Olds would move his factory to Detroit, so Olds agreed. Then Henry Ford built his plant in Detroit, too. Soon other car companies opened factories in and around Detroit. Detroit became the automotive center of the world. As a result Detroit came to be known as the Motor City.

Try It

Copy the chart below. Then complete the chart with causes and effects from the paragraph on page 262.

CAUSE AND EFFECT CHART

Smith promised to loan Olds money.	▶	Olds agreed and moved to Detroit.
	▶	
	▶	
	▶	
	▶	

What questions help you identify cause and effect?

Apply It

■ Review the steps for understanding cause and effect in Learn It.

■ Read the paragraphs below. Then use a chart to show the causes and effects.

In 1973 the OPEC nations started an oil embargo. Without OPEC oil, the United States had a gasoline shortage. As a result gas prices soared. People began buying smaller cars that used less gas. Detroit produced mostly big cars, but Japanese companies made small cars. As more people bought Japanese cars, Michigan auto companies suffered. Because the Detroit companies were not selling enough cars, they had to lay off workers. By 1974 one in four Detroit autoworkers was out of work.

Chapter 9

Michigan's Economics

You Are There

"My own dream for a hit factory was shaped by principles I learned on the . . . assembly line. . . . I wanted a place where a kid off the street could walk in one door an unknown and come out another a recording artist—a star."

Berry Gordy was a Detroit autoworker. Then he became a songwriter. He started Motown Records in Detroit in 1959.

Motown made hit records by artists like Stevie Wonder, Diana Ross, and the Jackson Five. It became a successful business. In this chapter you will learn how businesses work. You will learn how they help Michigan's economy grow.

Berry Gordy ▶

MN

IA

1 Pleasantview School

2 Migrant Worker

Lake Superior

Marquette•

Sault Ste. Marie•

CANADA

N
W · E
S

0 25 50 miles
0 25 50 kilometers

WI

Escanaba•

Traverse
City•

Au Sable River

*Manistee
River*

Lake
Michigan

*Muskegon
River*

Lake
Huron

Saginaw
4

•Flint

*Grand
River*

★Lansing

3

1

Eastpointe•

2

•Battle Creek

St. Joseph River

Detroit•

•Tecumseh

Lake Erie

IL

**Working in
Michigan**

Van Buren county
National boundary
State boundary
★ State capital
• Other city

3 **Cereal plant**

4 **Japanese Cultural Center**

265

Minding a Business

What things do people think about when they start a business?

VOCABULARY

> free enterprise
> market economy
> entrepreneur
> human capital
> capital resources
> investor
> opportunity cost

VOCABULARY STRATEGY

Word Origins Consume means "to use up." What do you think a **consumer** is?

READING STRATEGY

Cause and Effect Copy the chart below. Fill it in with causes and effects in the lesson.

MICHIGAN GLCE

E1.0.1
E1.0.2
E1.0.4

The students in Mrs. Cardillo's class wanted to make something special to sell at this year's school craft show. They came up with an idea for a product that no one else had. But that was just the first step. They had to make it and sell it. They worked hard. They had fun and they also learned a lot about owning a business.

Mrs. Cardillo and students at Pleasantview School in Eastpointe, Michigan ▼

Ⓐ Starting a Business

In the United States, anyone can run a business. The business has to be allowed by law. We call this right the **free enterprise** system.

A business that makes or sells goods is a producer. A business that does a service for people is a producer, too. The owners of a business can choose what to make and sell. They can choose the service they want to do.

Consumers make choices, too. Consumers are people who buy a product or a service. They decide what to buy and how much they will pay. The free enterprise system is also called a **market economy**.

Choosing the Product

Mrs. Cardillo's class in Eastpointe decided they wanted to start a business. They would become **entrepreneurs** (ahn truh pruh NURZ). Entrepreneurs are people who start and run their own businesses.

Each year the school had a crafts show. The class decided to make something to sell at the crafts show.

Now the class needed an idea for what to make. It had to be something people would buy. It had to be something that didn't cost much to make.

▲ The class held a contest to design the best cover for their cookbook.

The class had many ideas. They finally decided to make a cookbook. "We didn't think anyone else would be selling cookbooks," said Kirk Heilman. That was important, because the class wanted to make something no other class would be selling. Their cookbook would be special.

✔ **QUICK CHECK** Why did the class decide to make a cookbook? *Cause and Effect*

Students typed each recipe. (left)
They made copies of the pages (above)
and put the pages in order.

B Producing a Product

The class soon learned that producing a product takes many resources. First they needed people, or **human capital**. Students and their ideas were the human capital. Next the class needed machines to make the product. They used computers, printers, and a copy machine for **capital resources**.

The class needed money, too. Where would they get the money to buy paper and machines?

Many companies borrow money to get started. **Investors** are people who give money to a company. They expect to get some money back in return.

The investor for the cookbook was the school principal. She donated paper for the cookbooks. She let the class use the school copy machine. She loaned the students money. Then they could buy what they needed to make the books. That money had to be paid back.

Making the Cookbooks

The students got to work. First they had to get recipes. They asked their families for their best recipes. They asked their friends, too. Soon they had a good collection, with recipes like "Mom's Super Chicken Soup," "Kirk's Favorite Cake," and "Grandpa's Sunday Waffles."

▲ The covers were covered with plastic to strengthen them. Each set of pages got a cover.

▲ Other students used a special machine to bind the pages into a book.

Next the students typed the recipes. They made sure there were no mistakes. Finally they printed them.

Then the class put the recipes in order. The first section had recipes with fish. The next section had meat. The third section had soups. The last section had desserts.

Students made 50 copies of each page. They put the pages in order. Then they made an assembly line to make the books quickly.

Selling the Product

The cookbooks were finished! The class made ads so people would know about it. Their posters had lines like "A cookbook your Mom must have." They made announcements from the school office into all the classrooms. They wanted lots of people to know about their product.

Now the class had to price the books. They had to make enough money to pay the principal back. But they had to make a profit, too. A profit is the money left after all the costs are paid. People would not buy the books if the price was too high. The class decided to ask $3 for each book.

The class knew there would be many things for sale. Customers could not buy everything. They would have to make trade-offs. The value of what a person gives up to buy something else is called the **opportunity cost**. Imagine that a person has to choose between a cookbook and a pen. If the person buys the cookbook, and not the pen, the pen is the opportunity cost.

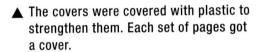

QUICK CHECK What things did students think about when they decided on the price for their cookbook? *Summarize*

C Business Success

Finally it was time for the crafts show. Mrs. Cardillo's class set up a booth near the gym door. It was the first thing people saw when they arrived.

By the last day of the crafts show, they sold every book! The class took more orders. Later they printed more books. In all, the class sold 75 cookbooks.

They paid back the principal. They made a profit of more than $120.

The class voted how to use the money. They wanted to help pay for a class field trip. Kiarra McFerrin was happy with the cookbook project. "It was a very good way to earn money. It also taught me that for a business to succeed, people have to work together."

✓ **QUICK CHECK** What is one reason the cookbook sale was a success?
Cause and Effect

▲ Students told customers why they should buy the cookbook.

What You Learned

Ⓐ In a free enterprise system, people can start their own businesses.

Ⓑ Producing a product uses different kinds of resources and involves manufacturing.

Ⓒ A successful business meets expenses and makes a profit.

★ Focus Lesson Review

1. **Focus Question** What things do people think about when they start a business?

2. **Vocabulary** Write one sentence for each vocabulary term.
   entrepreneur   human capital
   free enterprise

3. **Economics** What are some of the choices that Mrs. Cardillo's class had to make in starting their business?

4. **Critical Thinking** **Draw Conclusions** How do consumers influence what producers charge for a product?

5. **Reading Strategy** **Cause and Effect** Use the chart to show 3 reasons the cookbook business was a success.

6. **Write About** **THE BIG IDEA** To create their product, the class needed human resources, natural resources, and capital resources. How did students meet each of these needs?

7. **Link to Math** The students charged $3 for one cookbook and $5 for two. How much did someone who bought two cookbooks save?

Make Decisions

A **decision** is a choice about what to do. In Lesson 1 you read about how a class made business decisions. You make decisions as a consumer, too. One important decision consumers may make is whether to use **incentives**, or a reduced, or sale, price of the item.

1 Learn It

- To make a decision, know your goal. Your goal is what you want to happen.

- Identify your **options**, or choices. For any decision, you will have at least two choices.

- Predict the results of each option.

- Choose the option that will help you reach your goal.

2 Try It

Read the paragraph at the top right. Then answer the questions.

- What might Janelle's goal be?

- What are her options? Does she have other options?

- What might happen if Janelle buys the jacket on sale?

- What else should Janelle think about before deciding?

Janelle wants to buy a jacket that costs $60. She also needs money for a class trip next week. Janelle has a decision to make. She can pay cash for the jacket, or she can wait until the jacket is on sale.

If she buys the jacket when it is on sale, she will have more cash for the trip. However, if Janelle waits until the jacket goes on sale, the store may no longer have any jackets left in her size or in the color she wants.

3 Apply It

- Think of a decision you have made recently. Then use the steps in Learn It to tell about your options.

A Living from the Land

How does Michigan use its natural resources to provide goods and services?

In 1900 about one in three people in Michigan worked on a farm. Today about one person in fifty works on a farm. Agriculture is still important here. About one fourth of Michigan's land is farmed.

Michigan is a top producer of some fruits and vegetables. They grow blueberries and apples. They grow cucumbers, onions, and soybeans, too. Michigan also grows more cherries than any other state.

VOCABULARY

specialize
migrant worker
service industry

VOCABULARY STRATEGY

Word Origins The word *service* has the same origin as *serve* and *servant*. What kind of businesses do you think are in the **service industry**?

READING STRATEGY

Identify Main Idea and Details Use the chart to identify the main idea and details of the lesson.

MICHIGAN GLCE

E1.0.1
E1.0.3
E1.0.5
E2.0.1

Ⓐ Michigan Agriculture

One hundred years ago, most farms in Michigan were small family farms. They grew only what the family needed. Today most farms **specialize**. That means they grow one or two crops.

Crops grown here are sold to other states. For example, blueberries grown in Michigan are sold in Georgia. Georgia is a leading producer of peanuts. Many of Georgia's peanuts are sold here in Michigan.

▼ Michigan's natural resources make it a leading state for agriculture.

Migrant Workers

Michigan farmers depend on about 50,000 migrant and seasonal workers to harvest the crops. **Migrant workers** move from place to place for jobs. They plant or harvest crops. Many of these workers are Mexican or Mexican American.

Some former migrants have bought farms of their own. They live in Michigan year round. Others keep working as seasonal workers. The workers harvest crops in the South in the winter. Then they return to Michigan in the spring.

✓ **QUICK CHECK** How has farming in Michigan changed in the last 100 years?
Main Idea and Details

▲ Today Michigan protects its lumber industry by replanting its forests.

Ⓑ Using Resources

You know that lumber was once an important industry in Michigan. Michigan trees became a valuable resource because there was a scarcity of lumber. Scarcity means a shortage.

The lumber industry grew fast during the 1800s. Michigan's forests were cut down. The wood was used to build towns in the Midwest and West. New trees were not planted. Michigan's forests almost disappeared.

Mining was important, too. Michigan mines had metals. There was copper, iron, gold, and silver. They also had gypsum, slate, salt, coal, and limestone.

Today, Michigan is still a big producer of minerals. About 20,000 people work in mining. These workers produce iron ore, cement, and sand. They also produce gravel and crushed stone.

Logging Makes a Comeback

In the mid-1900s people in Michigan began to plant the forests again. Now, logging in Michigan is a strong industry again. Much of the wood from the forests is made into paper.

Some people recycle newspapers and phone books. To recycle paper helps use less wood from Michigan forests.

Serving Visitors

Michigan has many natural resources. People come to sail on the rivers and lakes. They come to walk in the forests. Tourism is the business of taking care of people who visit Michigan. It makes jobs for many Michigan people.

Tourism is a **service industry**. It means people take care of other people. People work at hotels and campgrounds. They work at camping stores and ski lodges. They rent out boats and cars. They have jobs as tour guides. They own bait shops, too. Tourism is Michigan's second-largest industry.

✓ **QUICK CHECK** Why are Michigan's forests important to the tourist industry?
Draw Conclusions

What You Learned

A Michigan's agriculture is big business. Migrant workers help to grow and harvest many of Michigan's crops.

B Mining and lumber remain important industries in Michigan. Tourism is the second-leading industry in the state.

▲ **Michigan's lakes and rivers attract many tourists.**

★ Focus Lesson Review

1. **Focus Question** How does Michigan use its natural resources to provide goods and services?

2. **Vocabulary** Write one sentence for each vocabulary term.
   **migrant worker   specialize
   service industry**

3. **Geography** What part of Michigan produces lumber?

4. **Critical Thinking Compare and Contrast** How is farming in Michigan today different from the way it was in the past?

5. **Reading Strategy Identify Main Idea and Details** Use the chart to identify main idea and details about the timber industry.

6. **Write About THE BIG IDEA** If you could work with Michigan's natural resources, what kind of job would you like to do?

7. **Link to Language Arts** Tourism includes visits to museums, concerts, and sports stadiums. Write a paragraph telling a story of your experience at one of these places. Include details that describe the place or event.

Manufacturing in Michigan

What goods do Michigan workers produce?

VOCABULARY

competition
corporation
robotics
microtechnology
biotechnology

VOCABULARY STRATEGY

Prefixes The prefix **micro-** means "very small." A microscope is used to examine very small things. What do you think **microtechnology** is?

READING STRATEGY

Summarize Use the chart below to summarize the information in the lesson.

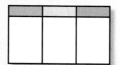

MICHIGAN GLCE

E1.0.5
E3.0.1

What is made in Michigan? Michigan companies make cars and cereal. They make desks and chairs. They make vacuum cleaners, too. For a long time, many jobs came from the auto industry. Cars are still important. But Michigan is developing new industries, too. Let's take a look at what Michigan makes.

Many breakfast cereals are manufactured in Michigan. ▼

Ⓐ Made in Michigan

Michigan people work in farming and mining. They also work in logging and tourism. Of course, these are not the only kinds of jobs that Michigan has. One in every six working people in Michigan makes something. They manufacture products. Michigan workers make chemicals, medicines, and furniture. They make sugar, automobiles, and cereal, too.

Cereal Kings

Millions of Americans eat cereal every day. All kinds of cereals are made in Battle Creek, Michigan. It is called the Cereal Capital of the World!

Post Toasties
A sweet, crisp food made of Pearly White Corn

▲ An early advertisement for Post cereal

John and Will Keith (W.K.) Kellogg started it all back in 1894. Both men were working at a hospital in Battle Creek. They discovered a way to make grains into flaked cereal. You can read more about W.K. Kellogg on page 282.

Charles W. Post learned about the cereal while he was in the Battle Creek hospital. Later Post and Kellogg each built factories close to the grain fields and the railroads. The two companies were in **competition**. That means they tried to win customers from each other. Today the Kellogg and Post companies are still leading cereal manufacturers.

QUICK CHECK How did Battle Creek become the center of the cereal manufacturing industry? *Summarize*

Ⓑ A Changing Industry

Michigan is the top auto manufacturer in the United States. It has been on top for more than 100 years. Three big auto **corporations** have their headquarters in or near Detroit. A corporation is a business. It belongs to many people. Each person owns a small part of the company.

Competition

You have read about the 1973 oil embargo. It made gasoline scarce, or hard to get. This meant gas cost more to buy. In the mid-1970s Americans began to buy cars from other countries. The cars were smaller than American cars. They used less gas. Fewer cars made in Michigan were sold. This caused auto plants to close. Many Michigan workers lost their jobs. These workers became unemployed.

Detroit car companies fought back. They made better products. They made smaller cars. They made engines that used less gas. Soon gas was easy to get again. Americans wanted their large cars back. So automakers made minivans and SUVs.

Still, by 2005 about one in three new cars was made by an Asian company. Today, many "foreign" cars have parts made in Michigan. Some of these cars are put together in Michigan. Michigan automakers are also making new "hybrid" cars. These cars use both electric and gas power. This saves fuel. Michigan's automobile industry continues to change.

QUICK CHECK How has Michigan's auto industry changed? *Summarize*

Large American cars (below) faced competition from foreign cars like this Volkswagen (right).

Michigan's Economy

Michigan's economy depends on many different industries. The map shows where Michigan's products are manufactured. The circle graph below shows the major industries in which people work.

Michigan Manufacturing

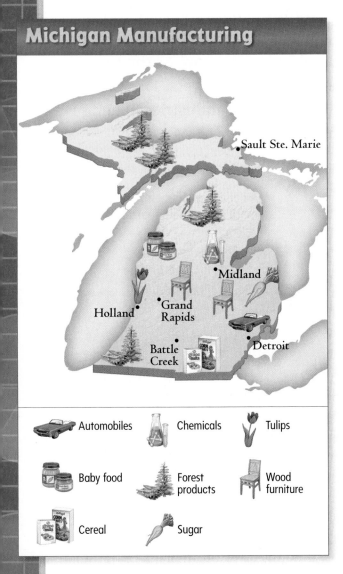

Sault Ste. Marie

Midland

Holland

Grand Rapids

Battle Creek

Detroit

Automobiles

Chemicals

Tulips

Baby food

Forest products

Wood furniture

Cereal

Sugar

Michiganians in Industry

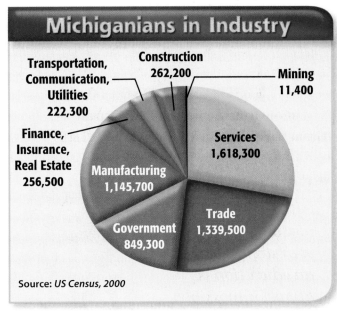

Transportation, Communication, Utilities 222,300

Construction 262,200

Mining 11,400

Finance, Insurance, Real Estate 256,500

Services 1,618,300

Manufacturing 1,145,700

Trade 1,339,500

Government 849,300

Source: *US Census, 2000*

Think About Manufacturing

1. More than 5 million Michiganians work. In which industry do most people work?

2. Which city is famous for producing cereal?

3. Based on the map and the graph, in which part of Michigan do you think the most people live?

Technology for the Future

Computers and other technologies have changed the way goods are made. In the past workers easily could get a good job. They did not have to go to college. Today Michigan's industries need skilled workers. There are few jobs for people who do not go to college. Read below what one executive tells young people.

New Ways

Michigan's schools work together with its industries. For example, teachers at the University of Michigan talk with the car companies. Michigan State University is a large research center. They do agricultural research. Students at these and other schools learn important skills.

Billions of dollars are spent in Michigan to do research and make new things. Tens of thousands of people work in research jobs. Research helps companies grow. As they grow, they need more workers. This growth helps Michigan's industries. It helps Michigan's future.

PRIMARY SOURCES

Laura Carlisle
a quote from Achieving Your Dream
Great Lakes Region Vice President, AT&T

"Achieving your dream with an education is possible. Achieving your dream without an education is almost impossible. Staying in school is the most important step you can take to achieving your dream."

Write About It! Why does Laura Carlisle advise students to stay in school?

A college education is becoming more and more important. ▼

New Fields of Research

Today robots often are used to make things or do tasks. A robot can do things that would be dangerous for humans. A robot can do a job the same way each time. Michigan is a leader in **robotics**. Robotics is the study of how machines can be used to make things. Robots have changed how goods are made.

Michigan is also doing research in **microtechnology**. This is called "small tech." It deals with tiny machines. A hearing aid could become the size of a pinhead. A computer could become smaller than a telephone!

Michigan companies lead medical research. They lead drug research, too. They are studying **biotechnology**. This means using living cells to make new medicine. These new fields move us forward. They improve how we live.

QUICK CHECK How has technology changed jobs and life in Michigan? *Summarize*

What You Learned

A Cereal production is an important Michigan industry.

B The American auto industry has changed in response to competition from foreign carmakers.

C Michigan is a leader in research and development, robotics, microtechnology, and biotechnology.

Focus Lesson Review

1. **Focus Question** What goods do Michigan workers produce?

2. **Vocabulary** Write one sentence for each vocabulary term.
   biotechnology   microtechnology
   competition   robotics

3. **Geography** Why did both Post and Kellogg build their plants in Battle Creek?

4. **Critical Thinking** **Identify Fact and Opinion** Tell whether the following statement is a fact or opinion. Explain.

   "Michigan's future depends on high-tech industries."

5. **Reading Strategy** **Summarize** Reread the section "A Changing Industry" on page 278. Use the chart to summarize the section.

6. **Write About** THE BIG IDEA Why might microtechnology and biotechnology be important industries for Michigan's future?

7. **Link to Art** Design a cereal box for a new type of cereal. Use an 8.5 × 11-inch sheet of paper. Try to use art or graphics to get kids to want to buy your product without offering prizes.

Will Keith Kellogg 1860–1951

When Will Keith Kellogg was 14 years old, he went to work in his father's broom business. Will's older brother was Dr. John Kellogg. He was the chief doctor at a hospital called the Battle Creek Sanitarium. A few years later, Will joined him there.

In 1894 the brothers were experimenting. They wanted to make a healthy food for the patients. They pressed cooked wheat through rollers. It made sheets of dough. One day they left a pot of cooked wheat too long. It dried out. They pressed the wheat anyway. It came out as flakes! The patients loved the new flaked cereal.

Later Will Kellogg started his own cereal company. He was an excellent businessman. By the time he retired in 1929, he had a fortune. In 1930 he started the W.K. Kellogg Foundation. The foundation has given away millions of dollars. It helps people in Battle Creek and around the world. Kellogg said,

"*Use the money as you please, so long as it promotes the health, happiness, and well-being of children.*"

 Write About It! Why do you think W.K. Kellogg gave away so much money?

LOG ON For more biographies, visit: www.macmillanmh.com

The Life of Will Keith Kellogg

1850	1875	1900	1925	1950	1975

1860 Will Keith Kellogg born

1894 Will and John Kellogg invent flaked cereal

1906 Starts the Kellogg Company

1930 Establishes the W.K. Kellogg Foundation

1951 W.K. Kellogg dies

CITIZENSHIP
DEMOCRACY IN ACTION

C5.0.1   P3.3.1
P3.1.1   P4.2.1
P3.1.3   P4.2.2

Take a Stand

In the past, many Michigan communities started the school year at different times. State lawmakers wrote a new bill. They wanted to have all Michigan schools start after Labor Day. They thought this bill would help tourism. Now more families can travel during Labor Day weekend. Other lawmakers were against the new bill. They thought the state shouldn't tell cities when to start the school year. In 2005 the bill became a law.

Michiganian lawmakers took a stand on the Labor Day law. Read these steps to learn how you can take a stand.

Build Citizenship

1. **Get informed** about an issue from newspapers or the Internet, or by talking to other people.

2. **Look at both sides.** Before taking a stand on an issue, think of reasons to be for or against it.

3. **Make a decision** after asking yourself, "What makes more sense to me?" and "Can I support my stand?"

4. **Take a stand** to be for or against the issue.

Think About It

1. How could you learn more about an issue?

2. Along with students, which groups of people are most affected by the Labor Day law?

3. This law helps the state's tourism industry make more money. Should states pass laws just because they would help local businesses? Explain your answer.

Write About It!

List four things you could do to convince others to join you in your stand.

283

How does Michigan trade with other countries?

VOCABULARY

interdependent
international trade
export
import
partnership

VOCABULARY STRATEGY

Root Words Import and **export** both come from the Latin word for *carry.* The prefix **im-** makes the word *import,* something carried in. What do you think an *export* is?

READING STRATEGY

Summarize Use the chart below to summarize this lesson.

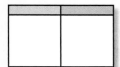

MICHIGAN GLCE

E2.0.1
E3.0.1

Michigan Trades with the World

Where were your shoes made? What about the electronic games you like to play? Have you had a banana in the last few days? Many things you wear, use, and eat come from thousands of miles away. That is because Michigan trades with the world!

Ⓐ A Smaller World

Long ago the things you needed came from places close to home. Goods did not go far from where they were made. Then transportation improved. People were able to trade with businesses and manufacturers that were far away.

Large cargo ships like this one carry goods into and out of Michigan. ▼

Today countries of the world are **interdependent**. They depend on each other to meet their needs and wants. One way they do this is by trading with other countries. This is called **international trade**.

Michigan's Trading Partners

Michigan shares a border with Canada. People and products can easily go between Michigan and Canada. Michigan **exports** vehicles, car parts, and furniture to Canada. Exports are goods sold or traded to another country.

Imports are goods brought in from another country. They are for people to sell or use. Michigan imports car parts, natural gas, and metal from Canada. Many Canadians come to visit Michigan each year, too. In fact Canada is Michigan's biggest trading partner.

Michigan imports goods from other places, too. The broccoli you eat may have come from Mexico. Some of the airplanes at Detroit Metropolitan Airport may have been made in France.

QUICK CHECK Why do countries trade with each other? *Summarize*

B World Partners

As you have seen, automakers work with each other. Some Michigan car makers are partners with other car makers around the world. A **partnership** is a business run by two or more people. They share the profits. They share the losses, too.

General Motors has a partnership with the Shanghai Auto Industry Corporation in China. Chrysler LLC, in Auburn Hills, has many partners. It works with companies in Germany, China, and India.

Manufacturers from other countries do research with people in Michigan. Hyundai is a Korean car maker. They expanded a plant near Ann Arbor. Now they can work on new technology. Some researchers try to find ways to make cars use less gas. Others work on ways to make cars that do not use gas.

Sister Cities

Some Michigan cities do more than trade goods with other countries. They trade ideas and friendship with "sister cities." Sister city exchanges help people make friends around the world.

The Friendship Garden and a tea ceremony (inset) at the Japanese Cultural Center, Saginaw

For example, students from Novi, Michigan, went to Japan. They visited hosts in their sister city, Owani. In Saginaw you can visit the Japanese Cultural Center. It has a teahouse and garden. People in Saginaw and its sister city Tokushima, Japan, shared the costs of building the center. New ways to travel and communicate make the world seem like a "smaller" place.

Lansing has four sister cities. They are on different continents. In Africa its sister city is Akuapim, Ghana. People in Lansing are trying to help their friends in Akuapim. They have collected more than 20,000 books. The books are sent to libraries in Ghana.

Lansing collected books to help schools and libraries in Ghana. ▶

The people of Lansing help improve health in Ghana. They have sent more than $1 million in medical equipment.

QUICK CHECK What are some ways countries work together? *Summarize*

What You Learned

A Michigan trades internationally, sending exports to and receiving imports from many countries.

B Michigan's auto industry works closely with auto industries in other countries. Countries around the world also exchange ideas and friendship.

Focus Lesson Review

1. **Focus Question** How does Michigan trade with other countries?

2. **Vocabulary** Write one sentence for each vocabulary term.
   export   interdependent
   import   international trade

3. **Geography** What does Michigan's location have to do with Canada being its leading trading partner?

4. **Critical Thinking** **Draw Conclusions** How do you think cities benefit from sister city programs?

5. **Reading Strategy** **Summarize** Use the chart to summarize the part of this lesson titled "A Smaller World."

6. **Write About THE BIG IDEA** Why do nations trade with other nations?

7. **Link to Culture** Do some research about Japan to find out a little about its customs. Write a paragraph that explains one custom.

Chapter 9 Review

FOCUS Vocabulary Review

Copy the sentences below on a separate sheet of paper. Use the list of vocabulary words to fill in the blanks.

competition	imports
exports	investors

1. _____ loan money to businesses in order to make a profit.

2. Michigan's _____ include natural gas and metal.

3. One of Michigan's leading _____ to Canada is motor vehicle parts.

4. _____ between companies can give customers better products.

5. **Test Preparation** When countries trade with each other to get what they need and want, they are _____.

   A **self-sufficient**   C **entrepreneurs**
   B **independent**   D **interdependent**

FOCUS Comprehension Check

6. What does an entrepreneur do?

7. Name three products grown in Michigan.

8. Name some products of Michigan's forests.

9. Which city is the center of Michigan's cereal industry?

10. Which country is Michigan's largest trading partner?

11. In what part of Michigan is iron mining an important industry?

12. Name some jobs related to tourism.

13. **Critical Thinking** How do Michiganians today take better care of forest resources than they did in the past?

14. **Critical Thinking** Use what you know about the lake effect to explain why Michigan is a leader in agriculture.

FOCUS Use the Time Line

Use the time line below to answer each question.

15. How many years does this time line cover?

16. How many years ago did the Kelloggs invent a flaked cereal?

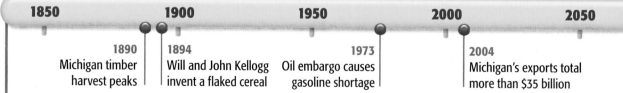

1850	1900	1950	2000	2050

1890 Michigan timber harvest peaks

1894 Will and John Kellogg invent a flaked cereal

1973 Oil embargo causes gasoline shortage

2004 Michigan's exports total more than $35 billion

Make Decisions

Write a complete sentence to answer each question.

A business owner may ask an investor for a loan so that he or she can improve the business. To make a profit, the investor will charge interest on the loan. That means the business owner must pay back the amount of the loan plus a fee. There is always the risk that the business owner might not make enough money to pay back the loan. An investor thinks carefully before making the decision to loan money, because she or he wants to be sure that the business owner can pay it back.

17. What is the investor's goal?

18. What do you think the investor needs to know before loaning money?

Using Primary Sources

Read the interview with Berry Gordy below. Write a complete sentence to answer each question.

❝ My own dream for a hit factory was shaped by principles I learned on the . . . assembly line. At the plant, cars started out as just a frame, . . . until they emerged at the end of the line—brand spanking new cars. . . . I wanted the same concept for my company, only with artists and songs and records. I wanted a place where a kid off the street could walk in one door an unknown and come out another a recording artist . . . a star! ❞

19. What did Berry Gordy compare the process of creating a star to?

20. Why is this quote a primary source?

Hands-on Activity

21. Create an Advertisement Suppose you have your own business. Create an advertisement for your business. It could be either a TV or magazine advertisement.

Write About Economics

22. Narrative Choose a Michigan business and do research about how it was started. Then write a narrative that tells the history of the business.

LOG ON For help with the process of writing, visit: www.macmillanmh.com

Chapter 10

Michigan's Government

You Are There

"I believe that truth is the glue that holds government together, not only our government but civilization itself."

Gerald Ford said these words in 1974. That was the year he became President of the United States. Gerald Ford grew up in Grand Rapids. He was the first person from Michigan to become President.

In this chapter you will learn about some important ideas. These ideas make the United States strong. You will find out how these ideas hold our country together.

Gerald Ford ▶

MN

IA

MO

1 Holland Tulip Festival

2 United States Capitol Building

N
W   E
S

Michigan Today

— Michigan boundary
— National boundary
— Other state boundary
⊛ National capital
★ State capital
• Other city
🏛 State capitol building
🏛 National capitol building

Lake Superior

MICHIGAN

CANADA

Lake Huron

WI

Lake Ontario

NY

Lake Michigan

Holland •
①   ③ ★ Lansing
Dearborn •
④

Lake Erie

PA

NJ

IL

IN

OH

DE

Washington, ⊛ MD
D.C.   ②

WV

VA

KY

③ **Michigan State Capitol**

④ **City Council of Dearborn, Michigan**

Our Core Values as Americans

What values do Americans share?

VOCABULARY

core democratic
   values
common good
representative
   government
patriotism
justice
equality

VOCABULARY STRATEGY

Root Words The root of **patriotism** is the Greek word *patrios,* meaning "of one's fathers." What do you think love of country has to do with fathers?

READING STRATEGY

Identify Main Idea and Details Use the chart to show how Americans live by core democratic values.

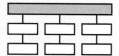

MICHIGAN GLCE

H3.0.2
C1.0.1
C5.0.1
G4.0.2
G4.0.4

The Declaration of Independence was signed in 1776. It said that Americans wanted freedom from Great Britain. Freedom is an important American value. Working together is another important American value. Working together makes us strong. Benjamin Franklin was one of the men who signed the Declaration of Independence. He thought about these values. He once said,

" *We must all hang together, or most assuredly we shall all hang separately.* **"**

These young people are celebrating their country. ▼

Ⓐ Our Democratic Values

For many years Great Britain ruled the 13 North American colonies. In 1776 the people living in the colonies decided they wanted to be free. Some of them signed the Declaration of Independence. It told the world that the colonies had the right to be free from Great Britain.

The Declaration says the government gets its power from the people. The government must work for the people. All people have rights and no one can take these away.

Three of these rights are life, liberty, and the pursuit of happiness. Life means that we have the right to live free from harm. Liberty means that we can say and think what we like. The third right is the pursuit of happiness. People should be able to do what makes them happy.

These three important rights are our **core democratic values**. They are values held by all Americans. Many Americans have fought and sometimes died for these values.

Rights and Responsibilities

Along with our rights, Americans have responsibilities. All people have rights, so it is important that we respect the rights of others. We should follow our laws. We should vote. We should learn about what is happening in our community.

QUICK CHECK Which American values can we find in the Declaration of Independence? *Main Idea and Details*

293

▲ Immigrants from Holland brought the tulip to Michigan.

ⓑ The Common Good

Americans believe it is important to work for the **common good**, or what is best for all people. People have a right to be happy. But they also need to think about the common good. Sometimes people do not agree about what is best for all.

In 2004 a business wanted to build a store near Charlevoix (SHAHR luh voy) Township. The new store would be built in the woods. Some people felt that the store was against the common good. They worked to stop the store from being built. The business listened to the people. It decided not to build the store there.

Different people can have very different ideas about the common good. One job of Michigan's government is to help decide what is best when people do not agree.

A Diverse State

Michigan has many different people who came from different places.

Some people came from Holland, in Europe. They settled in what is today Holland, Michigan. A Tulip Festival is held there each year. People go to the festival to remember their culture.

Later people came from Arab countries to work in Michigan. Many work for car companies in cities such as Dearborn.

Getting Involved

We can make sure that our country lives up to its values. One way to do this is by voting. When people vote, they pick leaders who they think share their values. These leaders become our **representative government**.

The people of Michigan vote for local leaders. They vote for leaders to run our state. They also vote for leaders to run our national government.

Responsible citizens learn what is happening in the government. Before they vote, they learn about the people who want to be leaders.

Patriotism is the love of one's country. Voting is an act of patriotism. Have you ever waved an American flag? Have you watched a Fourth of July parade? These are other ways to show patriotism.

You are patriotic when you say the Pledge of Allegiance. You are patriotic when you do things that show important American values. You are patriotic when you are fair and when you tell the truth. You are patriotic when you work with others.

When you are older, you may join the military. That, too, is a patriotic act. You may teach others about important ideas in your community.

Talking about important issues is patriotic. This is a way to work for the common good in your community or state. When you do things to help your community, your state, or your country, you are being patriotic.

QUICK CHECK Why is it important for citizens to stay informed? *Main Idea and Details*

PRIMARY SOURCES

Calvin Coolidge
President of the United States • 1923–1929

❝*Patriotism is easy to understand in America; it means looking out for yourself by looking out for your country.*❞

Write About It! What do you think Coolidge meant when he defined patriotism?

ⓒ Justice, Equality, and the Rule of Law

Our state is made up of different people with different ideas. Sometimes, people disagree. When they do, they use laws to help them find an answer. Americans believe in the rule of law. This means that all of us must obey laws. Even the President must obey laws. If a law does not work, or harms people, we can change it.

Our laws are the same for all people. **Justice**, or fair treatment, is important in our laws. If people think they or others have been treated unfairly, they can go to court and get justice.

Telling the truth is important. It is a part of our laws. People must tell the truth in court. That way, no one will go to jail because of something that is not true. They must tell the truth when they sell something. That way, people are not tricked out of their money. Our government must also tell the truth.

Fighting for Equality

Equality means treating all people fairly. Fairness is an important value for Americans. It is an idea talked about in the Declaration of Independence. There have been times, though, when some Americans were not treated equally.

Michigan police officers help enforce the rule of law. ▼

Michigan grew fast during the 1800s land rush. More people moved in. They pushed American Indians out. Americans were not fair to enslaved Africans either.

People have stood up for their rights. They fought for equality. They told others to live up to our country's values.

QUICK CHECK Why is it important for the President to follow the rule of law? *Draw Conclusions*

Michiganians attended a rally in 2004 to encourage young people to vote. ▶

What You Learned

A The Declaration of Independence is the source of many of our core democratic values.

B There are many ways to be patriotic, such as voting and helping others.

C Americans share core democratic values, including justice, truth, equality, and the rule of law.

Focus Lesson Review

1. **Focus Question** What values do Americans share?

2. **Vocabulary** Write one sentence for each vocabulary term.
common good	**justice**
equality	**patriotism**

3. **Citizenship** Why is it important for Americans to vote?

4. **Critical Thinking Make Decisions** Explain why you agree or disagree with the statement "It is not fair for people to decide where a business can or can't build."

5. **Reading Strategy Identify Main Idea and Details** Use the chart to show some of the ways you can be patriotic.

6. **Write About** 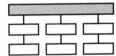 How do our core democratic values help Americans meet their needs?

7. **Link to Language Arts** Americans can vote in presidential elections when they turn 18. Do you think younger people should have the right to vote? Write a paragraph explaining your opinion.

Our Nation's Government

How does the United States government work?

VOCABULARY

democracy
citizen
federal
legislative branch
executive branch
judicial branch

VOCABULARY STRATEGY

Word Origins The word **democracy** comes from the Greek word for people. What kind of government do you think a democracy is?

READING STRATEGY

Summarize Use the chart below to summarize how our national government works.

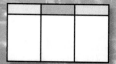

MICHIGAN GLCE

C5.0.1

James Madison helped write our Constitution. He hoped that Americans would always look to the Constitution. There they would find answers to the problems of their time. As Madison said in 1787:

> "In framing a system which we wish to last for the ages, we should not lose sight of the changes which ages will produce."

The United States Capitol building ▼

Ⓐ Our Nation's Government

The United States is a **democracy**. This means our government is run by the people. A **citizen** is a person who belongs to a country. In a democracy, citizens vote for people to represent them in the government. A citizen can be born in the country. Or a person can become a citizen of our country.

Our Constitution is the plan for our government. The words "We the people" mean that the government is run by the people.

The Constitution set up a **federal** system of government. This means that power is shared among national, state, and local governments. The Constitution lists the powers of the national government. It gives all other powers to state governments.

The Constitution gives the citizens of our country certain rights. They can say or think what they want. They can practice any religion they want. Citizens also have the right to own property, to vote, and to run for office. Our government must protect these rights. It must be fair to all citizens. It must treat them all the same.

Our national government is sometimes called federal government. It has three different branches, or parts. Each does different things. Each also has some power over the other two. This way, no single branch can become too powerful.

QUICK CHECK What kind of government does the Constitution set up? *Summarize*

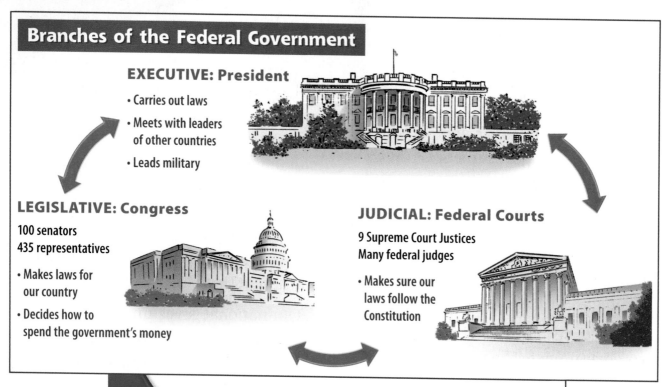

Branches of the Federal Government

EXECUTIVE: President
- Carries out laws
- Meets with leaders of other countries
- Leads military

LEGISLATIVE: Congress
100 senators
435 representatives
- Makes laws for our country
- Decides how to spend the government's money

JUDICIAL: Federal Courts
9 Supreme Court Justices
Many federal judges
- Makes sure our laws follow the Constitution

DIAGRAM Skill ▸ Which branch decides how to spend the government's money?

ⓑ The Three Branches

The **legislative branch** makes laws. The **executive branch** enforces laws. The **judicial branch** decides what the laws mean. Each branch can only do its own job. The President is part of the executive branch. So the President does not make laws. The executive branch can only enforce law.

The Legislative Branch

Congress is the legislative branch of our government. Congress has two houses, or parts. The Senate has 100 members, two from each of the 50 states. The House of Representatives has 435 members. Michigan has 15 representatives in the House of Representatives.

States with more people have more representatives. California is the state with the most people. It has 53 representatives. Congress makes new laws for our country. Congress is also in charge of taxes. It decides what to do with the tax money. Congress can also say when the country is at war.

The Executive Branch

The President is the head of the executive branch. The executive branch carries out the law. The President also runs our military. The President meets with leaders of other countries. The executive branch also runs other parts of the government, such as education and transportation.

Voters choose a President every four years. When voters choose a President, they also get a Vice President. The Vice President takes over as President if the President can no longer work. A term is four years. A President can only serve two terms.

The Judicial Branch

The judicial branch decides how the law works. This branch is made up of many judges. They work in courts all around the country. The Supreme Court is the top court in the land. It has nine judges, called Justices. Justices serve for life. When a Justice stops working, the President picks a new Justice. Congress has to agree with the President about who is picked.

QUICK CHECK Why do you think Supreme Court Justices must be approved by Congress? *Draw Conclusions*

▲ Visitors to Washington, D.C., can see the original copy of the Constitution.

What You Learned

A The United States is a democracy in which citizens choose their leaders by electing them.

B The Constitution divides the powers of the national government into three different branches.

Focus Lesson Review

1. **Focus Question** How does the United States government work?

2. **Vocabulary** Write one sentence for each vocabulary term.
   - citizen
   - democracy
   - federal
   - legislative branch

3. **Citizenship** Why does the Constitution begin with the words "We the people"?

4. **Critical Thinking Draw Conclusions** Why do you think the Supreme Court has an odd number of Justices?

5. **Reading Strategy Summarize** Use the chart to summarize the section titled "The Judicial Branch."

6. **Write About THE BIG IDEA** Which branch of the national government do you think does the most to meet people's needs? Please explain your answer.

7. **Link to Math** Michigan has 15 members in the House of Representatives. California has 53. Who represents more people, a Michigan representative or a California representative?

C5.0.1

Should There Be Special Rules for Who Is Elected President?

The Constitution has rules about who can be President. A person who wants to be President must be born in the United States. Some people want to change the Constitution. They want to give people born in other countries a chance to become President. Here are three ideas about who should be able to run for President.

"Every American citizen should have the chance to become President. . . . Most importantly he or she needs to teach the world about nonviolence so people will stop fighting."

Redha Muhsen
Dearborn, Michigan

"I don't think that people need to be born here. . . . A person's ideas matter more than where they were born. A person who runs for President should have good ideas about how to improve the United States."

Keagen Herzog
Grandville, Michigan

"We should not be in a hurry to change the Constitution. A person who was born in this country would be more familiar with our democracy and the way we do things here than somebody who was born in a different country. . . ."

Kayla Jennings
Lansing, Michigan

Build Citizenship

1. Why do you think the Constitution requires that Presidents be born in the United States?

2. Why would the Constitution have to be changed before a citizen born outside the United States could run for President?

3. What do you think are the most important qualifications a person needs to run for President?

Think About It

1. What reasons does Kayla Jennings give for her opinion?

2. In what ways do Redha Muhsen and Keagen Herzog agree?

3. What other points of view might people have on this issue?

Write About It!

Do you think citizens born in other countries should be able to run for President? Why or why not? Give reasons for your answer.

Our State's Government

VOCABULARY

issue
bill
veto

VOCABULARY STRATEGY

Foreign Words In Latin, **veto** means "I forbid." If Congress approves a law and the President vetoes it, what do you think has happened?

READING STRATEGY

Compare and Contrast Use the diagram to compare and contrast the government of Michigan with the government of the United States.

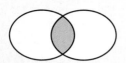

MICHIGAN GLCE

C1.0.1
C2.0.1
C3.0.2
C3.0.3
C3.0.4
C3.0.5

Anyone can work to change things. A group of students in Niles changed something. They found out that Michigan did not have a state reptile. They thought the painted turtle should be the state reptile. They told other people about their idea. Before long, Michigan decided to name the painted turtle the state reptile!

Ⓐ Government Power

As you have read, the Constitution says how the government of our country works. It gives power to the federal government as well as the 50 states.

Our country's founders wrote the Constitution in 1787. At that time each state was run by its own government. The founders wanted to have a strong federal government, too. Its job would be to protect the whole country. It would also print money and collect taxes. The founders gave state governments other powers.

State governments protect individual rights. They work for the common good. State governments make laws for the state. A state government can decide what its schools will teach. It can decide the rules for its roads.

Paying for Services

As you have read, our federal government collects taxes. State governments collect taxes, too. They use the money they collect to pay for goods and services.

States also make money in other ways. They collect fines for things like traffic tickets. They also collect fees for licenses. State governments then use this money for services. The building of roads and schools is a service. Health care is another service.

QUICK CHECK How did the powers of the states change when the Constitution was written? *Compare and Contrast*

The Michigan House of Representatives chamber ▼

B Three State Branches

Michigan has a state constitution. It is like the United States Constitution. It has three branches: legislative, executive, and judicial.

The Legislative Branch

Michigan's legislative branch makes laws for the state. It has two parts. People in the state pick its members. The state's Senate has 38 members. The state's House of Representatives has 110 members.

The legislative branch has to think about many issues. An **issue** is a subject important to the people in the state. Schools are an important issue. Health is also important.

It was once against Michigan's laws to bring medicine to school. But some students needed to have medicine when they were at school.

One mother spoke up about changing the law. A group of Michigan Representatives worked together on a **bill**. A bill is a plan for a law. The bill would allow students who needed medicine to bring it to school. Michigan's House and Senate passed the bill.

Then the bill went to Michigan's governor to sign. The governor can **veto**, or turn down, a bill. The House and Senate can still pass it if two thirds of them vote for it again. The governor signed this bill. You can follow the steps in the chart on the next page.

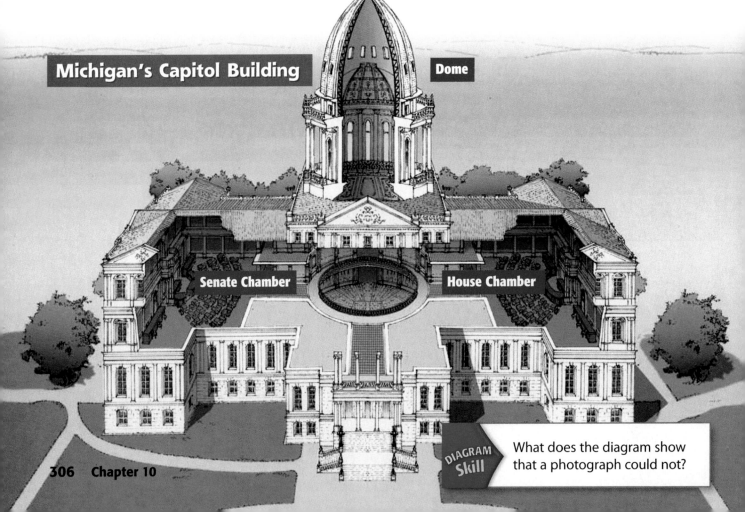

Michigan's Capitol Building

Dome

Senate Chamber

House Chamber

DIAGRAM Skill What does the diagram show that a photograph could not?

The Executive Branch

The governor is the head of the state's executive branch. Michigan's people elect a governor every four years. Jennifer Granholm is our governor. People elect other officials in the executive branch, too.

The governor works with state officials to make sure that Michigan runs well. The governor signs or turns down bills. Like the President, the governor picks people to help run the state.

The Judicial Branch

Michigan's judicial branch decides how to use the state's laws. Judges and courts make up the judicial branch.

Michigan has district courts. It also has 57 circuit courts. Cases begin in one of these two courts. People who feel that a court's decision is wrong can go to the State Court of Appeals. If a person still feels a decision is wrong, he or she can go to the Michigan Supreme Court.

There are seven justices on Michigan's Supreme Court. They decide if the state's other courts have made the right decisions. The justices listen to and talk about the facts. Then they give their decision. They can decide that another court's decision was wrong if it did not agree with the state's law or constitution.

QUICK CHECK Explain what is meant by a veto. *Summarize*

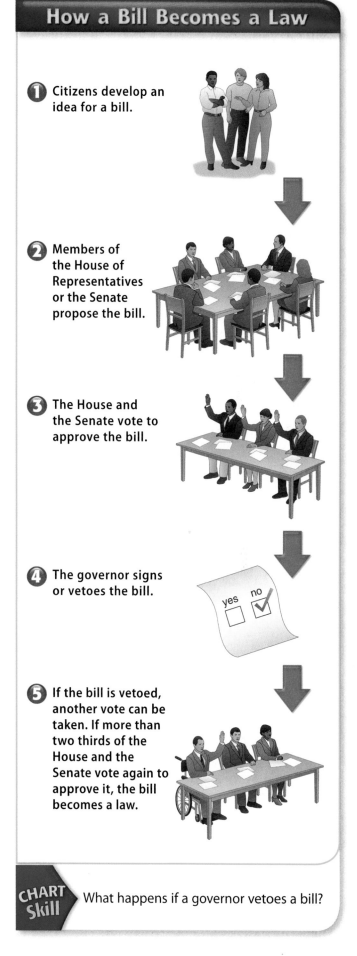

How a Bill Becomes a Law

1. Citizens develop an idea for a bill.

2. Members of the House of Representatives or the Senate propose the bill.

3. The House and the Senate vote to approve the bill.

4. The governor signs or vetoes the bill.

5. If the bill is vetoed, another vote can be taken. If more than two thirds of the House and the Senate vote again to approve it, the bill becomes a law.

CHART Skill What happens if a governor vetoes a bill?

Michigan and You

Michigan's state government represents its people. For a state's government to work, everyone must take part. You should know when your government is talking about an important issue. You should work to change the things you feel are not right. Just like legislators, people can speak out or write about the issues that matter to them.

Anyone can give ideas for new laws. If you think a state law needs to change, you can write your state legislator. You can ask a legislator to support a new law. Every person has a voice. Anyone can make a change for the better.

✓ **QUICK CHECK** How can a single citizen make a difference in Michigan?
Summarize

What You Learned

A The United States Constitution divides powers between the states and the national government.

B Michigan's constitution sets up legislative, executive, and judicial branches.

C Citizens are an important part of state government.

Focus Lesson Review

1. **Focus Question** How does the Michigan state government work?

2. **Vocabulary** Write one sentence for each vocabulary term.
   issue   bill
   veto

3. **Government** Should the state or the national government decide what children need to learn in school? Explain your answer.

4. **Critical Thinking Problem Solving** What could you do to get a legislator to support an issue that is important to you?

5. **Reading Strategy Compare and Contrast** Use the diagram to compare and contrast the roles that legislators and individuals can play in Michigan's government.

6. **Write About THE BIG IDEA** How does the governor meet the needs of a state's citizens?

7. **Link to Language Arts** Suppose the state legislature was considering a bill to make snowmobiling illegal in Michigan. Write a letter to your state representative explaining why you think the bill should pass or should fail.

Jennifer Granholm 1959–

Jennifer Granholm is the 47th governor of Michigan. She was born in Canada. Her family moved to California when she was young. She dreamed of becoming a star. After high school she moved to Los Angeles to become an actor. By the time she turned 21, though, Granholm did not want to be an actor.

Granholm had become an American citizen. She went to college in California. Then she went to Harvard Law School. She became a lawyer. In 1987 she moved to Michigan.

In 1998 the people of Michigan elected Granholm to be attorney general. Her job was to make sure Michigan was safe. Granholm worked to take criminals off the streets. She stopped criminals who stole from people. She stopped gas stations that made people pay too much money. In 2002 the people of Michigan elected Granholm to be governor. She became Michigan's first female governor. The people elected Granholm again in 2006. She said she wanted to be a role model for Michigan's young people:

> **❝** *It's a good message for our daughters and our sons that the face of leadership doesn't always have to look the same.* **❞**

 Write About It! How did Jennifer Granholm show leadership?

LOG ON For more biographies, visit: www.macmillanmh.com

The Life of Jennifer Granholm

1950	1970	1990	2010
1959 Jennifer Granholm born	**1987** Graduates from Harvard Law School	**1998** Elected Michigan Attorney General	**2002** Elected Michigan Governor

The LIBRARY of CONGRESS

VOCABULARY

official document
authority

Understand Official Documents

An **official document** has information that has been approved by one or more people. An official document is made by a person who has **authority**. Authority is power given to someone or something by someone else.

Official documents can be a window to the past. They tell us things that have happened, such as a baby being born. The Constitution is an official document. So are birth certificates, wills, and licenses.

Proclamation

A proclamation is one kind of official document. A person who has authority makes a proclamation. A proclamation is a way to announce something. It might be issued to announce a change in the way the government will do something. It might honor someone or announce a holiday.

 Learn It

Read the steps below to learn how to find information in official documents.

- Scan for the date and place the document was signed.

- Identify the authority that issued the document.

- Look for a raised seal. Without this seal many documents are not considered legal.

- Read the document.

A Proclamation

Fifty years ago the State of Nebraska instituted the observance of a day set apart for tree planting. This day was known as Arbor Day, and its observance has become general throughout the nation. It is a day of sentiment, reverence and faith—sentiment in the acknowledgment of the tender susceptibility of man toward all the living things of the out-of-doors; reverence inspired within us by the sturdiness of the oak, the majesty of the pine, the beauty of the elm and the splendor of the leaf bearing branches of the maple with its seasons of changing color and form; a well grounded faith in the productive energy of nature's generous creative forces.

To us of Michigan, Arbor Day is of particular significance. Time was when our forests outshone in splendor and magnificence those of any other State. Today, through the utilization of this natural product and the devastation wrought by forest fires, these forests have to a large extent disappeared, though we still have many thousands of acres of beautiful forest land.

Therefore, by virtue of the authority vested in me as

Governor of the State of Michigan, I do hereby designate Friday, May Fifth, 1922, as Arbor Day, and I request that exercises appropriate to the day be held in all our schools.

Given under my hand and the Great Seal of the State this twenty-first day of April, in the year of our Lord, one thousand nine hundred and twenty-two, and of the Commonwealth the eighty-sixth.

Alex J. Groesbeck,
Governor.

By the Governor:

Charles J. DeLand.
Secretary of State.

2 Try It

- Read the proclamation.
- What does this proclamation do?
- What is Arbor Day?
- Who issued this proclamation?

3 Apply It

- Give some examples of an official document.
- Why is this document a primary source?

Field Trip to  Lansing

Lansing

Detroit was once the capital of Michigan. In 1847 Lansing became the new capital. It did not become a city until 1859 though. Today people from all around Michigan visit the capital city.

 Oldsmobile Park ▶

You can cheer for the Lansing Lugnuts baseball team here, and watch fireworks shows during the season.

2 Capitol Building ▼

The massive Capitol building opened in 1879. A statue of Austin Blair, governor during the Civil War, stands outside.

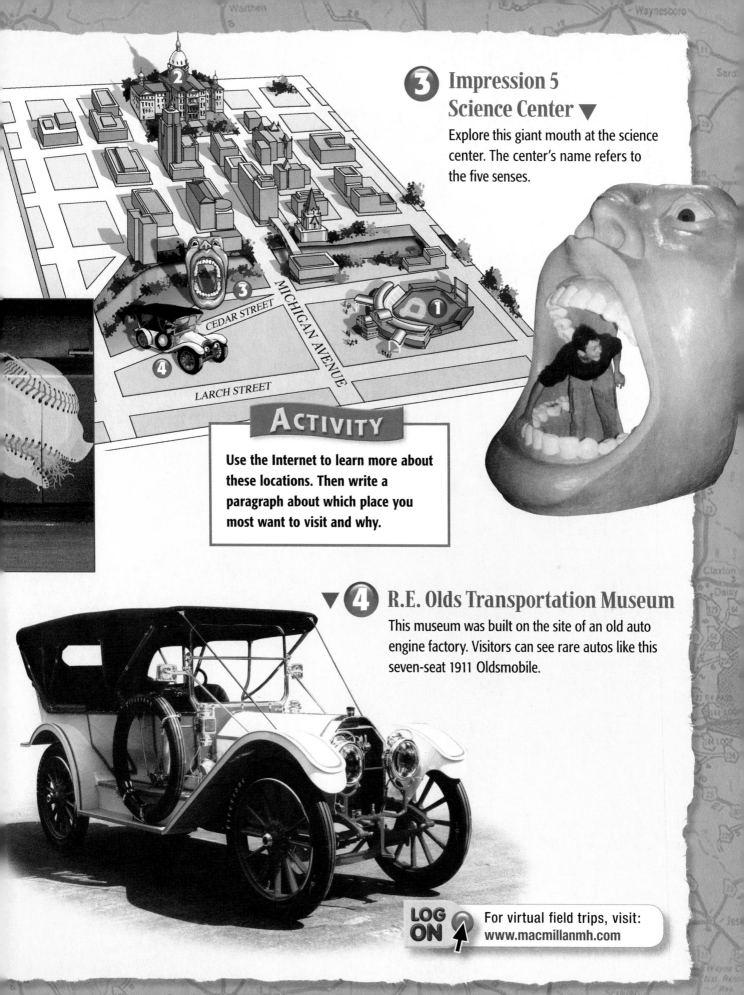

3 Impression 5 Science Center ▼

Explore this giant mouth at the science center. The center's name refers to the five senses.

CEDAR STREET

MICHIGAN AVENUE

LARCH STREET

ACTIVITY

Use the Internet to learn more about these locations. Then write a paragraph about which place you most want to visit and why.

▼ 4 R.E. Olds Transportation Museum

This museum was built on the site of an old auto engine factory. Visitors can see rare autos like this seven-seat 1911 Oldsmobile.

LOG ON — For virtual field trips, visit: www.macmillanmh.com

Focus Lesson 4

How do local governments work?

VOCABULARY

budget
county
charter
city council
mayor
city manager

VOCABULARY STRATEGY

Foreign Words Charter comes from the Latin word *charta*, which means "a sheet of paper." A **charter** is a document that gives rights or powers.

READING STRATEGY

Compare and Contrast Use the diagram to compare and contrast local government and state government.

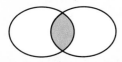

MICHIGAN GLCE

H3.0.2	C3.0.3
C3.0.1	C3.0.4
C3.0.2	P4.2.1

Local Government

A streetlight is out on a busy corner. Who comes to fix it? The playground equipment in the city park needs painting. Who takes care of that? A tree blows over in a storm and blocks a city street. Whose job is it to take the tree away? A downtown store is on fire. Who comes to fight the fire?

So many jobs! Who can do them, and who will pay for them? The answer is local government.

Ⓐ Local Government and You

You live in a place with a local government. Local governments run towns and cities.

Like our state government, local governments raise money from taxes, fines, and fees. They use this money to pay for services. They pay people to keep our streets clean. They pay people to pick up our garbage.

People work for your local government. City workers do many jobs to help a city run. They take care of parks and streetlights. Your local government runs schools and police and fire departments, too.

◄ Fighting fires is an important service of local government.

Local governments decide how to spend the money they raise. They make a plan called a **budget**. It tells them how much money will be raised and how it will be spent.

County Government

Our country has 50 states. Michigan also has smaller parts called **counties**. Michigan has 83 counties. Each county has a government. Counties take care of county roads. They also run jails and parks. Each county government has three branches.

A county board of commissioners makes up the legislative branch. The commissioners pass certain kinds of laws for the county.

A county executive or manager may run a county's executive branch. Other county jobs are sheriff and clerk.

Counties also have a judicial branch. County courthouses are part of the judicial branch.

QUICK CHECK How is county government similar to national government? *Compare and Contrast*

❷ Cities and Towns

Most people in Michigan live in cities or towns. But what makes them cities and towns? They each have a **charter**. This is an official document approved by Michigan's government. A charter gives people or groups certain rights. A city's charter says the kind of government it will have.

Michigan's towns and cities do not all have the same kind of government. Some have a town or **city council** to be the legislative branch.

Large cities might have a **mayor** elected by the people. A mayor heads a city's executive branch.

Some small towns pay a person to run their town. This person is called a town administrator or **city manager**.

How a City Works

Dearborn is a city of 97,000 people. It is in Wayne County, in southeastern Michigan. The Ford Motor Company is in Dearborn. Jobs making cars are very important to the people of Dearborn.

John B. O'Reilly, Jr. is Dearborn's mayor. He became mayor in 2006 when the mayor before him died. Before that he ran Dearborn's city council for almost 20 years. In 2007 a special election was held. Dearborn's people picked O'Reilly to be mayor.

Departments of Local Government

 Fire Department provides ambulance, fire, and rescue services

 Parks and Recreation Department maintains parks

 Planning Department plans for city projects

 Police Department keeps citizens safe

 Public Health Department helps citizens fight disease

 Building Inspection Department grants permits for new buildings, inspects plans

 Environmental Services Department collects garbage and recycling

 Finance Department collects taxes, handles city money

 Maintenance Department repairs streets, signs, traffic lights

CHART Skill What department would you call if a traffic light was broken?

The 2005 Dearborn City Council ▶

Dearborn has a city council. It makes up the city's legislative branch. It has seven members. Every four years the city's people pick council members. It is the city council's job to make a budget. The council decides how much tax people should pay. It also decides on the city services it pays.

City Courts

Cities have a judicial branch, too. City courts carry out the city's laws. If a person gets a ticket for driving too fast, they go to a city court.

City courts also hear cases about small crimes that have happened in the city.

QUICK CHECK What does a city charter do? *Summarize*

Then and Now   Michigan Schools

THEN In 1908, in this one-room schoolhouse near East Grand Rapids, children from different grades sat together. Until 1905 schools had to be open only three months a year.

NOW Michigan students today go to school nine months a year. They sit with other children from their own grade, and many rooms have computers.

Write About It! How were the classrooms of the early 1900s different from the classrooms of today?

Working Together

In 2002 people began to notice that Michigan's ash trees were dying. The problem was an insect. The Emerald Ash Borer (EAB) can kill ash trees. When the EAB came to Michigan, the government acted. Federal, state, and local governments worked together. The federal government gave Michigan money. Michigan used the money to fight the EAB.

The state government made new rules about the wood from ash trees. It stopped people from selling the wood. The new rules have helped to keep the EAB from spreading.

The Emerald
Ash Borer ▶

County governments met to learn about the EAB. Local officials told people about the problem. All levels of government are working together to stop the EAB and save Michigan's ash trees.

QUICK CHECK How did national, state, and local government work together to help save Michigan's ash trees? *Summarize*

What You Learned

Ⓐ Local government affects our lives every day. People pay taxes to pay for city services.

Ⓑ Most of Michigan's local governments have three branches.

Ⓒ Governments at all levels can work together to solve Michigan's problems.

Focus Lesson Review

1. **Focus Question** How do local governments work?

2. **Vocabulary** Write one sentence for each vocabulary term.
   budget   county
   charter   mayor

3. **Economics** Why do governments need budgets?

4. **Critical Thinking Identify Fact and Opinion** Is the following statement a fact or an opinion? *Michigan's problems are best solved at the local level.* Explain your answer.

5. **Reading Strategy Compare and Contrast** Use the diagram to compare and contrast how national and local governments responded to the EAB problem.

6. **Write About THE BIG IDEA** How does local government meet the needs of people in trouble?

7. **Link to Science** Why is it important to cut down and dispose of ash trees infested with the Emerald Ash Borer?

C2.0.1
C5.0.1
P3.1.1
P3.1.2
P3.1.3
P3.3.1
P4.2.1

Express Your Opinion

In the last chapter (page 283), you read about a proposed law that would make all Michigan public schools start after Labor Day. You also learned how to take a stand on that law. Now you will express your opinion. It is not enough to just state your opinion, however. You need to be able to support your opinion.

Apply Democratic Values

People both for and against this law have made arguments based on our core democratic values. You will use a core democratic value to support your position, too.

1. **Review our core democratic values.** You may want to turn back to pages 292–297. As you review, ask yourself which value or values support your stand.

2. **Decide which value supports your stand.** For instance, you might decide that the law supports the common good, or that it helps people in the pursuit of happiness.

Apply Social Studies Knowledge

3. **Use your knowledge of history, geography, civics, or economics to support your position.** For instance, some people say the law is good for Michigan's economy because it will help tourism.

4. **Use facts.** Find information that will support your position. If you think the law is good for tourism, what data are there proving that this is true? Remember, the data you use must support your position.

Now follow these steps to express your opinion about an issue using what you know about social studies and core democratic values.

Share Your Opinion

1. **Write your first sentence.** Your first sentence should state your position clearly.

2. **Support your position.** Now include the information that supports your position. Use the data you found, a core democratic value, and social studies knowledge.

3. **Check your work.** Be sure the information you included is not too general, and does not go against your position.

Think About It

1. People who work in the tourism industry say they support the Labor Day law because families should be able to take longer summer vacations. What core democratic value might they use to support their stand?

2. How is the debate about the Labor Day law an example of people having different ideas about the common good?

3. Create a bar graph showing whether students in your class are for or against this issue. Look at the graph. What do you think is the reason for the result?

Write About It!

Using what you have learned, write a letter to your local newspaper expressing your opinion on an issue people are debating in your school or community.

Vocabulary Review

Copy the sentences below on a separate sheet of paper. Use the list of vocabulary words to fill in the blanks.

authority	patriotism
citizen	veto

1. Only a _____ can vote in United States elections.

2. The school band showed _____ when it marched in the July 4th parade.

3. The governor doesn't agree with this bill, so she plans to _____ it.

4. The state has the _____ to send criminals to jail.

5. **Test Preparation** The mayor's office will prepare a(n) _____ showing how it plans to get and spend money.

   A **budget**   C **issue**
   B **charter**   D **bill**

Comprehension Check

6. What was the purpose of the Declaration of Independence?

7. What are core democratic values?

8. Which branch of the national government makes new laws?

9. Which branch of the national government commands the military?

10. How do local governments use the tax money they collect?

11. **Critical Thinking** In the United States Senate, Michigan and Wyoming each have two senators, even though Michigan's population is ten times larger. Do you think we should change how many senators each state has? Explain your answer.

12. **Critical Thinking** How can young people affect the government of their communities?

Use the Time Line

Use the time line below to answer each question.

13. How many years was it between the signing of the Declaration of Independence and the writing of the Constitution?

14. Which came first—a President from Michigan or a female governor in Michigan?

1775	1850	1925	2000
1776 Declaration of Independence signed in Philadelphia	1787 U.S. Constitution written	1974 Gerald Ford of Michigan becomes 38th U.S. President	2002 Jennifer Granholm elected Michigan governor

Official Documents

Use the Proclamation by the Governor of Michigan, May 5, 1922 to answer the questions.

> ❝ *Fifty years ago the State of Nebraska instituted [began] the observance of a day set apart for tree planting. This day was known as Arbor Day, and its observance has become general throughout the nation . . . by virtue of the authority vested in me as Governor of the State of Michigan, I do hereby designate Friday, May 5, 1922, as Arbor Day, and I request that exercises appropriate to the day be held in all our schools.* ❞

15. How does the governor ask the state to observe Arbor Day?

16. What does the governor mean when he writes that observance of Arbor Day has become "general throughout the nation"?

   A It is observed in the United States and in other countries.

   B It has become the nation's most important holiday.

   C It is observed in most places in the United States.

   D It is ignored by most people.

Make Decisions

Read the passage. Then answer the questions.

Kenan wants to buy a computer game that costs $40. He will not have the money until he gets paid from his part-time job at the end of the month. Kenan's brother Daryll will loan him the money if Kenan agrees to pay Daryll back $45. Think about the options that Kenan has, and what he should do.

17. What options does Kenan have?

18. How much interest is Daryll charging Kenan for the loan?

   A $40   **C** $35

   B $45   **D** $5

19. Make a Poster In small groups, create posters about core democratic values that show why these values are worthwhile. Each group should work on a different value. Then display your posters in the classroom or hall.

20. Persuasive Suppose there was a hall of fame for leaders. Think of a leader you have read about in this book whom you admire. Then write a letter to the Leadership Hall of Fame. Explain why the leader you admire should become a member of the hall of fame.

 For help with the process of writing, visit: www.macmillanmh.com

Unit 5 Review and Test Prep

Comprehension and Critical Thinking Check

Write one or more sentences to answer each question.

1. What **natural resources** have helped to shape Michigan's economy?

2. What do **migrant workers** do?

3. What is a **service industry**?

4. How has **technology** changed jobs in Michigan?

5. How is **international trade** important to Michigan's economy?

6. Provide an example from the unit that shows how countries today are **interdependent**.

7. Where can citizens go to seek **justice**?

8. How is the Michigan state government a **representative government**?

9. **Critical Thinking** What do you think is the best way for people to show **patriotism**? Explain your answer.

10. **Critical Thinking** Would you rather be **mayor**, governor, or President? Why?

Reading Skills Check

Identify Cause and Effect

Copy this graphic organizer. Recall what you read in this unit about Michigan's economy. Use the graphic organizer to help you identify cause-and-effect relationships about how the state meets its needs.

11. What caused Michigan to develop a large lumber industry?

12. What is the effect of many tourists visiting Michigan?

13. What happened because Olds, Ford, and other companies opened auto factories near Detroit?

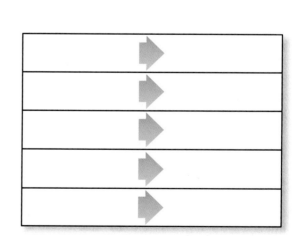

Use the map and what you already know to answer the questions.

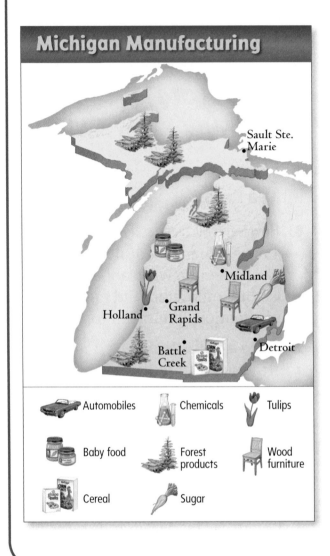

Michigan Manufacturing

- Automobiles
- Baby food
- Cereal
- Chemicals
- Forest products
- Sugar
- Tulips
- Wood furniture

14. Why do you think Michigan is a leading producer of paper and furniture?

A Immigrants needed a lot of paper and furniture.

B Those products are made from trees.

C French fur traders made furniture and paper.

D Henry Ford opened many furniture and paper factories.

15. What do you think is the BEST reason that tulips are grown in Holland, Michigan?

A American Indians in the area used to grow tulips there.

B W.K. Kellogg founded a tulip-growing business in the town in 1905.

C The city was founded by Dutch immigrants, and the tulip is part of their culture.

D The tulip is the official state flower of Michigan.

Write About Economics and Government

16. Persuasive Create a travel brochure that shows Michigan's tourist attractions. Include both outdoor activities and attractions in cities.

17. Expository Suppose you have just been elected governor of Michigan. Write a speech telling citizens what you hope to accomplish during your time in office. Include references to the core democratic values you learned about in this unit.

18. Persuasive Think of an issue that affects people in your community. Write a proposal to present to the public and to elected officials. Your proposal should describe the problem and suggest how citizens and government can deal with the problem.

LOG ON

For help with the process of writing, visit:
www.macmillanmh.com

REVIEW
THE BIG IDEA

How do people in our state meet their needs?

Write About the Big Idea

A Report

Think about the things you read about Michigan's economy and government in Unit 5. Then complete the graphic organizer below by filling in details.

Use information from your graphic organizer and other sources to write a report of several paragraphs. In it, explain some of the ways Michigan meets its needs.

Economy	Government
1. Free enterprise 2. 3. 4.	1. Our nation's government 2. 3.

Write a Report

1. Plan
- Choose either economic needs or government to write about.
- Use the Internet to find more information about your topic.

2. Write a First Draft
- Introduce your topic.
- Add paragraphs that give facts, details, and examples of the ways Michigan meets this need.
- Write a conclusion.

3. Revise and Proofread
- Read your report. Be sure all sentences and paragraphs tell about your topic.
- Check that your first paragraph has a good introduction. Be sure your final paragraph includes a conclusion.
- Check spelling and punctuation.
- Rewrite your report neatly before handing it in to your teacher.

ACTIVITY

Speak About the Big Idea

A Big Idea Newscast

Suppose you are a television reporter. You will report about an event that affects Michgan's economy. It can be an event from the past or a current event. Use your graphic organizer or your report for ideas.

Prepare Work with a partner. You and your partner will be "co-anchors" of a nightly news program. Rehearse your presentation of your topic.

Present Each pair of broadcasters will report on the news event. Be sure to report on what the event is, and what caused the event. You should also tell what the effects of the event might be.

LAUNCH PAD For help with the Big Idea activity, visit: www.macmillanmh.com

Read More About the Big Idea

Start Your Own Business!

Use this Leveled Reader to learn about how you and your friends can make money with your own business.

Getting out the Vote

Read this Leveled Reader to learn about the voting process and the history of voting rights.

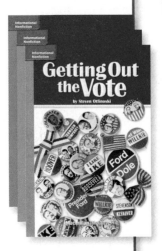

Making Laws: A Look at How a Bill Becomes a Law

by Sandy Donovan What if you had an idea for a new law? Find out about the process that turns an idea into a bill and then a law.

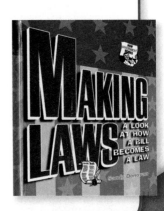

Citizenship Handbook

Good citizens know the Founding Documents of the United States – the Declaration of Independence and the Constitution of the United States.

- The **Declaration of Independence** describes the ideas of our country, the beliefs that support our nation.
- The **Constitution** tells the rules for how our nation will be governed.
- **Amendments**, or changes, to the Constitution show how American ideas about government have changed over the years.
- The first ten amendments, the **Bill of Rights**, list the rights of every American citizen.

This Citizenship Handbook includes explanations of the Founding Documents. Use the blue explanations to help you understand what it means to be an American citizen.

Being a Good Citizen

In your textbook, you have read biographies of people from Michigan. On each BIOGRAPHY page you saw one of the eight words below. These words help define what it means to be a good citizen, and they are the qualities people look for in their leaders. These words describe how to be a good citizen in your home, school, community, state, and country.

COURAGE being brave in the face of difficulty

FREEDOM making choices and holding beliefs of one's own

HONESTY telling the truth

JUSTICE working toward fair treatment for everyone

LEADERSHIP showing good behavior that others will follow

LOYALTY showing support for people and one's country

RESPECT treating others as you would like to be treated

RESPONSIBILITY being worthy of trust

The *Declaration of Independence*

By the summer of 1776, American colonists had been at war with Great Britain for 14 months. During that time colonists debated whether they were fighting to gain more rights from Great Britain or for independence. As the fighting went on, more and more colonists argued that peace with Britain was no longer possible. In June 1776 members of the Second Continental Congress asked Thomas Jefferson (1743–1826) of Virginia to write a statement explaining why the colonies ought to be independent. Read the Declaration of Independence that Jefferson wrote and the notes of explanation beside it. Notice Jefferson's ideas about government, rebellion, and people's rights. Notice also what unjust acts he accuses King George III of Great Britain of having committed against the colonists. How do King George's actions take away the rights that Jefferson believes people and governments should have?

The Preamble

Sometimes people need to break away from their home country and form their own country.

A Declaration of Rights

We believe that all people are created equal and have basic rights that can never be taken away. They are the right to live, to be free, and to look for happiness.

People create governments to preserve these basic rights.

When in the course of human events, it becomes necessary for one people to dissolve the political bands which have connected them with another, and to assume, among the Powers of the earth, the separate and equal station to which the Laws of Nature and of Nature's God entitle them, a decent respect to the opinions of mankind requires that they should declare the causes which impel them to the separation.

We hold these truths to be self-evident, that all men are created equal, that they are endowed by their Creator with certain unalienable Rights, that among these are Life, Liberty, and the pursuit of Happiness.

That, to secure these rights, Governments are instituted among Men, deriving their just Powers from the consent of the governed.

That, whenever any Form of Government becomes destructive of these ends, it is the Right of the People to alter or to abolish it, and to institute new Government, laying its foundation on such Principles, and organizing its powers in such form, as to them shall seem most likely to effect their Safety and Happiness.

Prudence, indeed, will dictate that Governments long established should not be changed for light and transient causes; and, accordingly all experience hath shown, that mankind are more disposed to suffer, while evils are sufferable, than to right themselves by abolishing the forms to which they are accustomed. But, when a long train of abuses and usurpations, pursuing invariably the same Object, evinces a design to reduce them under absolute Despotism, it is their right, it is their duty, to throw off such Government, and to provide new Guards for their future security.

Such has been the patient sufferance of these Colonies; and such is now the necessity which constrains them to alter their former Systems of Government. The history of the present King of Great Britain is a history of repeated injuries and usurpations, all having in direct object the establishment of an absolute Tyranny over these States.

To prove this, let Facts be submitted to a candid world.

He has refused his Assent to Laws the most wholesome and necessary for the public good.

He has forbidden his Governors to pass Laws of immediate and pressing importance, unless suspended in their operation till his Assent should be obtained; and when so suspended, he has utterly neglected to attend to them.

He has refused to pass other Laws for the accommodation of large districts of People, unless those People would relinquish the right of Representation in the Legislature, a right inestimable to them and formidable to tyrants only.

He has called together legislative bodies at places unusual, uncomfortable, and distant from the depository of their Public Records, for the sole purpose of fatiguing them into compliance with his measures.

People have the right to change their government, get rid of it, and form a new one if their government does not preserve their basic rights.

People should not change governments except for important reasons, such as the misuse of power. When this happens, people have the right and duty to form a new government.

A List of Abuses

It is time for the colonies to break away. For years King George III of Great Britain has ruled the colonies badly while he was trying to gain control over them.

He has:

• refused to sign needed laws passed by the colonists or to allow his governors in America to pass important laws.

• refused to recognize large voting districts unless the people living in them give up their right to be represented in the legislature, or lawmaking body.

• ordered lawmakers in the colonies to meet in unusual or hard to get to places to try to get them to accept his rule.

He would not allow colonists to:

- meet in legislatures or hold new elections.

- settle the West or emigrate.

- create courts in some places.

The king also:

- forced colonial judges to obey him.

- sent officials to the colonies who mistreated people and demanded unfair taxes.

- kept soldiers in the colonies in times of peace and tried to give them power over colonial legislatures.

- with other British officials, passed laws for the colonies that the colonists did not want.

- forced colonists to house and feed British soldiers.

- protected soldiers who murdered colonists by not punishing them or giving them fake trials.

- cut off American trade.

- demanded taxes the colonists never agreed to.

- would not allow colonists accused of crimes to be tried by jury.

He has dissolved Representative Houses repeatedly, for opposing, with manly firmness, his invasions on the rights of the people.

He has refused for a long time, after such dissolutions, to cause others to be elected; whereby the Legislative Powers, incapable of Annihilation, have returned to the People at large for their exercise; the State remaining in the mean time exposed to all the dangers of invasion from without, and convulsions within.

He has endeavoured to prevent the Population of these States; for that purpose obstructing the Laws of Naturalization of Foreigners; refusing to pass others to encourage their migration hither, and raising the conditions of new Appropriations of Lands.

He has obstructed the Administration of Justice by refusing his Assent to Laws for establishing judiciary Powers.

He has made judges dependent on his Will alone, for the tenure of their offices, and the amount and payment of their salaries.

He has erected a multitude of New Offices, and sent hither swarms of Officers to harass our People, and eat out their substance.

He has kept among us, in times of Peace, Standing Armies, without the Consent of our legislature.

He has affected to render the Military independent of and superior to the Civil Power.

He has combined with others to subject us to a jurisdiction foreign to our constitution, and unacknowledged by our laws; giving his Assent to their Acts of pretended Legislation:

For quartering large bodies of armed troops among us:

For protecting them, by a mock Trial, from Punishment for any Murders which they should commit on the Inhabitants of these States:

For cutting off our Trade with all parts of the world:

For imposing Taxes on us without our Consent:

For depriving us, in many cases, of the benefits of Trial by jury:

For transporting us beyond Seas to be tried for pretended offences:

For abolishing the free System of English Laws in a neighbouring Province, establishing therein an Arbitrary government, and enlarging its Boundaries, so as to render it at once an example and fit instrument for introducing the same absolute rule into these Colonies:

For taking away our Charters, abolishing our most valuable Laws, and altering fundamentally the Forms of our Governments:

For suspending our own Legislatures, and declaring themselves invested with Power to legislate for us in all cases whatsoever.

He has abdicated Government here, by declaring us out of his Protection and waging War against us.

He has plundered our seas, ravaged our Coasts, burnt our towns, and destroyed the Lives of our People.

He is at this time transporting large Armies of foreign Mercenaries to compleat the works of death, desolation and tyranny, already begun with circumstances of Cruelty & perfidy scarcely paralleled in the most barbarous ages, and totally unworthy the Head of a civilized nation.

He has constrained our fellow Citizens taken Captive on the high Seas to bear Arms against their Country, to become the executioners of their friends and Brethren, or to fall themselves by their Hands.

He has excited domestic insurrections amongst us, and has endeavoured to bring on the inhabitants of our frontiers, the merciless Indian Savages, whose known rule of warfare, is an undistinguished destruction of all ages, sexes and conditions.

In every stage of these Oppressions We have Petitioned for Redress in the most humble terms: Our repeated Petitions have been answered only by repeated injury. A Prince, whose character is thus marked by every act which may define a Tyrant, is unfit to be the ruler of a free People.

- brought colonists falsely accused of a crime to Great Britain to be put on trial.

- ended British laws in the Ohio River Valley and recognized this area as French territory (forcing the colonists living there to obey harsh French laws).

- took away important laws and the charters that made our governments legal and changed our governments.

- ended our legislatures and claimed to have the right to pass laws for us.

King George III gave up his right to rule the colonies when he failed to protect us and went to war against us.

He has:

- robbed American ships at sea, forced captured sailors to join the British navy, and burned down our towns.

- brought foreign soldiers to the colonies to commit cruel acts against us.

- tried to persuade enslaved people in the colonies to rebel and Native Americans to fight the colonists.

Statement of Independence

For years we have asked King George III to correct these problems, without success. The king is an unfair ruler who is not fit to rule a free people.

We have told the British about our problems and about the unfair laws passed by their government. We hoped they would help us because they believe in justice, are related to us, and have much in common with us. We were wrong. We must, therefore, break away from Great Britain and create our own country.

Nor have We been wanting in attention to our British brethren. We have warned them from time to time of attempts by their legislature to extend an unwarrantable jurisdiction over us. We have reminded them of the circumstances of our emigration and settlement here. We have appealed to their native justice and magnanimity, and we have conjured them by the ties of our common kindred to disavow these usurpations, which, would inevitably interrupt our connections and correspondence. They too have been deaf to the voice of justice and of consanguinity. We must, therefore, acquiesce in the necessity, which denounces our Separation, and hold them, as we hold the rest of mankind, Enemies in War, in Peace Friends.

We, therefore, the Representatives of the United States of America, in General Congress Assembled,

Signers	Button Gwinnett (Ga.)	William Hooper (N.C.)	John Hancock (Mass.)
	Lyman Hall (Ga.)	Joseph Hewes (N.C.)	Samuel Chase (Md.)
	George Walton (Ga.)	John Penn (N.C.)	William Paca (Md.)
		Edward Rutledge (S.C.)	Thomas Stone (Md.)
		Thomas Heyward, Jr. (S.C.)	Charles Carroll of Carrollton (Md.)
		Thomas Lynch, Jr. (S.C.)	George Wythe (Va.)
		Arthur Middleton (S.C.)	Richard Henry Lee (Va.)
			Thomas Jefferson (Va.)
			Benjamin Harrison (Va.)
			Thomas Nelson, Jr. (Va.)
			Francis Lightfoot Lee (Va.)
			Carter Braxton (Va.)

appealing to the Supreme judge of the world for the rectitude of our intentions, do, in the Name, and by Authority of the good People of these Colonies, solemnly publish and declare, That these United Colonies are, and of Right ought to be Free and Independent States; that they are Absolved from all Allegiance to the British Crown, and that all political connection between them and the State of Great Britain, is and ought to be totally dissolved; and that as Free and Independent States, they have full Power to levy War, conclude Peace, contract Alliances, establish Commerce, and to do all other Acts and Things which Independent States may of right do. And for the support of this Declaration, with a firm reliance on the protection of divine Providence, we mutually pledge to each other our Lives, our Fortunes and our sacred Honour.

In the name of the American people, we, members of the Continental Congress, state that the United States is no longer a colony of Great Britain. Instead, it is an independent country. This gives it the right to make war and peace, make agreements with other countries, trade with them, and do all the things that free countries do. We support this Declaration of Independence by promising each other our lives, our fortunes, and our honor.

Robert Morris (Pa.)
Benjamin Rush (Pa.)
Benjamin Franklin (Pa.)
John Morton (Pa.)
George Clymer (Pa.)
James Smith (Pa.)
George Taylor (Pa.)
James Wilson (Pa.)
George Ross (Pa.)
Cæsar Rodney (Del.)
George Read (Del.)
Thomas McKean (Del.)

William Floyd (N.Y.)
Philip Livingston (N.Y.)
Francis Lewis (N.Y.)
Lewis Morris (N.Y.)
Richard Stockton (N.J.)
John Witherspoon (N.J.)
Francis Hopkinson (R.I.)
John Hart (N.J.)
Abraham Clark (N.J.)

Josiah Bartlett (N.H.)
William Whipple (N.H.)
Samuel Adams (Mass.)
John Adams (Mass.)
Robert Treat Paine (Mass.)
Elbridge Gerry (Mass.)
Stephen Hopkins (R.I.)
William Ellery (R.I.)
Roger Sherman (Conn.)
Samuel Huntington (Conn.)
William Williams (Conn.)
Oliver Wolcott (Conn.)
Matthew Thornton (N.H.)

The Constitution of The United States

Explanation and Summary

The following text explains the meaning of the Constitution and its Amendments. Crossed out sentences are no longer in effect.

Preamble

The people of the United States make this Constitution to form a stronger nation; to ensure peace, justice, and liberty; to defend its citizens; and to improve the lives of its people.

Article 1

Congress has the power to make laws. It is made up of the Senate and the House of Representatives.

1. Members of the House of Representatives are elected every two years by voters in each state.

2. A member of the House of Representatives must be at least 25 years old, a U.S. citizen for at least seven years, and live in the state he or she represents.

3. The number of Representatives for each state is based on the number of people who live in that state. Every ten years a census, or count, must be taken to determine the population of each state. (This census included indentured servants but not most Native Americans. Each enslaved person was counted as three-fifths of a free person. Today all people are counted equally.)

Preamble

We the people of the United States, in order to form a more perfect Union, establish justice, insure domestic tranquility, provide for the common Defense, promote the general welfare, and secure the blessings of liberty to ourselves and our posterity, do ordain and establish this Constitution for the United States of America.

Article 1. The Legislative Branch

Section 1. The Congress

All legislative powers herein granted shall be vested in a Congress of the United States, which shall consist of a Senate and House of Representatives.

Section 2. The House of Representatives

1. The House of Representatives shall be composed of members chosen every second year by the people of the several states, and the electors in each state shall have the qualifications requisite for electors of the most numerous branch of the state legislature.

2. No person shall be a Representative who shall not have attained to the age of twenty-five years, and been seven years a citizen of the United States, and who shall not, when elected, be an inhabitant of that state in which he shall be chosen.

3. Representatives and ~~direct taxes~~ shall be apportioned among the several states which may be included within this Union, according to their respective numbers, ~~which shall be determined by adding to the whole number of free persons, including those bound to service for a term of years, and excluding Indians not taxed, three-fifths of all other persons.~~ The actual enumeration shall be made within three years after the first meeting of the Congress of the United States, and within every subsequent term of ten years, in such manner as they shall by law direct. The number of Representatives shall not exceed one for every 30,000, but each state shall have at least one Representative; ~~and until~~

such enumeration shall be made, the state of New Hampshire shall be entitled to choose three, Massachusetts, eight, Rhode Island and Providence Plantations, one, Connecticut, five, New York, six, New Jersey, four, Pennsylvania, eight, Delaware, one, Maryland, six, Virginia, ten, North Carolina, five, South Carolina, five, and Georgia, three.

4. When vacancies happen in the representation from any state, the executive authority thereof shall issue writs of election to fill such vacancies.

5. The House of Representatives shall choose their Speaker and other officers; and shall have the sole power of impeachment.

4. Special elections called by the state's governor must be held to fill any empty seat in the House of Representatives.

5. Members of the House of Representatives choose their own leaders. Only they have the power to impeach, or accuse, government officials of crimes in office.

Section 3. The Senate

1. The Senate of the United States shall be composed of two Senators from each state, chosen by the legislature thereof, for six years; and each Senator shall have one vote.

1. Each state has two Senators. Each one serves a term of six years and has one vote in the Senate. (State legislatures elected Senators. The Seventeenth Amendment changed this. Senators are now elected directly by the people.)

2. Immediately after they shall be assembled in consequence of the first election, they shall be divided as equally as may be into three classes. The seats of the Senators of the first class shall be vacated at the expiration of the second year, of the second class at the expiration of the fourth year, and of the third class at the expiration of the sixth year, so that one-third may be chosen every second year; and if vacancies happen by resignation, or otherwise, during the recess of the legislature of any state, the executive thereof may make temporary appointments until the next meeting of the legislature, which shall then fill such vacancies.

2. One-third of the Senate seats are up for election every two years. (The Seventeenth Amendment changed the way empty seats are filled.)

3. No person shall be a Senator who shall not have attained to the age of thirty years, and been nine years a citizen of the United States, and who shall not, when elected, be an inhabitant of that state for which he shall be chosen.

4. The Vice President of the United States shall be president of the Senate, but shall have no vote, unless they be equally divided.

5. The Senate shall choose their other officers, and also a president pro tempore, in the absence of the Vice President, or when he shall exercise the office of the President of the United States.

3. To be a Senator, a person must be at least 30 years old, a U.S. citizen for at least nine years, and live in the state he or she represents.

4. The Vice President is in charge of the Senate but votes only to break a tie.

5. Senators choose their own leaders. When the Vice President is absent, the Senate leader is called the President pro tempore (prō tem´pə rē), or temporary President.

6. The Senate holds all impeachment trials. When the President is impeached, the Chief Justice of the Supreme Court is the judge for the trial. A two-thirds vote is needed for conviction, or judgment of guilt.

7. Impeached officials convicted by the Senate can be removed from office and barred from serving again in government. Regular courts of law can decide other punishments.

1. State lawmakers make the rules for Congressional elections. Congress can change some of these rules.

2. Congress meets at least once a year, beginning in December. (The Twentieth Amendment changed this date to January 3.)

1. The Senate and House of Representatives decide if their members were elected fairly and are qualified. Half the members of each house of Congress must be present for Congress to do most business. Absent members can be required to attend meetings of Congress.

2. Each house of Congress may set rules and punish members for breaking them. A two-thirds vote is needed to expel, or force out, a member.

3. Each house of Congress keeps and publishes a record of its activities. Secret matters may be left out of this record. If one-fifth of the members demand it, a vote on any matter will be published.

4. During a session of Congress, neither house can stop meeting for more than three days or decide to meet somewhere else unless the other house agrees.

6. The Senate shall have the sole power to try all impeachments. When sitting for that purpose, they shall be on oath or affirmation. When the President of the United States is tried, the Chief Justice shall preside; and no person shall be convicted without the concurrence of two-thirds of the members present.

7. Judgment in cases of impeachment shall not extend further than to removal from office, and disqualification to hold and enjoy any office of honor, trust or profit under the United States; but the party convicted shall nevertheless be liable and subject to indictment, trial, judgment and punishment, according to law.

Section 4. Elections and Meetings of Congress

1. The times, places and manner of holding elections for Senators and Representatives shall be prescribed in each state by the legislature thereof; but the Congress may at any time by law make or alter such regulations, ~~except as to the places of choosing Senators~~.

2. The Congress shall assemble at least once in every year ~~and such meeting shall be on the first Monday in December, unless they shall by law appoint a different day~~.

Section 5. Rules of Procedure for Congress

1. Each house shall be the judge of the elections, returns and qualifications of its own members, and a majority of each shall constitute a quorum to do business; but a smaller number may adjourn from day to day, and may be authorized to compel the attendance of absent members, in such manner, and under such penalties as each house may provide.

2. Each house may determine the rules of its proceedings, punish its members for disorderly behavior, and with the concurrence of two-thirds, expel a member.

3. Each house shall keep a journal of its proceedings, and from time to time publish the same, excepting such parts as may in their judgment require secrecy; and the yeas and nays of the members of either house on any question shall, at the desire of one-fifth of those present, be entered on the journal.

4. Neither house, during the session of Congress, shall, without the consent of the other, adjourn for more than three days, nor to any other place than that in which the two houses shall be sitting.

Section 6. Privileges and Restrictions of Members of Congress

1. The Senators and Representatives shall receive a compensation for their services, to be ascertained by law, and paid out of the Treasury of the United States. They shall in all cases, except treason, felony and breach of the peace, be privileged from arrest during their attendance at the session of their respective houses, and in going to and returning from the same; and for any speech or debate in either house, they shall not be questioned in any other place.

2. No Senator or Representative shall, during the time for which he was elected, be appointed to any civil office under the authority of the United States, which shall have been created, or the emoluments whereof shall have been increased during such time; and no person holding any office under the United States, shall be a member of either house during his continuance in office.

Section 7. How Laws Are Made

1. All bills for raising revenue shall originate in the House of Representatives; but the Senate may propose or concur with amendments as on other bills.

2. Every bill which shall have passed the House of Representatives and the Senate, shall, before it become a law, be presented to the President of the United States. If he approve he shall sign it, but if not he shall return it, with his objections to that house in which it shall have originated, who shall enter the objections at large on their journal, and proceed to reconsider it. If after such reconsideration two-thirds of that house shall agree to pass the bill, it shall be sent, together with the objections, to the other house, by which it shall likewise be reconsidered, and if approved by two-thirds of that house, it shall become a law. But in all such cases the votes of both houses shall be determined by yeas and nays, and the names of the persons voting for and against the bill shall be entered on the journal of each house respectively. If any bill shall not be returned by the President within ten days (Sundays excepted) after it shall have been presented to him, the same shall be a law, in like manner as if he had signed it, unless the Congress by their adjournment prevent its return, in which case it shall not be a law.

3. Every order, resolution, or vote to which the concurrence of the Senate and House of Representatives may be necessary (except on a question of adjournment) shall be presented to the President of the United States; and before the same shall take effect, shall be approved by him, or being disapproved by him, shall be repassed by two-thirds of the Senate and House of Representatives, according to the rules and limitations prescribed in the case of a bill.

---

1. Each member of Congress receives a salary from the U.S. government. Except for very serious crimes, no member can be arrested in the place where Congress is meeting. Members cannot be arrested for anything they say in Congress.

2. Senators and Representatives may not hold any other job in the federal government while they serve in Congress.

1. All money and tax bills must begin in the House of Representatives. The Senate can later pass or change these bills.

2. After a bill, or suggested law, passes both houses of Congress, it goes to the President. If the President signs the bill, it becomes a law. If the President vetoes, or rejects, the bill, it goes back to Congress. A President's veto can be overridden, or upset, if Congress votes again and two-thirds of the members of each house vote in favor of the bill. The bill becomes a law. If the President does not sign or vetoes a bill within ten days (not counting Sundays) of first receiving it, the bill becomes a law. If Congress stops meeting before ten days have passed, however, the bill does not become a law. (This last type of action is called a "pocket veto.")

3. Every act passed by Congress must be given to the President either to sign or veto. The only exception is when Congress votes to adjourn, or stop meeting.

Congress has the power to:

1. raise and collect taxes to pay debts and to protect and serve the country. However, federal taxes must be the same everywhere in the United States;

2. borrow money;

3. control trade with foreign nations, between states, and with Native Americans;

4. decide how people can become U.S. citizens and make laws dealing with people and businesses unable to pay their debts;

5. print money, decide its value, and decide the standards of weights and measures;

6. punish people who make counterfeit, or fake, money and bonds;

7. set up post offices and roads for the delivery of mail;

8. protect the rights and creations of scientists, artists, authors, and inventors;

9. create federal, or national, courts lower than the Supreme Court;

10. punish crimes committed at sea;

11. declare war;

12. form and support an army, but the money set aside to do this can be for no more than two years;

13. form and support a navy;

14. make rules for the armed forces;

15. call the militia (today called the National Guard) to make sure federal laws are obeyed, put down rebellions, and fight invasions;

16. organize, arm, and discipline the National Guard, though states have

Section 8. Powers Granted to Congress

1. The Congress shall have power to lay and collect taxes, duties, imposts and excises, to pay the debts and provide for the common defense and general welfare of the United States; but all duties, imposts and excises shall be uniform throughout the United States;

2. To borrow money on the credit of the United States;

3. To regulate commerce with foreign nations, and among the several states, and with the Indian tribes;

4. To establish a uniform rule of naturalization, and uniform laws on the subject of bankruptcies throughout the United States;

5. To coin money, regulate the value thereof, and of foreign coin, and fix the standard of weights and measures;

6. To provide for the punishment of counterfeiting the securities and current coin of the United States;

7. To establish post offices and post roads;

8. To promote the progress of science and useful arts, by securing for limited times to authors and inventors the exclusive right to their respective writings and discoveries;

9. To constitute tribunals inferior to the Supreme Court;

10. To define and punish piracies and felonies committed on the high seas and offenses against the law of nations;

11. To declare war, ~~grant letters of marque and reprisal~~, and make rules concerning captures on land and water;

12. To raise and support armies, but no appropriation of money to that use shall be for a longer term than two years;

13. To provide and maintain a navy;

14. To make rules for the government and regulation of the land and naval forces;

15. To provide for calling forth the militia to execute the laws of the Union, suppress insurrections and repel invasions;

16. To provide for organizing, arming, and disciplining, the militia, and for governing such part of them as may be employed in the service of the United States, reserving to the states respectively, the appointment of the officers, and the authority of training the militia according to the discipline prescribed by Congress;

17. To exercise exclusive legislation in all cases whatsoever, over such district (not exceeding ten miles square) as may, by cession of particular states, and the acceptance of Congress, become the seat of the government of the United States, and to exercise like authority over all places purchased by the consent of the legislature of the state in which the same shall be, for the erection of forts, magazines, arsenals, dockyards, and other needful buildings;—and

18. To make all laws which shall be necessary and proper for carrying into execution the foregoing powers, and all other powers vested by this Constitution in the government of the United States, or in any department or officer thereof.

Section 9. Powers Denied to Congress

1. ~~The migration or importation of such persons as any of the states now existing shall think proper to admit, shall not be prohibited by the Congress prior to the year one thousand eight hundred and eight, but a tax or duty may be imposed on such importation, not exceeding ten dollars for each person.~~

2. The privilege of the writ of habeas corpus shall not be suspended, unless when in cases of rebellion or invasion the public safety may require it.

3. No bill of attainder or ex post facto law shall be passed.

4. No capitation, or other direct, tax shall be laid, unless in proportion to the census or enumeration herein before directed to be taken.

5. No tax or duty shall be laid on articles exported from any state.

6. No preference shall be given any regulation of commerce or revenue to the ports of one state over those of another; nor shall vessels bound to, or from, one state, be obliged to enter, clear, or pay duties in another.

7. No money shall be drawn from the Treasury, but in consequence of appropriations made by law; and a regular statement and account of the receipts and expenditures of all public money shall be published from time to time.

the power to appoint officers and train soldiers in the National Guard;

17. govern the capital and military sites of the United States;

18. make all laws necessary to carry out the powers of Congress. (This is called the "elastic clause" because it stretches the powers of Congress.)

Congress does not have the power to:

1. stop enslaved people from being brought into the United States before 1808. In 1808, the first year trade was allowed, Congress passed a law banning it;

2. arrest and jail people without charging them with a crime, except during a rebellion or emergency;

3. punish a person who has not had a trial or has done something wrong that was not against the law when the person did it;

4. pass a direct tax (such as an income tax) unless it is in proportion to the population. (The Sixteenth Amendment allowed an income tax);

5. tax goods sent out of a state;

6. favor ports of one state over ports of another state; nor can a state tax the ships of another state that enter its borders;

7. spend money without passing a law and keeping a record of what is spent;

8. give someone a title of nobility (such as king or queen); nor may a worker in the federal government accept a gift or title from a foreign government.

State governments do not have the power to:

1. make treaties, print money, or do anything forbidden in Section 9 of the Constitution, above;

2. tax goods sent into and out of a state unless Congress agrees;

3. keep armed forces, go to war, or make agreements with other states or countries unless Congress agrees.

Article 2

1. The President has the power to execute, or carry out, the laws of the United States. The President and Vice President together serve a term of four years.

2. The President is chosen by electors from each state. Today these electors are chosen by the voters and are called the Electoral College. The number of electoral votes for each state is decided by adding up the number of the state's Senators and Representatives.

3. (This part of the Constitution describes the first way the President and Vice President were elected. The Twelfth Amendment changed this method. Originally, the person who

8. No title of nobility shall be granted by the United States; and no person holding any office of profit or trust under them, shall, without the consent of the Congress, accept of any present, emolument, office, or title, of any kind whatever, from any king, prince, or foreign state.

Section 10. Powers Denied to the States

1. No state shall enter into any treaty, alliance, or confederation; grant letters of marque and reprisal; coin money; emit bills of credit; make anything but gold and silver coin a tender in payment of debts; pass any bill of attainder, ex post facto law, or law impairing the obligation of contracts, or grant any title of nobility.

2. No state shall, without the consent of the Congress, lay any imposts or duties on imports or exports, except what may be absolutely necessary for executing its inspection laws; and the net produce of all duties and imposts, laid by any state on imports or exports, shall be for the use of the Treasury of the United States; and all such laws shall be subject to the revision and control of the Congress.

3. No state shall, without the consent of Congress, lay any duty of tonnage, keep troops, or ships of war in time of peace, enter into any agreement or compact with another state, or with a foreign power, or engage in war, unless actually invaded, or in such imminent danger as will not admit of delay.

Article 2. The Executive Branch

Section 1. Office of President and Vice President

1. The executive power shall be vested in a President of the United States of America. He shall hold his office during the term of four years, and, together with the Vice President, chosen for the same term, be elected, as follows:

2. Each state shall appoint, in such manner as the legislature thereof may direct, a number of electors, equal to the whole number of Senators and Representatives to which the state may be entitled in the Congress; but no Senator or Representative, or person holding an office or trust or profit under the United States, shall be appointed an elector.

3. ~~The electors shall meet in their respective states, and vote by ballot for two persons, of whom one at least shall not be an inhabitant of the same state with themselves. And they shall make a list of all the persons voted for, and of the number of votes for each; which list they shall sign and certify, and transmit sealed~~

to the seat of the government of the United States, directed to the president of the Senate. The president of the Senate shall, in the presence of the Senate and House of Representatives, open all the certificates, and the votes shall then be counted. The person having the greatest number of votes shall be the President, if such number be a majority of the whole number of electors appointed; and if there be more than one who have such majority, and have an equal number of votes, then the House of Representatives shall immediately choose by ballot one of them for President; and if no person have a majority, then from the five highest on the list the said House shall in like manner choose the President. But in choosing the President, the votes shall be taken by states, the representation from each state having one vote; a quorum for this purpose shall consist of a member or members from two-thirds of the states, and a majority of all the states shall be necessary to a choice. In every case, after the choice of the President, the person having the greatest number of votes of the electors shall be the Vice President. But if there should remain two or more who have equal votes, the Senate shall choose from them by ballot the Vice President.

received the most electoral votes became President and the person who received the next highest number became Vice President.)

4. The Congress may determine the time of choosing the electors, and the day on which they shall give their votes; which day shall be the same throughout the United States.

4. Congress decides when Presidential electors are chosen and when they vote. Electors vote on the same day throughout the country. (Today people vote for the electors every four years on the Tuesday after the first Monday of November.)

5. No person except a natural born citizen, or a citizen of the United States, at the time of the adoption of this Constitution, shall be eligible to the office of the President; neither shall any person be eligible to that office who shall not have attained to the age of thirty-five years, and been fourteen years a resident within the United States.

5. To be President, a person must be a citizen born in the United States, at least 35 years old, and have lived in the United States for at least 14 years.

6. In case of the removal of the President from office, or of his death, resignation, or inability to discharge the powers and duties of the said office, the same shall devolve on the Vice President, and the Congress may by law provide for the case of removal, death, resignation, or inability, both of the President and Vice President, declaring what officer shall then act as President, and such officer shall act accordingly, until the disability be removed, or a President shall be elected.

6. If the President leaves office or can no longer serve, the Vice President becomes President. If there is no Vice President, Congress may decide who becomes President. (The Twenty-Fifth Amendment changed the way these offices are filled.)

7. The President shall, at stated times receive for his services, a compensation, which shall neither be increased nor diminished during the period for which he shall have been elected, and he shall not receive within that period any other emolument from the United States, or any of them.

7. The President receives a salary that cannot be raised or lowered while in office. The President can receive no other gift or salary from the country or its states while in office.

8. Before taking office, the person elected President takes an oath to carry out the laws of the country and to defend the Constitution.

1. The President is in charge of the armed forces and state militias. The President can demand written advice and opinions of the people in charge of each executive department (the President's Cabinet). The President also has the power to pardon, or free, people convicted of federal crimes, except in cases of impeachment.

2. The President has the power to make treaties, but they must be approved by two-thirds of the Senate. The President also has the power to name ambassadors, important government officials, and judges of the Supreme Court and other federal courts, with the approval of the Senate.

3. The President has the power to fill empty offices for a short time when the Senate is not meeting.

The President must tell Congress from time to time what the condition of the country is. (This speech is called the State of the Union address and is given once a year, usually in late January.) In this message, the President recommends ways to improve the country. The President can also, in time of emergency, call Congress to meet. When Congress cannot decide whether or not to stop meetings, the President can make this decision. The President receives foreign officials, makes sure the country's laws are carried out, and appoints officers in the armed forces.

8. Before he enter on the execution of his office, he shall take the following oath or affirmation:—"I do solemnly swear (or affirm) that I will faithfully execute the office of President of the United States, and will to the best of my ability, preserve, protect and defend the Constitution of the United States."

Section 2. Powers Granted to the President

1. The President shall be Commander in Chief of the Army and Navy of the United States, and of the militia of the several states, when called into the actual service of the United States; he may require the opinion, in writing, of the principal officer in each of the executive departments, upon any subject relating to the duties of their respective offices, and he shall have power to grant reprieves and pardons for offenses against the United States, except in cases of impeachment.

2. He shall have power, by and with the advice and consent of the Senate, to make treaties, provided two-thirds of the Senators present concur; and he shall nominate, and by and with the advice and consent of the Senate, shall appoint ambassadors, other public ministers and consuls, judges of the Supreme Court, and all other officers of the United States, whose appointments are not herein otherwise provided for, and which shall be established by law; but the Congress may by law vest the appointment of such inferior officers, as they think proper, in the President alone, in the courts of law, or in the heads of departments.

3. The President shall have power to fill up all vacancies that may happen during the recess of the Senate, by granting commissions which shall expire at the end of their next session.

Section 3. Duties of the President

He shall from time to time give to the Congress information of the state of the Union, and recommend to their consideration such measures as he shall judge necessary and expedient; he may, on extraordinary occasions, convene both houses, or either of them, and in case of disagreement between them, with respect to the time of adjournment, he may adjourn them to such time as he shall think proper; he shall receive ambassadors and other public ministers; he shall take care that the laws be faithfully executed, and shall commission all the officers of the United States.

Section 4. Removal from Office

The President, Vice President and all civil officers of the United States, shall be removed from office on impeachment for, and conviction of, treason, bribery, or other high crimes and misdemeanors.

Article 3. The Judicial Branch

Section 1. Federal Courts

The judicial power of the United States shall be vested in one Supreme Court, and in such inferior courts as the Congress may from time to time ordain and establish. The judges, both of the Supreme and inferior courts, shall hold their offices during good behavior, and shall, at stated times, receive for their services, a compensation, which shall not be diminished during their continuance in office.

Section 2. Powers of Federal Courts

1. The judicial power shall extend to all cases, in law and equity, arising under this Constitution, the laws of the United States, and treaties made, or which shall be made, under their authority; to all cases affecting ambassadors, other public ministers and consuls; to all cases of admiralty and maritime jurisdiction; to controversies to which the United States shall be a party; to controversies between two or more states; between a state and citizens of another state; between citizens of different states, between citizens of the same state claiming lands under grants of different states, and between a state, or the citizens thereof, and foreign states, citizens or subjects.

2. In all cases affecting ambassadors, other public ministers and consuls, and those in which a state shall be party, the Supreme Court shall have original jurisdiction. In all the other cases before mentioned, the Supreme Court shall have appellate jurisdiction, both as to law and fact, with such exceptions, and under such regulations as the Congress shall make.

3. The trial of all crimes, except in cases of impeachment, shall be by jury; and such trial shall be held in the state where the said crimes shall have been committed; but when not committed within any state, the trial shall be at such place or places as the Congress may by law have directed.

The President, Vice President, and other non-military officials may be impeached, or accused of committing crimes, and removed from office if found guilty.

Article 3
The judicial power, or the power of courts to make decisions, is held by the Supreme Court and by lower federal, or national, courts created by Congress. Supreme Court and other federal judges hold office for life if they act properly. Judges receive a salary that cannot be lowered.

1. Federal courts have authority over:
a) all laws made under the Constitution;
b) treaties with foreign governments;
c) cases involving:
  • matters occurring at sea;
  • the federal government;
  • different states or citizens of different states; and
  • foreign citizens or governments.
  (The Eleventh Amendment partly limits which cases federal courts can hear.)

2. In cases involving either states or ambassadors and government officials, the Supreme Court only makes a judgment. All other cases begin in lower courts but may later be appealed to, or reviewed by, the Supreme Court.

3. All criminal cases, except those of impeachment, are judged by trial and jury in the state where the supposed crime took place. If a crime occurs outside of any state, Congress decides where the trial takes place.

1. Treason is the crime of making war against the United States or helping its enemies. To be found guilty of treason, a person must confess to the crime or two witnesses must swear to having seen the crime committed.

2. Congress decides the punishment for treason. Relatives of people convicted of treason cannot also be punished for the crime.

Article 4
Each state must respect the laws, records, and court decisions of other states. Congress may pass laws to help carry out these matters.

1. Citizens are guaranteed all their basic rights when visiting other states.

2. A person charged with a crime, who flees to another state, must be returned to the state where the crime took place if the governor of the state demands it.

3. A person enslaved in one state, who flees to another state, is still enslaved and must be returned to the person's owner. (The Thirteenth Amendment, which outlawed slavery, overturned or took away the need for this section of the Constitution.)

1. Congress may let new states become part of the United States. No new state can be formed from another state or by joining parts of other states, unless Congress and the legislatures of the states involved approve.

2. Congress has the power to make laws and rules for territories and government properties of the United States.

Section 3. The Crime of Treason

1. Treason against the United States shall consist only in levying war against them, or in adhering to their enemies, giving them aid and comfort. No person shall be convicted of treason unless on the testimony of two witnesses to the same overt act, or on confession in open court.

2. The Congress shall have power to declare the punishment of treason, but no attainder of treason shall work corruption of blood, or forfeiture except during the life of the person attainted.

Article 4. *Relations Among the States*

Section 1. Recognition by Each State of Acts of Other States

Full faith and credit shall be given in each state to the public acts, records, and judicial proceedings of every other state. And the Congress may by general laws prescribe the manner in which such acts, records and proceedings shall be proved, and the effect thereof.

Section 2. Rights of Citizens in Other States

1. The citizens of each state shall be entitled to all privileges and immunities of citizens in the several states.

2. A person charged in any state with treason, felony, or other crime, who shall flee from justice, and be found in another state, shall on demand of the executive authority of the state from which he fled, be delivered up, to be removed to the state having jurisdiction of the crime.

3. No person held to service or labor in one state, under the laws thereof, escaping into another, shall, in consequence of any law or regulation therein, be discharged from such service or labor, but shall be delivered up on claim of the party to whom such service or labor may be due.

Section 3. Treatment of New States and Territories

1. New states may be admitted by the Congress into this Union; but no new state shall be formed or erected within the jurisdiction of any other state; nor any state be formed by the junction of two or more states, or parts of states, without the consent of the legislatures of the states concerned as well as of the Congress.

2. The Congress shall have power to dispose of and make all needful rules and regulations respecting the territory or other property belonging to the United States; and nothing in this Constitution shall be so construed as to prejudice any claims of the United States, or of any particular state.

Section 4. Guarantees to the States

The United States shall guarantee to every state in this Union a republican form of government, and shall protect each of them against invasion; and on application of the legislature, or of the executive (when the legislature cannot be convened) against domestic violence.

Article 5. Amending the Constitution

The Congress, whenever two-thirds of both houses shall deem it necessary, shall propose amendments to this Constitution, or, on the application of the legislatures of two-thirds of the several states, shall call a convention for proposing amendments, which, in either case, shall be valid to all intents and purposes, as part of this Constitution, when ratified by the legislatures of three-fourths of the several states, or by conventions in three-fourths thereof, as the one or the other mode of ratification may be proposed by the Congress; provided that ~~no amendment which may be made prior to the year one thousand eight hundred and eight shall in any manner affect the first and fourth clauses in the Ninth Section of the First Article; and that~~ no state, without its consent, shall be deprived of its equal suffrage in the Senate.

Article 6. Debts, Federal Supremacy, Oaths of Office

Section 1. Prior Debts of the United States

All debts contracted and engagements entered into, before the adoption of this Constitution, shall be as valid against the United States under this Constitution, as under the Confederation.

Section 2. The Supreme Law of the Land

This Constitution, and the laws of the United States which shall be made in pursuance thereof; and all treaties made, or which shall be made, under the authority of the United States, shall be the supreme law of the land; and the judges in every state shall be bound thereby, anything in the constitution or laws of any state to the contrary notwithstanding.

Section 3. Oaths of Office

The Senators and Representatives before mentioned, and the members of the several state legislatures, and all executive and judicial officers, both of the United States and of the several states, shall be bound by oath or affirmation, to support this Constitution; but no religious test shall ever be required as a qualification to any office or public trust under the United States.

The federal government guarantees that the people of each state have the right to elect their leaders. It also promises to protect each state from invasion, rebellion, and acts of violence.

Article 5
There are two ways to make amendments, or changes, to the Constitution: two-thirds of each branch of Congress can ask for an amendment; or, two-thirds of the state legislatures can call an official meeting to ask for an amendment. Three-fourths of the state legislatures or three-fourths of special state conventions must approve the suggested amendment for it to become part of the Constitution. No state can be denied its equal vote in the Senate without its approval. No amendment could be made before 1808 that affected either the slave trade or certain direct taxes.

Article 6
The United States government promises to pay back all debts and honor all agreements made by the government under the Articles of Confederation.

The Constitution and all the laws and treaties made under it are the supreme, or highest, law in the United States. If state or local laws disagree with federal law, the federal law must be obeyed.

All officials of the federal and state governments must promise to support the Constitution. A person's religion may never be used to give a person a job in the U.S. government or to take it away.

Article 7
The Constitution will become law when special conventions in 9 (of the 13 original) states approve it.

This Constitution is completed by the agreement of everyone at this convention on September 17, 1787.

The people present have signed their names below.

Article 7. Ratification of the Constitution

The ratification of the conventions of nine states, shall be sufficient for the establishment of this Constitution between the states so ratifying the same.

Done in convention by the unanimous consent of the States present the Seventeenth day of September in the year of our Lord one thousand seven hundred and eighty seven, and of the Independence of the United States of America the Twelfth.

In witness whereof we have hereunto subscribed our names.

George Washington, President and deputy from Virginia

DELAWARE
George Read
Gunning Bedford, Jr.
John Dickinson
Richard Bassett
Jacob Broom

MARYLAND
James McHenry
Daniel of St. Thomas Jenifer
Daniel Carroll

VIRGINIA
John Blair
James Madison, Jr.

NORTH CAROLINA
William Blount
Richard Dobbs Spaight
Hugh Williamson

SOUTH CAROLINA
John Rutledge
Charles Cotesworth Pinckney
Charles Pinckney
Pierce Butler

GEORGIA
William Few
Abraham Baldwin

NEW HAMPSHIRE
John Langdon
Nicholas Gilman

MASSACHUSETTS
Nathaniel Gorham
Rufus King

CONNECTICUT
William Samuel Johnson
Roger Sherman

NEW YORK
Alexander Hamilton

NEW JERSEY
William Livingston
David Brearley
William Paterson
Jonathan Dayton

PENNSYLVANIA
Benjamin Franklin
Thomas Mifflin
Robert Morris
George Clymer
Thomas FitzSimons
Jared Ingersoll
James Wilson
Gouverneur Morris

Attest: William Jackson, Secretary

Amendments to the Constitution

Amendment 1. Freedom of Religion, Speech, Press, Assembly, and Petition (1791)

Congress shall make no law respecting an establishment of religion, or prohibiting the free exercise thereof; or abridging the freedom of speech, or of the press; or the right of the people peaceably to assemble, and to petition the government for a redress of grievances.

Amendment 1
Under the First Amendment, Congress cannot make laws that:
1) set up an official religion; or prevent people from practicing their religion;
2) stop people from saying what they want;
3) stop people from printing what they want;
4) prevent people from gathering peacefully and asking the government to listen to their problems and to correct them.

Amendment 2. Right to Keep Weapons (1791)

A well-regulated militia being necessary to the security of a free state, the right of the people to keep and bear arms shall not be infringed.

Amendment 2
People have the right to keep weapons and be part of the state militia (today the National Guard).

Amendment 3. Protection Against Quartering Soldiers (1791)

No soldier shall, in time of peace, be quartered in any house, without the consent of the owner, nor in time of war, but in a manner to be prescribed by law.

Amendment 3
During peacetime, people cannot be forced to house and feed soldiers in their homes. During war, Congress may set other rules.

Amendment 4. Freedom from Unreasonable Search and Seizure (1791)

The right of the people to be secure in their persons, houses, papers, and effects, against unreasonable searches and seizures, shall not be violated, and no warrants shall issue, but upon probable cause, supported by oath or affirmation, and particularly describing the place to be searched, and the persons or things to be seized.

Amendment 4
To search a person's home or property, the government must get a search warrant, or special approval, describing exactly what place is to be searched and what items are expected to be found.

Amendment 5. Rights of Persons Accused of a Crime (1791)

No person shall be held to answer for a capital, or otherwise infamous, crime, unless on a presentment or indictment of a grand jury, except in cases arising in the land or naval forces, or in the militia, when in actual service in time of war or public danger; nor shall any person be subject for the same offense to be twice put in jeopardy of life or limb; nor shall be compelled in any criminal case to be a witness against himself, nor be

Amendment 5
A person cannot be charged with a serious crime unless a grand jury (a group of citizens appointed to study criminal evidence) decides that a good reason exists for a trial. (The only exceptions are cases involving people in the armed forces.) A person judged innocent by a court of law cannot be tried again for the same crime.

People on trial cannot be forced to testify, or speak in court, against themselves. A person cannot have life, liberty, or property taken away unless fairly decided by a court of law. If the government takes away property for the use of the public, a fair price must be paid to the owner.

Amendment 6

In all criminal cases, a person accused of a crime has the right to a fast, public trial by a fair jury in the place where the crime took place. All persons accused of a crime have the right to:
• know the charges against them;
• hear the evidence and witnesses against them;
• call witnesses in their defense;
• have a lawyer.

Amendment 7

A person has the right to a trial by jury in civil, or noncriminal, cases involving more than $20.

Amendment 8

The government cannot ask for very high bail, or deposit of money, from a person accused of a crime. People convicted of crimes cannot be fined an unfairly high amount, nor be punished in a cruel or unusual way.

Amendment 9

The rights of the people are not limited to those stated in the Constitution.

Amendment 10

Powers not given the U.S. government and not forbidden to the states are left to the states or to the people.

deprived of life, liberty, or property, without due process of law; nor shall private property be taken for public use, without just compensation.

Amendment 6. *Right to a Jury Trial in Criminal Cases (1791)*

In all criminal prosecutions, the accused shall enjoy the right to a speedy and public trial, by an impartial jury of the state and district wherein the crime shall have been committed, which district shall have been previously ascertained by law, and to be informed of the nature and cause of the accusation; to be confronted with the witnesses against him; to have compulsory process for obtaining witnesses in his favor, and to have the assistance of counsel for his defense.

Amendment 7. *Right to a Jury Trial in Civil Cases (1791)*

In suits at common law, where the value in controversy shall exceed twenty dollars, the right of trial by jury shall be preserved, and no fact tried by a jury shall be otherwise re-examined in any court of the United States than according to the rules of the common law.

Amendment 8. *Protection from Unfair Fines and Punishment (1791)*

Excessive bail shall not be required, nor excessive fines imposed, nor cruel and unusual punishments inflicted.

Amendment 9. *Other Rights of the People (1791)*

The enumeration in the Constitution, of certain rights, shall not be construed to deny or disparage others retained by the people.

Amendment 10. *Powers of the States and the People (1791)*

The powers not delegated to the United States by the Constitution, nor prohibited by it to the states, are reserved to the states respectively, or to the people.

Amendment 11. Limiting Law Cases Against States (1798)

The judicial power of the United States shall not be construed to extend to any suit in law or equity, commenced or prosecuted against one of the United States, by citizens of another state, or by citizens or subjects of any foreign state.

Amendment 12. Election of President and Vice President (1804)

The electors shall meet in their respective states, and vote by ballot for President and Vice President, one of whom, at least, shall not be an inhabitant of the same state with themselves; they shall name in their ballots the person voted for as President, and in distinct ballots the person voted for as Vice President, and they shall make distinct lists of all persons voted for as President, and of all persons voted for as Vice President, and of the number of votes for each, which lists they shall sign and certify, and transmit, sealed, to the seat of government of the United States, directed to the President of the Senate; the President of the Senate shall, in the presence of the Senate and House of Representatives, open all the certificates and the votes shall then be counted; the person having the greatest number of votes for President shall be the President, if such number be a majority of the whole number of electors appointed; and if no person have such majority, then from the persons having the highest numbers not exceeding three on the list of those voted for as President, the House of Representatives shall choose immediately, by ballot, the President. But in choosing the President, the votes shall be taken by states, the representation from each state having one vote; a quorum for this purpose shall consist of a member or members from two-thirds of the states, and a majority of all the states shall be necessary to a choice. And if the House of Representatives shall not choose a President whenever the right of choice shall devolve upon them, before the fourth day of March next following, then the Vice President shall act as President, as in the case of the death or other constitutional disability of the President. The person having the greatest number of votes as Vice President, shall be the Vice President, if such number be a majority of the whole number of electors appointed, and if no person have a majority, then from the two highest numbers on the list, the Senate shall choose the Vice President; a quorum for the purpose shall consist of two-thirds of the whole number of Senators, and a majority of

Amendment 11
A state government cannot be sued in a federal court by people of another state or a foreign country.

Amendment 12
This amendment changed the method of choosing a President and Vice President. The new method is called the Electoral College. Candidates for President and Vice President now run for office together, and each elector casts only one vote. (Before, candidates for President and Vice President ran for office separately, and each elector cast two votes.) Under the Electoral College, people called electors meet in their home states. Electors choose one person for President and a different person for Vice President. (One of the people voted for must be from a different state than the elector.) These electoral votes are then sent to the U.S. Senate where they are counted. The person who receives more than half the electoral votes for President is elected President. The person who receives more than half the electoral votes for Vice President is elected Vice President. If no person receives more than half the electoral votes for President, the House of Representatives chooses the President. A list of the top three vote-getters is sent to the House of Representatives. From this list, each state casts one vote for President. The person who receives more than half the votes in the House of Representatives is elected President. If no person receives more than half the vote, the Representatives vote again. If the Representatives fail to elect a President by March 4 (later changed to January 20), the Vice President serves as President. If no person receives at least half the

electoral votes for Vice President, no one becomes Vice President and a list of the top two vote-getters is sent to the Senate. From this list, the Senators then vote for Vice President, with each Senator entitled to one vote. The person who receives more than half the votes in the Senate becomes Vice President. Qualifications for the office of Vice President are the same as those of President.

Amendment 13

1. Slavery is outlawed in the United States.

2. Congress can pass any laws necessary to carry out this amendment.

Amendment 14

1. This amendment made formerly enslaved people citizens of both the United States and the states in which they lived. No state can deny any citizen the basic rights given in the Fifth Amendment. All states must treat people equally under the law.

2. The number of a state's Representatives in Congress can be lowered if the state prevents qualified citizens from voting. (This section aimed to force states in the South to allow African Americans to vote.)

the whole number shall be necessary to a choice. But no person constitutionally ineligible to the office of President shall be eligible to that of Vice President of the United States.

Amendment 13. Slavery Outlawed (1865)

Section 1. Abolition of Slavery

Neither slavery nor involuntary servitude, except as a punishment for crime whereof the party shall have been duly convicted, shall exist within the United States, or any place subject to their jurisdiction.

Section 2. Enforcement

Congress shall have power to enforce this article by appropriate legislation.

Amendment 14. Rights of Citizens (1868)

Section 1. Citizenship

All persons born or naturalized in the United States and subject to the jurisdiction thereof, are citizens of the United States and of the state wherein they reside. No state shall make or enforce any law which shall abridge the privileges or immunities of citizens of the United States; nor shall any state deprive any person of life, liberty, or property, without due process of law; nor deny to any person within its jurisdiction the equal protection of the laws.

Section 2. Representation in Congress

Representatives shall be apportioned among the several states according to their respective numbers, counting the whole number of persons in each state, ~~excluding Indians not taxed~~. But when the right to vote at any election for the choice of electors for President and Vice President of the United States, Representatives in Congress, the executive and judicial officers of a state, or the members of the legislature thereof, is denied to any of the ~~male~~ inhabitants of such state, being ~~twenty one years of age and~~ citizens of the United States, or in any way abridged, except for participation in rebellion, or other crime, the basis of representation therein shall be reduced in the proportion which the number of such ~~male~~ citizens shall bear to the whole number of ~~male~~ citizens ~~twenty one years of age~~ in such state.

Section 3. Penalties for Confederate Leaders

No person shall be a Senator or Representative in Congress, or elector of President and Vice President, or hold any office, civil or military, under the United States, or under any state, who, having previously taken an oath, as a member of Congress, or as an officer of the United States, or as a member of any state legislature, or as an executive or judicial officer of any state, to support the Constitution of the United States, shall have engaged in insurrection or rebellion against the same, or given aid or comfort to the enemies thereof. But Congress may, by vote of two-thirds of each house, remove such disability.

Section 4. Responsibility for Public Debt

The validity of the public debt of the United States, authorized by law, including debts incurred for payment of pensions and bounties for services in suppressing insurrection or rebellion, shall not be questioned. But neither the United States nor any state shall assume or pay any debt or obligation incurred in aid of insurrection or rebellion against the United States ~~or any claim for the loss or emancipation of any slave~~; but all such debts, obligations, and claims shall be held illegal and void.

Section 5. Enforcement

The Congress shall have power to enforce, by appropriate legislation, the provisions of this article.

Amendment 15. Voting Rights (1870)

Section 1. Black Suffrage

The right of citizens of the United States to vote shall not be denied or abridged by the United States or any state on account of race, color, or previous condition of servitude.

Section 2. Enforcement

The Congress shall have power to enforce this article by appropriate legislation.

Amendment 16. Income Tax (1913)

The Congress shall have the power to lay and collect taxes on incomes, from whatever source derived, without apportionment among the several states, and without regard to any census or enumeration.

3. Any Confederate official who took part in the Civil War cannot again hold any federal or state office. But Congress can remove this restriction by a two-thirds vote.

4. All money borrowed by the U.S. government to fight the Civil War is to be paid back. No debts the Confederate states or the Confederate government made to pay for the Civil War are to be paid back by the federal or state governments. No money would be paid to anyone for the loss of people they once held in slavery.

5. Congress can pass laws needed to carry out this amendment.

Amendment 15
1. No federal or state government can stop people from voting because of their race or color, or because they were once enslaved. The purpose of this amendment was to give black men the right to vote.

2. Congress can pass laws needed to carry out this amendment.

Amendment 16
Congress has the power to collect an income tax no matter what the population of a state is.

Amendment 17

1. Senators are to be elected by the voters of each state. (This amendment changed the method by which state legislatures elected Senators as outlined in Article 1, Section 3, Clause 1, of the Constitution.)

2. Special elections can be held to fill empty seats in the Senate. State legislatures may permit the governor to name a person to fill an empty seat until the next election.

3. This amendment does not affect the election or term of office of any Senator in office before the amendment becomes part of the Constitution.

Amendment 18

1. Making, selling, or transporting alcoholic, or intoxicating, drinks in the United States is illegal. (This amendment was called the Prohibition Amendment because it prohibited, or banned, the use of alcohol.)

2. Both Congress and the states can pass laws needed to carry out this amendment.

3. This amendment is to become part of the Constitution only if it is approved within seven years. (It was repealed, or canceled, by the Twenty-First Amendment.)

Amendment 17. Direct Election of Senators (1913)

Section 1. Method of Election

The Senate of the United States shall be composed of two Senators from each state, elected by the people thereof, for six years; and each Senator shall have one vote. The electors in each state shall have the qualifications requisite for electors of the most numerous branch of the state legislatures.

Section 2. Vacancies

When vacancies happen in the representation of any state in the Senate, the executive authority of such state shall issue writs of election to fill such vacancies: provided that the legislature of any state may empower the executive thereof to make temporary appointments until the people fill the vacancies by election as the legislature may direct.

Section 3. Those Elected under Previous Rules

~~This amendment shall not be so construed as to affect the election or term of any Senator chosen before it becomes valid as part of the Constitution.~~

Amendment 18. Prohibition of Alcoholic Drinks (1919)

Section 1. Prohibition

~~After one year from the ratification of this article the manufacture, sale, or transportation of intoxicating liquors within, the importation thereof into, or the exportation thereof from, the United States and all territory subject to the jurisdiction thereof for beverage purposes is hereby prohibited.~~

Section 2. Enforcement

~~The Congress and the several states shall have concurrent power to enforce this article by appropriate legislation.~~

Section 3. Time Limit on Ratification

~~The article shall be inoperative unless it shall have been ratified as an amendment to the Constitution by the legislatures of the several states, as provided in the Constitution, within seven years from the date of the submission hereof to the states by the Congress.~~

Amendment 19. Women's Right to Vote (1920)

Section 1. Women Made Voters

The right of citizens of the United States to vote shall not be denied or abridged by the United States or by any state on account of sex.

Section 2. Enforcement

Congress shall have power to enforce this article by appropriate legislation.

Amendment 20. Terms of Office (1933)

Section 1. Start of Terms of Office

The terms of the President and Vice President shall end at noon on the 20th day of January, and the terms of Senators and Representatives at noon on the 3rd day of January, of the years in which such terms would have ended if this article had not been ratified; and the terms of their successors shall then begin.

Section 2. Meeting Time of Congress

The Congress shall assemble at least once in every year, and such meeting shall begin at noon on the 3rd day of January, unless they shall by law appoint a different day.

Section 3. Providing for a Successor of the President-Elect

If at the time fixed for the beginning of the term of the President, the President-elect shall have died, the Vice President-elect shall become President. If a President shall not have been chosen before the time fixed for the beginning of his term, or if the President-elect shall have failed to qualify, then the Vice President-elect shall act as President until a President shall have qualified; and the Congress may by law provide for the case wherein neither a President-elect nor a Vice President-elect shall have qualified, declaring who shall then act as President, or the manner in which one who is to act shall be selected, and such person shall act accordingly until a President or Vice President shall have qualified.

Section 4. Elections Decided by Congress

The Congress may by law provide for the case of the death of any of the persons from whom the House of Representatives may choose a President whenever the right of choice shall have devolved upon them, and for the case of the death of any of the persons from whom the Senate may choose a Vice President whenever the right of choice shall have devolved upon them.

Section 5. Effective Date

Sections 1 and 2 shall take effect on the 15th day of October following the ratification of this article.

Amendment 19

1. No federal or state government can stop people from voting because of their sex. This amendment granted women the right to vote.

2. Congress can pass laws needed to carry out this amendment.

Amendment 20

1. The President and Vice President begin their terms on January 20. This date is called Inauguration Day. The terms of members of Congress begin on January 3. (Originally their terms began on March 4.)

2. Congress must meet at least once a year beginning at noon on January 3. However, Congress may pick a different day to first meet.

3. If the person elected President dies before taking office, the Vice President becomes President. If no person is elected President before the term of office begins, or if the person elected President does not have the skills or experience to serve, then the Vice President acts as President until a President is chosen. If both the person elected President and the person elected Vice President are not approved, Congress selects the President.

4. If, during the time Congress is choosing the President and Vice President, one of these two people dies, Congress may pass a law deciding how to choose the President and Vice President.

5. Sections 1 and 2 of this amendment take effect on the fifteenth day of October after this amendment becomes part of the Constitution.

Section 6. Time Limit on Ratification

~~This article shall be inoperative unless it shall have been ratified as an amendment to the Constitution by the legislatures of three-fourths of the several states within seven years from the date of its submission.~~

This amendment is to become part of the Constitution only if it is approved within seven years by three-fourths of the state legislatures.

Amendment 21. Repeal of Prohibition (1933)

Section 1. Prohibition Ends

The Eighteenth article of amendment to the Constitution of the United States is hereby repealed.

Section 2. Protection of State and Local Prohibition Laws

The transportation or importation into any state, territory, or possession of the United States for delivery or use therein of intoxicating liquors, in violation of the laws thereof, is hereby prohibited.

Amendment 21

1. The Eighteenth Amendment is repealed, or no longer in effect.

2. Any state or territory of the United States may pass prohibition laws.

3. This amendment is to become part of the Constitution only if state conventions approve it within seven years.

Section 3. Time Limit on Ratification

~~This article shall be inoperative unless it shall have been ratified as an amendment to the Constitution by conventions in the several states, as provided in the Constitution, within seven years from the date of the submission hereof to the states by the Congress.~~

Amendment 22. President Limited to Two Terms (1951)

Section 1. Limit on Number of Terms

No person shall be elected to the office of the President more than twice, and no person who has held the office of President, or acted as President, for more than two years of a term to which some other person was elected President shall be elected to the office of the President more than once. ~~But this Article shall not apply to any person holding the office of President when this Article was proposed by the Congress, and shall not prevent any person who may be holding the office of President, or acting as President, during the term within which this Article becomes operative from holding the office of President or acting as President during the remainder of such term.~~

Amendment 22

1. No person can be elected President more than two times. No person can be elected President more than once who has served more than two years of another President's term. This amendment does not affect any President who is in office when this amendment becomes part of the Constitution.

2. This amendment is to become part of the Constitution only if three-fourths of the state legislatures approve it within seven years.

Section 2. Time Limit on Ratification

~~This Article shall be inoperative unless it shall have been ratified as an amendment to the Constitution by the legislatures of three-fourths of the several states within seven years from the date of its submission to the states by the Congress.~~

C30

Amendment 23. Presidential Elections for the District of Columbia (1961)

Section 1. Presidential Electors in the District of Columbia

The District constituting the seat of Government of the United States shall appoint in such manner as the Congress may direct: A number of electors of President and Vice President equal to the whole number of Senators and Representatives in Congress to which the District would be entitled if it were a State, but in no event more than the least populous State; they shall be in addition to those appointed by the States, but they shall be considered, for the purposes of the election of President and Vice President, to be electors appointed by a State; and they shall meet in the District and perform such duties as provided by the Twelfth article of amendment.

Section 2. Enforcement

The Congress shall have power to enforce this article by appropriate legislation.

Amendment 24. Poll Tax Ended (1964)

Section 1. Poll Taxes Not Allowed in Federal Elections

The right of citizens of the United States to vote in any primary or other election for President or Vice President, for electors for President or Vice President, or for Senator or Representative in Congress, shall not be denied or abridged by the United States or any state by reason of failure to pay any poll tax or other tax.

Section 2. Enforcement

The Congress shall have the power to enforce this article by appropriate legislation.

Amendment 25. Presidential Succession (1967)

Section 1. Filling the Vacant Office of President

In case of the removal of the President from office or of his death or resignation, the Vice President shall become President.

Section 2. Filling the Vacant Office of Vice President

Whenever there is a vacancy in the office of the Vice President, the President shall nominate a Vice President who shall take the office upon confirmation by a majority vote of both houses of Congress.

Section 3. Disability of the President

Whenever the President transmits to the President pro tempore of the Senate and the Speaker of the House of Representatives his written declaration that he is unable to discharge the powers

---

Amendment 23

1. People living in Washington, D.C. (the District of Columbia), have the right to vote in Presidential elections. The number of electoral votes of Washington, D.C., can never be more than the number of electoral votes of the state with the fewest number of people.

2. Congress can pass any laws necessary to carry out this amendment.

Amendment 24

1. No person can be kept from voting in a federal election for failing to pay a poll, or voting, tax or any other kind of tax.

2. Congress can pass any laws necessary to carry out this amendment.

Amendment 25

1. If the President dies, resigns, or is removed from office, the Vice President becomes President.

2. If the office of Vice President becomes empty, the President names a new Vice President, with the approval of both houses of Congress.

3. If the President is unable to carry out the powers and duties of office, the President may tell the leaders of Congress. The Vice President then serves as Acting President. The

President may return to office only when he or she tells the leaders of Congress that he or she can again carry out the powers and duties of office.

4. If the Vice President and at least half the Cabinet, or a special committee, inform the leaders of Congress that the President cannot carry out the powers and duties of office, the Vice President immediately becomes Acting President. If the President tells the leaders of Congress that he or she is able to serve as President, he or she again becomes President. But if, within four days, the Vice President and at least half the Cabinet (or a special committee) tell the leaders of Congress that the President still cannot carry out the powers and duties of office, the President does not return to office. Instead, Congress must meet within 48 hours. In the next 21 days, Congress must decide if the President is able to carry out the powers and duties of office. If two-thirds of both houses of Congress vote that the President is unable to serve, the President is removed from office and the Vice President becomes Acting President. If two-thirds do not vote this way, the President stays in office.

Amendment 26

1. This amendment gives people who are at least 18 years old the right to vote.

2. Congress can pass laws needed to carry out this amendment.

Amendment 27

There can be no law changing the salaries of members of Congress until after the next election of the House of Representatives.

and duties of his office, and until he transmits to them a written declaration to the contrary, such powers and duties shall be discharged by the Vice President as Acting President.

Section 4. When Congress Designates an Acting President

Whenever the Vice President and a majority of either the principal officers of the executive departments or of such other body as Congress may by law provide, transmit to the President pro tempore of the Senate and the Speaker of the House of Representatives their written declaration that the President is unable to discharge the powers and duties of his office, the Vice President shall immediately assume the powers and duties of the office as Acting President. Thereafter, when the President transmits to the President pro tempore of the Senate and the Speaker of the House of Representatives his written declaration that no inability exists, he shall resume the powers and duties of his office unless the Vice President and a majority of either the principal officers of the executive departments or of such other body as Congress may by law provide, transmit within four days to the President pro tempore of the Senate and the Speaker of the House of Representatives their written declaration that the President is unable to discharge the powers and duties of his office. Thereupon Congress shall decide the issue, assembling within 48 hours for that purpose if not in session. If the Congress, within 21 days after receipt of the latter written declaration, or, if Congress is not in session, within 21 days after Congress is required to assemble, determines by two-thirds vote of both houses that the President is unable to discharge the powers and duties of his office, the Vice President shall continue to discharge the same as Acting President; otherwise, the President shall assume the powers and duties of his office.

Amendment 26. Vote for Eighteen-Year-Olds (1971)

Section 1. Voting Age

The right of citizens of the United States, who are 18 years of age or older, to vote shall not be denied or abridged by the United States or any state on account of age.

Section 2. Enforcement

The Congress shall have the power to enforce this article by appropriate legislation.

Amendment 27. Limits on Salary Changes (1992)

No law, varying the compensation for the services of the Senators and Representatives, shall take effect, until an election of Representatives shall have intervened.

Reference Section

The Reference Section has many parts, each with a different type of information. Use this section to look up people, places, and events as you study.

Governors of Michigan

STATE GOVERNORS	TERM	STATE GOVERNORS	TERM
Stevens T. Mason	1835–1840	Aaron T. Bliss	1901–1904
William Woodbridge	1840–1841	Fred M. Warner	1905–1910
J. Wright Gordon	1841	Chase Osborn	1911–1912
John S. Barry	1842–1846	Woodbridge N. Ferris	1913–1916
Alpheus Felch	1846–1847	Albert E. Sleeper	1917–1920
William L. Greenly	1847	Alexander J. Groesbeck	1921–1926
Epaphroditus Ransom	1848–1850	Fred W. Green	1927–1930
John S. Barry	1850–1851	Wilbur M. Brucker	1931–1932
Robert McClelland	1852–1853	William A. Comstock	1933–1934
Andrew Parsons	1853–1854	Frank D. Fitzgerald	1935–1936
Kinsley S. Bingham	1855–1858	Frank Murphy	1937–1938
Moses Wisner	1859–1860	Frank D. Fitzgerald	1939
Austin Blair	1861–1864	Luren D. Dickinson	1939–1940
Henry H. Crapo	1865–1868	Murray D. Van Wagoner	1941–1942
Henry P. Baldwin	1869–1872	Harry F. Kelly	1943–1946
John J. Bagley	1873–1876	Kim Sigler	1947–1948
Charles Croswell	1877–1880	G. Mennen Williams	1949–1960
David Jerome	1881–1882	John B. Swainson	1961–1962
Josiah W. Begole	1883–1884	George W. Romney	1963–1969
Russell Alger	1885–1886	William G. Milliken	1969–1982
Cyrus G. Luce	1887–1890	James J. Blanchard	1983–1990
Edwin B. Winans	1891–1892	John Engler	1991–2002
John T. Rich	1893–1896	Jennifer M. Granholm	2003–
Hazen S. Pingree	1897–1900		

Michigan Counties

COUNTY NAME	COUNTY SEAT	YEAR FORMED	COUNTY NAME	COUNTY SEAT	YEAR FORMED
Alcona	Harrisville	1869	Lake	Baldwin	1871
Alger	Munising	1885	Lapeer	Lapeer	1833
Allegan	Allegan	1835	Leelanau	Leland	1863
Alpena	Alpena	1857	Lenawee	Adrian	1826
Antrim	Bellaire	1863	Livingston	Howell	1836
Arenac	Standish	1883	Luce	Newberry	1887
Baraga	L'Anse	1875	Mackinac	Saint Ignace	1849
Barry	Hastings	1839	Macomb	Mount Clemens	1818
Bay	Bay City	1858	Manistee	Manistee	1855
Benzie	Beulah	1869	Marquette	Marquette	1848
Berrien	St. Joseph	1831	Mason	Ludington	1855
Branch	Coldwater	1833	Mecosta	Big Rapids	1859
Calhoun	Marshall	1833	Menominee	Menominee	1861
Cass	Cassopolis	1829	Midland	Midland	1850
Charlevoix	Charlevoix	1869	Missaukee	Lake City	1871
Cheboygan	Cheboygan	1853	Monroe	Monroe	1817
Chippewa	Sault Ste. Marie	1827	Montcalm	Stanton	1850
Clare	Harrison	1871	Montmorency	Atlanta	1881
Clinton	Saint Johns	1839	Muskegon	Muskegon	1859
Crawford	Grayling	1879	Newaygo	White Cloud	1851
Delta	Escanaba	1861	Oakland	Pontiac	1821
Dickinson	Iron Mountain	1891	Oceana	Hart	1851
Eaton	Charlotte	1837	Ogemaw	West Branch	1875
Emmet	Petoskey	1853	Ontonagon	Ontonagon	1848
Genesee	Flint	1836	Osceola	Reed City	1869
Gladwin	Gladwin	1875	Oscoda	Mio	1881
Gogebic	Bessemer	1887	Otsego	Gaylord	1875
Grand Traverse	Traverse City	1851	Ottawa	Grand Haven	1837
Gratiot	Ithaca	1855	Presque Isle	Rogers City	1871
Hillsdale	Hillsdale	1835	Roscommon	Roscommon	1875
Houghton	Houghton	1846	Saginaw	Saginaw	1835
Huron	Bad Axe	1859	St. Clair	Port Huron	1821
Ingham	Mason	1838	St. Joseph	Centreville	1829
Ionia	Ionia	1837	Sanilac	Sandusky	1848
Iosco	Tawas City	1857	Schoolcraft	Manistique	1871
Iron	Crystal Falls	1885	Shiawassee	Corunna	1837
Isabella	Mount Pleasant	1859	Tuscola	Caro	1850
Jackson	Jackson	1832	Van Buren	Paw Paw	1837
Kalamazoo	Kalamazoo	1830	Washtenaw	Ann Arbor	1826
Kalkaska	Kalkaska	1871	Wayne	Detroit	1815
Kent	Grand Rapids	1836	Wexford	Cadillac	1869
Keweenaw	Eagle River	1861			

Robin Williams is an actor and comedian who grew up in Bloomfield Hills. He has starred in movies such as *Mrs. Doubtfire* and *Good Will Hunting*, for which he won an Academy Award.

Serena Williams is a professional tennis player. She was born in Saginaw but moved to California as a young girl. Williams was the number-one tennis player in the world in 2002, and she has won each of the sport's four Grand Slam tournaments.

Helen Thomas of Detroit is a journalist who has reported from the White House since 1961. For many years, as the senior White House reporter, she asked the first question during Presidential press conferences.

Julie Krone of Benton Harbor is a pioneering female jockey. In 1993 she won the Belmont Stakes and became the first woman rider ever to win one of the three races that make up the sport's Triple Crown.

Stevie Wonder is a singer, songwriter, and musician from Saginaw who has been blind nearly since birth. He recorded his first hit single when he was 12 years old. He was also part of the successful campaign to make Dr. Martin Luther King, Jr.'s birthday a national holiday.

Sam Raimi of Franklin is the director of movies including *Spider-Man* and *Spider-Man 2*. He got his start in films directing horror movies in the 1980s.

Benjamin Carson of Detroit is a famous brain surgeon. In 1987 he made medical history by separating a pair of twins born joined at the back of the head. He has also toured the country speaking to young people about achieving their dreams.

Aretha Franklin is famous for her soul, gospel, and rhythm and blues recordings such as "Respect" and "Chain of Fools." Franklin grew up in Detroit, and got her start in the choir of the New Bethel Baptist Church, where her father was the minister.

Famous Michiganians

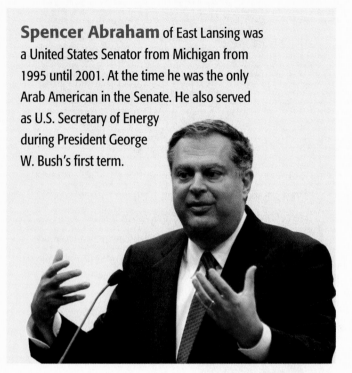

Spencer Abraham of East Lansing was a United States Senator from Michigan from 1995 until 2001. At the time he was the only Arab American in the Senate. He also served as U.S. Secretary of Energy during President George W. Bush's first term.

Ruth Behar is a writer, poet, and professor of anthropology at the University of Michigan. She has written about her experiences as a Cuban, a woman, and a Jew. *Latina* magazine named her one of the 50 Latinas who made history in the twentieth century.

Chris Van Allsburg of Grand Rapids is a writer and illustrator of books for children. Some of his most popular books, including *Jumanji*, *The Polar Express*, and *Zathura*, have been made into movies.

Terry McMillan of Port Huron is one of America's best-selling writers. Her books include *Waiting to Exhale*, which became a film in 1995. She has also helped to bring attention to young African American writers.

Lily Tomlin of Detroit is an actor and comedian who has won six Emmy Awards for her work on television. She was also the voice of Ms. Frizzle in the popular cartoon *The Magic School-Bus*.

Magic Johnson of Lansing is a member of the Basketball Hall of Fame. As a star of the Los Angeles Lakers in the 1980s, his teams won five championships. Today he is a businessman who has built movie theaters and shopping centers in several cities.

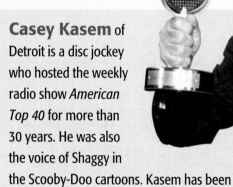

Casey Kasem of Detroit is a disc jockey who hosted the weekly radio show *American Top 40* for more than 30 years. He was also the voice of Shaggy in the Scooby-Doo cartoons. Kasem has been active in the Arab American community.

Diana Ross of Detroit is one of America's most successful pop singers. She got her start as a member of the Motown group the Supremes in the 1960s, and then became a solo artist. In all, 18 of her songs have been number-one hits.

Michigan Symbols

▲ **STATE SEAL**
The word *Tuebor* on the Michigan state seal means "I will defend."

▲ **STATE FLAG**
The bald eagle on the flag represents the United States. The elk and the moose represent Michigan.

◄ **STATE WILDFLOWER**
Dwarf Lake Iris
Most of the world's Dwarf Lake Irises grow in Michigan, but the flower is threatened by shoreline development. The flower was chosen in 1998 to draw attention to Michigan's conservation efforts.

STATE MAMMAL
White-tailed Deer
White-tailed deer live in wooded areas and can run at speeds of up to 30 miles an hour. They are also excellent leapers and swimmers. ▼

▲ **STATE FISH**
Brook Trout
Brook trout are found in the cold, clear water of streams, lakes, and ponds throughout Michigan. They are most often found in spring-fed streams.

◀ **STATE REPTILE**
Painted Turtle
Painted turtles spend their days sunning themselves on logs. They stack themselves on top of each other. As many as 50 can fit on one log at the same time!

STATE BIRD ▶
American Robin
The robin is the state's best-known and best-loved bird. In 1931 Michiganians voted overwhelmingly to make it the state bird.

▲ **STATE FLOWER**
Apple Blossom
The apple blossom became our state flower in 1987. Blossoming apple trees add much to the beauty of Michigan's landscape. Some apple trees are even native to our state.

◀ **STATE TREE**
White Pine
The white pine is an evergreen that has a bluish-green color. It adds an elegant beauty to Michigan's landscape.

R9

Michigan and United States 1600-2009

1600 · **1700**

Michigan Events

1620
Etienne Brulé
explores Michigan

1701
Antoine de la Cadillac
founds Detroit

1763
Pontiac's Rebellion

1600 · **1700**

United States Events

1607
English settlers start
Jamestown, Virginia
colony

1621
English settlers and
American Indians hold
the first Thanksgiving

1673
Marquette and Jolliet reach
the Mississippi River

1763
French and
Indian War

1800   **1900**   **2000**

1837
Michigan
becomes a state

1863
24th Michigan
fights at Gettysburg

1903
Henry Ford
founds the Ford
Motor Company

1973
Coleman Young
elected mayor
of Detroit

2006
Jennifer
Granholm
re-elected
governor

1800   **1900**   **2000**

1776
British colonies declare
independence

1865
Civil War ends

1920
Women gain
the right
to vote

1941
United States
enters World
War II

2008
Barack Obama
elected
President

Gazetteer

This Gazetteer is a geographical dictionary that will help you to pronounce and locate the places discussed in this book. Latitude and longitude are given for cities and some other places. The letters and numbers tell you where each place first appears on a map (m.) or in the text (t.).

Pronunciation Key									
a	at	ē	me	ō	old	ū	use	ng	song
ā	ape	i	it	ô	fork	ü	rule	th	thin
ä	far	ī	ice	oi	oil	ù	pull	th	this
âr	care	îr	pierce	ou	out	ûr	turn	zh	measure
e	end	o	hot	u	up	hw	white	ə	about, taken, pencil, lemon, circus

Albion (al′ bē ən) A town in southeastern Michigan that was a stop on the Underground Railroad. (m. 155, t. 155)

Ann Arbor (an är′ bər) A city in the southeastern part of the Lower Peninsula; site of the University of Michigan; 42°N, 88°W. (m. A10, t. 155)

Antietam (an tē′ təm) A creek near the town of Sharpsburg, Maryland; site of a Civil War battle in 1862. (t. 164)

Appalachian Mountains (ap ə lā che ən moun′ tenz) Chain of mountains stretching from Canada to Alabama. (m. A5, t. 94)

Au Sable River (aw sô′ bəl riv′ ər) A river in the Lower Peninsula. (m. 31)

Battle Creek (bat′ əl krēk) A city in the south-central part of the Lower Peninsula; 42°N, 85°W. (m. G13)

Black Bottom (blak bot′ əm) A Detroit neighborhood where many African Americans lived in the early 1900s. (t. 181)

Buffalo (buf′ ə lo) A city in western New York on Lake Erie; the endpoint of the Erie Canal. (m. 119, t. 119)

Cass County (cas koun′ tē) A county in southwestern Michigan that became the home of many African Americans who fled slavery on the Underground Railroad. (t. 155)

Cassopolis (kə sop′ ə ləs) A community in the southwestern part of the Lower Peninsula. It was an important stop on one route in the Underground Railroad; 42°N, 86°W. (m. A12, t. 155)

Copper Harbor (kop′ ər här′ bər) A community at the northwestern tip of the Upper Peninsula; 47°N, 88°W. (m. G13)

Dearborn (dîr′ born) An industrial city in the southeastern part of the Lower Peninsula; 42°N, 83°W. (t. 182)

Detroit (dē troit′) The largest city in Michigan, in the southeastern part of the state; 42°N, 83°W. (t. 23)

Erie Canal (îr′ ē kə nal′) A canal in New York State that opened in 1825 and provided a water route between the Great Lakes and the Atlantic Ocean. (m. 107, t. 119)

Escanaba (es kań e ba) A city in the southeastern part of the Upper Peninsula; 46°N, 87°W. (m. G12)

Escanaba River (es kań e ba riv′ ər) A river in the Upper Peninsula. (t. 205)

Flint (flint) A city in the southeastern part of the Lower Peninsula; important site of automobile manufacturing; 43°N, 84°W. (m. G13, t. 23)

Fort Duquesne (fôrt du kān) A fort built by the French in 1754 where Pittsburgh stands today. (t. 92)

Fort Mackinac (fôrt mak' ə nô) A fort on Mackinac Island in the Straits of Mackinac, attacked by the British and Native Americans during the War of 1812; 45°N, 84°W. (m. 113)

Fort Miami (fôrt mī a' mē) A fort built by the French in 1679 on the Miami River in the Lower Peninsula. (m. 86, t. 84)

Fort Michilimackinac (fôrt mish ə le mak' ə nô) A fort on the northern tip of the Lower Peninsula, on the Straits of Mackinac. It was captured by Native Americans during Pontiac's Rebellion; 45°N, 84°W. (m. 81, t. 93)

Fort Pontchartrain (fôrt pon' chər trān) A French settlement established in 1701 in what is now Michigan. It is the site of the present city of Detroit; 42°N, 83°W. (m. 86, t. 86)

Fort St. Joseph (fôrt sānt jō' zəf) A fort built in 1718 by the French, near the present city; 41°N, 86°W. (m. 97, t. 96)

Fort Sumter (fôrt sum' tər) A fort guarding the entrance to the harbor in Charleston, South Carolina, site of the first battle of the Civil War. (t. 142)

Frenchtown (french town) A French settlement established about 1785 on the River Raisin in southeastern Michigan; present-day Monroe; 42°N, 83°W. (m. 113, t. 113)

Gettysburg (get' ēz burg) A town in southern Pennsylvania that was the site of a major Union victory during the Civil War. (m. 145, t. 163)

Grand Rapids (grand rap' idz) A city in southwestern Michigan; the second-largest city in the state; 43°N, 85°W. (m. G13, t. 23)

Grand River (grand riv' ər) A river that flows through Lansing and Grand Rapids on its way to Lake Michigan. (m. A10, t. 15)

Great Lakes (grāt lāks) The world's largest freshwater lakes, between the northern United States and Canada. The Great Lakes are Lake Superior, Lake Michigan, Lake Huron, Lake Erie, and Lake Ontario. (m. A3, t. 13)

Hancock (han' kok) A town in the Upper Peninsula that began as an iron mining camp. (m. A10)

Houghton (hōt' ən) A city in the Upper Peninsula. In the late 1800s, it was a center for the mining and logging industries. Today it draws many tourists; 47°N, 88°W. (m. G12, t. 33)

Huron Mountains (hyur' on mount' ənz) A mountain range in the Upper Peninsula, containing Mount Arvon. (m. A10)

Ishpeming (ish pem' ing) A town on the Upper Peninsula that began as an iron mining town; 46°N, 88°W. (m. 127)

Isle Royale (īel rôi' əl) An island in Lake Superior off the north coast of the Upper Peninsula; now a national park; 48°N, 89°W. (m. A10)

Jackson (jak' sən) A city in the south-central part of the Lower Peninsula; 42°N, 84°W. (m. A10, t. 155)

Kalamazoo (kal ə mə zü') A city in southwestern Michigan that became a center for the lumber industry; 42°N, 86°W. (m. G13, t. 23)

Keweenaw Peninsula (kē' win ô pə nin' sə lə) A peninsula in the northwestern Upper Peninsula; the site of many rich copper mines. (m. G12, t. 30)

Lake Erie (lāk îr' ē) The southernmost of the Great Lakes. It borders the southeastern part of the Lower Peninsula. (m. A3, t. 13)

Lake Huron (lāk hyur' ən) The second-largest of the Great Lakes. It forms part of Michigan's eastern border. (m. A3, t. 13)

Lake Michigan (lāk mish′ i gən) The third-largest of the Great Lakes. It forms the western border of the Lower Peninsula. (m. A3, t. 13)

Lake Ontario (lāk on târ′ ē ō) The smallest of the Great Lakes, and the only one that does not border Michigan. (m. A3, t. 13)

Lake St. Clair (lāk sānt clâr) A lake northeast of Detroit on the border between the United States and Canada. (m. A10)

Lake Superior (lāk sə pîr′ ē ər) The largest of the Great Lakes. It borders most of the northern part of Michigan. (m. A3, t. 13)

Lansing (lan′ sing) The capital of Michigan, in the south-central part of the Lower Peninsula; 43°N, 85°W. (m. G11, t. 23)

Lexington (lek′ sing tən) A town in eastern Massachusetts; site of one of the earliest battles of the American Revolution. (t. 99)

Mackinaw City (mak′ ə nô sit′ ē) A city at the north-central tip of the Lower Peninsula; 46°N, 85°W. (m. A10)

Manistee River (man ə stē′ riv′ ər) A river that flows through the northwestern Lower Peninsula and empties into Lake Michigan. (m. A10)

Manistique (man ə stēk′) A city in the south-central part of the Upper Peninsula; 46°N, 86°W. (m. A10)

Marquette (mär ket′) A city on the northern shore of the Upper Peninsula, important for iron mining; 47°N, 87°W. (m. G12, t. 21)

Marshall (mär′ shəl) A community in southeastern Michigan; 42°N, 84°W. (t. 146)

Mississippi River (mis ə sip ē riv ər) A river in the Central United States, flowing from Minnesota to the Gulf of Mexico; the second-longest river in the United States. (m. A3, t. 84)

Monroe (man rō′) Formerly Frenchtown, a city in the southeastern corner of the Lower Peninsula. It was the site of a battle during the War of 1812; 42°N, 83°W. (m. A10, t. 113)

Montgomery (mont gum′ ə r ē) Capital of Alabama. (t. 240)

Mount Arvon (mount är′ von) Michigan's highest peak, in the western part of the Upper Peninsula; 47°N, 88°W. (p. A10)

Muskegon (mə skē′ gən) An industrial city on Lake Michigan, in the western part of the Lower Peninsula; 43°N, 86°W. (m. G13)

Muskegon River (mə skē′ gən riv′ ər) A river of the Lower Peninsula; it begins in Houghton Lake and flows southwest into Lake Michigan at Muskegon. (m. A10, t. 15)

New France (nü frans) French possessions in North America from 1609 to 1763. It included large parts of what are now Canada and the United States. (m. 83, t. 82)

Niles (nīlz) A city near the site of Fort St. Joseph in the southwestern part of the Lower Peninsula; 42°N, 86°W. (m. A10)

North Manitou Island (nôrth man′ ə tü ī lənd) One of two islands in Lake Michigan that are part of Sleeping Bear Dunes National Lakeshore. (m. A10, t. 7)

Northwest Territory (nôrth west′ ter′ i tôr ē) The land claimed by the United States after the Revolutionary War and organized as a territory in 1787. It included the present states of Illinois, Indiana, Michigan, Ohio, and Wisconsin. (m. 109, t. 109)

Norton Mounds (nôr tən moundz) Burial mounds built by Hopewell American Indians near Grand Rapids. (m. 46, t. 46)

Novi (no′ vi) A city in south-central Michigan. (t. 287)

Pronunciation Key									
a	at	ē	me	ō	old	ū	use	ng	song
ā	ape	i	it	ô	fork	ü	rule	th	thin
ä	far	ī	ice	oi	oil	u̇	pull	th	this
âr	care	îr	pierce	ou	out	ûr	turn	zh	measure
e	end	o	hot	u	up	hw	white	ə	about, taken, pencil, lemon, circus

Parma (par′ mə) A town in southeastern Michigan that was a stop on the Underground Railroad. (m. 155, t. 155)

Pictured Rocks National Lakeshore (pik′ chərd roks nash′e nəl lāk′ shôr) Lakeshore on the Upper Peninsula, on Lake Superior; 46° N, 86° W. (m. G12)

Pontiac (pon′ tē ak) A city in the southeastern part of the Lower Peninsula, named for the Odawa chief who led Pontiac's Rebellion in 1763; 43°N, 83°W. (m. A10, t. 23)

Porcupine Mountains (pôr′ kyə pīn moun′ tənz) Mountains, popular for skiing, in the northwestern part of the Upper Peninsula. (m. G12)

Port Huron (pôrt hyur′ ən) A community on the eastern part of the Lower Peninsula. It was a stop on the Underground Railroad; 43°N, 83°W. (m. A10)

Put-in-Bay (pùt in bā) A bay of South Bass Island in Lake Erie, site of a War of 1812 naval battle; 42°N, 83°W. (m. 107, t. 114)

Quebec (kwi bec′) A city in Canada on the St. Lawrence River; it began as a trading post founded by de Champlain in 1608. (m. A8, t. 82)

Raisin (rā′ zin) A town in the southeastern corner of the Lower Peninsula that was the site of a battle during the War of 1812; 41°N, 83°W. (t. 159)

Saginaw (sag′ ə nô) An industrial city in the eastern part of the Lower Peninsula, on the Saginaw River; 43°N, 84°W. (m. A10, t. 126)

Saginaw Bay (sag′ ə nô bā) An inlet of Lake Huron on the eastern shore of the Lower Peninsula. (m. A10)

Saginaw River (sag′ ə nô riv′ ər) A river on the Lower Peninsula. It flows into Saginaw Bay, an inlet of Lake Huron. (m. A10)

St. Ignace (sānt ig′ nəs) A city on the southeastern shore of the Upper Peninsula. Today this city is a popular summer resort; 46°N, 85°W. (m. G12, t. 84)

St. Marys River (sānt mâr′ ēz riv′ ər) A body of water that connects Lake Superior to Lake Huron; forms a border separating Michigan from Canada. (m. A10, t. 24)

Sault Ste. Marie (sü sānt mə rē′) A city on the St. Marys River in the eastern part of the Upper Peninsula; site of the Soo Canal; 46°N, 84°W. (m. G12, t. 24)

Sleeping Bear Dunes (slē′ ping bâr dünz) A national park on the shore of Lake Michigan in the northwestern part of the Lower Peninsula. (m. 11, t. 14)

South Manitou Island (sowth man′ ə tü ī′ lənd) One of two islands in Lake Michigan that are part of Sleeping Bear Dunes National Lakeshore. (m. A10, t. 7)

Straits of Mackinac (strāts əv mak′ ə nô) The narrow body of water between the Upper and Lower peninsulas that connects Lake Michigan with Lake Huron. (m. A10, t. 24)

Toledo Strip (tə lē′ dō strip) A piece of land in northern Ohio that includes the port of Toledo. In the 1830s it was claimed by both Michigan and Ohio. (m. 107, t. 125)

Traverse City (trav′ ərs sit′ ē) A city in the northwestern part of the Lower Peninsula known for cherry production; 46°N, 86°W. (m. G13, t. 22)

Willow Run (wil′ ō run) A town in Michigan that was the site of a huge airplane plant during World War II; near Ypsilanti; 42°N, 84°W. (m. 229, t. 231)

Ypsilanti (ip sə lant′ ē) An industrial city in the southeastern part of the Lower Peninsula; 42°N, 84°W. (m. 229, t. 231)

Biographical Dictionary

The Biographical Dictionary will help you to pronounce the names of and to identify the key people in this book. The page number tells you where each name first appears in the text.

Pronunciation Key

a	at	ē	me	ō	old	ū	use	ng	song
ā	ape	i	it	ô	fork	ü	rule	th	thin
ä	far	ī	ice	oi	oil	u̇	pull	th	this
âr	care	îr	pierce	ou	out	ûr	turn	zh	measure
e	end	o	hot	u	up	hw	white	ə	about, taken, pencil, lemon, circus

A

Anderson, Marge (an′ dur sən), 1932– Leader of her band of Ojibway from 1991 to 2005 who worked to keep Ojibway traditions alive. (p. 5)

B

Blackbird, Andrew (blak bûrd), 1822–1908 Odawa writer, historian, and translator. (p. 4)

Blair, Austin (blâr), 1818–1894 Governor of Michigan during the Civil War. (p. 139)

Brulé, Etienne (brü lā′, ā tyen), 1592–1632 French explorer who sailed up Lake Huron, the St. Marys River, and Lake Superior in 1620; the first European to explore present-day Michigan. (p. 83)

C

Cadillac, Antoine de la (kȧ′ dē yȧk, an′ twän), 1658–1730 French colonial commander and the founder of Detroit in 1701. (p. 86)

Carleton, Will (kärl′ tun), 1845–1912 Popular Michigan poet of the 1800s who wrote about frontier life. (p. 118)

Cartier, Jacques (kär′ tyā, zhäk), 1491–1557 French explorer who became the first European to navigate the St. Lawrence River in 1535. (p. 82)

Cass, Lewis (kas), 1782–1866 Michigan governor from 1813 to 1831 who persuaded American Indians to sell large amounts of their land to the Michigan government. (p. 115)

Champlain, Samuel de (sham plān′), 1567–1635 French explorer and mapmaker who founded Quebec City and sent out explorers to the area around present-day Michigan in search of the Northwest Passage. (p. 82)

Chandler, Elizabeth (chan′ dlər), 1807–1834 Quaker woman who was a leader in the abolitionist movement in Michigan. (p. 138)

Clark, George Rogers (klärk), 1752–1818 Revolutionary War general and frontier leader who defeated the British at Fort Vincennes in 1779. (p. 100)

Columbus, Christopher (kə lum′ bəs), 1451?–1506 European explorer who reached North America while sailing west in search of Asia in 1492. (p. 82)

Conyers, John, Jr. (kän′ yûrz), 1929– Member of the U.S. House of Representatives from Michigan since 1964. (p. 242)

Crane, Caroline Barlett (krān), 1858–1935 Progressive reformer from Kalamazoo who worked to bring an end to unclean conditions in meatpacking houses during the late 1800s. (p. 208)

Crosswhite, Adam (kross′ wīte), 1799–1878 Formerly enslaved person who escaped with his family in 1844 to Marshall, Michigan, where they were protected from slave catchers by the community. (p. 146)

Custer, George (kus′ tər), 1839–1876 Leader, from Monroe, of the Michigan Cavalry Brigade during the Civil War. (p. 162)

D

Davis, Jefferson (dā′ vis), 1808–1889 United States Senator who was president of the Confederate States of America from 1861 to 1865. (p. 161)

DeBaptiste, George (də bap tēst′), 1815?–1875 African American "conductor" on Michigan's Underground Railroad who helped enslaved people escape to freedom. (p. 139)

Douglass, Fredrick (dug′ ləs), 1817–1895 Abolitionist and writer who led the attack on slavery in the middle 1800s. (p. 149)

E

Edison, Thomas Alva (ed′ ə sən), 1847–1931 Inventor of hundreds of items, including the light bulb and the record player. He grew up in Port Huron. (p. 176)

Edmonds, Sarah Emma (ed′ məndz), 1841–1898 Woman from Flint who disguised herself as a man and fought in several battles during the Civil War. (p. 144)

Ettawageshik, Frank (et a wa gē′ shik), 1949– Odawa pottery maker and former chairman of the Little Traverse Bay band who re-created a way of making pottery used hundreds of years ago. (p. 5)

F

Ford, Gerald R., Jr. (fôrd), 1913–2006 Native of Grand Rapids who was first elected to represent Michigan in the U.S. House of Representatives in 1948; became Vice President of the United States in 1973; served as the thirty-eighth President of the United States from 1974 to 1977. (p. 258)

Ford, Henry (fôrd), 1863–1947 Founder of the Ford Motor Company in 1903. He also introduced assembly-line techniques that made automobiles affordable for the average American. (p. 196)

G

Goodridge, Glenalvin, Wallace, and William (gůd rij), 1829–1922 Brothers living in East Saginaw who became famous for their photographs of white and African American citizens and Michigan tourist attractions. (p. 183)

Gordy, Berry, Jr. (gôr′ dē), 1929– Promoter of the "Motown Sound" through his record company, Motown, which recorded such stars as Stevie Wonder, the Supremes, and the Temptations. (p. 264)

Granholm, Jennifer (gran′ holm), 1959– In 2002 became the first woman to be elected as Michigan's governor. (p. 259)

H

Hamilton, Henry (ham′ əl tən), 1740?–1796 British commander in Detroit during the American Revolution. (p. 100)

Harrison, William Henry (har′ ə sən), 1773–1841 American general who led the recapture of Detroit for the United States during the War of 1812; ninth President of the United States. (p. 108)

Haviland, Laura (hav′ ə lənd), 1808–1898 Conductor on Michigan's Underground Railroad who helped enslaved people escape to freedom. (p. 156)

Hemingway, Ernest (hem′ ing wā), 1899–1961 American writer whose books include *The Old Man and the Sea* and who spent childhood summers in the Upper Peninsula. (p. 20)

Houghton, Douglass (hōt′ ən), 1809–1845 Scientist whose report that there were large copper deposits in the Keweenaw Peninsula led to the development of the copper industry in Michigan during the 1800s. (p. 128)

Hull, William (hul), 1753–1825 First governor of the Michigan Territory, from 1805 to 1812. (p. 110)

J

Jefferson, Thomas (jəf′ er sən), 1743–1826 Third President of the United States, from 1801 to 1809, and the author of the Declaration of Independence. (p. 110)

Jolliet, Louis (jo′ lē ā), 1645–1700 French explorer who sailed with Jacques Marquette through the Great Lakes and down the Mississippi River to the Arkansas River in 1673. (p. 84)

Kellogg, Will Keith (kel' og), 1860–1951 Battle Creek businessman who invented corn flakes and founded the Kellogg Company. (p. 258)

Key, Francis Scott (kē), 1779–1843 Writer of "The Star-Spangled Banner" during the War of 1812. The poem later became the national anthem. (p. 112)

King, Martin Luther, Jr. (king), 1929–1968 Important civil rights leader during the 1950s and 1960s; in 1963 he visited Detroit and made a speech in front of 125,000 people. (p. 197)

La Salle, Robert (lə sal'), 1643–1687 French explorer who founded Fort Miami, the first European fort in the Lower Peninsula. (p. 84)

Lincoln, Abraham (ling' kən), 1809–1865 Sixteenth President of the United States; led the country during the Civil War. (p. 158)

Malcolm X (mal' kəm), 1925–1965 African American civil rights leader in the early 1960s. (p. 239)

Marquette, Jacques (mär ket', zhäk), 1637–1675 French missionary and explorer who founded Sault Ste. Marie and St. Ignace in the 1660s. (p. 74)

Mason, Stevens T. (mā' sən), 1811–1843 The "boy governor" who began serving as Secretary of the Michigan Territory when he was only 20 years old. He became acting governor of the Michigan Territory in 1834 when he was 23 years old. (p. 75)

McCoy, Elijah (mə koi'), 1843–1929 Detroit inventor of a number of devices, including the "oil cup," which helped trains to run more smoothly. (p. 171)

Murphy, Frank (mûr' fē), 1890–1949 Mayor of Detroit from 1930 to 1933, and governor of Michigan from 1936 to 1939. Joined United States Supreme Court in 1940. As mayor he worked to help families hurt by the Great Depression. (p. 219)

Nicolet, Jean (nik ə lā'), 1598–1642 French explorer of the shoreline of the Upper Peninsula in 1634. (p. 83)

Olds, Ransom E. (ōldz), 1864–1950 Founder of the world's first automobile factory, which began operating in 1899 in Lansing. (p. 211)

Palmer, Thomas W. (pôl' mər), 1830–1913 United States Senator from Detroit who gave the first Senate speech in favor of woman's suffrage in 1885. (p. 208)

Parks, Rosa (pärkz), 1913–2005 African American who fought segregation on city buses in Montgomery, Alabama, in 1955. (p. 197)

Perry, Oliver Hazard (per' ē), 1785–1819 American naval officer who defeated the British in the Battle of Put-in-Bay during the War of 1812; he said, "We have met the enemy and they are ours." (p. 75)

Pingree, Hazen (ping' grē), 1840–1901 Mayor of Detroit and governor of Michigan in the late 1800s who tried to make life better for working people. (p. 196)

Pontiac (pōn' tē ak), 1720?–1769 Odawa chief who united American Indians against the British in 1763; leader of what became known as Pontiac's Rebellion; later worked to bring about peace between American Indians and the British. (p. 74)

Post, Charles W. (pōst), 1854–1914 Started the Post cereal company in Battle Creek. (p. 277)

Pronunciation Key

a	at	ē	me	ō	old	ū	use	ng	song
ā	ape	i	it	ô	fork	ü	rule	th	thin
ä	far	ī	ice	oi	oil	u̇	pull	th	this
âr	care	îr	pierce	ou	out	ûr	turn	zh	measure
e	end	o	hot	u	up	hw	white	ə	about, taken, pencil, lemon, circus

Reuther, Walter (rü′ thər), 1907–1970 President of the United Auto Workers union from 1946 to 1970. (p. 197)

Roosevelt, Franklin Delano (rōz′ ə velt), 1882–1945 President of the United States during the Great Depression and World War II. (p. 219)

Sable, Jean du (dü säb′ lə, zhän), 1750?–1818 Haitian-born American from the Great Lakes region who was captured by the British as a suspected spy during the American Revolution. (p. 74)

Schoolcraft, Henry Rowe (skül′ kraft), 1793–1864 Geographer and geologist who studied Michigan's land and American Indian cultures. (p. 4)

Shaw, Anna Howard (shô), 1847–1919 Leader of the women's rights movement in Michigan who grew up in Big Rapids; as a result of Shaw's and other people's work, the Michigan Constitution was changed in 1918 to allow women to vote. (p. 196)

Stowe, Harriet Beecher (stō), 1811–1896 Novelist who wrote *Uncle Tom's Cabin* in 1851. The book convinced many people that slavery should be abolished. (p. 149)

Taub, Shelley Goodman (tob), 1939– Michigan State Representative who helped pass a law in 2004 that allows students with asthma to bring inhalers to school. (p. 259)

Tecumseh (tə kum′ sə), 1768–1813 Shawnee chief who tried to organize American Indians in order to slow down the advance of American settlement on their lands; ally of the British during the War of 1812. (p. 75)

Tenskwatawa (ten skwə ta′ wa), 1775?–1837 Shawnee religious leader known as "the Prophet," who worked with his brother, Tecumseh, to try to slow the advance of American settlement on American Indian lands. (p. 111)

Truth, Sojourner (truth), 1797?–1883 Former enslaved person whose real name was Isabella Baumfree; settled in Battle Creek and became a famous speaker in support of the abolition of slavery; also spoke powerfully in support of women's rights. (p. 138)

Tubman, Harriet (tub′ mən), 1820?–1913 Abolitionist, Underground Railroad conductor, and spy for the Union Army during the Civil War. She helped hundreds of enslaved Africans escape to freedom. (p. 140)

Washington, George (wô′ shing tən), 1732–1799 First President of the United States, from 1789 to 1797. He fought in the French and Indian War and led the Continental Army during the American Revolution. (p. 92)

Wayne, Anthony (wān), 1745–1796 American general who, in 1794, defeated American Indians at the battle of Fallen Timbers in Ohio; this led to the signing of the Treaty of Greenville, in which American Indians agreed to give up large areas of land in southeastern Michigan. (p. 110)

Woodward, Augustus (wūd′ wərd), 1774–1827 Territorial judge who designed the new city of Detroit after its terrible fire in 1805. (p. 110)

Young, Coleman (yung), 1918–1997 Detroit's first African American mayor; was elected to office in 1973; was a union member and state senator before becoming mayor. (p. 197)

Biographical Dictionary

Glossary

This Glossary will help you to pronounce and understand the meanings of the vocabulary terms in this book. The page number at the end of the definition tells where the term first appears.

abolitionist (ab ə lish′ən ist) A person who worked to end slavery. (p. 147)

adapt (ə dapt′) Change to suit the environment. (p. 34)

alliance (ə lī′əns) An agreement between two or more countries, or groups to work together in doing something. (p. 83)

amendment (ə mend′mənt) A formal change made according to official rules. (p. 208)

archaeologist (är kē ol′ə jist) A scientist who studies artifacts to learn how people lived in the past. (p. 45)

arsenal (är′sə nəl) A place where weapons are made or stored. (p. 231)

artifact (är′ti fakt) An object made or used by people in the past. (p. 26)

assembly line (ə sem′blē līn) A way of working in which workers and machines are arranged so that each worker does one job in turn. (p. 213)

authority (ə thôr′i tē) Power given to someone or something by another source. (p. 310)

band (band) A small group of people. (p. 52)

barter (bär′tər) To trade goods for other goods without using money. (p. 85)

bill (bil) A plan for a law. (p. 306)

biotechnology (bī ō tek nol′ə jē) Technology that uses living cells to create new medicines. (p. 281)

boundary (bound′ə rē) A line or physical feature that shows where one place ends and another begins. (p. 13)

boycott (boi′kot) A refusal to do business with a company or to buy a product. (p. 240)

brigade (bri gād′) A large group of soldiers. (p. 162)

budget (buj′it) A plan for using money. (p. 315)

canal (kə nal′) A human-made waterway. (p. 119)

capital resources (kap′i təl rē′sôr sez) The machines needed to produce something. (p. 268)

cash crop (kash krop) A crop that is grown to be sold. (p. 171)

cavalry (kav′əl rē) A group of soldiers fighting on horseback or from tanks. (p. 162)

charter (chär′tər) A document that gives people or groups certain rights or powers. (p. 316)

citizen (sit′ə zən) A person who is born in a country or who has earned the right to become a member of a country by law. (p. 299)

city council (sit′ē kown′səl) The main body of the legislative branch of a town or city. (p. 316)

city manager (sit′ē man′i jər) A person hired to run a small town or community. (p. 316)

civil rights (siv′əl rīts) The rights of all people to be treated equally under the law. (p. 240)

circle graph (sûr′kəl graf) A graph that shows how the parts of something make up the whole. (p. 174)

clan (klan) A group of families descended from the same ancestor. (p. 52)

climate (klī′mit) The pattern of weather a place has over time. (p. 30)

closed shop (klōzd shop) A business where all workers must join a union. (p. 222)

colony (kol′ə nē) A place that is ruled by another country. (p. 82)

common good (kom′ən gůd) What is best for everyone. (p. 294)

competition (kom pi tish′ən) The rivalry between two or more businesses striving for the same customers. (p. 277)

compromise (kom′prə mīz) An agreement in which each side gives up part of what it wants. (p. 125)

confederacy (kən fed′ər ə sē) A group united for a common purpose. (p. 51)

Confederacy (kən fed′ər ə sē) The Confederate States of America. (p. 160)

consequence (kon′si kwəns) A result. (p. 117)

constitution (kon sti tü′shən) A plan of government. (p. 125)

core democratic values (kôr dem ə kra′tik val′ûz) The basic ideas that unite all Americans. (p. 293)

corporation (kôr pə rā′shən) A business that belongs to many people, each of whom owns a small share of the company. (p. 278)

county (koun′tē) One of the sections that a state is divided into. (p. 315)

culture (kul′chər) The art, beliefs, and customs shared by a group of people. (p. 46)

decision (di sizh′ən) A choice about what to do. (p. 271)

degree (di grē′) The unit of measure of lines of latitude and longitude on a map. (p. 48)

democracy (di mok′rə sē) A government that is run by the people who live under it. (p. 299)

development (di vel′əp mənt) A group of houses or other buildings planned and built together. (p. 248)

dictator (dik′tā tər) A person who rules a country without sharing power. (p. 231)

dictionary (dik′shən er′ē) A reference book that gives meanings of words. (p. 58)

discrimination (di skrim ə nā′shən) An unfair difference in the way people are treated. (p. 173)

diverse (di vûrs′) Made up of a variety of people. (p. 172)

drumlin (drum′lin) A small egg-shaped hill left behind by glaciers. (p. 14)

duration (dûr ā′shun) The length of time during which something continues. (p. 201)

economy (i kon′ə mē) The way a region uses and produces natural resources, goods, and services to meet a group's needs and wants. (p. 179)

ecosystem (ē′kō sis təm) All the living and nonliving things in a certain area. (p. 16)

elevation (el ə vā′shən) The height of land above sea level. (p. 18)

Emancipation Proclamation (i man sə pā′shən prok lə mā′shən) President Abraham Lincoln's 1862 decree that said all enslaved people living in the Confederate states were free. (p. 164)

embargo (em bär′gō) A restriction that a government or an organization puts on the importing and exporting of certain goods. (p. 247)

encyclopedia (en sī klə pē′dē ə) A book or set of books that gives information about people, places, things, and events. (p. 58)

entrepreneur (än trə prə nûr′) A person who starts and runs his or her own business. (p. 267)

equality (i kwol′i tē) Being treated equally. (p. 296)

executive branch (eg zek′yə tiv branch) The branch of government that carries out laws. (p. 300)

expedition (ek spi dish′ən) A journey of exploration. (p. 82)

export (ek′spôrt) Something sold or traded to another country. (p. 285)

fact (fakt) A statement that can be proven true. (p. 151)

federal (fed′ə rəl) A system of government that shares power between national, state, and local governments. (p. 299)

fortification (fôr tə fi kā′shən) Something that strengthens, like a wall. (p. 100)

free enterprise (frē en′tər prīz) The economic system that allows people to own and run any kind of business they want to, as long as the business is allowed by law. (p. 267)

frontier (frun tîr′) The far edge of a country, where people are just beginning to settle. (p. 91)

fugitive (fū′ji tiv) A person who has escaped. (p. 148)

glacier (glā′shər) A huge sheet of ice that moves slowly across the land. (p. 14)

global grid (glô′bəl grid) Crisscrossing latitude and longitude lines used to locate places on Earth. (p. 48)

graph (graf) A drawing that shows relationships between information. (p. 174)

Great Depression (grāt di presh′ən) The period of American history in the 1930s when business was slow and many people were out of work. (p. 218)

guide words (gīd wûrdz) Words at the top of each page of a dictionary that tell you the first and last words defined on the page. (p. 58)

historian (his tor′ē ən) A person who studies the past. (p. 26)

human capital (hū′mən kap′i təl) The people and ideas needed to produce something. (p. 268)

illegal (i lē′gəl) Against the law. (p. 147)

immigrant (im′i grənt) A person who comes to a new country to live. (p. 126)

import (im′pôrt) A good brought in from another country for sale or use. (p. 285)

impressment (im pres′mənt) The act of forcibly making someone enroll in the military. (p. 113)

incentive (in sen′tiv) The opportunity to buy something for a lesser price. (p. 271)

industry (in′də strē) All the businesses that make one kind of product or provide one kind of service. (p. 21)

integrate (in′ ti grāt) To make open to people of all races. (p. 242)

interdependent (in tər di pen′dənt) Relying on one another to meet needs and wants. (p. 285)

interest (in′tər ist) The fee a person must pay when money is borrowed. (p. 271)

international trade (in tər nash′ə nəl trād) Trade between nations. (p. 285)

Internet (in′tər net) A worldwide computer network. (p. 58)

investor (in vest′ər) A person or company that invests money. (p. 268)

issue (ish′ü) A subject that is being discussed or considered. (p. 306)

judicial branch (jü dish′əl branch) That part of government that interprets laws or decides what they mean. (p. 300)

justice (jus′tis) Fair treatment. (p. 296)

keyword (kē′wûrd) A topic word that helps you find information on the Internet. (p. 236)

kinship (kin′ship) A family relationship. (p. 62)

lake effect (lāk i fekt′) The effect a lake has in changing the weather nearby. (p. 32)

large-scale map (lärg skāl map) A map that shows many details of a small area. (p. 96)

latitude (lat′ə tüd) Distance measured on the earth's surface north and south of the equator. (p. 48)

legislative branch (lej′is lā tiv branch) The branch of government that makes laws. (p. 300)

liberty (lib′ər tē) The condition of being free from restriction or control. (p. 148)

line graph (lin graf) A graph that shows how something has changed over time. (p. 174)

longhouse (lônghous) A long wooden building in a American Indian village in which many related families lived. (p. 62)

longitude (lôn′ji tüd) Distance measured on the earth's surface east and west of the prime meridian. (p. 48)

lumberjack (lum′bər jak) A person who cuts down trees and transports timber to sawmills. (p. 126)

manufacturer (man yə fak′chər er) A business that uses machinery to make products. (p. 171)

map scale (map scāl) A scale that uses a unit of measure, such as an inch, to represent real distance on Earth. (p. 96)

market economy (mär′kit i kon′ə mē) Another name for the free enterprise system. (p. 267)

mass production (mas prə duk′shən) The process of making large numbers of one product quickly. (p. 212)

mayor (mā′ər) The elected head of the executive branch of a town or city. (p. 316)

meridian (mə rid′ē ən) A line of longitude. (p. 48)

microtechnology (mī krō tek nol'ə jē) The development of tiny machines and objects. (p. 281)

migrant worker (mī'grənt wur'kər) A person who moves from place to place to harvest different crops as they ripen. (p. 273)

migrate (mī'grāt) To move from one place to another. (p. 50)

missionary (mish'ə ner ē) A person who teaches religious beliefs to others who have different beliefs. (p. 84)

mosque (mosk) A Muslim place of worship. (p. 182)

natural resource (nach'ər əl rē'sôrs) Something found in the environment that people can use. (p. 21)

nonrenewable resource (non ri nü'ə bəl ri zôrs') A natural resource that cannot be replaced. (p. 248)

Northwest Passage (nôrth'west' pas'ij) A water route through North America to the Pacific Ocean. (p. 82)

official document (ə fish'əl dok'yə mənt) A document containing information that has been agreed upon by one or more people or institutions and issued by someone in authority. (p. 310)

opinion (ə pin'yən) A statement that tells what someone feels or believes. (p. 151)

opportunity cost (op ər tü'ni tē kost) The value of what someone gives up in order to buy something else. (p. 269)

option (op'shən) A choice you can make to solve a problem. (p. 117)

ordinance (ôr'din əns) A rule, law, or decree. (p. 109)

Paleo-Indian (pā lē ō in'dē ən) The ancient people who were the first humans to arrive in Michigan. (p. 45)

parallel (par'ə lel) A line of latitude. (p. 48)

partnership (pärt'nər ship) A business run by two or more people who share the profits and the losses. (p. 286)

patriotism (pā'trē ə tiz əm) Love and loyal support of one's country. (p. 295)

peninsula (pə nin'sə lə) Land that has water on three sides. (p. 13)

pioneer (pī'ə nēr) A person who is one of the first people to settle in a region. (p. 110)

plantation (plan ta'shən) A large estate or farm worked by laborers who live there. (p. 147)

population (pop yə lā'shən) The number of people who live in a place or an area. (p. 22)

precipitation (pri sip i tā'shən) The moisture that falls to the ground as rain, snow, sleet, or hail. (p. 31)

primary source (prī'mer ē sôrs) Spoken or written accounts from a person who has seen or experienced an event. (p. 26)

prime meridian (prīm mə rid'ē ən) On a map, the starting place for measuring distance from east to west. (p. 48)

proclamation (prok lə mā'shən) An official public announcement. (p. 94)

Progressives (prə gres'ivz) A group of politicians at the end of the 1800s who worked to make changes to help the neediest people. (p. 207)

racist (rā'sist) Believing that one human race is better than another race. (p. 239)

ration (rash'ən) To limit the use of goods or resources. (p. 232)

raw materials (rô mə tîr'ē əls) Goods from nature used to make other products. (p. 171)

rebellion (ri bel'yən) A struggle against a government or other authority. (p. 93)

recycle (rē sī'kəl) To use something over again instead of throwing it away. (p. 248)

reference materials (ref'ər əns mə tîr'ē əls) Books and other sources that contain facts about many different subjects. (p. 58)

reform (ri form') To improve the way government is run. (p. 207)

regiment (rej'ə mənt) A military unit made up of men from the same area. (p. 164)

region (rē'jən) An area with common features that set it apart from other areas. (p. 21)

renewable resource (ri nü'ə bəl ri sôrs') Natural resources that can be replaced. (p. 248)

representation (rep ri zen tā'shən) A voice in a government. (p. 98)

representative government (rep ri 'zent ət iv gəv arn mənt) A government where voters elect national, state, and local leaders who represent their needs and ideas. (p. 295)

Glossary

reservation (res ûr vā'shən) Land set aside by the government as settlements for American Indians. (p. 115)

revolution (rev ə lü'shən) The overthrow of a government. (p. 98)

riveter (riv'it ər) A worker who fastens pieces of metal together with rivets, or bolts. (p. 232)

robotics (rō bôt'iks) The study of the design of machines used in manufacturing. (p. 281)

scarcity (skâr'si tē) A shortage of goods or resources. (p. 232)

sea level (sē lev'əl) The level of the surface of the sea. (p. 18)

secede (si sēd') To withdraw from or formally leave a group or country. (p. 158)

secondary source (sek'ən der'ē sôrs) Spoken or written accounts of an event that come from a person who did not see or experience the event. (p. 26)

segregate (seg' ri gāt) To keep groups of people apart from one another. (p. 239)

self-reliant (self ri lī'ənt) Able to take care of oneself. (p. 121)

service industry (sûr'vis in'də strē) An industry that serves people. (p. 275)

slavery (slā'və rē) The practice of keeping people against their will and forcing them to work without pay. (p. 109)

small-scale map (smôl skāl map) A scale map that covers a large area but cannot include many details. (p. 96)

solution (sə lü'shən) Another word for *answer*. (p. 117)

specialize (spesh'ə līz) To concentrate on just one activity, such as to grow just one or two crops on a farm. (p. 273)

steamboat (stēm'bōt) A boat powered by steam. (p. 119)

stockade (stok ād') A tall fence of upright posts used to protect an area. (p. 62)

stock market (stok mär'kət) A market where shares of companies are bought and sold. (p. 218)

strait (strāt) A narrow channel of water that connects two larger bodies of water. (p. 13)

strike (strīk) To stop working until demands for better working conditions are met. (p. 222)

suffrage (suf'rij) The right to vote. (p. 208)

suspension bridge (sə spen'shən brij) A bridge supported by cables hung from towers. (p. 247)

tax (taks) Money paid to a government for its support. (p. 98)

technology (tek nol'ə jē) The use of skills, tools, and machines to meet people's needs. (p. 171)

territory (ter'i tôr ē) Land owned by a country either within or outside the country's borders. (p. 91)

time line (tīm līn) A diagram that shows when events took place. (p. 88)

tourism (tur'iz əm) The business of providing services to travelers. (p. 21)

township (toun'ship) A subdivision of land six miles by six miles in size. (p. 109)

trading post (trā'ding pōst) A store in an unsettled area where goods and services are traded. (p. 82)

treaty (trē'tē) A formal agreement between nations. (p. 92)

Underground Railroad (un dər ground' rāl'rōd) The system of secret routes used by people escaping slavery. (p. 155)

unemployed (un em ploid') Not having a job. (p. 218)

union (ūn'yən) A group of workers who join together to improve their pay and working conditions. (p. 220)

URL The address of a particular Web site on the Internet. (p. 236)

veto (vē'tō) The power of the executive branch to reject a bill passed by the legislature. (p. 306)

vision (vi' zhun) Something imagined or dreamed. (p. 53)

voyageur (voi ə zhər') French-speaking fur trappers who transported furs from the trading posts to Quebec. (p. 85)

Web site (web sīt) A location on the World Wide Web. (p. 236)

wigwam (wig'wom) A dome-shape home made of bark and young trees. (p. 52)

World Wide Web (wûrld wīd web) A collection of information on the Internet. (p. 236)

Index

*This index lists many topics that appear in the book, along with the pages on which they are found. Page numbers after a *c* refer you to a chart or diagram; after a *g*, to a graph, after an *m* , to a map, after a *p*, to a photograph or picture, and after a *q*, to a quotation.

Index

Credits

309: www.gophouse.com, Michigan Gov. 310: Richard Hamilton Smith/CORBIS. 311: (t) Library of Congress, Printed Ephemera Collection; (b) Library of Congress, Printed Ephemera Collection. 312: (t) Lansing State Journal; (b) Gordon R. Gainer/Dembinsky Photo Associates. 313: (t) Courtesy of Travel Michigan.gov / William Houp; (b) R.E. Olds Transportation Museum, Lansing, Michigan. 314-315: Bill Grimshaw / AP Wide World. 317: (t) Dearborn Michigan city council; (bl) State Archives of Michigan; (br) Chris Honros/Getty Images. 318: AP Wide World/Michigan State University

R4: (tl) Nick Laham/Getty Images Sport; (tr) Reuters; (bl) Bill Janscha/AP Wide World; (cr) Rebecca Roth/Getty Images. R5: (tl) ArenaPal / Topham / The Image Works; (tr) Stephane Cardinale/People Avenue/Corbis; (cl) RAVEENDRAN/AFP/Getty Images; (br) Chris Pizzello/Reuters/CORBIS. R6: (tl) Courtesy Ruth Behar; (tr) Reuters; (cr) Petre Buzoianu/CORBIS; (bl) Bryce Duffy/CORBIS. R7: (tl) AP Wide World; (tr) Douglas Kirkland/CORBIS; (tl) Mark Mainz/Getty Images; (br) Bettmann/CORBIS. R8: (tl) Fotosearch; (cl) Claudia Adams/Alamy; (bl) Tierblid Okapia/ Photo Researchers Inc.; (tr) Fotosearch; (br) Stephen J. Krasemann/Photo Researchers Inc. R9: (tl) Harry Engels/Animals Animals; (bl) Richard Shiell/Animals Animals; (tr) Arthur Morris/CORBIS; (cr) Dennis MacDonald/PhotoEdit Inc. R10: (tl) The Granger Collection; (tr) Superstock; (bl) Bettmann/CORBIS; (br) The Granger Collection. R11: (tl) Painting by Don Troiani, www.historicalartprints.com; (tr) www.gophouse.com, Michigan Gov; (bl) The Granger Collection; (bc) Smith College Sophia Smith Collection; (br) Mandel Ngan/AFP/Getty Images.

ACKNOWLEDGMENTS

Grateful acknowledgment is given to the following authors, composers, and publishers. Every effort has been made to trace the ownership of all copyrighted material and to secure the necessary permissions to reprint these selections. In the case of some selections for which acknowledgment is not given, extensive research has failed to locate the copyright holders.

Through Indian Eyes, by Reader's Digest, edited by Jill Maynard. Copyright © 1995 by The Reader's Digest Association. Published by The Reader's Digest Association, Inc. All Rights Reserved. Used by Permission.

The Legend of Sleeping Bear, by Kathy-jo Wargin. Illustrated by Gijsbert van Frankenhuyzen. Copyright © 1998 by Sleeping Bear Press. Used by Permission.

Three Stories & Ten Poems, by Ernest Hemingway. Copyright © 1977 by Contact Publishing Company. Published by Contact Publishing Company. All Rights Reserved. Used by Permission.

Road Crews Battle Winter Storm, by Lisa M. Reed. From Iron Mountain Daily News, December 11, 2003. Found on website: <http://www.ironmountaindailynews.com/Archives/top_news_archives/lclnewsarchives-1203.html#11> Used by Permission.

The Role of Ojibwe Elders, by Beatrice Taylor. From Mille Lacs Band of Ojibwe website: <http://www.millelacsojibwe.org/cultureColumn.asp?id=117> Used by Permission.

Testimony before the National Gambling Impact Study Commission, by Marge Anderson, November 9, 1998. Found on website: <http://indiangaming.org/library/studies/1061-Anderson_Mille_Lacs.pdf> Used by Permission.

McGraw-Hill School Dictionary, Edited by Robert B. Costello, Editor in Chief. Copyright © 1998 by McGraw-Hill School Division. All Rights Reserved. Used by Permission.

The Wendat Confederacy, August 27, 1999. Found on website: <http://www.wyandot.org/confederacy.html> Used by Permission.

The White Pine of This Century is Water, by Frank Ettawageshik. From the Michigan Environmental Council website: <http://www.mecprotects.org/MER/FEB05/whitepine.htm> Used by Permission.

Cover Permission for **The Legend of Mackinac Island**, by Kathy-jo Wargin. Illustrations by Gijsbert van Frankenhuyzen. Copyright © 1999 by Sleeping Bear Press. Published by Sleeping Bear Press. All Rights Reserved.

Cover Permission for **The Birchbark House**, Text and Illustrations by Louise Erdrich. Copyright © 1999 by Louise Erdrich. Published by Hyperion Books for Children. All Rights Reserved.

Cover Permission for **A Curious Glimpse of Michigan**, by Kevin and Stephanie Kammeraad. Illustrations by Ryan Hipp. Text Copyright © 2004 by Kevin and Stephanie Kammeraad. Illustrations Copyright © 2004 by Ryan Hipp and Kevin Kammeraas. Published by EDCO Publishing, Inc. All Rights Reserved.

French Pioneers 1534-1759, from A Book of Americans, by Rosemary and Stephen Vincent Bénet. Copyright © 1933 by Rosemary and Stephen Vincent Bénet. Published by Rinehart & Company, Inc. Used by Permission.

Pontiac and the Indian Uprising, by Howard H. Peckham. Copyright © 1947 by Princeton University Press. Published by Princeton University Press. All Rights Reserved. Used by Permission.

America the Beautiful: Michigan, by R. Conrad Stein. Copyright © 1987 by Regensteiner Publishing Enterprises, Inc. Published by Children's Press. All Rights Reserved. Used by Permission.

Cover Permission for **A Place Called Home: Michigan's Mill Creek Story**, by Janie Lynn Panagopoulos. Illustrated by Gijsbert van Frankenhuyzen. Copyright © 2001 by Mackinac Island State Park Commission. Published by Sleeping Bear Press. All Rights Reserved.

Cover Permission for **Jacques Marquette and Louis Jolliet**, by Jeff Donaldson-Forbes. Copyright © 2002 by The Rosen Publishing Group, Inc. Published by The Rosen Publishing Group, Inc. All Rights Reserved.

Cover Permission for **A Pioneer Sampler**, by Barbara Greenwood. Illustrated by Heather Collins. Text Copyright © 1994 by Barbara Greenwood. Illustrations Copyright © 1994 by Heather Collins/Glyphics. Published by Houghton Mifflin Company. All Rights Reserved.

Harriet Tubman, from Honey, I Love and Other Love Poems, by Eloise Greenfield. Text Copyright © 1978 by Eloise Greenfield. Illustrations Copyright © 1978 by Diane and Leo Dillon. Published by Thomas Y. Crowell Company. Used by Permission.

New Jersey Multi-Ethnic Oral History Project Interview with Mildred Arnold, by Giles Wright, August 19, 1980. Transcribed by Pat Thomas.

Pioneers, by Martin W. Sandler. Copyright © 1994 by Eagle Productions, Inc. Published by HarperCollins Publishers. All Rights Reserved. Used by Permission.

Irene Jordan, from **"Voices of Michigan,"** December 26, 1999. The Detroit News website: <http://www.detnews.com/specialreports/1999/roots/1226voices0/1226voices0.htm> Copyright © 1999 by The Detroit News. Used by Permission.

Field to Factory: Afro-American Migration, 1925-1940, by Spencer R. Crew. Copyright © 1987 by the Smithsonian Institution. Published by the National Museum of American History, Smithsonian Institution. All Rights Reserved. Used by Permission.

Cover Permission for **Pink and Say**, by Patricia Polacco. Copyright © 1994 by Babushka, Inc. Published by Penguin Young Readers Group. All Rights Reserved.

Cover Permission for **Civil War**, by John Stanchak. Text Copyright © 2000 by John Stanchak. Copyright © 2000 by Dorling Kindersley Publishing, Inc. Published by Dorling Kindersley Publishing, Inc. All Rights Reserved.

Cover Permission for **The Great Migration**, by Jacob Lawrence. Copyright © 1993 by The Museum of Modern Art, New York, and The Phillips Collection. Published by HarperCollins Publishers. All Rights Reserved.

Willow Run, by Patricia Reilly Giff. Copyright © 2005 by Patricia Reilly Giff. Published by Random House, Inc. Used by Permission.

In My Merry Oldsmobile, Words by Vincent Bryan. Music by Gus Edwards. Copyright © by Warner Chappell Music, Inc. All Rights Reserved. Used by Permission.

Michigan: A History of the Great Lakes State, by Bruce A. Rubenstein and Lawrence E. Ziewacz. Copyright © 1981, 1995, 2002 by Harlan Davidson, Inc. Published by Harlan Davidson, Inc. All Rights Reserved. Used by Permission.

Brother, Can You Spare a Dime, Words by Yip Harburg. Music by Gorney Harburg. Copyright © Warner Chappell Music, Inc. All Rights Reserved. Used by Permission.

Walter Reuther, by Irving Bluestone, December 7, 1998. From Time 100 website: <http://www.time.com/time/time100/builder/profile/reuther.html> Used by Permission.

"Troops Surround Plants Following Riots in Flint," by Russell B. Porter. Copyright © by The New York Times, February 2, 1937. All Rights Reserved. Used by Permission.

Duration Blues, Words and Music by Johnny Mercer. Copyright © 1944 by The Johnny Mercer Foundation. Published by WB Music Corp., Warner Chappell Music Inc. All Rights Reserved. Used by Permission.

About Malcolm X, from CMG Worldwide. Copyright © the Estate of Malcolm X. Found on website: <http://www.cmgww.com/historic/malcolm/about/bio3.html> Used by Permission.

A Call to Conscience: The Landmark Speeches, edited by Clayborne Carson and Kris Shepard. Copyright © 2001 by IPM/Warner Books. Used by Permission.

Interview with Rosa Parks, from **Rosa Parks: How I Fought for Civil Rights**. From Scholastic Inc. website: <http://216.182.167.201/rosa/interview.htm> Used by Permission.

Cover Permission for **Along Came The Model T! How Henry Ford Put the World on Wheels**, by Robert Quackenbush. Copyright © 1978 by Robert Quackenbush. Published by Parents' Magazine Press. All Rights Reserved.

Cover Permission for **From the Back of the Bus to the Front of a Movement**, by Camilla Wilson. Copyright © 2001 by Camilla Wilson. Published by Scholastic Inc. All Rights Reserved.

Cover Permission for **Rosie the Riveter**, by Penny Colman. Copyright © 1995 by Penny Colman. Published by Random House, Inc. All Rights Reserved.

Purple Mountain Majesties: The Story of KatharineLee Bates and "America the Beautiful," by Barbara Younger. Text Copyright © 1998 by Barbara Younger. Illustrations Copyright © 1998 by Stacey Schuett. Published by the Penguin Group. All Rights Reserved.

Motown Artists Dancing in the Streets, from Motown Historical Museum. Found on website: <http://www.motownmuseum.com/mtmpages/perform.html> Used by Permission.

Foundations, from Learning to Give. Found on website: <http://www.learningtogive.org/materials/foundations/foundations.asp> Used by Permission.

Who's News, by Lorrie Lynch. From USA Weekend website: <http://www.usaweekend.com/o3_issues/030202/030202whosnews.html> Used by Permission.

The Wreck of the Edmund Fitzgerald, Words and Music by Gordon Lightfoot. Copyright © 1976 by Moose Music Inc. All Rights Reserved. Used by Permission.

Cover Permission for **Vote!** by Eileen Christelow. Copyright © 2003 by Eileen Christelow. Published by Houghton Mifflin Company. All Rights Reserved.

Cover Permission for **Mail by the Pail**, by Colin Bergel. Illustrations by Mark Koenig. Text and Illustrations Copyright © 2000 by Colin Bergel and Mark Koenig. Published by Wayne State University Press. All Rights Reserved.

Cover Permission for **Making Laws: A Look at How a Bill Becomes a Law**, by Sandy Donovan. Copyright © 2004 by Sandy Donovan. Published by Lerner Publications Group. All Rights Reserved.

About the Cover:
Front: The Detroit skyline (top) is shown here as seen across the Detroit River from Canada. The St. Joseph lighthouse (bottom) marks the entrance to the St. Joseph River. Back: The Michigan State Capitol Building in Lansing, completed in 1879, is a National Historic Landmark.

Michigan Social Studies
Grade Level Content Expectations

History

H3 History of Michigan (Through Statehood)
Use historical thinking to understand the past.

H3.0.1 Identify questions historians ask in examining the past in Michigan (e.g., What happened? When did it happen? Who was involved? How and why did it happen?)

H3.0.2 Explain how historians use primary and secondary sources to answer questions about the past.

H3.0.3 Describe the causal relationships between three events in Michigan's past (e.g., Erie Canal, more people came, statehood).

H3.0.4 Draw upon traditional stories of American Indians (e.g., Anishinaabeg - Ojibway (Chippewa), Odawa (Ottawa), Potawatomi; Menominee; Huron Indians) who lived in Michigan in order to make generalizations about their beliefs.

H3.0.5 Use informational text and visual data to compare how American Indians and settlers in the early history of Michigan adapted to, used, and modified their environment.

H3.0.6 Use a variety of sources to describe interactions that occurred between American Indians and the first European explorers and settlers in Michigan.

H3.0.7 Use a variety of primary and secondary sources to construct a historical narrative about daily life in the early settlements of Michigan (pre-statehood).

H3.0.8 Use case studies or stories to describe how the ideas or actions of individuals affected the history of Michigan.

H3.0.9 Describe how Michigan attained statehood.

H3.0.10 Create a timeline to sequence early Michigan history (American Indians, exploration, settlement, statehood).

Geography

G1 The World in Spatial Terms
Use geographic representations to acquire, process, and report information from a spatial perspective.

G1.0.1 Use cardinal directions (north, south, east, west) to describe the relative location of significant places in the immediate environment.

G1.0.2 Use thematic maps to identify and describe the physical and human characteristics of Michigan.

G2 Places and Regions
Understand how regions are created from common physical and human characteristics.

G2.0.1 Use a variety of visual materials and data sources to describe ways in which Michigan can be divided into regions.

G2.0.2 Describe different regions to which Michigan belongs (e.g., Great Lakes Region, Midwest).

G4 Human Systems
Understand how human activities help shape the Earth's surface.

G4.0.1 Describe major kinds of economic activity in Michigan today, such as agriculture (e.g., corn, cherries, dairy), manufacturing (e.g., automobiles, wood products), services and tourism, research and development (e.g., Automation Alley, life sciences corridor, university communities), and explain the factors influencing the location of these economic activities. (E)

G4.0.2 Describe diverse groups that have come into a region of Michigan and reasons why they came (push/pull factors). (H)

G4.0.3 Describe some of the current movements of goods, people, jobs or information to, from, or within Michigan and explain reasons for the movements. (E)

G4.0.4 Use data and current information about the Anishinaabeg and other American Indians living in Michigan today to describe the cultural aspects of modern American Indian life; give an example of how another cultural group in Michigan today has preserved and built upon its cultural heritage.

G5 Environment and Society
Understand the effects of human-environment interactions.

G5.0.1 Locate natural resources in Michigan and explain the consequences of their use.

G5.0.2 Describe how people adapt to, use, and modify the natural resources of Michigan. (H)

Civics and Government

C1 Purposes of Government
Explain why people create governments.

C1.0.1 Give an example of how Michigan state government fulfills one of the purposes of government (e.g., protecting individual rights, promoting the common good, ensuring equal treatment under the law).

C2 Values and Principles of American Government
Understand values and principles of American constitutional democracy.

C2.0.1 Describe how Michigan state government reflects the principle of representative government.